Pious and Rebellious

Pious and Rebellious

Jewish Women in Medieval Europe

Avraham Grossman

*Translated from the Hebrew
by Jonathan Chipman*

Brandeis University Press
Waltham, Massachusetts

PUBLISHED BY UNIVERSITY PRESS OF NEW ENGLAND
HANOVER AND LONDON

Brandeis University Press

Published by University Press of New England,

One Court Street, Lebanon, NH 03766

www.upne.com

© 2004 by Brandeis University Press

This book was published with the generous support of the Lucius N. Littauer Foundation, Inc.; the Institute of Jewish Studies at the Hebrew University of Jerusalem; the Tauber Institute for the Study of European Jewry through the support of the Valya and Robert Shapiro Endowment at Brandeis University; and the Hadassah-Brandeis Institute through the support of the Donna Sudarsky Memorial Fund.

Printed in the United States of America

5   4   3   2   1

Library of Congress Cataloging-in-Publication Data

Grossman, Avraham.

[Ḥasidot u-mordot. English]

Pious and rebellious : Jewish women in Medieval Europe / Avraham Grossman ; translated from the Hebrew by Jonathan Chipman. — 1st ed.

p.   cm. — (Tauber Institute for the Study of European Jewry series) (Brandeis series on Jewish women)

Includes bibliographical references and index.

ISBN 1–58465–391–4 (cloth : alk. paper) — ISBN 1–58465–392–2 (pbk. : alk. paper)

1. Women in Judaism—Europe—History—To 1500. 2. Jewish women—Europe—History. 3. Women—Legal status, law, etc. (Jewish law) 4. Judaism—Europe—History—To 1500. 5. Hasidism. 6. Middle Ages. I. Title. II. Series.

BM729.W6G7613   2004

305.48'892404'0902—dc22

2004003029

The Tauber Institute for the Study of European Jewry Series

Jehuda Reinharz, *General Editor*
Sylvia Fuks Fried, *Associate Editor*

The Tauber Institute for the Study of European Jewry, established by a gift to Brandeis University from Dr. Laszlo N. Tauber, is dedicated to the memory of the victims of Nazi persecutions between 1933 and 1945. The Institute seeks to study the history and culture of European Jewry in the modern period. The Institute has a special interest in studying the causes, nature, and consequences of the European Jewish catastrophe within the contexts of modern European diplomatic, intellectual, political, and social history.

Gerhard L. Weinberg, 1981
World in the Balance: Behind the Scenes of World War II

Richard Cobb, 1983
French and Germans, Germans and French: A Personal Interpretation of France under Two Occupations, 1914–1918/1940–1944

Eberhard Jäckel, 1984
Hitler in History

Frances Malino and Bernard Wasserstein, editors, 1985
The Jews in Modern France

Jehuda Reinharz and Walter Schatzberg, editors, 1985
The Jewish Response to German Culture: From the Enlightenment to the Second World War

Jacob Katz, 1986
The Darker Side of Genius: Richard Wagner's Anti-Semitism

Jehuda Reinharz, editor, 1987
Living with Antisemitism: Modern Jewish Responses

Michael R. Marrus, 1987
The Holocaust in History

Paul Mendes-Flohr, editor, 1987
The Philosophy of Franz Rosenzweig

Joan G. Roland, 1989
Jews in British India: Identity in a Colonial Era

Yisrael Gutman, Ezra Mendelsohn, Jehuda Reinharz, and Chone Shmeruk, editors, 1989
The Jews of Poland between Two World Wars

Avraham Barkai, 1989
From Boycott to Annihilation: The Economic Struggle of German Jews, 1933–1943

Alexander Altmann, 1991
The Meaning of Jewish Existence: Theological Essays 1930–1939

Magdalena Opalski and Israel Bartal, 1992
Poles and Jews: A Failed Brotherhood

Richard Breitman, 1992
The Architect of Genocide: Himmler and the Final Solution

George L. Mosse, 1993
Confronting the Nation: Jewish and Western Nationalism

Daniel Carpi, 1994
Between Mussolini and Hitler: The Jews and the Italian Authorities in France and Tunisia

Walter Laqueur and Richard Breitman, 1994
Breaking the Silence: The German Who Exposed the Final Solution

Ismar Schorsch, 1994
From Text to Context: The Turn to History in Modern Judaism

Jacob Katz, 1995
With My Own Eyes: The Autobiography of an Historian

Gideon Shimoni, 1995
The Zionist Ideology

Moshe Prywes and Haim Chertok, 1996
Prisoner of Hope

János Nyiri, 1997
Battlefields and Playgrounds

Alan Mintz, editor, 1997
The Boom in Contemporary Israeli Fiction

Samuel Bak, paintings
Lawrence L. Langer, essay and commentary, 1997
Landscapes of Jewish Experience

Jeffrey Shandler and Beth S. Wenger, editors, 1997
Encounters with the "Holy Land": Place, Past and Future in American Jewish Culture

Simon Rawidowicz, 1998
State of Israel, Diaspora, and Jewish Continuity: Essays on the "Ever-Dying People"

Jacob Katz, 1998
A House Divided: Orthodoxy and Schism in Nineteenth-Century Central European Jewry

Elisheva Carlebach, John M. Efron, and David N. Myers, editors, 1998
Jewish History and Jewish Memory: Essays in Honor of Yosef Hayim Yerushalmi

Shmuel Almog, Jehuda Reinharz, and Anita Shapira, editors, 1998
Zionism and Religion

Ben Halpern and Jehuda Reinharz, 2000
Zionism and the Creation of a New Society

Walter Laqueur, 2001
Generation Exodus: The Fate of Young Jewish Refugees from Nazi Germany

Yigal Schwartz, 2001
Aharon Appelfeld: From Individual Lament to Tribal Eternity

Renée Poznanski, 2001
Jews in France during World War II

Jehuda Reinharz, 2001
Chaim Weizmann: The Making of a Zionist Leader

Jehuda Reinharz, 2001
Chaim Weizmann: The Making of a Statesman

ChaeRan Y. Freeze, 2002
Jewish Marriage and Divorce in Imperial Russia

Mark A. Raider and Miriam B. Raider-Roth, editors, 2002
The Plough Woman: Records of the Pioneer Women of Palestine

Ezra Mendelsohn, 2002
Painting a People: Maurycy Gottlieb and Jewish Art

Alan Mintz, editor, 2002
Reading Hebrew Literature: Critical Discussions of Six Modern Texts

Haim Be'er, 2002
The Pure Element of Time

Yehudit Hendel, 2002
Small Change: A Collection of Stories

Thomas C. Hubka, 2003
Resplendent Synagogue: Architecture and Worship in an Eighteenth-Century Polish Community

Uzi Rebhun and Chaim I. Waxman, 2003
Jews in Israel: Contemporary Social and Cultural Patterns

Gideon Shimoni, 2003
Community and Conscience: The Jews in Apartheid South Africa

Iris Parush, 2004
Reading Jewish Women: Marginality and Modernization in Nineteenth-Century Eastern European Jewish Society

Haim Be'er, 2004
Feathers

Avraham Grossman, 2004
Pious and Rebellious: Jewish Women in Medieval Europe

Brandeis Series on Jewish Women

Shulamit Reinharz, *General Editor*
Joyce Antler, *Associate Editor*
Sylvia Barack Fishman, *Associate Editor*

The Brandeis Series on Jewish Women is an innovative book series created by The Hadassah-Brandeis Institute. BSJW publishes a wide range of books by and about Jewish women in diverse contexts and time periods, of interest to scholars, and for the educated public. The series fills a major gap in Jewish learning by focusing on the lives of Jewish women and Jewish gender studies.

Marjorie Agosín
Uncertain Travelers: Conversations with Jewish Women Immigrants to America, 1999

Rahel R. Wasserfall, editor
Women and Water: Menstruation in Jewish Life and Law, 1999

Susan Starr Sered
What Makes Women Sick? Militarism, Maternity, and Modesty in Israeli Society, 2000

Pamela S. Nadell and Jonathan D. Sarna, editors
Women and American Judaism: Historical Perspectives, 2001

Ludmila Shtern
Leaving Leningrad: The True Adventures of a Soviet Émigré, 2001

Jael Silliman
Jewish Portraits, Indian Frames: Women's Narratives from a Diaspora of Hope, 2001

Judith R. Baskin
Midrashic Women: Formations of the Feminine in Rabbinic Literature, 2002

ChaeRan Y. Freeze
Jewish Marriage and Divorce in Imperial Russia, 2002

Mark A. Raider and Miriam B. Raider-Roth, editors
The Plough Woman: Records of the Pioneer Women of Palestine, 2002

Elizabeth Wyner Mark, editor
The Covenant of Circumcision: New Perspectives on an Ancient Jewish Rite, 2003

Kalpana Misra and Melanie S. Rich, editors,
Jewish Feminism in Israel: Some Contemporary Perspectives, 2003

Farideh Goldin
Wedding Song: Memoirs of an Iranian Jewish Woman, 2003

Rochelle L. Millen
Women, Birth, and Death in Jewish Law and Practice, 2003

Sylvia Barack Fishman
Double or Nothing? Jewish Families and Mixed Marriage, 2004

Iris Parush
Reading Jewish Women: Marginality and Modernization in Nineteenth-Century Eastern European Jewish Society, 2004

Avraham Grossman
Pious and Rebellious: Jewish Women in Medieval Europe, 2004

Shulamit Reinharz and Mark A. Raider, editors
American Jewish Women and Zionism, 2004

Tamar Ross
Expanding the Palace of Torah: Orthodoxy and Feminism, 2004

Contents

Preface

This study deals with the status of the Jewish woman in Europe during the High Middle Ages (1000–1300). For certain subjects I used later sources, in some cases even from the late Middle Ages, where these helped to provide a fuller description of reality, given that customs, ceremonies, and institutions do not change easily.

The discussion is conducted from a broad historical perspective, covering a wide variety of aspects of women's situation in medieval Jewish society: the image of woman, the structure of the family unit, age at marriage, woman's position in family and society, her place in economic and religious life, her education, her role in family ceremonies, violence against women, the position of the divorcée and the widow in society, and other topics. Strong inner connections link this entire range of subjects.

During this period, a distinct improvement occurred in the status of Jewish women in Europe relative to their status during the Talmudic period and in Muslim countries. This improvement relates both to the economic activity of Jews during that period and to developments in neighboring Christian society, expressed in a wide range of areas. Women were far more successful than has been imagined thus far. If, during the twelfth century, they are described as "pious," "pure," and "holy," in tribute to their central role in the acts of martyrdom during the First Crusade (1096), by the second half of the thirteenth century some of the sages complained about their "haughtiness," calling them "arrogant," "licentious," and "rebellious." The changes in their status and the attempts to impede their steps lie in the center of this work.

This is the first study to deal in a comprehensive way with the subject of the medieval Jewish woman, whereas dozens of books and hundreds of articles have been written about the status of Christian women during that same period. The main cause of the relatively limited scholarly study of the status of Jewish women has to do with the nature of the sources. Notwithstanding their important place in family and in society, the voices of Jewish women as such were barely heard. Their actions spoke in their stead. Not only is there no extant work created by a Jewish woman during the medieval period (a period that lasted nearly one thousand years), but not so much as a single book from that period deals with her status in the family and society. The relevant sources in print and in manuscript are widely dispersed. There is need to locate them, to ascertain their correct text, to identify their authors, and to carefully analyze them, while noting the internal connections among them and constantly comparing them with the reality in the non-Jewish environment. Finally, we need to examine the transformations that occurred in the stance of the medieval sages as compared to the approach that emerges from the Talmudic literature and the responsa of the Babylonian Geonim. On more than one occasion, I was confronted by the question, to what extent a general picture may be constructed on the basis of isolated testimony.

I utilized printed and manuscript sources from many different areas: Jewish law (halakhah), biblical exegesis, responsa, philosophical and ethical works, secular and sacred poetry, chronicles, folk literature, archival material, gravestones, and decorations. The synthesis of information taken from varied sources, the correlation of the data contained therein and its careful examination, while referring to the reality of the surrounding Gentile society, allow us to sketch a picture of the status of Jewish women in medieval Europe, even if this picture is at times only a fragmentary one.

I tried to draw an exact and balanced picture and not to prettify what was at times a quite unfortunate reality, avoiding a tendentious approach that would examine developments on the basis of only some of the sources. It seems to me that bringing a comprehensive picture of things as they were, with its light and darkness, is the firm basis upon which any discussion must be based, not only of the reality of times long past, but also for what can be learned of the future. In any event, the commonly heard phrase, "the dark Middle Ages," does not describe the status of Jewish women in medieval Europe. Alongside the numerous shadows there were also lights, and in several respects (such as the sanctions employed against violent husbands), the status of the Jewish woman in those days was preferable even to that found today.

This book is an abridged translation of my Hebrew book, *Ḥasidot u-Mordot: Nashim Yehudiyot be-Eropah be-Yemei ha-Beinayim,* published by the Zalman Shazar Center for Jewish History in 2001, now in its third printing. Due to considerations of space, I deleted approximately two-fifths of the material found in that edition, mostly quotations from primary sources, as well as much of the scholarly apparatus and bibliography. Those who seek a more comprehensive picture are referred to the Hebrew edition.

It is my pleasant task to express my thanks to those who assisted in the preparation of this book: Rabbi Jonathan Chipman, who translated the book faithfully and capably, at times also contributing comments on substantive matters; Professor David Berger, who read the manuscript and offered many important comments; Cheryl Tallan, who read the first seven chapters of the manuscript with great care; Professor Jehuda Reinharz, General Editor of the Tauber Institute series, for his appreciation of my work; Sylvia Fuks Fried, Executive Director of the Tauber Institute, who handled the preparation of the book for press with great dedication; the staffs of Brandeis University Press and University Press of New England, for their faithful work. In funding the translation, I was assisted by contributions from the Institute of Jewish Studies of the Hebrew University of Jerusalem; the Lucius N. Littauer Foundation; and the Tauber Institute of Brandeis University.

A. G.
Jerusalem
May 2003

Pious and Rebellious

Introduction

1. The Historical Background

T he status of the Jewish woman in the Middle Ages was affected by three main factors: the biblical and Talmudic heritage; the situation in the non-Jewish society within which the Jews lived and functioned; and the economic status of the Jews, including the woman's role in supporting the family. The biblical heritage is not unequivocal, and may be interpreted in different ways. Over the last generation, a number of works have been written emphasizing the feminist aspect in biblical interpretation, and seeking egalitarian elements between man and woman, some of them bearing an apologetic orientation—a subject that goes beyond the framework of our discussion. For our purposes, the Talmudic heritage is more important than the biblical one. Jews in the Middle Ages were convinced that the Bible must be understood according to the accepted interpretation of the *tannaim* and *amoraim* (sages of the Mishnaic and Talmudic period). They saw themselves as a "holy congregation" committed to the time-honored Jewish religious tradition. The sages' opinions concerning woman—her modesty, her faithfulness to her husband, her way of life—were seen as part of a binding, sanctified tradition whose source lay in the books of Scripture and in the thought of Jewish sages throughout the generations. But the economic, cultural, and social reality of the Diaspora also had a very great impact upon their mental world, and a constant tension existed between the Talmudic tradition and reality.

In terms of family life generally, and the status of women in particular, the atmosphere in the neighboring Gentile society exerted a great influence. German Hasidism described this well, in stating that the Jews behave in each place according to the practice of their Christian neighbors. Hence, they admonished

Jews to examine the degree of modesty of their non-Jewish neighbors before deciding where to make their residence, because their sons and daughters would imitate the behavior of the local Gentiles.[1] The discussions found in the body of this book, concerning the entire gamut of those areas of life related to the status of the Jewish woman, indicate the truth of this statement.

The third factor, the economic situation of the Jews and the role played by the wife in supporting the family, is extremely significant, and is of greater importance than is generally assumed by research. The primary conclusion of this work is that the profound economic change that occurred in Jewish society in the Middle Ages, and its transformation into a bourgeois or petit-bourgeois society, exerted a stronger positive influence upon the status of the Jewish woman than any other factor. We cannot elaborate here upon the profound economic transformation that took place in the socio-economic situation of the Jews generally, as this is a far-reaching change that influenced all aspects of the Jewish way of life. From the time of their origin as a nation, Jews engaged primarily in agricultural work. Such is the picture reflected in the Bible, the Mishnah, and the Talmud. There were merchants and artisans among them, but the majority of the people earned their livelihood from working the soil. In the eighth century c.e., a great transformation took place, beginning in Babylonia and the other Muslim countries, and spreading from there to the entire Jewish world. The Jews abandoned agricultural work, were concentrated in the cities, and became a group whose main source of income was commerce and financial activity. This was one of the decisive transformations in the history of the Jewish people, with far-reaching implications for its society and culture.

This change in economic structure also influenced the image of Jewish society. A good illustration of this may be seen in the words of Rav Sherira Gaon. In his day, the second half of the tenth century, Jewish women in Baghdad no longer engaged in the kinds of tasks that the village women continued to do; hence, the husband could no longer force his wife to perform them, even though these tasks are listed in the Mishnah as incumbent upon the woman.[2] A similar reality existed during that same period in various cities of North Africa and Egypt, as follows from the sources preserved in the Cairo Genizah.

The transformation in Spain began later and received its greatest impetus during the course of the eleventh and twelfth centuries in the wake of the Reconquista. Many Jews abandoned their locales and moved to the cities, in which trade was flourishing and a livelihood was available. As we shall see in chapter 4, these frequent migrations and travels had a great influence on Jewish family life in Muslim Spain.

The Jews of Christian Europe assumed an important role in local and international trade. In practice, their taking of residence and becoming established in different countries had its roots in economic activity. From the twelfth century on, many of them began to engage in money lending. Jewish women took an active part in both commerce and money lending, and when the husbands were absent from home—which happened frequently and often for lengthy periods—they conducted all of the family business and were also responsible for raising the children. This economic change greatly affected their status within the family and society generally, a point to which we shall return in chapter 5.

It follows from all this that any study whose purpose is to examine the status of the Jewish woman must refer to the three above-mentioned factors in relation to each and every subject. These developments indicate a real change in the woman's status, as the Jews did not easily deviate from the biblical and Talmudic tradition that they considered sacrosanct. Hence, in this book I have begun the treatment of each topic with a brief discussion of the biblical and Talmudic heritage and of the situation in the surrounding Gentile environment, both Christian and Muslim. So as not to make these excessively lengthy, I did not enter into a detailed elucidation and sufficed with a brief outline of the main points alone, particularly in light of the fact that extensive literature is available about the status of Christian women in the Middle Ages.

With the growth of the European cities in the twelfth and thirteenth centuries, an improvement occurred in the status of Christian women within the high bourgeois society. Some Jews were also part of the elite classes. They saw themselves as free and were used to imitating the way of life of the high bourgeoisie, and to a certain extent even that of the nobility. The wives of the nobility, the knights, and the high bourgeoisie enjoyed a high social status. There were also women from noble families who ran duchies.[3] Did they continue to enjoy this power during the twelfth and thirteenth centuries, when the improvement in the position of the Jewish woman in Germany and France reached its peak? Many researchers believe that a certain decline took place in the status of the noblewomen during this period, a theory that has recently been opposed by Theodore Evergates. The latter gathered together several different studies that refuted the theory in question, proving that the aristocratic women maintained their position into the twelfth and thirteenth centuries, particularly during periods of absence of their husbands.[4]

The situation in Jewish society was similar. Women in Germany and northern France filled similar functions in family and social life, particularly during their husbands' absences on the occasion of extensive commercial travels.

2. Sources

Anyone who sets out to examine the status of Jewish women in the Middle Ages confronts a great difficulty: namely, that the voice of the women themselves is never heard. Not only are there no works written by Jewish women (with the exception of a few isolated poems), but not a single book from the period deals with her status in the family or in society. The relevant sources in print and in manuscript are of diverse nature and widely dispersed. One needs to locate them, to identify their authors, to discover the inner connections among them, and, above all else—to undertake a careful analysis of them, while taking note of the changes that occurred in halakhic rulings and custom as opposed to that found in Talmudic literature and in the Geonic responsa, as well as in parallel developments in the neighboring Gentile society. The small number of sources conveys great importance to each one of them. However, the question frequently arises as to whether we are permitted to construct a general picture on the basis of such isolated testimonies.

The most fruitful source for researching this subject is halakhic literature, in all its branches, and particularly the responsa. The questions arose from everyday life, so that the reality portrayed therein—and particularly that found in the words of the interlocutor as he presents his question in all innocence—is of the greatest importance for determining the everyday reality in the various places. Nevertheless, study of the responsa demands great caution: in determining the correct text, identifying the respondent, examining the historical background, and deriving proper conclusions.

I also made use of general halakhic works. While these are based upon the Talmudic rulings, so that the picture that emerges from them generally does not reflect the changes that took place in the status of Jewish women during the Middle Ages, they do give hints of the changes and deviations from the rulings of the Talmudic sages and Babylonian Geonim. These are indicative of the developments, and at times also of their causes, from which follows their great value. Another important source is the exegetical literature of the Bible and Talmud. The manner of confronting those texts that deal with women reflects the spiritual world of the exegete. Moreover, those great sages who were accepted as true authorities also influenced subsequent generations. The same holds true for Talmudic commentaries. Things in praise or denigration of woman found in the commentaries of Rashi, the Tosaphists, and other commentators from Spain, Provence, and other Diaspora centers influenced subsequent generations. The abundance of halakhic sources, as against the relative paucity of other sources, is the reason for the place of honor given in this book to halakhic-legal aspects of the problem.

Sources of a more problematic nature include folk literature, *maqamot,* and love and wine poetry composed by authors and poets in Spain, Italy, and Provence. The *maqamot* and other poems generally convey a negative picture of women, but it is doubtful whether these descriptions are a faithful picture of reality or merely literary conventions. Even if the second possibility is the case, it is still unclear whether these descriptions were perceived by contemporaries and by those who lived in subsequent generations in that way. Literary critics are still in disagreement as to the full meaning of the message that follows from the repeated use of these motifs.[5]

A similar doubt also exists regarding ethical literature. Repeated admonitions concerning the immodesty of women and of men may be indicative of reality, but they are also delimited by the author's mentality and his own conceptual world. Admonitions to preserve modesty are not in themselves evidence of rife immodesty. Such insistence must also be interpreted against the background of the author's world-view. I nevertheless did make extensive use of these sources, particularly of *Sefer Ḥasidim,* albeit with an awareness of and attention to the above-mentioned suspicion.

Greater doubt exists as to the degree of reliability of the chronicles concerning the anti-Jewish persecutions in Ashkenaz in 1096, in which women occupied a major place, for which reason I devoted a detailed discussion to them in chapter 9. Archival sources are of great importance, but most of these relate to the late Middle Ages.

Taking together the entire range of information, both those that are explicit and those only alluded to in these sources, correlating the information found therein, and studying them with care, while referring to the general historical background, it is possible to create a picture—albeit fragmentary—of the position of Jewish women in the High Middle Ages.

It is more difficult to reconstruct the silent voice of women. Their actions speak on their behalf, but the meaning of these actions is not always altogether clear. I shall bring one example to concretize my words. R. Yom Tov Ibn Ish-bili (Ritba), one of the outstanding Spanish sages at the end of the thirteenth and first quarter of the fourteenth century, was asked to issue a legal ruling concerning a woman towards whom fate had been cruel. Her husband had abandoned her some time after their wedding and for many years she was left a "chained" woman, unable to marry. Two witnesses then appeared, testifying that they had heard that her husband had died in a far-away place. The woman remarried, but this marriage was not successful and she was divorced. She then married a third time, this time happily, and gave birth to a daughter. Some time later, her first husband, who had been considered dead, suddenly appeared. The Court ruled that she needed to divorce both husbands—the first and the third—and that her daughter was to be considered as a bastard. (As her first husband was in fact alive, her third marriage was retroactively treated as adulterous.) The third husband refused to support the wife and daughter, claiming poverty. In her bitterness, the woman took her daughter and placed her on the doorstep of the home of her third husband, the child's father.[6]

What is the significance of this harsh story? Is it in fact indicative of the woman's cruelty and alienation from her daughter, as suggested by the questioner, or may it be in fact a kind of cry of pain over her plight, and perhaps a plea for financial support? Why is she alone responsible for supporting her daughter, after all the suffering she's been through? The questioner related with understanding to the father, who suffered financial difficulties, and in a negative way toward the mother. The respondent was unable to help the woman, nor to allow her third husband to take her back.

The unfortunate woman, who during the course of her life had received three divorce writs, and whose only daughter was defined as a bastard, with all that implies, needed to carry alone on her shoulders the burden of her child's support—and all this without any wrongdoing, as she had remarried on the basis of two witnesses who testified to her first husband's death. True, one is speaking of an objectively difficult situation, but the inquirer does not betray any empathy for the woman's situation. We find here a detailed description of a tragic situation, without a single word from the mother herself, making it impossible to clearly interpret the meaning of her actions.

3. The Chronological and Geographical Framework

The restriction of this study to the subject of the status of Jewish women in Europe stems primarily from the state of research. The status of Jewish women in the Mediterranean countries has been studied in meticulous detail by Shlomo Goitein and Mordechai Friedman.[7] Even though Goitein relied primarily upon the Cairo Genizah documents and only in a limited way upon the Babylonian Geonic responsa literature, there is no reason to return to that subject. The great wealth of sources in the Genizah makes it possible to paint an overall picture of the place of the woman in family and society. Regarding certain topics, I have compared the situation in Europe with that which follows from the Genizah sources, particularly the Geonic responsa. Such a comparison can highlight the changes that occurred in Europe. The Babylonian Talmud was accepted, no later than the tenth century, as an obligatory binding source throughout Jewry. The Geonic responsa and their halakhic works were also understood in Europe as sources of great importance, imbued with a certain sacral character. The willingness to deviate from them nevertheless in certain specific cases may thus be indicative of changes in the conception of the woman's role in society and family.

This study deals primarily with the High Middle Ages, that is, with the years 1000 to 1300, even though many sources from a later period are also discussed. The delineation of the time period as beginning from the year 1000 is based upon the state of the sources. While there was Jewish settlement in Spain already at the beginning of the Middle Ages, and in Germany from the beginning of the ninth century, written sources from these centers—as from other centers in Europe—are extant only from the period following the establishment of the major centers of Torah toward the end of the tenth century (in Spain, already in the middle of that century). The information concerning the role of the woman in the responsa of R. Moses ben Hanokh, who was active in Spain in the mid-tenth century, and of R. Meshullam ben Kalonymus, who was active in Italy at that same time, are scarce and one cannot utilize them for even a general examination of the status of the woman.

Our focus upon the eleventh to thirteenth centuries derives from two factors: the desire not to cast our net too widely, and the nature of the sources. Hardly any information of worth is available concerning the situation of Jewish women in Ashkenaz in the fourteenth century. Only toward its end and during the fifteenth century do women again appear in the Ashkenazic responsa literature. This situation was influenced by the deterioration of the political and security situation of the Jews that began with the edicts of Innocent III at the beginning of the thirteenth century and reached its low point in the persecutions of Rindfleisch in 1298 and of Armelder in 1336, and in the harsh persecutions during the period of the Black Death in the mid-fourteenth century. During the course of this violence, thousands of Jews were killed and many communities were destroyed. The decline in the political situation of the Jews led to a partial retrenchment in the status of Jewish women as well.

In Spain, the picture is drawn somewhat more broadly. There, I referred to sources from the first half of the fourteenth century as well, as the transformations in the status of the Jewish woman in Spain were not as sharp and striking as in Germany and France. The decline in the political stature of the Jews there likewise was slower. In the history of Spanish Jewry, the fourteenth century has been described by Yitzhak Baer as a period of "decline," that reached its nadir in the harsh persecutions of 1391.

I nevertheless referred to the responsa of sages from both Ashkenaz and Spain after the year 1300. It is the nature of social frameworks not to change quickly. While there is need for a careful reading of these sources, it is also reasonable to assume that the way of life described therein reflects to a large extent that which was characteristic of earlier days.

Careful and thorough study of the various genres of halakhic sources (Talmud, Geonic literature, and works of the *rishonim*) requires examination of the text, comparison of sources and their devolution, and clarification of the various positions. To avoid excessive length, I elaborated upon these problems only when such explanations were useful for understanding developments and changes in the status of the woman. The same held true for the use of secondary literature. Hundreds of books and articles have been written about the status of women in Christian Europe during the Middle Ages, and several dozen concerning the Muslim family. Here, too, I only referred to those studies that would, in my opinion, shed light on parallel or contrasting developments in Jewish society.

CHAPTER ONE

The Image of the Woman:
Partner or the "Other"?

"Women are a nation unto themselves" is more than simply a clever turn of phrase.[1] Many men in medieval Jewish, Christian, or Muslim society saw woman as a different creature, inferior to themselves and having different character traits. This perspective found backing from Holy Scripture—which enjoyed great weight in the Middle Ages—from philosophy, and even from medical descriptions. This perception was an integral part of the overall view of the medieval world, which denied equality among human beings: Some people are of superior pedigree and of higher status and deserve special privileges. The feudal regime was based upon such a social structure. The division into classes was understood, not only as good and helpful to society, but as just and fitting in the eyes of God as well. This world view was shared by sages and thinkers, and hence greatly influenced the status of women in the Middle Ages, including that of the Jewish woman.

As noted in the introduction, the status of Jewish women within society and family and the attitude toward them were determined by three main factors: the biblical and Talmudic heritage, the attitude toward women in the neighboring Christian and Muslim societies within which the Jews lived and acted, and the role of the woman in supporting the family and in running household affairs. While the first two factors were often detrimental to the woman, the third was to her benefit. True, the Midrash and Talmud do say many things in praise of women, but other statements denigrate her, stemming from equally great and venerated Torah sages. The reality of Christian and Muslim society also generally weighed down her status and influenced it in a negative way, numerous examples of which will be cited below in our discussion of various subjects. By contrast, the third factor, the economic one, tended to act as an equalizing factor between the members of the couple, enhancing the perception of the Jewish woman as a "partner" in building the family unit. This last factor is more powerful than might be suspected. The threads that bind husband and wife together with bonds of mutual love and admiration are often influenced more by the sense of mutuality and the feeling that they are building their home together, than by the statements of wise men, great in Torah and wisdom as they may be.

The institution of marriage was understood by Judaism in an extremely favorable light, both from the individual viewpoint of the man and from that of its function in the world:

They taught: Whoever has no wife is in a situation lacking in goodness, without help, without joy, without blessing, without atonement . . . even without peace . . . without life . . . nor is he a complete person . . . [2] Until a person is twenty the Holy One blessed be He sits and waits for the man to marry. Once he reaches the age of twenty and has not married, He says: May his bones swell up.[3]

Among those considered to be "excommunicated from heaven," the rabbis included "a Jewish man who has no wife."[4] Such statements, and many others like it, combine the ideal of fulfilling the commandment of procreation with the desire to save the man from illicit sexual relations.

The Church theory of marriage is totally different. Already in medieval Christianity, celibacy was perceived as the preferred and chosen path. Even when medieval churchmen developed a more positive theory concerning marriage, stressing its sacramental aspect, they still maintained that celibacy was preferable. Such thinkers as Peter Lombard and Thomas Aquinas even advised the marriage partners to arrive at a mutual agreement to refrain from sexual relations in the framework of the marriage. Indeed, some women chose this path even against the will of their husbands, a point to which we shall return in chapter 11.

Jewish law completely precludes a unilateral decision by one of the marriage partners to refrain from sexual relations with the other; one who does so is defined as a *mored* or *moredet* ("rebellious husband or wife"). Moreover, abstinence is forbidden even should both partners agree. The Talmud and the Midrash cite various stories concerning people—including noted scholars—who refrained from sexual relations and in the end were overcome by their physical need or desire.

But notwithstanding Judaism's positive attitude toward the institution of marriage, this does not necessarily imply a positive image of woman as such. One may still marry a woman and have children with her even if one's valuation of her is extremely low.

In the present chapter, we shall examine the "theory"—that is, the attitude of several of the outstanding Jewish sages of the Middle Ages—regarding the position of woman in law and in society. However, one must constantly remember the profound gap between theory and "reality," the realization of things in actual life. The words of many of the sages of the Talmud and the Middle Ages emphasize the negative aspect in the nature of women. Had this image been constructed from men's actual attitude toward their wives, it seems likely that the picture would be more positive. This has already been noted by Eileen Power in relation to the attitude of Christian thinkers toward women.[5] The subject is a very broad one, and we can only discuss here a few basic aspects of it. We shall begin by examining the five main arguments offered as rationale for the inferior position of women.

1. The Creation and the Superiority of Man

One of the arguments used to justify the inequality between the sexes and the special privileges enjoyed by the man is his superiority to the woman according to the biblical narrative of the Creation. This holds true in three respects: (i) he was created first, his body from the earth and his soul by God; (ii) not only was the woman created later, but she was created from man's rib, like something secondary to the principal thing—implying that, were there true equality between them, God would have selected a different process of creation; (iii) she is described from the onset as "a helpmate to him"—that is, he is the significant one and she is a kind of vessel or tool to assist him. This idea is shared by all three monotheistic religions: It already appears in the Midrash, is ubiquitous in the words of Jewish sages and Christian scholars in the medieval period, and is also alluded to in the Quran. I shall bring several examples to exemplify this idea from the words of medieval Jewish sages.

R. Abraham ben David of Posquières (Rabad), the greatest Provençal sage of the twelfth century, thought that the creation of woman from man's rib made her subordinate to him, while creating a profound psychological connection between the two partners, who are in practice one body:

For had male and female been created from the soil as were the other creatures, woman would have stood in relation to man as the female animal does in relation to the male, who does not accept the rule of the male and is not available to him for his use. . . ."And he shall cling to his wife and they shall be one flesh"—that is, it is fitting that she should always be with him and I [he] with her—that is, to be one flesh. It is therefore fitting that a man should love his wife like his own body, honor her and have compassion for her and protect her as he protects one of his limbs. And she, too, is required to serve him and to honor him and love him like her own soul, for she was taken from him.[6]

This basic idea—a combination of positive and negative interpretations of the Creation—repeats itself in the words of other medieval sages, although there were admittedly those who emphasized more strongly the negative element.

According to R. Levi ben Gershom (Ralbag; Provence, 1288–1344), man's elevated stature led to a situation in which the Creator gave him as wife one who was intellectually inferior to him so as to care for all his needs and the needs of his household ("she was created for his service"), allowing him to devote his time to study Torah and to reflect upon "the intellects." It was for this purpose that she was created.[7]

Ralbag's terminology is taken from the realm of servitude. In his opinion, from the very outset man was given greater wisdom than his wife. He is more dignified and has the ability to attain higher spiritual achievements, while the woman serves him as a tool. This idea is expressed even more strongly by R. Yitzhak Aboab, in whose opinion the woman's eyes need to be "lifted" toward her husband "like the eyes of a servant toward her mistress" (we shall cite his words below).

In the Midrash, these things are said about the Creation in general—the forces of nature and the animals who were created to serve human beings—while in their literal sense they refer to man and his wife. One of the Tosaphists explained the creation of woman from the rib of man in similar manner, namely, so that the woman would be subject to her husband in her ribs and subjugated to him.[8]

R. Bahye ben Asher (Spain, end of thirteenth century) repeated the idea that the woman was created to serve man, and that she is like a "tool" alone. In his opinion, it was not merely by chance that the serpent began by seducing the woman rather than her husband, for he knew that she was "matter" and was subsidiary to her husband: "For even though the female is taken from him and they were two, the female is not considered part of the creation, for she is no more than something secondary to the primary thing."[9]

The manner of her creation likewise influenced woman's nature. According to the sages and the medieval commentators, woman's creation from Adam's rib made her hard like a bone and less amenable to compromise, as opposed to the man who was created from soil, which is softer and less rigid. But, as mentioned, there were also those who saw a blessing in the creation of woman from man's rib. They emphasized not only her inferiority and dependence upon the man, but also the deep relation between them, because in their root they are one body.

According to R. Yitzhak Aboab, the Torah also requires the husband to love his wife, as a consequence of the very fact of her having been created from him: "And if he loves her like his body he fulfills the Torah, as is written, 'and they shall be one flesh'—that she is like one of his limbs."[10] But he also sees fit to admonish the woman that this fact must not blind her:

Even though the woman is the partner of the man, she should not consider her husband as a friend, but as a master. . . And the woman should love her husband and he will rule over her . . . And her eyes should be raised to him like the eyes of a maidservant to her mistress, then she shall be very precious and honored in his eyes.

R. Yitzhak Abravanel likewise emphasized the positive aspect in woman's creation from the rib, its purpose being to emphasize the equality and cooperation between the partners. God did not create the woman from his feet, which are a lowly part of the body, so that she not be viewed with contempt ("so that she not be like a servant in his eyes"); nor did He create her from the head, so that she not be to him like "the mistress of the house"; rather, He created her from the ribs, which are in the middle of the body, "so that she shall be in the house like him" [e.g., in terms of status]. He explicitly ignored rabbinic dicta concerning this very subject, to be discussed below, which saw woman's nature in a negative light due to her creation from the rib. But he also emphasized that one cannot speak of equality between them in concrete terms. In his opinion, the statement that man was created "in the image of God" is repeated twice, "to indicate that male and female are not equally made in the image of God, but man alone."[11] The woman was not created "in the image of God," meaning, that she is intellectually inferior. Similar interpretations may be found in the words of other medieval Jewish sages. To the best of my knowledge, there is not even one medieval Jewish biblical commentator or thinker who speaks of full equality between man and woman in the context of the account of the Creation, although the writings of some Spanish Kabbalists do contain some allusion to this idea.

An issue unto itself is the negative approach to women taken by the Jewish philosophers active in Spain and Provence, particularly in the fourteenth century. This is an extensive topic, and we shall suffice here with mentioning only the main elements of their thought. One might have anticipated that people close to philosophy and rationalism would in general express a more sympathetic attitude toward women, but the reality is quite different. The attitude of the mystics—Spanish Kabbalists and Ashkenazic pietists—was better than that of the philosophers. In his Bible commentary, Ralbag expressed a hostile attitude toward women. In his view, woman's intellectual ability is inferior to that of man and stands on an intermediate level between the animals and beasts and man.[12] Ralbag's principled position regarding the "weakness of woman's intellect" affects his attitude regarding various other areas, such as their exemption from some of the mitzvot and from studying Torah, their refraining from participating in the Song of the Sea ("for it is not fitting that women should gather to tell the praises of God, may He be exalted . . . because of their intellective lack").[13]

Another sage active in Provence during that same time whose attitude toward women was also negative was R. Jacob Anatoli. In his opinion, only men were created in the image of God. Similar, if not so extreme, outlooks are found in the sermons of other sages who were active in Spain and Provence during that period.[14]

A negative perception toward several of the qualities of women is also to be found in the teachings of those Jewish sages who belonged to the neo-Platonic circle in Jewish philosophy in the fourteenth century. True, they do not express themselves in a style that indicates actual disdain toward women, such as is found

in Ralbag and others, but as a result of their ascetic approach and their perception of physical contact with woman as harming the religious and intellectual
perfection of man, they saw the sexual attraction toward woman in a negative
light. This approach is discussed in detail by Dov Schwartz, who concludes:

Thinkers of this circle did not create a demonic image of the woman, although the image
of the feminine as reflected in their writings is not at all complimentary. At the same
time, it is clear that they did not refrain from condemning and denouncing. In terms
of the development of medieval ethical theories, the teaching of that circle is a significant phenomenon: no longer an approach in which sexual abstinence is an ideal for
individuals or prophets, nor an ascetic doctrine suggested by allusion to those who
understand, but rather, separation from woman as marking the path for all those who
seek wisdom and religious perfection. If there is not a demand for total withdrawal from
sexual life, there is a definite tendency in that direction.[15]

2. The Temptation in the Garden of Eden and the Superiority of Man

The story of the Garden of Eden seriously harmed woman's image in the eyes
of both Jewish and Christian thinkers. Christians described Eve as the symbol
of the sinful woman, as opposed to the pure and unblemished Mary. Jewish
sages saw her as responsible for the expulsion of Adam from the Garden of Eden,
for the great efforts subsequently needed in order for man to obtain his livelihood, and for his descent from the high level on which he had been. In the opinion of some, she was even responsible for the entry of death into the world.
Using harsh language, Rabbenu Bahye described man's fall in the wake of Eve:

"That God has made man straight" [Eccles 7:29]. That is, He created him entirely intellective, that he might follow reason alone in all his attributes; but when the woman
emerged from him and was taken from his rib, then he sinned and moved away from
the path of intellect because of her, for she misled him to think evil of the Lord . . .
and it was the woman who caused death to come to him and to the entire world. . .
Because he never sinned at all so long as he was by himself, until the woman came;
but once the woman came, sin came . . .[16]

The idea that Eve brought death and sin into the world is not new. It is already
found in the midrashic literature, while Christian scholars made extensive use
of it in their discussions of the status of woman and her place in society.

The Midrash, which states that the serpent seduced Eve and had sexual relations with her, further contributed to the negative perception of woman.
The "primeval sin" cast a certain contamination or lasciviousness upon the
human race.[17] She was seen as a symbol of lightheadedness and as the one who
seduced man throughout the course of history, having been so easily seduced
by the snake. The curse imposed upon the woman in wake of this sin—"and
your longing shall be to your husband, and he shall rule over you" (Gen. 3:16)—
lay in the center of the discussions of Jewish sages concerning this issue,

serving as justification for woman's inferiority. The following are a few examples of the power of this argument. According to Maimonides, the verse "he shall rule over you," is not only descriptive, but prescriptive: The man is commanded to dominate and rule over his wife, such being the will of the Creator following the sin in the Garden of Eden.[18]

R. David Kimhi (Radak) interpreted: "'He shall rule over you'—to command you as he wishes, *like a master to a slave*."[19] Nahmanides writes similarly on that verse: "He punished her that she shall greatly desire her husband ... and he shall keep her *as a maidservant*. ... and this is measure for measure. For she had given to her husband and he ate at her command, so her punishment is that she shall no longer be able to command him, but that he command over her regarding all, at his will."[20] R. Bahye ben Asher followed in his wake: "And it is the way of the servant to flee from his master so as not to be enslaved. But He decreed here that she should long for her husband and be subjugated to him, in the opposite of the [usual] custom ... that her husband should be like a prince and a ruler over her."[21] In *Sefer ha-Zohar*, Eve is depicted as the archetype of the primeval sin and as the symbolic origin of bad women as such, of whom it says in Ecclesiastes (7:26) "and I find woman more bitter than death." It was Eve who brought death into the world. Due to her primeval sin, which was the first one in the world, it was decreed upon her and upon women generally that their husbands should dominate them, and that only when the men are "culpable" do their wives rule over them.[22]

According to R. Yitzhak Aramah, even the change of the woman's name to "Eve" is a consequence of the sin in Eden. The name *ishah* ("woman") expressed a deep spiritual connection to her husband, *ish* ("man"), of whom she was a part. After she brought about decline and curse to the human race as whole, she was given the name Eve (*havah*, from the word *hay*, life), indicating her exclusive involvement with childbirth and raising children.[23] But despite woman's descent from her high level, Rabbenu Aramah emphasized that those women who are suitable are still able to reach high spiritual levels, and that childbirth is not the woman's only task.

Let us conclude with the interpretation of one of the Tosaphists. *Hadar Zeqenim* states that Adam sinned in that he saw the woman as his equal, and therefore was cursed by needing to labor for his livelihood:

The Holy One blessed be He thought it good that he [Adam] should sit calmly and engage in the service of God while she exert herself in all the labors. But Adam did not think thus, but rather [spoke of] 'the woman whom you gave with me'—i.e., as an equal to me. Therefore he shall have no calm and no rest: 'By the sweat of your brow you shall eat bread.'[24]

The very thought on the part of Adam that the woman was equal to him was perceived as a sin deserving of punishment.

These examples are from different places and different time periods, indicating how wide an impression Eve's sin left upon the status of women throughout the generations. On the other hand, one should not be misled by the comparison of woman to a "a maidservant" or "slave," such as we have found in some of the commentators mentioned. The authors used these expressions to describe the woman's dependence upon her husband and her duties toward him, particularly in the running of the household. The negative connotation usually attached to the words "servant" and "maidservant," carrying with them an attitude of contempt and derision, has no basis in the words of the sages in question; it is clear from the context that this is not what they intended. As mentioned, several of them even emphasized the respect that the husband needs to display toward his wife and that he must love her "as his own body." Nevertheless, one cannot minimize the negative burden of these remarks and the concept of the woman's basic inferiority in the wake of her sin, nor of the task destined for her as a tool for the advancement of the man, who is more sublime and elevated in the attainment of spiritual qualities. However, one cannot hang all of these interpretations on the wording of the verse, "And he shall rule over you." In some of the references mentioned, and in other similar works that we have not cited here, commentators went far beyond this in their descriptions of the inferior place of the woman in society.

3. Characteristics of Woman and the Superiority of Man

In various cultures, including that of Judaism, the woman is understood as having negative characteristics.[25] This factor is the most important and significant of all in accounting for discrimination against women and their perception as the "other." I am not referring here to events that occurred thousands of years ago or to the sin of the first woman, but of negative character traits that are supposedly found in women by virtue of their very nature, and which are not to be found—at least not to the same measure—among men. This perspective is not new. It is found in ancient cultures, including those of Greece and Rome, and also appears explicitly in the midrashic literature.

The fact that similar complaints were lodged against women in the literature of the *Fabliaux,* widespread in bourgeois circles in Christian Europe during the twelfth and thirteenth centuries, helped to implant them even further within the hearts of people in Jewish society. In this literature, women are described as stingy, lazy, covetous, egoistic, exploitative, attracted toward foolishness and debauchery, making their husbands' lives miserable, tending to engage in witchcraft, treacherous, unfaithful to their husbands, and more. Christian theologians emphasized, more so than did poets and writers, the negative aspect of women's sexual desire, while virgins and martyrs were invoked as the symbol of women who deserved great respect.

Medieval Jewish sages who dealt with the characteristics of women repeated the accusations leveled against them in the midrashic literature. At first glance, one is dealing here simply with a kind of literary activity, originating in the great respect given to the words of the sages of the Mishnah and Talmud—sources to which one ought not to relate historical significance with respect to the Middle Ages. But examination of things in their full context indicates that at least some of the sages accepted them literally. Moreover, their being gathered together and the intensive involvement in them gave them great force. Thus, for example, R. Yitzhak Aboab assembled in his book *Menorat ha-Maor*—a book that enjoyed great popularity—most of those midrashim that speak of women with contempt, while repeatedly admonishing his readers to choose as wives only those who are deserving and blessed with positive values, due to the negative qualities of many women. There was thus woven together an entire system that could damage the woman's image.

R. Nissim of Kairouan, one of the leading sages of Jewry in the Islamic countries during the eleventh century, elaborated upon the negative qualities of women in his book *Ḥibbur Yafeh meha-Yeshu'ah*, and he, too, admonished men to choose their wives most carefully. From his words, it follows that many women possess negative qualities and only a small number are fit and deserving. He even invoked the story of King Solomon, who proved to his wise men how correct he was in stating that one cannot find even one good woman among a thousand (Eccles. 7:28). It is described there how a certain woman, who was considered extremely faithful, was prepared to kill her husband, the father of her children, in order to marry Solomon. This story, which was repeated with slight variations in various medieval sources, carries a particularly harsh message as to the allegedly negative character of women. During the Middle Ages, many sages sought ways to interpret this verse ("and a woman among all these I have not found") in a non-literal sense and thereby to reject the harsh connotations that follow from it. The greatest of the Geonic sages, Rav Saadya Gaon, even found it necessary to stress that it is impossible that these things refer to all women, for "we have found among them pious prophetesses."[26] It is clear that his interest was more to educate his contemporaries than it was to interpret the literal meaning of Scripture.

There were also some, including Rashi, who interpreted this verse ("and a woman . . . I have not found") as condemning women, in the literal sense. Rashi took great pains, in both his Bible commentary and in his responsa, to admonish his readers to honor their wives and to see them as partners and not as "others," as we discussed above. But he also "gave in" and interpreted the verse as implying that King Solomon did not find a single woman who was perfectly upright, not even among one thousand women. When he wished to do so, Rashi would often deviate from close adherence to the literal sense, whether due to polemic with the Christian interpretation of the Bible, or to achieve a didactic objective, but in this case he did not do so. He too thought that a woman is more easily seduced than a man, and that there is need for great caution and insistence upon modesty.

The extent to which the negative view of women's character was deeply rooted may be inferred from the ease with which the sages were willing to deprecate the biblical heroines, and to level against them various accusations that had no real basis in the scriptural text. Thus, according to R. Isaac Abravanel, the story of the idol made by Micah was recorded in Judges 17 for one clear purpose: "The story of the silver and its matter was written so that we might learn from it six things. First, that most evil derives from women . . . and that women's vows are worthless."[27] He refers here to the behavior of Micah's mother; yet, anyone reading the account in the Book of Judges will find that the behavior of Micah and that of the people of the tribe of Dan was far more serious than that of Micah's mother. R. Menahem Hameiri, who was noted for his tolerance toward his non-Jewish environment, and who was greatly concerned with the honor of the Jewish woman, interpreted Proverbs 31:10: "'A woman of valor who shall find? She is more precious than pearls': Few find her . . . because perfection of character in women is rare."

One of the negative qualities of women extensively mentioned by the Sages is their supposed *lightheadedness:* that is, their tendency to talk a lot and the ease with which they may be seduced. This quality is mentioned in the Book of Proverbs, in Ben-Sira, in Talmudic and midrashic literature, and is repeated extensively by medieval authors. It is also repeated in the writings of Christian thinkers and poets. Women's lightheadedness is alluded to in an off-hand way, as if it were something obvious and well known to all. One of the particularly negative expressions is that mentioned in the book of Ben-Sira, whose words are also quoted in support by medieval sages. A daughter is described there as a false treasure, who disturbs her father's peace. Among the weighty charges brought by Ben-Sira is the tendency to be easily seduced, which is so great that she needs to be guarded. The lightheadedness of women is also used as part of the background to various discussions about their way of life. Their lightheadedness and willingness to be seduced are attributed by the sages to Eve's sin in the Garden, who was easily seduced by the serpent, who is the embodiment of the Satan; from the time of that event this tendency is connected with the nature of woman.

The perception of woman as having an uncontrollable sexual appetite is common to most human cultures, a point that has already been discussed at length by anthropologists and sociologists. In their opinion, this idea stems, among other things, from men's own feeling of being overwhelmed by woman's charms and their preference to attribute the weakness to women rather than to themselves.

This accusation is repeated many times in various places in Talmudic literature. One is not speaking here of only a theoretical accusation. The sages undertook various measures in order to guard women and to keep them away from "sin." But the great majority of the incidents concerning this subject recorded in the Talmud deal with men, rather than with women, who found it difficult to overcome their sexual impulse.

This statement is even more true regarding Jewish sages in the Middle Ages. Very few cases describe lightheaded women who in practice were easily seduced; there were far more men who "stumbled" in this sin. This holds true, not only of the responsa literature, but also of folk literature of various sorts.[28] Even R. Nissim ben Jacob, who dealt extensively with the negative qualities of women, reports many cases of concupiscent men who found it difficult to restrain themselves, as against the modesty of women. Even among the sages from the Neoplatonic circle in fourteenth-century Spanish Jewish philosophy, there were those who interpreted the sages' criticism against excessive closeness to women and the admonitions to distance oneself from them because of the fear of seduction, as being rooted specifically in man's weakness and not in woman's nature.[29]

Another negative quality of women, repeated numerous times by many of the Jewish sages, is their supposed lack of understanding and intelligence. According to R. Solomon Ibn Adret (Rashba), the woman served as a symbol of the person who is lacking in wisdom.[30]

The most important testimony regarding the discrimination against woman because of their character traits derives from the extensive discussion in the Midrash and Talmud and in the works of the medieval Jewish sages concerning the "bad wife." This is a technical term, widespread in Rabbinic literature, without there being any corresponding term for the man ("bad husband"). The sages enumerated in detail the characteristic of "bad wives," the danger inherent in them, the suffering of their husbands, and how to protect against them. While they also speak in praise of the "good wife," the descriptions of the harsh qualities found in the "bad wife" are particularly powerful. There is no intermediate stage. If the husband was "deserving," his wife is a helpmate to him; if not, she is disastrous for him. Thus, we read: "A bad wife is as hard as a cloudy day"; "How bad is a bad wife, for Gehinnom is compared to her"; "'The Lord gave into the hands of one whom I cannot withstand' [Lam. 1:14]—This refers to a bad wife with a large *ketubah*"; "Every bad thing—only not a bad wife!!"; "One who has a bad wife is saved from the sufferings of Gehinnom, because he has already paid for all his sins in this life"; and many other like statements. Hence, "It is a mitzvah to divorce an evil wife."[31] The Talmud mentions various sages—including some of the greatest tannaim and amoraim—who had bad wives. One searches in vain for a complementary discussion of the woman who suffers a "bad husband." The self-evident, axiomatic assumption is that many women suffer from defective characters and hence there is a need to specifically discuss this subject at length and not its counterpart. Anyone reading the numerous sources on this subject from the Talmudic and midrashic literature collected, for example, by R. Yitzhak Aboab in his *Menorat ha-Maor* will easily see the intensity of the phenomenon.[32]

Particularly impressive testimony of the accusation that women have bad characters is preserved in the literature of the *maqamot*—stories written in rhymed prose. Beginning from the end of the twelfth century, a number of authors of *maqamot*—particularly in Spain—dealt with the evil qualities that supposedly characterize women. Several of these, especially Judah Ibn Shabbetai's *Minhat Yehudah Sone ha-Nashim*, attributed to them all possible bad traits in the world. Admittedly, one is dealing here with a specific literary genre in which humor played a major role, which was constructed upon certain conventions and influenced by the non-Jewish environment, both Christian and Muslim. But the power of this phenomenon nevertheless calls for comment. Scholars have vigorously debated the question as to how much historical weight is to be given to this literary form, but clearly some degree of criticism of women is contained therein. To what extent these stories made an impression may be inferred from the reaction of Yitzhak, "the Lover of Women," on behalf of women and his defense of them against Yehudah. His intense reaction likewise indicates the impression these things made upon readers.[33]

Both in the secular poetry of the Jews of Spain and Italy, and in their belles-lettres generally, one finds echoes of the attitude that the character of women is negative. Already in the poetry of Emmanuel of Rome (ca. 1300 C.E.) this is expressed with great intensity.[34]

It is worth mentioning that the discussion by medieval Jewish scholars of the subject of "bad wives" is more ubiquitous in Spain and North Africa than in Germany and France. But one must relate to this finding with caution, as the literary nature of the sources contributed to it in a decisive way. Musar (ethical-admonitory) literature, "secular" poetry, and *maqamot* were widespread in Spain and Italy, but not in Ashkenaz (Franco-Germany), and the discussion of "bad wives" is more commonly found in this literature. But one must not forget that one is not dealing here with a blanket condemnation of all women. During the course of the extensive discussion of the issue of "bad wives," the sages also emphasized the virtues of "good wives," while advising one who is about to marry to carefully choose the most suitable woman. This literary solution provides only a partial explanation of the extensive nature of the discussion in Spain and North Africa. *Sefer Ḥasidim,* composed in Germany during the first half of the thirteenth century, is a work explicitly devoted to ethical guidance; as such, it is involved extensively in the status of the Jewish woman.[35] Nevertheless, it did not devote a special discussion to the "bad wife" nor does it depict women as an inferior group because of their character traits (except for the discussion of women involved in witchcraft, which is more extensive than that related to men). It would therefore appear that the permissiveness and openness that characterized the way of life of many Jews in Spain and Italy, combined with the existence of this literary genre borrowed from the surrounding Gentile society, left their mark.

The Talmud mentions extensively the attribute of beauty in women, seen as a positive trait, and the sages even extolled at some length the woman who adorns herself for her husband. The Iranian literature contemporaneous to that of the Talmud also drew a connection between woman's beauty and her designation as a "good wife."[36] During the Middle Ages, discussion of this facet (beauty) in the halakhic, ethical, and homiletical literature became limited, alongside the extensive involvement with it in secular poetry. The beauty of women was "exploited," so to speak, for love poetry, becoming part of a genre that many sages did not view with favor, and therefore limited their involvement therein.

Talmudic literature also mentions many positive traits of women, such as woman's pleasant voice, her more compassionate nature than that of men, her superior intuition, and other traits. Medieval sages also mentioned these traits, but they did not occupy as central or striking a place as we would have expected if the sages had indeed wished to say more positive things in praise of women.

4. Women and Sorcery

The understanding of women as being associated with magic and sorcery is very old and common to various different cultures. Anthropologists and sociologists have connected it with the phenomena of pregnancy and childbirth in women, on the one hand, and with the difficulty of the male world in dealing with their sexual desire for and attraction toward women, on the other. The placing of the blame upon women provided an easy solution. Sorcery is directly related to woman's image as seductress, which we discussed above. The woman is seen as the emissary of the devil, using magical powers to trap men in her net. In the folklore of various peoples, the image of the harlot is associated with that of the witch.

In Talmudic and midrashic literature, women are shown as closely connected with the world of magic. In *Masekhet Sofrim* it states: "[Even] the most proper of women is a sorceress." In *Avot* it says, "He who multiplies wives— multiples witchcraft." Two women sitting on opposite sides of a crossroad are engaged in magic. And so on, many such additional sayings in the tannaitic and amoraitic literature together, and particularly in the Babylonian Talmud. Even the daughters of great Babylonian sages were suspected of engaging in witchcraft.[37] There is no doubt that the powerful belief in witchcraft and in magical powers that was widespread in Sassanian Babylonia also affected Jewish society.

ויתבונן וקבל המ ותומעל אֹל ועל תתומתו ׳ ויקיעך הכזלך חיור׳ וייטע להבוייתה

כִּי אָנכֵ

וְהָשׁוֹב

הָטִיתָ ט

לְקֵטוֹב

אוֹיבִי

בְּעֵלְעֵדֵי

לָנֶשׁוֹב׳

וְאֵזְפֵרָה

חָדָם אֵל

קְרָאוּגי

פֵּנֵהֶמֵא

אוֹדוֹתָם

אֲגֵידָה וְלֹא אֶרְאֵם ׳ אֵשִׁיחָה יָצִרְהּ וְנַקֵבִיתָה אֲנַטְיוּבֵס אַבַּח חָסִירֵי׳
וּמְשִׁיחָי נַבֵּס ׳ אֲיֵירֵי עַמֵי פַּהֵקְרֵיענוּבֵי לְהָדִרְבֵּס ׳ ל״ב ׳׳

The Jewish woman as heroine. Judith decapitating Holofernes. Italy, circa 1470. This motif also appears in other illuminations in medieval Jewish manuscripts. MS. Rothschild 24, fol. 217, from the collection of the Israel Museum, Jerusalem.

In medieval Jewish society, we find strong echoes of the belief that women were engaged in witchcraft, particularly in folk literature and in the teaching of Ashkenazic pietists. On the other hand, in halakhic literature per se there are far fewer echoes of this, a phenomenon deserving the greatest attention. One of the repeatedly discussed motifs is the connection between a woman being so-to-speak easily seduced and her connection with demonic powers: "that the Satan was created together with the woman . . . and she is easily seduced."[38] The *Scroll of Ahima'az*—composed in Italy in the middle of the eleventh century—contains a description of a woman who turned a boy into a donkey and of women who ate children. These child-eating women were in fact demons, but the author describes them as disguising themselves as women and not as men. Great sages of the medieval period also believed in the powers of charms recited by women. Thus, for example, R. Simhah of Speyer—one of the great sages of Ashkenaz at the end of the twelfth and beginning of the thirteenth century—is described as needing a woman's charm in order to heal his eye. The extensive involvement of Muslim sages with rationalism substantially limited the impact of this subject on Jewish society in the Islamic countries during the tenth to thirteenth centuries. It flourished with great power in *Sefer Ḥasidim,* written in Germany in the thirteenth century, a fact that is hardly surprising, as one is speaking there of a period during which European society was increasingly immersed in folk beliefs. A certain retreat from rationalism took place in the twelfth century, and an anti-rationalistic approach began to spread in Europe.

The catastrophe that visited Europe at the middle of the fourteenth century with the outbreak of the Black Death further increased the fear of supernatural forces. Man found himself lost and helpless in the face of terrible natural disasters that he did not know how to explain, so he turned toward the supernatural for answers. Women, who had always been connected with witchcraft and Satan, gradually became the scapegoat, a process that reached its height in the fifteenth century. The involvement of many women in healing increased fear of them even further and augmented the accusation that they were engaged in magic. As mentioned, these accusations reached their height during the fifteenth and sixteenth centuries, victimizing many innocent women who were burned at the stake because of their alleged involvement in witchcraft.

Even *Sefer ha-Zohar,* in which the woman is shown in a relatively more favorable light, emphasized her connections with witchcraft out of a demonic impulse to kill and to destroy, and even propounds a detailed theory to explain the connection between women and witchcraft. Eve's seduction by the serpent and her union with him is the earliest source of wicked women; woman's magical powers originate from the contamination of the serpent, a power that acts primarily during the period of women's menstruation. While the Talmud does state that at the revelation at Sinai contamination ceased from within Israel, the commandment to study Torah was only given to men; moreover, after the sin of the Golden Calf the same contamination returned, and it is more difficult to separate the women from it than it is the men. Hence women are more involved in witchcraft than are men.[39] While medieval literature does occasionally mention men who engaged in witchcraft, their number is infinitesimal compared to that of women.

As mentioned, there is no medieval Jewish work in which witchcraft—and particularly women who engage in witchcraft—occupies as great a place as it does in *Sefer Ḥasidim.* While men are also portrayed there as engaging in magic, their number is much smaller, and they are hardly ever portrayed as harming others, whereas the damage done by women is great. For example, a certain woman enchanted the son of her neighbor, and therefore he regularly cried at night; women enchanted their cohorts so that they would be unable to conceive; one woman wanted to suck the blood of another woman; women performed magic using herbs, to see who would live and who would die; one of them disguised herself as a cat; some of them performed acts with the help of demons.[40]

Joseph Dan published thirty-one demonological stories from the writings of R. Judah he-Hasid, preserved in MS. Oxford-Bodleian 1567 and in MS. Günzburg 82. These also portray both men and women who engaged in magic, but the number of women—and especially those who harmed others—is much greater. The picture is portrayed there of a woman who killed others through magical means, of a woman who enchanted other women so that they might not conceive, and of women who lay with demons.[41]

Sefer Ḥasidim also describes an attempt to hurt a woman who was suspected of eating children. The pietist sage objected to this, and proposed to suffice with a threat alone.[42] Ashkenazic Jews rarely executed anyone, and the Hebrew sources do not contain any testimony of Jewish women who were executed by the Jewish courts for engaging in magic; in this respect, their lot was better than that of the Gentile women in the same environment during the fifteenth and sixteenth centuries, who suffered greatly from similar charges. But their image was harmed by the folk beliefs that influenced the general mentality of people.

5. The "Medical Inferiority" of Women and the Superiority of Men

The "inferiority" of women assumed a "scientific" nature. Medieval people, be they Jews, Christians, or Muslims, found additional justification for viewing women as inferior to men from contemporary medical theories.[43] This approach derived from the medical theory borrowed from Greek and Roman science, whose scientific ideas and outlooks were incorporated in scientific and medical works written by Jews, Muslims, and Christians, and even enjoyed a certain position of importance in works of an explicitly theological and ethical nature.

The woman was considered to be inherently inferior by her nature (the warmth of her body and the composition of her blood), her physiological characteristics not enabling her to be as perfect a creature as man. According to the Aristotelian view, the very belonging of women to the female sex influences their characteristics. Hence the woman tends more towards jealousy, to argumentativeness, to depression, to forgetfulness, and even to speaking falsehood. Witchcraft was one of the means intended to ease her confrontation with her weakness. In practice, these theories provided an explanation for sages during the ancient and medieval period (again—Christians, Muslims, and Jews), a "scientific" platform upon which to base their age-old theories about the superiority of the man.

Menstruation is a subject unto itself. This is a broad topic, about which a relatively large number of sources have been preserved and which is discussed at length in research literature.[44] We shall suffice here with a hint at the main things alone, related to the image of the woman. Even though one is dealing here with an explicitly physiological phenomenon, it had considerable negative impact upon the image of woman. It is difficult not to agree with the statement of Ron Barkaï:

It seems to me that there is no other physiological phenomenon which has been removed from its natural context and to which there have been attributed such mythological and supernatural dimensions, as happened to the monthly discharge of uterine tissue.[45]

Already in Greek culture, negative magical and therapeutic powers were attributed to menstrual blood, with Aristotle among those supporting this view. In the Midrash, the laws pertaining to menstruation are understood—alongside the commandments of separating *hallah* and lighting Shabbat candles—as punishment and atonement imposed upon the woman for her role in the primordial sin in Eden.

The biblical and Rabbinic prohibitions against sexual relations and other kinds of intimate contact with a menstruant woman were greatly expanded in folk culture. There are those who conjecture that this also reflected Karaite influence, although there is no unequivocal proof of this. A tractate written during the Geonic period, *Beraita de-Niddah,* whose origin is not altogether sufficiently clear, contains many stringent rules regarding the laws of menstruation. Our purpose here is not to deal with these, but to note the damage they caused to the image of the woman. Among other things, it is stated there in the name of the sages that even the speech that emits from the menstruant's mouth is impure, and that a man should avoid stepping on the soil upon which a menstruant woman had previously trodden. Generally speaking, although Christianity and Islam also held a negative attitude regarding sexual relations with a menstruant woman, they were not as strict in this matter as was Jewish halakhah.[46]

The Talmud brings the ruling of Rav Hunna: "Any labor that a woman does for her husband, a menstruant does for her husband, apart from pouring his wine, making his bed, and washing his face, hands and feet."[47] But during the Middle Ages, we find in the rulings of the Ashkenazic rabbis, and thereafter among the Sephardic sages, further customs of separation beyond those appearing in the words of Rav Hunna. Thus, for example, R. Eliezer ben Nathan (Raban) writes: "Today women are accustomed not to cook and not to bake during their menstruation." Two generations later, R. Yitzhak ben Moshe wrote in his book *Or Zaru'a:*

And in the name of the sages of Narbonne, my master the Rabyah wrote that they prohibit a menstruant from eating at the table of her husband ... And in whatever we are able to be strict, we are strict and distance ourselves from her, and we give her [separate] utensils and bowls and spoons and keys and linen and bedclothes to use during her days of impurity ... and there are women who refrain from entering the synagogue or from touching the scroll; while this is merely a stringency, they do well to do so.[48]

I. Ta-Shma has shown that the Ashkenazic sages were more stringent regarding customs of separation from the menstruant than were the Sephardic sages, following in the wake of the ancient Palestinian tradition. But in Spain and in other places, they were also strict regarding the laws of menstruation.

Folk customs made the attitude to the menstruant even worse, and there were some places where she was even forbidden to enter the synagogue. The opposition to these stringencies of such rabbis as Rav Sherira Gaon and Maimonides did not suffice to abolish folk customs whose source also lay in archaic fear of the phenomenon of menstrual blood and the attribution to women of magical powers. A late custom in Ashkenaz, of women refraining from reciting blessings during their menstruation, further harmed their image. They even refrained from reciting the blessing over Shabbat candles, even though the sages knew well that this custom was opposed to halakhah. Many of these strict customs originated among the women themselves, who imposed upon themselves various edicts that passed from mother to daughter, but it is highly doubtful whether this would undo the harm they caused to their image. The repeated admonitions by the Babylonian Geonim and of later sages against these stringencies, in themselves indicate the difficulty involved in countering this phenomenon. The power of accepted custom or practice was stronger than the authority of the rabbis.

In practice, we may distinguish three stages in the exacerbation of the attitude toward the menstruant: (a) prohibitions whose source lay in misgivings about becoming accustomed to intimacy, that is, avoidance of everyday physical contact between husband and wife that might lead to sexual contact; (b) prohibition against the menstruant touching food and utensils, due to the fear that she might render them impure. The source of this lies in the strictures of eating *hullin* (non-sacred food) in a state of ritual purity, observed in the Land of Israel not only during the Second Temple period, but for centuries after its destruction. These stringencies were observed at least in part even during the Geonic period; (c) withdrawal from the menstruant and from food and other objects she has handled because of "danger." Thus, menstrual blood was associated with magical forces.

6. The Obligation to Perform Mitzvot and the Superiority of Man

Halakhah (Jewish law) determined that women are exempt from the performance of certain *mitzvot* (religious obligations). Sages and scholars have suggested various explanations for this exemption; but whatever the reason may have been, the woman's image was harmed thereby. The fulfillment of the *mitzvot*, which originated from the Holy Scriptures, was understood as indicative of the status of a Jewish person. The comparison found in the Talmud in this connection between "women, slaves, and minors," who are exempt from certain obligations that others are obligated to perform, certainly did not enhance their image. One may assume that women's self-image was likewise harmed. While the words of Jewish women from the Middle Ages have hardly reached us (with the exception of some letters from the Cairo genizah and several other important fragments), so that we do not know from a first-hand source what their reaction was, it is difficult to imagine that this did not harm their image. Parents, generally speaking, preferred sons. Already at an early age, the Jewish girl knew that her parents prayed that God would "bless them with male children." Those who had only daughters received felicitations for sons, such as "May God bless you with something to uplift your hearts."[49] Despite the fact that she reached her majority and became obligated to perform the *mitzvot* at age twelve, a year earlier than her brothers, no festive ceremony was conducted in her honor, nor were there any external symbols to indicate this—such as the donning of tefillin, being included in the quorum (*minyan*) for prayer, being called to the reading of the Torah, or a festive meal to honor the occasion—as was the case for her brother.[50] The exemption from some of the *mitzvot* emphasized her inferiority even more. We shall suffice with one example of the connection between woman's obligation to fulfill only some of the *mitzvot* and her perception as inferior in comparison to the man.

R. David Ibn Shushan, who lived during the late Middle Ages, devoted a special halakhic-philosophical tract to the question as to whether Jewish women enjoy "survival of the soul"—that is, afterlife—as they do not perform a large part of the *mitzvot*: "One needs to examine whether according to the view of the Torah the woman's soul survives or not, because there are arguments on behalf of the woman's soul surviving [after death], and other aspects to suggest that the opposite is the case." After a long and convoluted discussion, he arrived at the conclusion that women also have a portion in the World to Come, as they help their husbands and allow them to engage in Torah. This idea as such is not new, but already appears in the Talmud.[51] However, the fact that an enlightened Jewish sage found it necessary to discuss this question at length, drawing extensively upon philosophic thought, calls for explanation.

Offhand, one might argue that the issue of the meaning of women's exemption or non-performance of *mitzvot* was quite distant from the hearts of both men and women, as they were born into a reality that had been practiced by the Jewish people for centuries and in every locale, and that was understood as an integral part of the Jewish cultural heritage over the generations. But the sources indicate that this was not the case. Jewish women in Ashkenaz (Franco-Germany) demanded the privilege, not only of performing *mitzvot* from which they were exempt, but also of blessing over them, notwithstanding the serious concern that such a blessing might be considered a "blessing in vain" or an "unnecessary blessing." During the eleventh century, some of these women began at their own initiative to fulfill some of the *mitzvot* in which they were not obligated and to recite the blessing over them. R. Yitzhak Halevi permitted them to do so.[52]

His wording, "If they wish to do so . . . we do not prevent them" indicates that the women were the initiators and that, in the opinion of R. Yitzhak Halevi, the head of the yeshiva in Worms in the mid-eleventh century and one of Rashi's teachers, they are not to be opposed. This is thus a kind of retroactive agreement. Their initiative indicates that the matter was important to them and that they felt deprived. It would seem that the background to their initiative was a general improvement in the status of Jewish women in Ashkenaz during that period. It is also possible that the religious revival among the Christian women in their surrounding environment augmented this.[53] Many of the sages of Ashkenaz and France ratified R. Yitzhak Halevi's ruling, among them R. Jacob Tam, the leading Tosaphist. A few opposed it because of their concern with "unnecessary blessings," an opinion supported by most of the Sephardic sages, including Maimonides. About one hundred years later, we find sages who agreed to include women in the quorum of three or ten needed for the "invitation" to Grace after Meals—a subject to which we shall return in chapter 8.

7. Expressions in Praise of Women and their Perception as "Partner"

We have noted the damage done to the image of the woman in various areas, and brought numerous examples of statements in condemnation of the woman and justifying her "inferiority" vis-à-vis the man. But there were also expressions by the sages in praise of women and of their perception as a "partner." However, one is not speaking here of a fully developed, well-based theoretical structure, such as that which existed regarding the five subjects mentioned above, or of an explicit statement regarding their right to equality. Nevertheless, these expressions are of great importance, especially against the background of the discrimination described above, which was based upon interpretation of the Scriptures and of God's will.

We shall suffice with three examples from different areas and from different time periods. The most explicit one is that of Rashi, in whose opinion marriage is of the nature of a holy covenant made between the two partners. In his interpretation of Malachi 2:14–15, he explains that the woman is "the seed of God," from which there follows the obligation to behave toward her with great respect. These brief remarks by Rashi display his great respect for the institution of marriage. Among the traditional medieval Bible commentators, I have not found any other thinkers who followed in Rashi's path, in terms of constructing a clear, well-established structure. According to Rashi's interpretation of the above verse in Malachi, God created both Adam and Eve, from which it follows that the

women are "the seed of God." Generally speaking, the medieval sages interpreted this powerful expression as referring to the sons whom a man seeks and
wishes: Children are "the seed of God." Rashi differs. In later editions, Rashi's
language was "corrected" by the printers, who substituted the word "and he"—
that is, the man—is "the seed of God." But manuscripts indicate that the
reading "and she" is the correct one, as is also implied by the context. Moreover,
in Rashi's commentary on the Torah, there is no hint of the inferiority of the
woman against the background of her creation from Adam's rib, and that too
is not merely a matter of chance. In his commentary on the Creation chapters
in Genesis, Rashi consistently refrains from citing midrashim that speak in contempt of the woman, despite the fact that he brought many other midrashim
related to the Creation in general.

On the other hand, he does bring there midrashim that praise women, and he
especially stressed their devotion during the enslavement in Egypt and their love
for the Land of Israel, which saved them from the sin of the spies and from their
punishment. Unlike their husbands, they did enjoy the privilege of entering the
Land of Israel: "because they treasured the land." He likewise stresses the high level
of the daughters of Zelophehad, who saw what Moses was not privileged to see.[54]

Particularly interesting is one of his responsa that indicates the extent to
which Judaism, in his opinion, required the husband not only to honor his wife,
but also the great reward forthcoming to one who behaves towards her with
love and friendship. He was asked about a husband who wished to divorce his
wife without paying her *ketubah* money, on the basis of the argument that when
he married her she had scars on her face that she concealed by means of makeup,
and hence the marriage was "an erroneous purchase"—that is, undertaken under
false premises. Evidence sent to Rashi confuted the husband's testimony, to
which he reacted with great vehemence. But he did not suffice with a discussion of the halakhic aspect and with ruling in favor of the woman, but also took
the opportunity to admonish the husband. Rashi's remarks about the merits of
a husband who behaves properly toward his wife are of particular interest:

And the man showed that his actions were done for ill, and revealed that he is not of
the seed of Abraham our father, whose way is to have compassion on other people—all
the more so for his wife who had entered into a covenant with him . . . And happy is
he to be with her and to acquire through her the life of the World to Come . . .[55]

Marriage is an act of "covenant" between husband and wife, with all of the
intense emotional and spiritual baggage implied by this concept. The Holy One
blessed be He is the witness to the upholding of this covenant. Particularly
remarkable is Rashi's statement that had the man behaved decently toward
his wife he would "acquire through her the life of the World to Come." The idea
that a man may receive a reward in the afterlife thanks to his good relations with
his wife is not found in the midrashic or Talmudic sources. Possibly, Rashi may

have seen it as a direct consequence of the "covenant" made between the two partners in which God also takes part, as according to the midrash He rests his Shekhinah between them and He is the third partner in the covenant of marriage.[56] Thus, each of the partners who develops and cultivates the marriage ipso facto enjoys the blessing of the third partner, namely, God. But this is not an isolated case. From other comments of Rashi in his Bible and Talmud commentary, one can see his attitude of respect and value toward the woman. Rashi's daughters and granddaughters enjoyed a position of great honor and respect within the family. It follows that his sons-in-law continued in his tradition.

The second example is from *Sefer ha-Zohar*. Unlike the approach of Rashi, which has thus far not been discussed at all in the research literature, the position of women in the *Zohar* has been discussed in great detail. I shall therefore suffice here with a brief sketch of the main points. The relations between God and the Shekhinah are similar to those between husband and wife. The Shekhinah does not rest upon a person and the multitude of blessings is not drawn down from above except through the joining together of male and female; if one does not marry, his soul does not merit to be included within the realm of Divine holiness in the life of the World to Come.

The woman is thus the reflection of the Shekhinah. The man is privileged to be attached to the Shekhinah by virtue of his connection to his wife. Only when the house is properly established and the two partners perform marital relations with love and affection does God rest His Spirit upon them. Their perfect union, to the point of their becoming one body and one soul, is a condition of their receiving holiness and of the Shekhinah dwelling upon them. The two partners help to bring down holiness from its supernal place. Thus, the perfection of the man and the fulfillment of his mission in the world depend upon the woman and his way of life with her. She is a full partner in fulfilling his purpose upon the earth. The husband is required to make his wife happy and to acknowledge her virtues, for it is through her virtue and by her means that he enjoys the supernal mating with the Shekhinah. A person's prayer is also more readily accepted by God when he is married.

The importance of love in married life is stressed repeatedly in *Sefer ha-Zohar*. The husband must take account of his wife's desires and rights in the realm of marital relations:

The man must come to the place for lying together which the woman has prepared for him. And even if his bed is more comfortable and pleasant than hers he must forego it; even if he has a bed of gold and embroidered linens to sleep on, and she makes his bed with rocks on the ground and with a covering of straw, he should leave his own bed and sleep by his wife.[57]

In the portrayal of the Garden of Eden in *Sefer ha-Zohar*, women—and especially the four matriarchs—are depicted as being on a very high level. The

equality between men and women in the Garden of Eden, even if it is not complete, is far greater than that accepted on the earth. Women even merit there to
engage in *mitzvot* that they did not perform in this world, and with greater
depth. Of special interest is the description of the union of the souls in the World
to Come, analogous to the union of bodies in this world. In connection with
this description, it is explained that even a union "of cleaving of desire" of
two partners in this world has blessed fruits. Abraham and Sarah created pure
souls from their union of desire even before Isaac was born to them:

> When souls cleave to one another, they make fruits and lights emerge from them and
> they become as lamps, and these are the souls of the proselytes who convert ... Through
> the union of desire of those two righteous people (i.e., Abraham and Sarah) there were
> born the souls of the proselytes, during the time they were in Haran, as the righteous
> do in the Garden of Eden.[58]

It is emphasized there that all this takes place on the condition that there was
desire of both the husband and wife together. The soul of the husband awaits
his partner in Paradise, and upon the death of the wife there is a renewed union
between the partners.

The description generally, and especially the high level of women in Paradise
and their union with the soul of the men with its blessed fruits, was bound to
improve the image of the women. Even if in this world they do not occupy
the same position as men in religious worship, they shall do so in the next world
and merit the highest levels. The speech of the souls who were born to Abraham and Sarah in this world when their union was "with desire" was likely to
emphasize the high level of the institution of marriage and to refute the view
of the Neo-Platonic circle in fourteenth century Spanish Jewish philosophy,
which saw sexual relations in a negative light and called to limit them insofar
as possible, as noted above.

The sexual life of husband and wife was a subject of great importance in the
world of the Kabbalists. Images from the sexual life were extensively used in
their descriptions of the Divine *Sefirot*. The sexual act was perceived as a sublime act that serves as a metaphor for the relations between the human soul and
the supernal realms. The act, performed between two marital partners, is understood as a mystical participation in those same spheres.[59]

The understanding of the institution of marriage in the thought of the Kabbalists was likely to improve the woman's image and to emphasize the importance of her place within the family. They saw marriage as a sacral act creating
an eternal connection between the partners. A profound mutual relation remains
between them even if the husband predeceases his wife. They therefore held a
negative attitude toward the remarriage of a widow. While this outlook may
harm the living woman, the widow, who is expected to remain forever in
her widowhood, it serves to improve her overall image. She is bound to her

husband by delicate but powerful fibers of her soul and is part of an eternal sacral covenant, comparable to the covenant between God and Israel. Some of the phrases chosen by the Kabbalists to express this relationship are very powerful, such as: "A man's wife is like a candle that has been lit from him, and the two of them are one candle. The light of this one emerges from that; if one of them dies down it is lit from the second light, because the light is one."[60]

On the other hand, *Sefer ha-Zohar* also speaks a good deal about "bad wives," of the superiority to which the man is generally entitled within the home, and of the involvement of women in acts of witchcraft—from all of which it is clear that one is not to see it as reflecting a world in which there is complete equality between husband and wife.

The third example of praise expressed toward women is taken from R. Gedaliah Ibn Yihya, a prominent sixteenth century Italian sage, who at the end of his life moved to Alexandria in Egypt. He wrote a special work, still extant in a manuscript, in praise of women. In this work, he discourses at great length concerning their historical virtues and their positive character. They are noted for wisdom, decency, and uprightness. He likewise rebuffs the attacks upon them. Even regarding the temptation in the Garden of Eden, he sought extenuating explanations for Eve and placed the blame upon Adam. The latter had heard directly from God that it was forbidden to eat of the fruit of the tree of knowledge, and therefore should have questioned Eve's proposal to eat of the fruit of the garden and not to accept her words.

8. Between Image and Reality

One could invoke many other examples of things said in praise of women, in particular *Sefer Ḥasidim*, which presents a positive image of woman and of the attitude which she deserves. But it is difficult to assume that the numerous, detailed descriptions of "evil women" and their negative qualities, as found in the exegetical, philosophical, and ethical literature, did not leave an impression upon the consciousness of people and did not hurt the image of women. But, in my opinion, it would be an error to describe the concrete status of the woman in her home and the complex of relations between herself and her husband on the basis of the theory mentioned, as is done extensively in research literature. One must not blindly accept the negative image of women as reflecting the actual attitude toward women in society and in the family. There is a profound gap between this image, which originates in the words of sages and poets, and reality. It is highly doubtful whether the husband and the members of the family generally saw their wife and mother in light of the description of Eve, who was later created from Adam's rib and who stumbled in the Garden of Eden. As mentioned, relations within the family were influenced by shared interests, by

the creation of a family unit, by raising children, by the woman's share in supporting the family, and by the specific character traits of the members of the
couple, more than they were by abstract descriptions. Moreover, it is doubtful
whether the above theories were known to all, as the expense of manuscripts
prevented the dissemination of these works among a wide public.

Anyone contemplating the relations between R. Eleazar of Worms and his
wife Dulca, who was killed when she sacrificed her life to save her husband and
her son, will not find a trace of the influence of the "discriminatory theories"
mentioned above. To the contrary, he will find full partnership and cooperation, intense relations of love, and mutual respect and admiration—and to this
one might add many further examples, including some in the Cairo Genizah.[61]

On the other hand, one may not ignore entirely the impression left by such
statements. Preachers made use of these descriptions, and their words were
absorbed by synagogue goers, especially given the fact that they had their source
in the words of outstanding sages.[62] But let us now turn to the other chapters
of this book, which shall be concerned with the concrete reality of woman's
position in medieval Jewish society.

CHAPTER TWO

Age at Marriage

T he age at which marriage took place in medieval Jewish society bore important implications for the structure of the family unit and the woman's status within the family. Several major questions relate directly to this issue, such as the degree of involvement of the woman in choosing her intended bridegroom, the involvement of the parents in the life of the new couple, the couple's place of residence, their degree of economic independence, the degree of fertility of the woman, the woman's education, and her relation to her husband. But despite the great importance of this subject, we do not have at hand the sources needed to conduct a thorough and properly documented examination of this question. The study required is of an explicitly statistical and demographic nature, and in the absence of documentary material, it is impossible to arrive at an unequivocal conclusion. Historians of family life in medieval Christian Europe are in that respect more fortunate: They enjoy the availability of richer and more varied sources, even if these too are not abundant.

Nevertheless, a careful examination of sources from the areas of halakhah, folk literature, and particularly of responsa literature from the Middle Ages, will enable us to draw a picture—even if only a partial one—regarding this question. These sources indicate that the age at marriage of the Jewish man, and especially that of the Jewish woman, was often quite young, particularly during the tenth to fourteenth centuries. Examination of the entire complex of sources available indicates that a transformation took place during the course of the Middle Ages. Numerous cases are described of marriage of young girls who had not yet reached sexual or mental maturity, including some who had not yet reached the age of twelve, the age considered by Jewish law to be that of puberty. The marriage age for men also decreased significantly, although it was usually higher than that for women. The phenomenon of child marriage was common in Jewish society in both the Muslim countries and in Christian Europe, more so than is generally assumed in the research literature. Even though the sources do not enable us to determine the exact number of these marriages, they do indicate the existence of harsh cases of child marriage in the literal sense, especially in Muslim Spain.[1]

This conclusion is not accepted by all scholars. S. D. Goitein, who examined the marriage age in Mediterranean Jewish society on the basis of the Cairo Genizah, concluded that child marriage was a rare phenomenon. He found few sources in the Genizah indicative of marriage of girls who had not yet reached physical or emotional maturity. He therefore concluded, not only that the phenomenon was a rare one, but that it was of no significance from a social viewpoint.[2] Those isolated cases that he found in the Genizah sources dealt mostly with orphan girls; hence, he conjectured that the phenomenon of child marriage was limited primarily to this group.

As he states explicitly, Goitein relied in his research upon the Genizah sources. His main argument is based on silence (*a silentio*)—that is, the fact that only a small number of sources dealt with the marriage of children who had not yet reached the age of twelve. Nevertheless, he too agreed that young women were generally married at a very early age.

It is worth noting that in the halakhic sources the concept "minor" (*qetana*) refers to a girl who had not reached the age of twelve years and a day, whereas *bogeret*, "pubescent maiden," refers to anyone past the age of twelve and a half. Hence the concept *bogeret*, found in the Genizah literature and in halakhic literature generally, may well refer to any girl who has reached this age, and not necessarily to a young woman who is mature from the mental, physical, or psychological viewpoint. As a result, the "mature" bride may in many cases also be quite young.

1. The Talmudic Heritage

The age of marriage in the Land of Israel and in Babylonia during the Mishnaic and Talmudic period is subject to some dispute among researchers. The assumption held widely in the past, that this age was quite low, has meanwhile been subject to considerable doubt. Decisive evidence either way is absent. In any event, with all due respect to the importance of this question, this is not our subject here; rather, we are concerned with the Talmudic heritage as it appears in the discussions of the medieval sages, and as it was understood in the consciousness of people living in the Middle Ages. What influenced the stance of Jewish sages in the Middle Ages was not the historical reality of the Talmudic period, but the statements by the tannaim and amoraim either in praise or disapprobation of early marriage.

Several Talmudic sages counseled that a person should marry his sons and daughters at a young age, and the Talmud and Midrash even contain clear testimony of the marriage of children.[3] On the other hand, there is also strong opposition in the Talmud to the marriage of young girls who have not yet attained intellectual and emotional maturity, and who are unable to judge for themselves the suitability and character of their intended husband, even though from a purely formal halakhic point of view the father is allowed to betroth his underage daughter and such a marriage is considered entirely valid. The Talmud (*Niddah* 13b) states that: "Those who play with female children delay the Messiah." This is an expression of clear opposition to sexual relations with girls who are not yet able to bear child, which are understood as "playing" rather than as proper marital relations. There is no mention there of the exact age of such girls, but it more or less overlaps the age of puberty at twelve, as mentioned above. In any event, the expression "play with female children" indicates the extent to which the phenomenon was understood as negative and deserving of condemnation.

In the name of the amora Rav—or, according to another tradition, in that of the Palestinian amora R. Eleazar—it is said: "A man is forbidden to marry off his daughter when she is underage, until she grows up and says, 'I want so-and-so.'"[4] This unequivocal formulation ("is forbidden") clearly indicates the opposition to the phenomenon of marrying off immature children and its total rejection from the moral viewpoint, even if it is legally valid. Moreover, the reason given for the prohibition—namely, the girl's right to express an opinion on the choice of her intended husband and to give her consent—carries important implications for the woman's status in the family and in society.

Intense opposition to the marriage of young girls is brought in the name of R. Shimon bar Yohai, that "Whoever marries off his daughter when she is young minimizes the bearing of children and loses his money and comes to bloodshed."[5] On the other hand, the Talmud and Midrash also cite the words of other sages in praise of early marriage, making it clear that there were disagreements among the sages regarding this issue.[6] In any event, the medieval rabbis saw no contradiction among these sources, being used to harmonizing different, conflicting sources. They read these sources as, on the one hand, opposing the marriage of a "minor"—i.e., one less than twelve years of age—and as opposed to delay in the marriage of a "mature girl"—one above twelve and a half—on the other. The conclusion reached by *Sefer Ḥasidim*, namely, that the ideal age for marriage of a maiden is thirteen, or slightly later (as we shall see below), could easily serve as a "compromise" among the different sources. In any event, those sources that oppose postponing the marriage of a "mature" maiden in no way negate the powerful impression left by the firm opposition of the sages to the marriage of a "minor" child before the age of twelve. This holds true particularly in relation to the opinion of Rav, to which the medieval sages referred extensively.

2. The Situation in Babylonia in the Eighth and Ninth Centuries

It follows from the Geonic literature that the Babylonian Geonim continued, in principle, the negative attitude to the marriage of young girls, even though from a legal viewpoint they acknowledged the validity of child marriage where the father had given his consent. Nevertheless, already in Geonic halakhic literature we begin to find more equivocal formulations. Some of these lack the firm opposition to the marriage of minors found in the above-mentioned remarks of Rav.[7] The prohibition against marrying a minor is described explicitly by one of the Geonim, not as one for which one is punished, but as merely an ethical injunction. One may also infer the opposition to marriage of underage orphans from the responsum of one of the Babylonian Geonim, who proposed that sanctions be taken against a religious court judge who officiated at the marriage of underage orphans.

This sanction, directed against a *dayan* who married an underage orphan, indicates the ubiquity of the phenomena and the difficulties encountered in the struggle against it. Nor were all the judges meticulous in their execution of the above-mentioned instructions of the Geonim. In any event, sources from as early as the ninth century already indicate that the phenomenon of marriage of young girls, including child marriage of those who had not yet reached the age of twelve, gradually increased and spread.

3. The Situation in Non-Jewish Society

In Christian Europe, child marriage was relatively rare. The Church established twelve years as the minimum age of marriage for girls (like the age of maturity in Judaism) and fourteen for boys, but they were not always insistent in observing this norm. Child marriage was not uncommon in aristocratic circles, particularly among the high aristocracy. This was due to the fear that, upon the father's death, the young girl would pass over to the guardianship of the owner of the estate, who would marry her off to whomever he wished, quite often even to elderly noblemen. Eileen Power has observed that these marriages were frequently arranged when the children were still in their cradles.[8] Indeed, as a rule members of the wealthy families married at an earlier age than did those from poor families. If the father of minor children died, the guardians responsible for the inheritance often married them off at a young age. At times, children whose marriages had been solemnized continued to live apart for several years, with their parents or with a guardian.

But these cases were a minority that characterized the higher strata of society; generally speaking, the marriage age in Medieval Europe was higher.[9] David Herlihy, invoking numerous examples to support his statement, concluded that the estimated average age of marriage of noblewomen in the twelfth century was between twelve and sixteen, while that of boys was older. During the late Middle Ages, the average marriage age was even higher.[10]

Herlihy also noted an additional finding, one of great importance for understanding developments within Jewish society. In Christian Europe, particularly in Italy, an important change took place. The marriage market for women grew smaller, as a result of which the size of the dowry that the parents of brides were expected to pay to the grooms increased. He conjectures that two factors may have led to this development. First, the functions fulfilled by women in the noble families and in the cities declined, as a result of which their importance as a factor contributing to the economic power of the family declined. I have already noted (above, in the introduction), that today some people question this conclusion regarding the power of women in aristocratic families. Second, the power of the "market of women" decreased. While parents attempted to marry off all their daughters, they only did so for some of their sons; a certain portion of the men went on the Crusades or entered the priesthood.[11] The inflation in the size of the dowries was a heavy burden for many people in the villages and in the cities, leading to a rise in marriage age. Poets and preachers protested against this, describing the great difficulties confronted by parents who set about to marry off their daughters. At the beginning of the fourteenth century, Dante also complained about this in his *Divine Comedy*. The Church even organized charitable enterprises to assist needy families in marrying their daughters; Herlihy offers examples of all of these.

A similar picture emerges from *Sefer Ḥasidim*. "Money" became a weighty consideration in marrying off daughters, and the size of the dowry that parents needed to provide increased. This book cites several examples of women who consulted with rabbis about how to marry off their daughters when they did not have enough money to pay a dowry for suitable husbands—a point to which we shall return when we deal with the economic status of women in chapter 6.

Muslim law does not restrict the age of marriage, so that marriage of young girls, even to old men, was not unusual. Jews lived alongside their Muslim neighbors, and there were frequently close economic, social and cultural contacts between them. In this situation, it was very difficult not to be influenced by what was widespread and conventional in the surrounding society, especially when this was accompanied by other weighty factors, as will be explained below.

4. The Situation in Jewish Society during the Tenth through Thirteenth Centuries

Sources from the tenth century on, from both Muslim countries and from Christian Europe, indicate that the phenomenon of early marriage, including child marriage, gradually spread and increased. The responsa literature contains many testimonies of the marriage of "minor" girls, that is, those who had not reached the age of twelve. Thus, many people ignored the opposition of Rav and other sages to this practice.

One ought to mention a methodological point of greatest importance for the study of responsa literature connected with our subject. The cases of child marriage mentioned in the responsa are not to be seen, in themselves, as covering the sum total of the reality of child marriage in Jewish communities. Such cases are merely examples, which appear in the responsa due to some unusual occurrence or aspect related to them. The questions did not arise because of the marriage of underage girls per se, but as a result of some other factor; thus, the respondent is not called upon to express his opinion on the subject of marriage of minors as such. The matter of their young age is mentioned almost in passing, alongside some other factor that elicited the question on the part of the sages that lay at the focus of discussion. That is, were it not for this other issue, those questions would not have been addressed to the sages. The evidence in these sources is to be seen as the testimony of one who is simply describing what happened (without any particular tendency or prejudice), which makes it of particularly great historical value. It follows from this that the marriage of minors was far more common than those "special" cases, problematic from the halakhic viewpoint, that appear in the responsa literature.

We may illustrate this by means of three questions that were addressed to R. Hanokh ben Moshe in Muslim Spain at the end of the tenth or beginning of the eleventh century.[12] A certain doubt had arisen regarding the proper manner of carrying out *miun,* or annulment, and not with regard to child marriage as such. Were it not for this doubt, they would not have turned to him at all.

In the second case, a certain doubt arose in connection with levirate marriage (*yibbum*) with the brother-in-law (see Deut. 25:5–10).

Dinah was orphaned from her father when she was a child about six years old. And her mother came and misled her and married her to Reuven, who was about forty years old, and she lived with him for about three years. This Reuven died, and she became subject to levirate marriage, [to the brother-in-law] who was about fifty years old and had a wife and sons.[13]

This important testimony concerning marriage of a young girl to a man older than herself by many decades would not have arisen and not been preserved had the husband not died. What elicited the question was the uncertainty regarding levirate marriage and the financial compensation due to the maiden.

The third question is a little bit different. It was not child marriage that led to uncertainty on the part of the inquirers, but rather the unusual circumstances described in the question. It refers there to a person who had died "and left a small son, still nursing at his mother's breast, and two daughters, the older about six and the younger about four years old. His widow became betrothed to a new husband while she was still nursing the son, and betrothed her two daughters to the brother and the son of that same husband."[14]

It seems clear that it was the marriage of the woman during the period of nursing (within twenty-four months after childbirth), in explicit contradiction to the halakhah, that elicited doubt on the part of the interlocutors. Another doubt may have emerged from the suspicion of forbidden marriage among relatives. But it seems most likely that they would not have questioned the rabbi concerning the marriage of minors per se, were it not for the issues of nursing and of consanguinity. R. Hanokh's position regarding this case is interesting, adamantly opposing the marriage of minors.

All these questions relate to the marriage of young children to older men when the girls are orphans. The same phenomenon also emerges from other sources and, as noted by Goitein, the same holds true for those few cases that he found in the Genizah literature. The strong opposition in Talmudic literature to the marriage of young girls to old men did not make much of an impression. It seems likely that the widow wanted to marry off her minor daughters quickly due to her own financial difficulties, in order to provide them with a warm home, and so that she herself would be able to remarry more easily. The same held true in those cases where the father was widowed and was left alone with his small daughters. Nevertheless, the phenomenon of marriage of minors to old men was not limited to orphans alone. The situation in the surrounding Muslim society left its mark on Jewish society as well.[15]

In my opinion, the phenomenon of child marriage gradually began to expand during the tenth and eleventh centuries, reaching its peak in the twelfth and thirteenth centuries—and this in Jewish communities both in the Muslim countries and in Christian Europe. R. Hanokh ben Moshe's opposition did not help. There were many cases of child marriage in Spain. The responsa literature of the twelfth and thirteenth centuries preserves dozens of testimonies to this, most of them mentioned in passing in the context of the testimony of a person simply describing a situation, from which we may infer even more strongly the large number of such marriages.

An important testimony appears in a question sent to Maimonides from Damascus. He was asked about a monetary dispute over inheritance between a brother and the husband of his sister, who had died. The girl's father wrote in his will that the girl was to be given a large sum of money at the time of her marriage, on condition that the marriage be "lawful"—that is, in accordance with halakhah. The girl was married when she was still a minor, and died shortly thereafter. The brother refused to give the husband the promised money, claiming that the marriage was not conducted in accordance with a Talmudic law, since the daughter was married while she was still underage. He argued that this was an explicit violation of the condition the father had specified in his will.

As against that, the husband argued that the term "lawful" was only intended to prevent transfer of the money at the time of her betrothal, prior to the solemnization of the marriage through her entering the *huppa,* and was not at all related to the age at marriage, relying upon "the custom of the Jews in Damascus to marry their daughters at the age of eight or nine."[16]

How is one to interpret the phrase "the custom in Damascus to marry their daughters at the age of eight or nine"? Was this the practice of the majority or only of individuals? True, one need not necessarily infer that this was the practice of the majority of the Jewish community. If, however, the custom was that of only a small number of individuals, it would be difficult to argue on its basis that the father's use of the word "by law" was intended to exclude her being merely engaged, and that it did not at all relate to the issue of child marriage. For this reason, the inquirer noted the accepted custom in Damascus. This halakhic argument indicates that the custom was common, but it is still difficult to say how common.[17] A careful reading of this important source indicates the strength of the phenomenon of child marriage. While it does not indicate the general practice throughout Jewry, as it explicitly states that it refers to the custom of Damascus alone, neither can we infer that in other places they behaved differently. The questioner described the custom in his own place, because that is what is relevant from the halakhic viewpoint, as "It all follows the custom of the place" and "custom overrides halakhah," the sense being that the father would not have ignored in his will the reality known to him from his own city.

One also finds in the responsa literature a discussion about how one conducts the marriage of a minor, described as an accepted, common custom. Another important testimony is preserved in the words of the Tosaphists. In their discussion concerning the above-mentioned statement of Rav that it is forbidden for a father to marry off his daughter when she is a minor, the *Tosafot* state that in their day they were not strict about this prohibition:

> But now we are accustomed to marry off our daughters even when they are minors. This is so, because every day the exile becomes stronger. Thus, if a person is able to provide his daughter with a dowry, perhaps at some later time he will be unable to do so, and his daughter will remain a spinster forever.[18]

Another reason was that offered by R. Peretz ben Elijah of Corbeil (second half of the thirteenth century) in the name of R. Meir of Rothenburg. In his opinion, the prohibition against marrying small children was only in force in Talmudic times, "when there were many Jews in one place. But now that we are few, we are accustomed to betrothing even a small child, lest [the prospective bridegroom] be taken by another."[19] In this case, too, we cannot determine exactly what the rabbis meant by saying "we are accustomed to ...," but it seems clear that this does not refer to the practice of unusual individuals alone, a reading for which there is support also from other sources. The fact that R. Meir of Rothenburg did not deal with this issue in a purely theoretical manner, but married off his own daughter before she was twelve years old, certainly influenced many other people: "And so did I do with my small daughter. I said to her: 'My daughter, accept your *qiddushin* if you wish.'"[20] If the greatest Ashkenazic scholar of the thirteenth century behaved in this way, why should others take heed of Rav's admonitions not to marry off a "minor"? Rabbenu Tam likewise testified that in his family they married off "minor" girls, that is, less than twelve years old. One may assume that the practice of prominent figures in the community influenced others. The desire to emulate the behavior of the elite group in society is a well-known and accepted social phenomenon.

In Italy, too, the marriage of young girls was common practice. From the responsa of R. Isaiah of Trani, it follows that in his day (the thirteenth century), young girls in Byzantium were betrothed at the age of four and five. For many years, Sicily was under Muslim rule, and traces of this rule were felt in Jewish society there even after it returned to Christian hands in 1091. The widespread practice in Muslim society, of marrying young girls to older husbands, influenced the Jews of Sicily as well. Nadia Zeldes, who examined archival sources in Sicily, summarized her findings as follows:

Jewish women were usually married at a young age to husbands many years older than themselves, as was customary in Christian society in Sicily as well. However, the marriage did not cause the separation of the woman from her birth family. This may be seen from their wills, in which the women preferred to bequeath their property to relatives rather than to relatives of the husband. The closeness to the nuclear family was an important consideration in the ability of the woman to be separated from her husband.[21]

Another testimony of the ignoring of Rav's prohibition against marrying off a young girl may be found in the halakhic codes of the twelfth and thirteenth century sages. The "theoretical" *pesaq* literature is by nature closer to the formulations of the Talmud. It follows that these testimonies are of great value. Thus, for example, Maimonides chose a less binding formulation than that given by the Talmud:

Even though the father has the right to betroth his daughter when she is a minor or when she is a maiden [*na'arah;* i.e., ages 12 to 12.5] to whomever he wishes, it is *not fitting* that he should do so. Rather, the Sages commanded that one should not betroth his daughter when she is a minor until she matures and says, I want so-and-so. It is likewise not fit that a man should betroth a minor girl, nor should he betroth a woman until he sees her and she is fit in his eyes, lest she not find favor in his eyes, and he will divorce her or lie with her even though he hates her.[22]

The phrases, "the Sages commanded" and "It is not fitting," are less forceful than the original language used in the Talmud, "it is forbidden." In *Sefer Ḥasidim* as well, the Talmudic prohibitions against marrying a minor are interpreted in a manner that diminishes their force. One may not take a minor in marriage in a situation where there is a mature maiden (*bogeret*) from a respected family that belongs to the sect of the pietists ("good"); it is preferable that one marry her, as she is able to bear children immediately. If one does not find a young woman of this type, it is permitted to marry a minor, provided that she is from a proper family. But even in such a case, one should ascertain that the girl not be below the age of thirteen, as that is an age that is fitting and suitable for marriage.[23]

We have only cited here a few examples. Dozens of other examples of marriage of minors appear in the responsa literature, the problem raised always being, not the marriage of minors per se, but the various side effects of this phenomenon.

Another important indication of the growth of the phenomenon of child marriage, specifically during this period, is found in the attempt by R. Menahem of Joigny—from the second half of the twelfth century—to prohibit a mother and brothers from marrying off their daughter/sister while the father was away from home, "in the province of the sea." According to R. Menahem, such marriages raise the question as to whether she is not already considered a married woman, because of the possibility that her father may have betrothed her to another during the course of his travels without informing anyone else of this. This clearly refers to the marriage of a "minor," because a mature maiden (*bogeret*) cannot be married off or betrothed by her father without her granting him permission to do so (even though there were some who permitted this as well). The concern expressed by R. Menahem is quite surprising. How can one prohibit the mother from marrying off her daughter on the basis of the remote suspicion that the father may have betrothed her? It is difficult to imagine that he would impose such a prohibition on the basis of such a rare and unlikely possibility, when this might greatly weigh upon the daughter's marriage prospects, as absences of merchant husbands on trading trips were often very lengthy. Therefore, we must conclude that it was not unusual for fathers to arrange marriages for their young daughters in absentia, while far away from home.

In many cases, a lengthy delay elapsed between betrothal and marriage because of the betrothal of minors. At times, the "wives" were so small that they did not even know how to make a bed. One of the disputes brought before the Rashba (R. Solomon Ibn Adret) originated in the girl's request—evidently at her parent's behest—that the husband buy a servant to make up the beds, "since she was small and her hands were not skilled at doing this task."[24]

The extensive involvement (including books presenting formulae of various kinds of documents, both printed and in manuscript) with the issue of annulment (*miun*) also tends to confirm our assumption that early marriage was quite common. For a daughter is entitled to "refuse"—that is, to nullify a marriage unilaterally—only if she was orphaned from her father and married by her mother or brothers before she was twelve years of age. Regarding this subject as well one needs to turn one's attention to the methodological aspect. The discussions on the subject of annulment found in the responsa do not deal with the issue per se, but only with various difficulties or doubts that arose in its connection. It follows that the cases brought in the responsa literature do not reflect the totality of all cases of *miun*.

From a comparison between the attitude toward *miun* of the Geonim with that of the twelfth- and thirteenth-century sages, one may infer the moving forward of the age of marriage. One of the Babylonian Geonim declared that he and his forebears were opposed to the marriage of underage orphan girls precisely because of the fear of *miun*. By contrast, the well-known Tosaphist R. Yitzhak ben Shmuel opposed this view. In his view, "there is no need for us to refrain from annulments," and hence no reason to oppose the marriage of minor orphans. Moreover, we may infer that the opposition to the marriage of men at an early age on the part of those sages who were steeped in rationalism was also not merely theoretical, but derived from the miserable reality that these people observed in their environment. Maimonides' comments on this matter can nevertheless be interpreted as merely theoretical—but only with difficulty:

It is the way of right-thinking people that first a man establishes for himself an occupation with which to support himself, and then buys a house to live in, and then marries . . . But the foolish person first marries, then seeks the wherewithal to buy a house, and only thereafter, at the end of his days, seeks an occupation or supports himself through charity.[25]

The marriage age for young boys or men goes beyond the framework of our present discussion. Some sources have also preserved evidence of marriage of "minor" males, but this phenomenon was rarer than in the case of girls. As a rule, that age was also brought forward. It would seem that the sages' admonitions to advance the age of marriage bore fruit. But we must exercise great caution in relying upon admonitions of this type. Just as one ought not to determine the actual age of marriage in Palestine during the Mishnaic and Talmudic age on the basis of the dictum, "Eighteen years of age to the marriage canopy," so is it difficult to entirely ignore the impression left by this statement on people over the course of generations.[26] The same holds true for the similar call of sages in the Middle Ages to advance the marriage of boys. For example: the statement by R. Yitzhak ben Shmuel, one of the leading Tosaphists, that a man should take care to marry his son "close to his maturation." Similarly in *Sefer Ḥasidim,* we read, "Take a wife while you are a minor, and likewise for your son . . . and make sure once they reach maturity that they are married, and find them a woman to marry; for if you delay, perhaps they will lie with the wives of their fellows or with alien women . . ."[27] "But as for the boys, you should marry them off before they are grown, lest they say like Samson: 'Take that one for me, for she is comely in my eyes.'"[28] R. Yitzhak Aboab stated that: "The best, most suitable, time for a match is as early as possible, before he is overwhelmed by his Urge."[29] In these words he relied upon various Talmudic sources, from which he found support for the view that one ought to bring forward the marriage age of men. He also explained why there is no contradiction between this statement and the advice to first devote time to study of Torah.

The various sources mentioned here from Musar literature, and others of a similar bent, are on the order of auxiliary support for our thesis. One cannot learn about the actual reality from them alone. The most impressive and important testimony concerning the proportions of this phenomenon is preserved, as mentioned above, in the numerous cases in the responsa literature and in their nature—that is, that they relate the things in passing, as an aside. These testimonies are common in the responsa literature from all the Jewish centers in the Middle Ages.[30] The conclusion that follows is that the usual age of marriage of girls in Jewish society was between twelve and sixteen, while many girls married at an earlier age, and there were even those who were given in marriage by their parents while they were still literally small children.

5. Factors Causing the Large Number of Childhood Marriages

Rav's comments condemning the marriage of minors—frequently quoted by medieval Jewish sages—are unequivocal. Once the delay in the coming of the Messiah was connected to the marriage of young girls, one certainly would have expected it to exert great influence on Jewish society. It follows from this that the ignoring of this advice also stemmed from weighty considerations. The reason brought in the *Tosafot*, "the Exile that grows stronger every day"—that is, the security and economic situation—fits the situation in the thirteenth to fifteenth centuries and, to a lesser extent, that of the twelfth century. However, it is very difficult to apply it to the situation in the tenth and eleventh centuries. But in principle, as we shall discuss below, changes in the social and economic conditions were indeed the most accepted explanation. Three main factors combined together to cause this retreat and change. First and foremost, one must remember the situation in the surrounding Muslim society, within which Jews lived and acted, and in which, as mentioned, marriage of young girls was a common phenomenon. There was great social closeness and cultural proximity between the Jews and their Muslim neighbors. In this reality, it was very difficult not to be influenced by the norms of the surrounding society.

We noted above that many cases of marriage of young girls were documented among the high aristocracy in Europe. While the Jews in Christian Europe did tend to imitate the way of life of the nobility and the knights in various matters, it seems highly doubtful whether the marriage of children may be attributed to this directly; it would appear that this factor was of only secondary importance. On the other hand, the greater supply of marriageable girls than that of boys, which increased the price of dowries, indirectly affected Jewish society. True, the basic data were different, as unlike Christian society the Jewish family was interested in the marriage of both sons and daughters. However, the desire to marry their daughters to bridegrooms from good families not only increased the value of the dowry, but also brought forward the age of marriage so as to "catch" a good husband. In any event, the main factor causing the increase in marriage of young girls in Jewish communities in Germany and France was socio-economic.

During the ninth to eleventh centuries many of the Jews of Germany and France—like many of the Jews in Muslim countries—engaged in international trade. This was a basic fact that left its mark in all areas of life. The extended journeys and absences from home greatly influenced the structure of the Jewish family, as will be seen in many chapters in this book. Due to the numerous journeys of Jewish tradesmen to other countries, and the grave dangers of the roads, they preferred to see their sons and daughters "arranged" in life as early as possible. Many of these merchants never returned from these journeys, as may be clearly seen from the responsa literature, including the extensive discussion of questions involving "anchored" wives (those unable to remarry because their husbands' whereabouts were unknown). This subject is also one that, in principle, ought to be included in what *Tosafot* described as "the exile that grows stronger from day to day": that is, the existence of special conditions that brought about intense social pressure and led to a change in the reality. But in fact, economic pressure was not the main cause of early marriage. On the contrary, it mostly affected well-established families that could easily allow themselves to "take care" of their children as long as possible.[31]

The fact that the marriage of children was customary even in the families of Jewish tradesmen and well-known scholars—and not only among families of orphans or those suffering from economic distress—is very important. This accelerated and expanded the spread of marriage at an early age. The fact that sons of a number of well-established and pedigreed families entered into marriage at a young age—or even made matches among one another—caused similar thoughts among others. The fear that "good" bridegrooms or "successful" brides (that is, those from wealthy and prominent families) would be "snatched up" led to the desire among others to make matches for their young children. Social phenomena of this type tend to be infectious, especially when the children of "good" families took part in these changes. As mentioned, even Rabbi Meir of Rothenburg—the leading Ashkenazic sage of the thirteenth century—married off his daughter before she reached the age of twelve.

The occupation of loaning money on interest, which spread throughout Jewish society in Christian Europe in the twelfth century and thereafter, allowed parents to create a strong economic basis for their children even when they were young, and at times even to involve them in their own businesses. The economic difficulty of young couples was the main factor leading to delay in marriage in Christian society in the cities, certainly among the lower social classes. The bridegroom needed to learn a profession before he could marry, and to this end a protracted period of study was required. The sons of those Jews who received help from their parents, who provided them with a certain basic working capital, were able to advance the age of marriage: Youths who wished to continue to study Torah could usually do so undisturbed. Their parents were able to help them, and later on, the wife also took part in the money lending business.

The third reason for this phenomenon is also a weighty one. The reason given by Rav, "until she grows up and says, I want so-and-so"—which lay at the basis of the prohibition against marriage of minors—was no longer in force. In the reality of medieval Jewish society, this reason no longer had any significance, as the parents chose the destined bridegroom themselves, without asking the girl. Her agreement was a purely formal act, lacking in all practical significance. This was the case even after the age of twelve. There is abundant evidence for this phenomenon, discussed at length below, in the next chapter.

Among the other factors leading to marriage at an early age, we have not mentioned that of sexual puritanism, the desire to limit insofar as possible the sexual tension to which maturing young people were subject. It is clear that this factor also exerted some influence, even though it is not an explanation for child marriage. This factor was of significance in advancing marriage age in Jewish society during the late Middle Ages, but not at the period under discussion here.

6. Results of Early Marriage

The phenomenon of marriage at an early age led to deleterious results in several areas of family life.

One consequence was the absolute dependence of the young couple on the parents for a considerable period, including total involvement of the parents in their personal life. A good illustration of this is found in one of the questions addressed to Maimonides, which tells of a nine-year-old girl who was married to a certain man and went to live with his parents within the framework of the extended family circle or clan. She suffered endless interference on the part of her mother-in-law, as well as other difficulties.[32] It is clear that the young couple was forced to live a number of years with the parents—usually with the husband's parents—and at times, due to sudden impoverishment of the supporting parents, they found themselves in considerable difficulty. The influence of the very young wife on family life during the early years of marriage was extremely small: she played no part in the choice of a partner, and was subjected to the will of her husband, who was usually older and more mature than she and, even more so, to the wishes of his parents. Only later, once she had given birth and was raising their children, did she rise to a position of influence and authority. On the other hand, this phenomenon enhanced the power of the patriarchal family: the extended family unit, the clan, occupied an important place in the life of Jewish society, and in the communal framework, as it did in Christian society in Europe during that same period.

At times, various difficulties resulted from incompatibility between the couple that only became evident after they grew up. It suddenly became clear that the girl was taller than her husband, that there was no emotional and mental compatibility between them, or the like. Thus, for example, in a responsa by R. Nissim of Gerondi, we read of "children" who were betrothed, and in the interim their sizes changed, until the bride was taller than the bridegroom, accentuating the tension between the two.[33]

Another source of disputes derived from economic changes that occurred in the family of the bridegroom or the bride, or resulting from the death of one of the parents. The parents frequently waited until the children grew up somewhat and only then was the marriage actually solemnized.

Postponement in formalizing the marriage of young children and the fear of one side backing out led to the imposition of serious economic sanctions upon the nullifying side, as we shall see in the next chapter.

Childbirth at an early age, before the young mother was prepared in either a physical or an emotional sense, could be another negative factor. It is nevertheless doubtful whether this sufficed to increase the number of children in the family in a significant way, due to the high infant mortality rate in the Middle Ages. Indeed, pregnancy and childbirth at an early age increased the number of mothers who died in childbirth. Initial sexual relations at an excessively young age likewise harmed the woman's health, as was already noted by the Tosaphists: "and several minor girls are ill from this."

Early marriage also placed limitations on the woman's education. This was particularly true of Muslim countries. A married woman's leaving her home was problematic. While the insistence on feminine modesty was not equally strict among all Jewish communities in the Muslim countries, there can be no doubt that a married girl's ability to go out and study was very limited. Jews in Christian Europe did not relate to the question of modesty and the right of the married woman to leave her home with the same strictness, but there too it seems quite likely that her ability to expand her education was quite limited— a point to which we shall return in chapter 7.

The phenomenon of beating wives may also have been exacerbated by marriage of girls at an early age. The fact that at times the wife was extremely young led the husband to relate to her as he would to his daughter. This was particularly true in those places where young girls were married to husbands significantly older than themselves, which was, as we have seen, a common phenomenon in Jewish society, and particularly in Muslim countries. Moreover, it may well be that the beating of the wife, which was a part of the life of the young couple, also continued thereafter.

These factors suffice to indicate the great importance of early marriage in shaping the character of Jewish society in the Middle Ages.

CHAPTER THREE

Engagement, Betrothal, and the Choice of a Marriage Partner

1. The Ceremonies and their Development

The marriage ceremony as practiced in medieval Jewish society consisted of three stages: engagement (*shiddukhin*), betrothal (*erusin*), and the formalization of the marriage (*huppah*). The engagement was a kind of framework agreement made prior to the wedding, in which the parties involved agreed to the time of the wedding, where the couple would live, and the financial arrangements.[1] This stage did not have a religious character, and did not include any blessings or other ritual act. Originally, the engagement was not even conducted publicly, but was made during private meetings between the parents of the bridegroom and those of the bride. The next two stages—betrothal or sanctification of the bride (*erusin* or *qiddushin*), and marriage (*nissuin* or *huppah*)—bore an explicitly religious character and included special blessings. The public nature of engagement and betrothal in the High Middle Ages were intended to prevent secret marriages, which were often love matches made without the parents' agreement.

Originally, there were two formal ceremonies, performed separately: betrothal and marriage; but in most Jewish communities, and specifically in Europe, the two ceremonies were united in the Middle Ages—as is done today as well—thus creating the need for an engagement ceremony, in which the parents of the bridegroom and those of the bride agreed upon the specific conditions of the marriage.[2]

The medieval sages already deliberated the question of the factors that led to the uniting of the two ceremonies, a question that continues to trouble scholars to this day. According to Rashi, the main reason was economic—the desire to reduce the expenses involved in providing a festive meal for numerous guests—

The Seven Blessings being recited at a wedding feast. The bride and groom are on either side of the rabbi, who recites the blessings over a cup of wine. At the wedding ceremony the groom took upon himself various obligations, including caring for his wife's needs and her honor, and loyalty to the community. MS. Rothschild 24, fol 121b, from the collection of the Israel Museum, Jerusalem.

as both ceremonies were conducted in the presence of many people.[3] In my opinion, the large number of marriages at a young age and the frequent journeys of intended husbands to distant places for commercial purposes, also contributed to the merging of these two ceremonies. Many brides were already betrothed when they were still children (before the age of twelve), and at times waited a lengthy period of time until the marriage was formalized. Some of the bridegrooms who temporarily left their homes for commercial journeys did not return at the appointed time, leaving the betrothed maidens effectively abandoned and considered as "chained wives." Dozens of accounts testifying to this phenomenon are preserved in the sources. The sages thus preferred to unite betrothal and marriage, adding a "secular" ceremony (engagement or *shiddukhin*) in which the conditions of the marriage were summarized between the two sides, but whose violation did not require a divorce writ (*get*), whereas breaking a betrothal did so. Simultaneously, they added certain economic sanctions to the engagement in order to strengthen its force. The extent to which such journeys and the consequent abandonment of young affianced women weighed upon Jewish society may be seen in a communal edict from eleventh-century Spain, establishing an explicit condition to be made at the time of *qiddushin* (*erusin*), automatically nullifying them were the bridegroom to be absent for more than one year.[4]

The desire to lend binding force to engagement and betrothal also found expression in the nature of the ceremony. In the High Middle Ages it was performed in public, usually in the synagogue, rather than in private homes, and included a festive meal with blessings. The fear of broken engagements led to the provision of financial guarantees on the part of both sets of parents, the side canceling the engagement being required to pay a large monetary penalty. This fear was particularly grave on the part of the parents of brides. While the girl was waiting for the formalization of her marriage and to go to live in her husband's home, available bridegrooms were "grabbed" by other maidens. If the agreement with their daughter was nullified, not only had she lost valuable time for naught, but a certain stigma and negative image became attached to her, as one whose engagement had been broken. Moreover, such cancellations often provoked rumors and gossip. Jewish society—especially in Germany and France—waged battle against this phenomenon in various ways. Thus, for example, Rashi tells that it was customary in his day in the communities of Germany and France for both sides to provide monetary guarantees that they would not cancel the engagement.[5]

The threat of a fine for one who cancelled an engagement also appears in documents from the Cairo Genizah.[6] In Spain, as well, it was widely accepted to write a special document at the time of the engagement, containing the threat of a fine against one who would nullify the agreement. Such a document is preserved in R. Judah Barzeloni's *Sefer ha-Shtarot* (late eleventh and early twelfth century), which even involves permission to make use of the Gentile authorities to force the one canceling the engagement to pay the fine, a fact indicative of the widespread nature of the phenomenon and the seriousness with which it was regarded. R. Judah Barzeloni even testified, that in his day, "it was customary in most places to ratify the engagement agreement and conditions by means of a *kinyan* [symbolic act of property transfer]." He added that there were those who sufficed with a verbal agreement, without imposing monetary sanctions upon the side violating the agreement.[7] As mentioned, Rashi also used this language in describing the custom in his milieu, "in the manner customary *in most* places," from which it follows that in those days there was no uniform, binding practice observed in all the Jewish communities in Europe, but only in most of them. And indeed, in a responsum from Spain—which may have been written by R. Joseph Ibn Avitur (late fifteenth century), the author rules that one may not impose a penalty for cancelling an engagement, a point to be discussed further below.

2. The Ban in Ashkenaz against Cancelling Engagements

An all-out war against breaking engagements was already conducted in Germany and in France in the eleventh century. Initially, the agreements between the two sides were reinforced by the imposition of monetary penalties and providing

guarantees. The agreement was confirmed by a handshake, which was considered a particularly strong kind of commitment. Finally, the sages even imposed
a ban upon one who reneged on an engagement agreement. These procedures
transformed the engagement from a private agreement between two parties,
which belonged to the realm of monetary law, to a serious ethical commitment
overseen by the communities.

The public nature of the engagement (which was conducted in the presence
of "the important men of the city"), the giving of guarantees, and the imposition of fines did not suffice. Rashi even ruled that corporal punishment should
be imposed upon a bridegroom who broke his promise. We cannot determine whether this act of beating was in fact accepted as a rule in Germany and
France in the event of broken engagements, or whether Rashi was particularly
strict in this case, consistent with his general concern for the honor and status
of Jewish women. An engagement document drawn up in England in 1271 not
only mentioned sanctions and the ban imposed upon one who cancelled an
engagement, but also included an oath imposed upon both to assure that
they would honor it.[8] The detailed wording of this document—like that of other
engagement documents—indicates the seriousness of the fear that the engagement might be broken, from which it follows that, despite all the means of dis-
suasion brought into play, there were those who failed to fulfill their promise
and backed out of the agreement made between the two sides. In another document made in England in 1249, the father of the bride even agreed to "force"
his daughter to marry "the above-mentioned Shlomo [i.e., the bridegroom]
at the specified time."[9]

The great detail in which the obligations undertaken between the sides were
enumerated indicates the great importance attributed to the ceremony of engagement, but also the mutual suspicion. Some of the documents from England and
France were even made in the presence of a "court of three" so that they would
have greater, more binding legal force, and not seem like a mere agreement
between laymen. This evidently refers to three of the guests invited to the engagement festivities who were chosen to serve as a court. These documents were
usually extremely detailed, including such matters as the amount of the dowry,
dwelling arrangements, support, the bride's trousseau, and other details.

When was this ban first imposed and what were the circumstances that led
to it? According to Freimann, the ban was very old and had already been introduced in the eleventh century, as part of the edict against polygamy attributed to R. Gershom Meor Hagolah.[10] According to Falk, this ban originated
later and was only composed in the thirteenth century. He inferred this, among
other things, from the fact that, in the above-mentioned responsum, Rashi did
not refer at all to a ban of this sort, even though he severely lambasted a certain
bridegroom who broke his engagement. From the edict attributed to Rabbenu
Gershom, it also follows that this ban was not necessarily automatically imposed

upon whoever violated an engagement. However, it is difficult to agree with Falk's conclusion on this point. From two of the sources mentioned (Rashi's responsum and R. Gershom's edict), it would seem that the ban referred to was not imposed automatically upon everyone who became engaged, but was imposed by agreement between the parties. In the above-mentioned responsum, Rashi writes regarding these guarantees that "the *early ones* behaved thus so as not to shame Jewish women." But as far as one can tell, this edict was unable to completely eliminate broken engagements. Since the making of matches involving minors was widely accepted in those days, there was a reasonable fear that, by the time they grew up, one or another side might back out due to economic, social, or personal factors. For that reason, an edict was then introduced prohibiting the breaking of engagements and obligating engaged men to marry their fiancées. This may be seen from a manuscript source in the JTS Library in New York. It states there that a certain young man from the community of Avallon who had "sanctified" a girl wanted to renege, and even took an oath, that if they were to force him to marry her under threat of *herem*, he would not obey the edict of the community.[11]

But one cannot state with certainty whether one is speaking here merely of engagement, or of actual betrothal. The fact that R. Yitzhak ben Yehudah—head of the yeshiva in Mainz after 1064—supported the *herem* and encouraged the members of his community to force the boy to marry the girl, as told in that same source, clearly indicates the tendency toward strictness. Those who instituted and initiated this communal edict well knew, that a marriage begun under such circumstances was unlikely to be particularly successful, and it was quite likely that the bridegroom would try to divorce his wife immediately after the wedding ceremony. The Talmud even forbids a person to marry a woman if he contemplates divorcing her after the wedding, even though from a formal legal viewpoint both the marriage and the divorce are valid.[12] However, they feared that the cancellation of the engagement would be taken as an indication of some sort of blemish in the family. Such worries seem to have increased following the pogroms in Western Europe between the years 1008 and 1012, which reached their height in the expulsion of the Jews from Mainz in 1012. The sources suggest that among the victims of these persecutions were some members of the Ashkenazic communities who converted to Christianity (including the son of Rabbenu Gershom, and possibly also the son of R. Simeon ben Isaac ben Abun). Others converted in the eleventh century and even later of their own free will, and the phenomenon was more widespread than initially thought by scholars.[13] In order that this not be considered a source of shame for the families involved, Rabbenu Gershom issued an edict, as mentioned, not to mention such apostasy. This fear seems to have been greater in Ashkenaz (Franco-Germany) than in other centers, not only due to the pogroms during the eleventh century, but also because of the small size of the communities. Rumors and gossip were known to all, and the breaking of an engagement could well be critical for the family involved. The communities battled in various ways against the spread of rumors of this and similar types, which were likely to damage the social standing of families and to create difficulties for the marriage of their children.

Elsewhere, the breaking of engagements was not treated with the same severity as it was in the communities of Ashkenaz and France in those days. In one of his responsa, Rav Saadya Gaon explicitly stated that a man is allowed to back out of an engagement, also stating explicitly that the cancellation of an engagement does not imply any aspersions upon the family:

> For in this generation we do not have monetary penalties for either shame or damages. For it is the custom of the world that several people may speak of marriage with the daughters of Israel, and they do not marry except the one who falls to their lot. Because the matching of a woman to a man is naught but an act of heaven.[14]

The fear of cancellation of engagement and betrothal was so great that some rabbis did not recite the Blessing over Betrothal on the occasion of the betrothal but postponed it to the occasion of the actual wedding, so that it not be a blessing in vain. R. Abraham ben R. Nathan Hayarhi—who travelled throughout the Jewish Diaspora during the second half of the twelfth century—also mentioned this custom, explaining that it originated in the fear of breaking of engagements. He was astonished by the custom of postponing the recitation of *Birkat Erusin,* as this caused the blessing not to be recited at its proper time.[15] Only the harsh reality and widespread occurrence of cancellation of engagements could explain this peculiar phenomenon.

The Christian Church was also opposed to the cancellation of engagements. It saw this not merely as a matter of monetary damages, but also as a religious-ethical sin, and the German tribes behaved in like manner.[16] It seems quite likely that there is a connection of some sort between the practice in the two societies, but the main factor mitigating the strictness of the Ashkanazic Jews seems to lie in a general tendency, widespread in Ashkenazic Jewish society in those days, of concern for the status of the woman and family pedigree.

Ze'ev Falk, who devoted a detailed study to the prohibition against cancelling engagements, attributed the strictness in Ashkenaz to the influence of the surrounding Christian society. The sanctity of betrothal, accepted in Christianity already in the earliest generations and whose violation was declared by the ecclesiastical council held in the city of Elvires in 300 to be a sin punishable by excommunication from the Christian congregation for a number of years, was also accepted in principle under German law. Both the church and the German tribes waged struggles for the honoring of engagements, especially during the eleventh century.

This view seems both reasonable and plausible, but there still remains the question as to why specifically in this period the Jews in Ashkenaz took such strict steps against the cancellation of engagements to the extent of imposing a ban, and why we do not find its like in other countries in which there was also strong Christian influence, such as Italy, Provence, and Spain after the Reconquista. In my opinion, only a combination of all the factors mentioned above—including the small size of the communities and their character—can serve as a full explanation for this phenomenon. The advance of the phenomena to the eleventh century, when the communities were very small in size and family pedigree played a very important role, also contributed to this.

3. Choice of Marriage Partner

As stated above in chapter 2, we find in the Talmud a statement by the amora Rav—one of the greatest amoraim and among the founders of the Torah center in Babylonia—prohibiting a person from betrothing his daughter while she is still a "minor" in order that she may express her opinion of her intended husband ("until she grows and says, I wish to be married to so-and-so"). The midrashic literature also contains support for this opinion, which the sages based upon the verse in Genesis 24:57: "Let us call the maiden and ask her."

But notwithstanding the extensive involvement of medieval Jewish sages with the words of Rav, their practical impact was rather weak and they were largely ignored. During the twelfth century and thereafter in Christian Europe, there was a firm, widespread opinion in support of marriage requiring the full agreement of both parties (to be discussed below), but this fact did not leave much of a mark on Jewish society. Only a small number of Jewish sages recognized the right of young sons or daughters to choose partners as they willed. The accepted norm in Jewish society, in both Muslim countries and in Christian Europe, was for the parents to choose the partner for their children. This reality follows from both popular literature and from the various genres of halakhic literature. Already the Babylonian Geonim described it as "immodesty" and "arrogance" for the girl to involve herself in the choice of a spouse against the wishes of her father, even if she is a mature woman "twenty years old."[17]

A halakhic work written in Judaeo-Arabic, several pages of which were preserved in the Cairo Genizah, explicitly states that Rav's words suited the reality of an earlier time, or that in Christian Europe at the time of the author, in which young women went about with their faces uncovered, but not that in Muslim countries. What good will it do the bridegroom if he sees her, since in any event she is completely covered? Maimonides wrote similar things regarding a claim of physical defects in a bride that had been hidden from her prospective husband.[18]

Rashba (R. Solomon Ibn Adret) was asked about the case of a person who had obligated himself to marry his granddaughter to a certain man. The agreement stated that if either side were to cancel the engagement agreement, they would be required to pay a fine. Surprisingly, the girl refused to accept her grandfather's choice. The grandfather refused to pay the fine, on the grounds that one was dealing here with an unusual event, which could be classified as *force majeure*. Rashba accepted his argument and exempted him from payment because "this is absolute *force majeure* . . . Because the girls always accept whomever is chosen by their father or relatives." Similar to this—albeit perhaps more extreme—is Rashba's statement that the father may force his young daughter to marry the man to whom he had sworn to give her, even if this was opposed to her own will.[19]

Indeed, an engagement document drawn up in England in the thirteenth century uses this formula ("to force") in its description of the obligation taken by the father upon himself: "The above-mentioned Yom Tov agreed by force of *herem* and command of the court and edict of the communities to *force* his daughter Ziona to go to the above-mentioned Shlomo and to fulfill all the conditions mentioned."[20]

The impact upon society as a whole of this reality, in which the choice of the bridegroom is made by the parents, may be inferred from the commentary of the well-know sage, R. Menahem Hameiri of Provence, contemporary of the Rashba. He interprets Rav's statement, that a man is not allowed to betroth his daughter when she is a minor and that one must wait until she grows up and chooses her own bridegroom, as follows:

And that which they said, "until she grows and says I want so and so," does not mean that *once she grows we need her to say "I want so-and-so,"* for the more she grows, the more she accepts anyone . . . Rather, the meaning is, "until she grows," and once she has grown we assume that whoever her father chooses is acceptable to her.[21]

This explanation is rather ironic. Hameiri turned Rav's opinion upside down, distorted its literal meaning, and interpreted it according to the reality of his own time. There is no need whatsoever to ask the grown daughter what she wants, since it is clear that the father's choice is convenient to her and acceptable to her! In this approach we find a change, not only from the words of the Talmud, but also from the outlook regnant during the Geonic period.

More complex was the approach of the Ashkenazic Hasidim. Concerning the marriage of young men, we read in *Sefer Ḥasidim:* "Sons should be married off by their father before they grow up, lest they say like Samson, 'Take her for me, for she is pleasing in my eyes (Jdg. 14:3).'"[22] That is, involvement of the bridegroom in the choice of his mate is seen in a negative light; he ought to prefer his parents' choice and rely upon their judgment. Nevertheless, the authors of the book are realistic in their approach. They know that the imposition of a marriage partner upon a son or daughter against his or her will is likely to cause severe repercussions in the future; therefore they asked the parents to take account of their children's wishes, at times even using harsh language against those parents who forced an unwanted husband upon their daughter. They knew the great power of love and advised to take it into account. This idea is repeated a number of times. Thus: "Do not match a young girl to an old man or to one who does not want her or one whom she does want... You should not marry her to an old man or to one who is contemptible in her eyes . . ." The love of a youth and a maiden, without the knowledge of the parents or even against their will, is not to be ignored.[23] Moreover, there is a concrete danger in ignoring the daughter's wish: If she is not satisfied with the husband whom her parents chose for her and if she does not love him, she is liable to seek lovers outside of the family. The power of love is so great, that even if the beloved "is not suitable" one should allow her to marry him.

As we find too in the case of other subjects in *Sefer Ḥasidim,* the authors advise a person to remember the counsel of Hillel: "That which is hateful to you, do not do to your neighbor." The authors advise the father to imagine how he would feel if he were forced to marry a woman against his will. Moreover, if the father pressures her to marry one whom she does not love, he will be held morally accountable if she strays from him.[24] The same holds true of sons: "He who has a dissolute son, if he is married to a woman whom he does not wish, will lie with other women. Therefore, he [the father] should leave him to his wish."[25] True, this approach is utilitarian. Consideration of the wishes of the son or daughter are not taken here out of acknowledgment of their feelings and desires. The "concession" to their will stems from the serious fear that if are not allowed to marry a partner who is loved and acceptable to them, they will seek happiness outside of the framework of the family, leading to promiscuity in Jewish society. In practice, whatever the motivation, there is a clear call here to the parents not to completely ignore their children's wishes.

On the other hand, the repeated exhortations on this theme indicate that many people did not behave in this way and forced their will upon their children. The Ashkenazic Hasidim were consistent in this "utilitarian" approach. Their justification, based upon the need for partners to find full sexual satisfaction, is based upon the fear that they would contemplate going with other partners, and not upon the needs of the individual and his personal satisfaction and happiness: "At the time that she lies in his breast that he gives her pleasure through intercourse, that she not think of other men, nor he of other women."[26]

R. Joseph Colon (Maharik), who was active in the rabbinate in Italy during the middle of the fifteenth century, was asked about a dispute between a father and son in which the parents thought that the son had chosen as a wife a girl whom they considered unsuitable, merely because of his love for her. R. Colon supported the son's right in principle to choose his own wife. The son said that his father had made him take an oath not to marry except according to his wishes, asking whether he was obligated by such an oath, and whether he needed to obey his father in this case due to the commandment to honor one's parents. R. Colon replied that the son was required to obey his father in this specific case due to the oath he had taken, but that otherwise the son would not be required to forego his love because of the requirement of honoring one's parents. Moreover, he emphasized that the father is not allowed to force his son to marry a woman against his will, because this is like a person "commanding his son to violate the words of the Torah," as the sages stated that a person may not marry a woman until he has seen her and she finds favor in his eyes, based upon the verse, "you shall love your neighbor as yourself."[27]

Particularly interesting is the responsum of R. Elijah Capsali, who was active in Italy during the first half of the sixteenth century. As has been demonstrated by Woolf, he based his view upon the precedent of the above-maintained responsum of R. Colon, expanded it, and added to it a rationale, characteristic of the education and mental world of a Jew who had been educated in Italy and who was influenced by the Renaissance culture. Capsali wrote:

> When his father commands him not to marry this one, it is as if he commands him to violate the words of the Torah . . . And if we say that the son is required to listen his father's and his mother's voice to marry a woman that he does not like, we find that this shall greatly increase hatred and strife within a man's house, which is against the law of our Holy Torah . . . And if he marries another woman whom he does not desire, all his days shall be miserable.[28]

Both these sages were influenced by the Renaissance in Italy, as may clearly be felt in their arguments. There may also be a certain connection between their stance in opposition to forced marriage and that accepted in Christian Europe in the twelfth and thirteenth centuries, as we shall see below. One may assume that many parents understood the need to take the wishes of their children into account, and did not force upon them marriage against their will. But, as mentioned, many others ignored this. Their primary criteria for the choice of spouses for their children were money, family lineage, and beauty. It is not for naught that these three subjects appear repeatedly in the comments on this matter by the Ashkenazic Ḥasidim.

A similar reality emerges from the description given by Ahimaaz, a man living in southern Italy in the eleventh century. The parents' will is decisive, and one does not ask the daughter's opinion. Not only did it frequently happen that they did not ask the maiden, but there were even cases in which the father betrothed her to a man whom he met during a commercial journey, without even informing the girl herself, the mother, or other members of the family. This practice emerges from many testimonies. One of the more important of these is R. Menahem ben Peretz of Joigny's statement in opposition to a ruling found in *Halakhot Gedolot*. The latter work states that a mother is allowed to marry her daughter when the father is far away for an extended period. Rabbenu Menaham disagreed, stating that a marriage of this type involved the possibility that the girl might already be married, as her father may have betrothed her to another man without telling anybody.[29] One is dealing here of a very remote sort of suspicion. If Rabbenu

Menaham had not actually encountered cases of fathers who betrothed their daughters without the knowledge of anyone else in the family, it seems unlikely that he would have raised such a far-fetched scenario, imposing a burdensome restriction upon family life and the marriage prospects of young girls, as it frequently happened that the father was absent from his home for extended periods of time.

This situation seems to have originated in the frequent trips of Jews for mercantile purposes. People met one another in distant places, got to know one another and became friends. This friendship in turn led to betrothals without the father being able to tell to his wife or to other members of the family. Rabbenu Tam opposed R. Menaham's ruling and supported that of the *Halakhot Gedolot*. He relied inter alia upon the fact that "you and I are both familiar with several cases in which people died in distant lands leaving small daughters, and they were married, and there are such cases in our family."[30]

Journeys to remote places on business were common and many people never returned to their homes. Even without the above halakhic difficulty, these journeys imposed a heavy burden upon family life, and Rabbenu Tam refused to impose the additional burden of the possibility that the father had betrothed his daughter—but the problem as such clearly existed.

In one of the questions addressed to Maimonides, his interlocutors related that, in their community, engagements were generally speaking not made in secret. They were accustomed to making an engagement into a public occasion, so as to avoid subsequent claims that the girl had already been promised to another. Nevertheless, from that source one may infer that such claims did in fact arise. The very fact of the considerable involvement with this question indicates that the problem was a real one. It relates there that an orphan maiden, who was of age, became engaged "in the presence of a large public," but two months later a person appeared "bearing a document stating that this maiden had been betrothed to him by her father when she was underage and that the father had received *qiddushin* from him . . ."[31]

Another indication of the complete ignoring of the daughter's wishes regarding the choice of a partner is preserved in a question addressed from Kairouan to Rav Sherira Gaon, dealing with a girl who had been betrothed separately by her father and brother to two different persons. The Gaon asks: "Which *qiddushin* shall be valid: the first one, in which she was betrothed by her brother while she was under her father's aegis, or the latter *qiddushin*, which was performed by the father himself?"[32] The daughter's wishes are not even mentioned here, as if they were not relevant to the subject at hand. If they had bothered to speak with her, perhaps she could have told them that she was already betrothed. A similar picture emerges from the folklore literature. One of the stories brought by R. Nissim ben Jacob of Kairouan (mid eleventh century) tells of a man who appeared on the evening of the wedding ceremony and declared that the bride had been promised to him years before by her father, and that he had a document testifying to this:

And the child was not yet of age . . . And I had an only son who is twenty years old. One day I took him in my hand, and I told him gently: My son, do what I advise you, and you shall acquire both this world and the World to Come. He said to me: Father, I shall not refuse you! I said to him: take this girl as a wife . . . and when the time came for the *huppah* I made a great feast. . . He [the guest] said: I weep for this girl, whom you wish to marry to your son who is from such-and-such a city, and I am from that same city. I have betrothed her and she is mine. But she was taken captive and I was taken captive after her, and here is the document of *qiddushin*.[33]

While this literary motif also appears in other sources and is a kind of accepted literary convention, its citation here by Rabbenu Nissim also teaches us something of the atmosphere of this period and an impression of the reality of the time.

As late as the period of the Renaissance in Italy, the authority of the parents in the choice of a marriage partner was still generally accepted. The edicts of R. Judah Mintz and his circle state that whoever initiated *qiddushin* with a maiden without the agreement of her parents was subject to the ban. The documents confirm the existence of a policy of marriages and alliances between the prominent families.[34]

We have only cited here a few limited examples, in order to make matters more coherent. Many similar cases from both Muslim countries and from Christian Europe have been preserved in the sources.

4. Consensual Marriage in Christian Europe

The imprecations in *Sefer Hasidim* to refrain from imposing marriage and to take account of the children's wishes in the choice of a partner, as discussed above, correspond to the dominant atmosphere among European thinkers of the time. During the High Middle Ages, there gradually grew in Church circles the recognition that the choice of a marriage partner should be made freely and not under compulsion. Already in 866, Pope Nicholas I affirmed the need for agreements on the part of both partners to a marriage. The sacramental quality of marriage strengthened this view. However, of particular ideological and practical importance were the thinkers who were active at the beginning of the twelfth century and thereafter. These scholars emphasized in principle the central importance of individual salvation and called not to focus upon the redemption of the collectivity. The placing of the individual in the center of religious activity gradually led to a broader recognition of his rights. Peter Abelard (1079–1143), one the great scholastics of the twelfth century, insisted on this point extensively. It was only natural that a discussion of the freedom of the individual would include a discussion of the right of the husband and wife to choose their partners by their own free will, without automatically acquiescing to the wishes of the parents, the family, or those holding authority in feudal society.[35] Gratian likewise saw great value in the agreement of the partners, in order to create a complete union between them. Around 1140, he stated explicitly that, if there is no agreement between the two partners, there is in effect no union between them.[36]

During the course of the twelfth century, the power of the individual in society grew, serving as a challenge to the authority of the patriarchal family and the feudal hierarchy.[37] Of special importance was the activity of Pope Alexander III, who was known for his great tenacity and his struggle to increase the authority of the Church. In the 1170s, he issued explicit instructions concerning the necessity of free consent of both partners about to be married. According to Brundage, Alexander III systematically attempted to reduce the authority of the parents and the feudal authorities over candidates for marriage, giving the couple themselves exclusive authority over their marriage. However, according to a number of scholars, the realization of this theory in practice was only partial. Nevertheless, everyone agrees that it was an important step and that it gradually found its expression in legislation as well. This doctrine was brought to the knowledge of the public through sermons preached by the priests, in which they emphasized the great importance of free choice of the partners to their marriage.[38]

After the Fourth Lateran Council in 1215, this tendency found clear expression in both ethical literature and in Church legislation. Among other things, owners of estates were forbidden to impose marriage upon widows who preferred not to remarry after their husband's death. John of Kent issued a call (around 1220) for partners whose parents had matched them when they were children to express their free consent to the marriage upon reaching maturity. Union of partners against their will was liable in his opinion to bear destructive consequences. As we have seen above, similar things were written at the same time by the Ashkenazic Hasidim.

Robert of Flamborough (early thirteenth century) stated that a double agreement was required in order for a marriage to be valid: agreement of the soul (*consensus animorum*) and agreement of the body (*consensus corporum*). Another preacher active during the same period, Thomas of Chobham, emphasized that external, verbal agreement of the two partners to marriage is insufficient, but that there must be agreement of the hearts. He emphasized that the right of free choice of partner applies to all levels of society, even slaves and serfs, and that they do not require the agreement of their masters. He devoted particular attention to the practical implementation of his theory, and counseled priests how to help people from the lower classes to marry according to their will, despite the opposition of their masters.

Forty years after Alexander III had emphasized the importance of free consent to marriage, this idea was given clear expression in canon law, even though

opposition to it continued on the part of secular society. Another enthusias-
tic champion of free choice of marital partners was Richard Wetheringset (ca.
1220), who demanded that the priests take care to ascertain that there was in
fact full mutual consent to marriage and that it was undertaken with the free
consent of both partners, or whether the consent was merely verbal, in
which case it was not valid. Another demand that he made of the priests was
that they bring the value of free will to the knowledge of the simple people. He
advised them how to overcome the opposition of the family and the feudal
lords and to refrain from participating in weddings that were not based
upon full mutual consent. In practice, this theory was already widely known
to many people by this period.

According to Jacqueline Murray, the activity of Thomas of Chobham and
Wetheringset were of particular importance in spreading this theory to the public throughout England. Testimonies were preserved of the refusal of serfs to
submit to their masters' pressure to marry partners they did not want. There is
clear evidence to indicate that the power and authority of the landlords in
this area became weakened. "Pastoral epistles" of this type were sent by the heads
of the Church both within England and outside it also in the thirteenth through
fifteenth centuries, increasing the power of the doctrine that championed the
freedom of the individual. Some researchers even think that the success of the
agitation on behalf of freedom of the individual in the choice of marriage partner and in other areas was greater than that originally intended by the Church,
and attempts were later made to restrict it to some degree.[39]

In sum, the Church strongly supported marriage based upon mutual agreement. It provided both ideological and practical support, and in effect increased
the power of the individual in general in medieval society. There is a certain
degree of irony in the fact that a number of Jewish sages of the thirteenth and
fourteenth centuries—including Rashba—ignored the advice given in the Talmud that one is not to allow marriage without the agreement of the couple,
while in their broader society this approach was gaining momentum, at least
in theory. Rashba's ruling, that due to his oath a father is required to impose
upon his daughter marriage to a particular man notwithstanding her refusal to
do so, is deserving of particular attention. Were he to have seen the daughter's
agreement as an important principle and an integral part of the laws of marriage, he could easily have classified the father's oath as one that was impossible to fulfill, as it involved nullifying a *mitzvah*. As we have already seen above,
R. Joseph Colon and R. Elijah Capsali saw one who forces his son to marry a
woman against his will as commanding him "to violate the words of the Torah."
Among the circles of those sages who were closer to rationalist thinking, there
was greater consideration of the daughter's wishes, if only due to pragmatic considerations. R. Levi ben Gershon (Ralbag), who often took negative positions
with regard to women, advised a certain person not to marry a woman who did

not want him, because otherwise the relations between them would be problematic and she might even be unfaithful to him.[40] While the reason given was pragmatic and not principled, it nevertheless expresses the recognition, if only partial,
of the value of the woman's free consent. Maimonides also seems to have supported such an approach, out of consideration of the woman's feelings. He ruled
that a woman is entitled to demand a divorce at any time on the grounds that
her husband is disgusting to her, as we shall see below in chapter 11, because one
cannot require her "to have intercourse with a man who is hateful to her." A person holding such a view will also take into consideration the woman's wishes in
the choice of a partner, and not force a husband upon her.

What were the factors that led to change, and why did medieval Jewish
sages so often ignore the counsel of the sages requiring consent of the children
to the choice of marriage partner? First and foremost, this must be attributed to
the large number of marriages at a young age. What point is there in obtaining
the agreement of young children? Do they possess rational judgement or significant emotions? Are not the parents' judgment and experience preferable? One
may assume that the parents frequently presented the young couple to one another
simply to fulfill the formal halakhic requirement of receiving their consent.

The second factor was also a weighty one. Family lineage and economic standing served as important factors in the choice of a partner. Families belonging
to the social and economic elite usually made marriages among one another;
we have already seen a similar phenomenon occurring within Christian society, especially from the end of the twelfth century on. In such a system of
relationships, the wishes of the children were given a secondary place. Explicit
testimony to the importance of the family's economic standing in the choice of
marriage partner may be found in *Sefer Ḥasidim*. The leaders of this sect repeatedly exhorted their followers to ignore economic factors and to choose marriage partners on the basis of "spiritual" and ethical factors (i.e., family pedigree,
punctilious observance of a religious way of life, and closeness to the pietist
group). Members of wealthy families also feared that youths who were not to
their liking would develop romantic connections with their daughters out of
economic motivations (to enjoy their wealth) and would persuade them to
ignore their parents' wishes and even to marry them secretly.

The numerous admonitions in *Sefer Ḥasidim* to take into consideration the
will of the children in the choice of partner shows how difficult it was to persuade people. The need of the families to set up an economic basis for their
young children so that they might earn a living from lending on interest further strengthened the tendency to seek marriage partners from wealthy families. Nevertheless, these numerous discussions indicate that the older the children
were, the more problematic were imposed marriages based upon the parents'
choice. Finally, we have seen above that the authors of *Sefer Ḥasidim*, despite
their excessive concern for family pedigree, advised parents to take into

consideration the will of their children, fearing that otherwise they might seek satisfaction outside of the family framework.

5. *The Institution of Matchmaking and Its Place in Jewish Society*

The development of the institution of professional matchmaking (*shadkhanut*) in medieval Jewish society is an interesting chapter in the history both of the family and of society, and is connected, among other things, with changes in marriage age and the minimal involvement of the prospective bridegroom and bride in the choice of a partner. The appearance of the professional matchmaker is quite late, being first mentioned in sources from Germany and France in the twelfth century. Its activity gradually increased until it became an important institution in Ashkenazic Jewish society, but the phenomenon is very rare in Sephardic sources, and paid professional matchmaking was not accepted in practice.[41]

From the remarks of R. Samson of Sens in the late twelfth and early thirteenth century, it seems that he was speaking of a new and somewhat disreputable profession in France. He even cites this fact as one of the reasons for the high fee that the *shadkhan* was entitled to receive for his efforts. It follows from his remarks that in the past people engaged in matchmaking for free, while in his day they took for it a substantial sum. In his opinion, this high fee derived not only from the lack of honor associated with the profession, but also from the talents demanded of the matchmaker. Discretion and powers of personal persuasion were important qualities demanded of the *shadkhan*, and not necessarily wisdom or established social status. On the other hand, from the comments of R. Simhah of Speyer, who was active in Germany during that same period, it seems that in his day matchmaking was already an accepted profession in Germany.[42] While the *shadkhan*'s main talent lay in his power of speech, in his ability to persuade the two sides, when he did find a choice bridegroom or bride, the value of his match was great. From *Sefer Ḥasidim*, which was composed in Germany at that same time, it follows that the profession of matchmaking was widespread:

A certain Jew wanted [to marry] a certain woman whom he loved and who loved him. And he sent matchmakers to her father and mother, and they said: Our daughter is not interested. But she sent him [a message] in secret: I wish [to marry] you, but my mother and father are involved in making another match.[43]

No one would speak directly with the girl's parents, but instead sent matchmakers to do so, in the hope that they would be more successful in the task of persuasion. The daughter's wishes did not play an important role in the parents' decision, and they ignored them. The social standing and economic situation of the bridegroom were more important. While we have seen that the Ashkenazic Hasidim did teach that one should take the children's wishes into consideration in choosing a partner, in reality things were usually different.

Throughout the course of the thirteenth century, the profession became more common, as may be seen from the responsa literature and particularly from the responsa of R. Meir of Rothenburg (Maharam) and his disciples. Unlike a number of other sages, Maharam attempted to reduce the fees paid to matchmakers, and ruled that there is no obligation to pay them "except for the cost of their efforts." In any event, Rabbenu Meir's attempts did not succeed for long. Not only did the profession of matchmaking become a popular one, but in the fourteenth century—and possibly already at the end of the thirteenth century—an interesting and important development of the greatest social significance took place in Germany and France. Matchmaking began to be an important activity of well-known Torah scholars, who took considerable sums of money for their services. In practice, this became a major source of income for the rabbis of that generation.

R. Johanan Trèves, rabbi of Paris during the second half of the fourteenth century, strongly criticized this phenomenon and described it in the harshest terms:

The lions roar for their spoils, and there is no one to save from their hand, and whoever insults their honor has no recourse . . . No one in the land is permitted to make a match for his son or daughter surreptitiously without the permission of the rabbis of their city, and to them gifts are brought.[44]

What are the conjectured reasons for this development in the institution of matchmaking? Why did this practice begin only in the twelfth century, then developing so rapidly that it became a known and respected profession in Ashkenazic Jewish society? This subject has not yet been discussed in research literature. It is difficult to find a single convincing explanation for this process; rather, a number of factors seem to have combined together. First and foremost, one needs to remember the role of family lineage and its important role in Ashkenazic Jewish society. From the eleventh century on, Torah erudition and family pedigree occupied a more significant place in this society than in any other Jewish society of that time. This phenomenon already finds clear expression in the chronicles of the murders that occurred during the First Crusade in 1096, and continues throughout the entire period. Due to the small size of the communities, members of prominent families often found it difficult to find a suitable marriage partner in the immediate environment, and there was need to seek a partner in a more distant community. The activity of the matchmakers was thus both local and trans-local.

Jacob Katz has shown that, at the end of the Middle Ages and the beginning of the modern period, Ashkenazic Jewish society was based upon strict social stratification, and hence the society was unable to allow the choice of a partner on the basis of a random chance meeting. He also pointed out an ironic phenomenon that was common at the time of the Haskalah, in the nineteenth century: namely, when a marriage took place as the result of an arranged match, this was hidden from others. This was so, because of the desire at that time to break with the way of life of traditional Jewish society.

The second factor contributing to the rise of the institution of matchmaking was also of great importance: marriage at a young age and the central place of the parents in the choice of a partner, as we discussed above. The parents usually did not consult with their children at all and arranged a partner for them according to their own understanding, the main criteria for their choice being family pedigree, Torah standing, and economic status. Direct appeal to the parents by a prospective partner involved a certain unpleasantness, and at times might also involve a humiliating rejection. Many testimonies of this have been preserved in the sources, particularly in *Sefer Ḥasidim*. There thus emerged the need for an "objective" intermediary who could "feel the pulse," investigate the economic situation of the respective families, and see if there was any point in proceeding with the match. Due to the central place occupied by the economic aspect of marriage agreements, it was easier for both sides to have a third party acting as middleman.

The third factor was the large number of divorces in Ashkenazic Jewish society, to be discussed below in chapter 11. An extraordinarily large number of couples in Ashkenazic Jewish society split up. In terms of chronology, there is full correspondence between the two phenomena: that is, the number of professional matchmakers increased during the thirteenth to fifteenth centuries, and during that same period the number of divorces grew, to the extent that the sages, led by R. Meir of Rothenburg, decided to combat the phenomenon with stringent means. It may be no coincidence that Maharam, who led the struggle to reduce the number of divorces, was the same one who attempted to reduce the fee paid to the matchmakers. The large number of divorces created abundant opportunity for the activity of matchmakers, who at times also served as a catalyst for the divorce of partners who were still hesitating whether or not to break up the family unit. Because of their desire to receive the high matchmaking fee and in order to beat out other matchmakers, matchmakers offered attractive alternatives to individuals who were still undecided whether to divorce, heaping praises upon the prospective bridegrooms and brides. Explicit testimony to this is preserved in the words of R. Seligman of Bingen, who bewailed the large number of divorces and lambasted the activity of the matchmakers as a vulture waiting for its prey, while the couple were still living together and had not yet divorced.

Due to the widespread occurrence of the phenomenon and its seriousness, Rabbenu Seligman proposed aggressive action against matchmakers who spoke of matches prior to the divorce:

They have made a breach in Israel . . . And we have issued an edict to whomever will listen to us not to speak of any matters of matches while the woman is still with the husband . . . and whoever aids or gives a hand to allow to engage in matchmaking under such circumstances . . . will have to render an account in the future . . . and he gives a hand to sinners and walks in the way of those that err.[45]

There were many well-established women in Ashkenazic Jewish society, widows and divorcées, who encountered difficulty in finding a new partner and were embarrassed to engage in any public efforts to that end. The families of these women did not always respond to their requests for help in finding a new partner and did not encourage them to do so, because they preferred that the woman's property remain within the family and not pass over into strange hands, and that she devote her time to her children. As a result, these women had need of an outsider to help them.

A fourth factor—which was particularly relevant in the fourteenth and fifteenth centuries—is the establishment of the rabbinate. The professional rabbis made a living primarily from various rabbinic functions that they performed.[46] Among these was matchmaking, which served as an important source of income. Once the rabbi of the community became an advisor, confidante, and prominent voice in matters of marriages, the dependence of people upon this institution increased. Any attempt to bypass the rabbi was likely to sour relations with him and be against their best interest.

The ascent of the matchmakers also had a significant negative side. The matchmaker's main interest was directed toward the profits and prestige he would receive, and not necessarily to the best interest of the couple. He was willing to exaggerate his praises of the bridegroom, the bride, and their families, while concealing significant facts that might be likely to discourage the sides. This habit served as fruitful ground for many folk stories and jests. In the responsa of R. Jacob Moellin (Maharil), we read of the complaint of a certain woman who was misled by the matchmakers. They told her that the man was handsome and wise and a Torah scholar, "and he was none of these."[47] Maharil did not accept her complaints, for she had seen him before the match was finalized. Moreover: "If he is not handsome this is not a defect, as even if he is ignorant and a boor, what of it? For if all Israel were sages, who would work and make a living." Society needs ordinary workmen and artisans, and not only learned people. Moreover, in his words, according to a Talmudic statement, a woman wants to marry a man even if he is not perfect, because staying single is very difficult for her. In brief, the matchmaker's promises to the woman were not seen as something binding. It is doubtful in my eyes, whether the sages who acted in Germany and France in the eleventh to thirteenth centuries would have accepted the arguments of Maharil, which do not express much respect for women.

CHAPTER FOUR

Monogamy and Polygamy

The question of the basic structure of the Jewish family unit in the Middle Ages—whether monogamous or polygamous—has been discussed more extensively in research literature than any other subject concerning the status of women at that time. Rabbenu Gershom Meor Hagolah's ban (*herem*) imposed against taking a second wife has aroused much interest and stood at the center of this research. Nevertheless, opinions are still divided among scholars, both regarding the question of the actual situation that prevailed in the various diasporas and that of the historical reality that gave rise to this ban.

1. The Biblical and Talmudic Heritage

It was common in Jewish society of the biblical period to have many wives and concubines. The patriarchs, the kings, and at times also the ordinary people behaved thus. While there were sects during the Second Temple period that thought that the Torah prohibits a person from taking additional wives, it seems quite clear that this is not the literal meaning of the texts, and that the Torah does not prohibit polygamy. Nevertheless, most families in Israel were monogamous. In Assyrian documents, in the Nuzi documents, and later on in Aramaic marriage documents of Jews from Alexandria, one occasionally finds conditions stipulated in the marriage document in which the husband commits himself not to take an additional wife. Such documents may have existed in Jewish society during the biblical period, but there is no explicit evidence for this.

According to a number of early sages and contemporary researchers, the words of the prophets contain clear hints that monogamy was understood as the ideal structure for the Jewish family, an approach that appears explicitly in the words of several Talmudic sages.[1] R. Yehudah ben Beteira even found evidence for the preference of monogamy in the account of the Creation. The fact that Adam was given only one wife indicates, in his opinion, that such is the ideal. The preference of monogamy is expressed in other midrashim as well.[2]

There was evidently a difference in the attitude toward polygamy between the Palestinean sages and those of Babylonia. Of special interest is the attitude of Rav Ami, one of the great Palestinean amoraim of the third century, who stated that "One who marries a second wife should divorce his first wife and pay her *ketubah* money." By contrast, the Babylonian amora Rabba, who lived at the same time, thought that a man may marry as many wives as he likes, so long as he is able to fulfill their needs.[3] It would seem that R. Ami did not mean to imply that in every case in which a man marries a second wife he is required to divorce the first, but simply to emphasize the right of the first wife to demand a divorce should she so wish and to receive full financial compensation as stipulated in the *ketubah*. If, however, she agrees to his marrying a second wife and is not interested in divorce, her husband is allowed to keep both wives.

The Babylonian Geonim followed the ruling of Rabba and permitted polygamy; moreover, it is clear that the phenomenon was common in their day, as it was common also in the neighboring Muslim society; however, it is difficult to determine just how common it was, on the basis of the few examples that have been preserved in the geonic responsa. The Genizah sources support the assumption that the phenomenon was quite common at that time too. Nevertheless, other Babylonian Geonim ruled as R. Ami did in a case where the husband suffered from impotence, claiming that he was "under a spell" and therefore unable to perform sexual relations with his wife. He sought permission to prove this by marrying a second wife (with whom, according to his words, he was not under a spell) and thereby exempt himself from paying the *ketubah* money to his first wife. Several Babylonian Geonim required him to divorce his first wife and to pay her *ketubah*, should she wish it.

A number of varied sources preserve testimonies concerning polygamy in Eretz Yisrael during the post-Talmudic period—in passages from *Sefer ha-Ma'asim shel bnei Eretz Yisrael* among others—but generally speaking the halakhic tradition in Eretz-Yisrael recognized the woman's right to insist on monogamy. According to Mordechai Akiva Friedman, this explains the fact that, in dozens of Palestinian *ketubot* from the Geonic period, no actual commitment on the part of the husband prevents him from marrying a second wife, nor is there even any discussion of the consequences of polygamous marriage. Since the Palestinean halakhah recognized the woman's right to demand a divorce writ (*get*) and *ketubah* in the event that her husband took a second wife, there was no need to stipulate this in writing.

On the other hand, abundant material on this subject is to be found in the Cairo Genizah sources. Friedman has devoted a detailed and well-documented study to this, and his findings are very interesting. The Jews of Egypt were accustomed to stipulating in the *ketubah* that the husband would not marry a second wife except with her agreement. It is likely that this condition was introduced primarily under pressure of wealthy parents who provided a generous dowry for their daughters, and were fearful that their money would be inherited by other wives or their sons. But this condition was unable to prevent the marriage of a second wife. Friedman found dozens of cases in the Genizah documents in which Egyptian Jews married a second wife notwithstanding the heavy penalties they were forced to pay to their first wives. In the main, these were wealthy people who belonged to the elite of society, but people from the middle and even from the lower classes also married a second wife. The commonness of this phenomenon in Muslim society doubtless left its impression.[4]

The relatively large number of Genizah sources concerning polygamy also gives us a glimpse of the inner world of the women whose husbands brought a "rival wife" into their home, a subject that will be discussed separately below.

2. *The Situation in Ashkenaz*

The Edict of Rabbenu Gershom

A major revolution in the attitude toward polygamy occurred in Franco-Germany during the eleventh century, when bigamy was prohibited not only in theory, but also in practice. Unlike Egypt, where economic sanctions or oaths were used at various times to enforce monogamy, in Ashkenaz an actual ban was placed upon anyone who married an additional wife. This was the most severe punishment in effect in Jewish communities during the Middle Ages. Moreover, this *herem* was evidently the most widely known one imposed in any Jewish community throughout the medieval period, one which, from the mid-twelfth century, was explicitly attributed to R. Gershom Meor Hagolah. The ban has been extensively discussed in research literature with regard to three aspects: (i) its time: Was it indeed imposed by Rabbenu Gershom, that is, about 1000 c.e.; (ii) its applicability: Does it apply to all cases of bigamy, or only those that do not involve "a case of *mitzvah*"?; (iii) what is the historical background for the edict?

Some scholars think that this edict against bigamy was not in fact promulgated by Rabbenu Gershom, but was introduced later on and attributed to him due to his prominent position. This theory is based primarily upon two arguments. First, that the *herem* was first attributed to Rabbenu Gershom only from the second half of the twelfth century on, and that there is not a single Rabbinic authority in Germany or France during the eleventh century who explicitly mentions the edict against marrying two women. On the face of it, there is even internal evidence against this in Rabbenu Gershom's own writings: namely, that in one of his responsa he permitted a husband to marry a second wife when his first one was barren.[5]

But this responsum does not really contradict Rabbenu Gershom's authorship of the ban: first, because the incident in question could have occurred before Rabbenu Gershom introduced the edict against bigamy. But, as it is specifically states there that the woman in question was barren, it is also plausible that his edict may not have applied "in a case of *mitzvah*"—that is, where it would abnegate the commandment of reproduction, to which great importance was attached in his day.

A question addressed to Rashi at the end of the eleventh century also describes a situation of a person who has married a second wife, but there too it refers to "a case of *mitzvah*," that is, of a barren woman: "and he stayed with her for ten years or more, like the words of the Sages, and then married another."[6] The fact that the man waited ten years and only then married a second wife—as stipulated in Talmudic law—supports the assumption that marrying a second wife was not easily allowed. But it is also clear that this is not an unequivocal proof.

Scholars have also invoked the words of R. Eliezer ben Nathan (Raban) to prove that the edict against polygamy was not introduced by Rabbenu Gershom, nor during the eleventh century. Raban, who was active in the mid-twelfth century, was the first sage to mention it, alongside the prohibition against divorcing a wife against her will. In his discussion of the statement of the amora Rabba, allowing a man to marry several wives, the Raban added: "and know that now that they have introduced the edict of the communities not to marry an additional wife and not to divorce a woman against her will, one may not do so."[7] He sees this *taqqanah* as an act of the "communities," without even mentioning Rabbenu Gershom. But this too is only an apparent contradiction. It seems quite likely that Rabbenu Gershom did not enact his edict alone, but did so in concert with several other sages. There was not a single sage in eleventh-century Ashkenaz who considered all of the communities to be obligated by his edicts. Even Rashi, the greatest sage in France, only made edicts for the community of Troyes alone.[8] Only later, when Rabbenu Gershom's name came to enjoy extraordinary respect and honor in Ashkenaz—to a large extent thanks to Rashi—he is alone mentioned as the author of the edicts.[9] Several of Rabbenu Gershom's edicts were reaffirmed and accepted as communal edicts at gatherings of Ashkenazic rabbis.[10] Confirmation of this type lent these edicts more strongly binding force than the individual edict of an early sage, however great and important he might have been. This also follows from a responsum written by R. Asher ben Yehiel (the Rosh) after he arrived in Spain:

There was a certain sage in our land named Rabbenu Gershom, and he introduced good edicts concerning matters of divorce, and he lived in the days of the Geonim, of blessed memory. And his edicts and regulations were firmly established as if they had been given at Sinai, because they were accepted and passed down from generation to generation.[11]

That is, only after the communities took upon themselves the edicts of Rabbenu Gershom did they become obligatory "like Torah from Sinai." Moreover, an examination of the attitude of the sages in Ashkenaz and France to the *herem* against bigamy reveals a clear development. During the first few generations, and into the twelfth century, they were not seen as universally binding, but they were prepared to allow a man to take a second wife relatively easily in "a case of *mitzvah*." Raban even thought that in the case of a "rebellious" wife, a husband ought to be allowed to marry a second wife immediately so that he would "not be 'anchored' [i.e., without a wife]" during the lengthy process of divorce.[12] Later on, there was a tendency to be strict in these cases as well and rabbis were reluctant to deviate from the edict against bigamy attributed to Rabbenu Gershom, giving it preference even over the commandment to "be fruitful and multiply." Clear evidence that already at the time of Raban the edict was attributed to Rabbenu Gershom may be inferred from the fact that, only a few years after Raban had referred to the ban by the term *taqqanat haqehilot* ("the edict of the communities"), it was described by his colleagues, the great rabbis of Ashkenaz, as "the *Herem* of Rabbenu Gershom."

Further support for the attribution of the edict to Rabbenu Gershom follows from the fact that all the outstanding sages of Ashkenaz from the late twelfth century on ascribed it to him, and especially from the fact that the outstanding disciples of Rashi, who were active at the end of the eleventh and the beginning of the twelfth century, portrayed Rabbenu Gershom as one who introduced edicts "for the entire Diaspora."[13] While there are many later additions in the literature of the school of Rashi, the context of the things here and the manner in which they are expressed indicates that this wording in fact originated with the disciples of Rashi, and that this style is characteristic of them. That is, at the beginning of the twelfth century—only three generations after his death— Rabbenu Gershom is described as one who enacted edicts "for the entire Diaspora." This is clear evidence of an early and well-established tradition that many edicts were issued from the hands of Rabbenu Gershom, or at his initiative in tandem with other rabbis, including those dealing with concrete problems. Had these problems been of only secondary importance, it is doubtful whether the title "one who makes edicts for the entire Diaspora" would have come into existence. In sum, to this day we do not have any unequivocal proof that Rabbenu Gershom in fact issued the edict against bigamy, but it is highly likely. Likewise, the formulation of the *taqqanot* of Rabbenu Gershom—the two mentioned and others—is not altogether clear. This resulted from the accepted practice in Ashkenaz of incorporating later sources within early texts in order to update and to adjust them to historical reality.

The Historical Background of the Ashkenazic Edicts against Polygamy

Scholars have pondered the question of the historical background of this edict, which on the face of it seems superfluous. There are many and varied kinds of extant sources from eleventh century Ashkenaz—halakhic rulings, commentaries, customs, liturgical poems, and chronicles—including memorial books containing the names of those killed during the First Crusade in 1096. In none of these varied sources is there any indication of anyone marrying a second wife during the lifetime of the first, with the exception of a few isolated cases that were evidently "cases of *mitzvah*," primarily those in which the first wife had been barren for more than ten years. This fact indicates that already during the eleventh century polygamy was not practiced in Germany. Special weight is to be given to the fact that, among all the chronicles concerning the pogroms of 1096 and the lists of those killed in those persecutions, not a single family is mentioned as having more than one wife! And one is speaking here of families, some of which were established already in the first half of that century.

From all this, one may conclude that monogamy was accepted as a general rule in eleventh century German Jewish society. If that was the case, why did Rabbenu Gershom find it necessary to issue his edict, backed by the severe sanction of *herem* (ban from the community)? It is difficult to see this as mere "decoration," as merely a declarative statement that the Jewish family in that period was absolutely monogamous. Sources indicate that the sages and communal leaders were led to enact edicts, involving change from previously existing halakhic practice and reality, only by the most vital urgent necessities. Five different solutions have been suggested by scholars:

According to S. Epenstein, at the beginning of the eleventh century and earlier, a certain migration of Jews from Oriental countries to Germany came with two wives, as was common among Jews in Muslim countries. But it is difficult to imagine that Rabbenu Gershom wanted these people to break up their family unit even before entering Ashkenaz, unless he feared that the Jews of Germany would learn from their behavior.

According to A. N. Z. Roth, there were those men among the German Jews themselves who had married two wives; hence the need for this edict. It is impossible to refute this possibility entirely but, as mentioned, there is no evidence for it in the considerable quantity of material extant for this period.

Salo Baron conjectures that, at that time, literary sources arrived from Oriental lands, containing documentation of official permission to marry more than one wife. There was a fear that these might influence the Jews of Germany to change their practice, as the halakhic literature of the Babylonian Geonim enjoyed great respect in all the Jewish Diasporas, including those of Christian Europe. Rabbenu Gershom and his associates saw a need to prohibit this.

Ze'ev Falk places this edict in the twelfth century, citing the main cause for its enactment as the influence of the reality of the Christian environs, in which it was forbidden by law to marry more than one woman. It seems reasonable to assume that this was an important factor and that there was a connection between the reality and tendencies in Christian society and those in Jewish society, but the question of the need for a formal edict remains. If in practice people in Ashkenaz married only one wife, than de facto the reality in Jewish society was identical to that in Christian society.

M. A. Friedman raised the possibility that Rabbenu Gershom's ban reflects an ancient Palestinean tradition of monogamy from the third century, which was preserved and passed over to Ashkenaz. This is possible, but for a period of centuries we find no testimony to this Eretz Yisrael tradition in the periphery of Italian-German Jewry, and in any event the basic question remains: Edicts were introduced in response to a real, felt need and not as a declarative act alone.[14]

It is difficult not to agree with the opinion of Falk and others, who contend that the reality in Christian society exerted some sort of influence—at least in terms of establishing suitable ground—for the edict against bigamy and the willingness to accept it by various different communities, not only in Germany but outside of it. The other theories may also contain a certain degree of truth. However, in my opinion, the main motivation for the edicts was connected with the economic activity of German Jewry during that period. Many were engaged in international trade and stayed for lengthy periods of time in remote lands, including Muslim countries. More extensive documentation for this phenomenon exists today than in the past, thanks to the correct identification of numerous anonymous sources in the responsa literature written by German sages during that same period. These sources provide a comprehensive picture of merchants who travelled often to distance places and were absent from their homes. This is especially true of the responsa of Rabbenu Gershom and of his disciple, Judah ha-Cohen, who were active in Mainz during the first half of the eleventh century.[15] The merchants stayed in different countries, including Provence, Spain, North Africa, and other Muslim countries. At times, their stays in these remote places continued for several years, as indicated by the responsa literature. This also explains the strange phenomenon of the penetration of technical commercial jargon used in the Muslim countries and originating in the Arabic language, into the language of the German sages during that period.[16] Explicit testimony of the power of this phenomenon and the burden it placed upon Jewish family life in Ashkenaz is found in the edict of R. Jacob ben Meir (Rabbenu Tam) from the mid-twelfth century, prohibiting any Jewish trader from being absent from his home for more than a year and a half, and requiring him to remain at home for at least half a year upon returning from his journey.[17]

The date of this edict is the middle of the twelfth century—that is, already after the high point of the Jews' activity in international trade, during the period of its decline—from which we may draw inferences regarding the length of such absences and their implications for family life during the tenth and eleventh centuries. If Rabbenu Tam permitted men to be absent for only eighteen months, we may assume that at times they were away for even longer periods of time. The prohibition against the husband travelling great distances if harmony does not prevail between him and his wife indicates that there were husbands who set off on long journeys and did not hasten to return, abandoning their wives in practice. This harsh reality reemerges in responsa of the Spanish sages from the eleventh and twelfth centuries and in the Genizah sources. It therefore should hardly be surprising if at times these Jewish merchants married a second wife while they were away from home for such extensive periods of time. This was fostered, not only by the reality of their life situation, but also by ancient and venerated sources from the Babylonian Talmud, which relates of great sages who were in the habit of marrying additional wives even during brief sojourns away from their homes; thus we are told about Rav and Rav Nahman.[18] If these two great amoraim could behave thus, during a brief absence within Babylonia itself, why should not Jews from Germany, remaining in Muslim countries for extended periods, allow themselves to do so? One need not add that the fact that in these countries the Muslims and even some of the Jews were accustomed to having more than one wife encouraged such marriages. Perhaps this was also influenced to some degree by the practice of the Shiite Muslims to marry a woman for a brief and limited time ab initio. And indeed, in the halakhic literature of Jewish sages who were active during that same period in Muslim countries, we find accounts of "foreign" men who came from afar to the local communities, married women for a certain period, and then returned home after divorcing their new wives or abandoning them for an extended period—until their next commercial jaunt. Explicit testimony of this appears in Maimonides' edict issued in Egypt during the twelfth century:

That Maimonides enacted edicts on behalf of the welfare of Jewish women; namely: that no woman be married to a foreign Jew, who is not from the community of Egypt, unless he brings proof that he is not married, or takes an oath to this effect on a Pentateuch. And any foreign man who married a woman here and wished to go out to another country is not allowed to leave, even if his wife agrees to this, until he writes her a divorce writ and gives it to her.[19]

Maimonides was well aware of the reality of husbands with wives in other places; therefore he required them to prove that they were bachelors before they could take a wife in Egypt. He ignored the permission granted in Muslim countries to marry more than one wife, knowing how common and difficult the phenomenon of protracted absence was for family life. The weapon of the ban, which in the Middle Ages also bore deep sacral significance, was understood by Rabbenu Gershom and his colleagues as the most effective weapon against this phenomenon, which led husbands not only to delay their return to Germany, but at times actually to abandon their wives, particularly when relations between them were in any event fragile. It was not for naught that Rabbenu Gershom emphasized that permission to go away was only granted to husbands whose home life was in order.

Particular importance was attached to the second half of Maimonides' edict, that prohibits an "alien" Jew from leaving Egypt, unless he writes a *get* to his wife, and this, even if his departure is done with the full agreement of the wife. Only the harsh reality of abandoning of wives for protracted periods could serve as the background for such an extreme edict, which weighed heavily upon those Jews who had immigrated to Egypt and engaged in trade, for in practice it did not allow them to leave their place without depositing a *get;* and this, at a time when many Jewish merchants from Egypt still frequently travelled away from their place for purposes related to their livelihood.[20]

The prevalent economic and social reality in the Jewish communities in Egypt and adjacent countries was similar, and therefore it is difficult to assume that the phenomenon did not also find its expression in other places and in earlier generations. Many sources from the responsa of the Alfasi indicate a similar milieu.

Our conjecture as to the connection between the protracted absences of Jewish tradesmen from Germany in distant places and Rabbenu Gershom's edict might be challenged by arguing that there is no evidence in Ashkenazic Jewish literature from the eleventh century of merchants who married additional wives while residing in far away places. But the vast majority of the sources that have come down to us from this period were written after Rabbenu Gershom's *taqqanah.* Moreover, it is difficult to assume that any sort of halakhic problem arose in Germany because of the fact that a husband married a woman far away. This second wife did not come back with him upon his return to Germany. Frequently, he even separated from her before his return, or even attempted to conceal the fact of his temporary marriage during his absence. This act did not raise any halakhic aspect that might have elicited questioning among the German sages. The natural place for doubts of this type to arise would be in those countries where he married the second wife. This woman suddenly found herself abandoned or in the process of divorce, without imagining in advance that she was dealing with a man who already had a wife and family elsewhere, as clearly follows from the responsa of the sages in the Muslim countries during the tenth to twelfth centuries, as it does from the above edict of Maimonides.

In discussing this edict, we need to take into consideration two additional facts related to the socio-economic structure of the Jewish communities in Germany during that period: the large number of wealthy merchants in the community; and the relatively high status of the Jewish woman in those communities, a status that was well established and better than that in any other Jewish center at the same time. In such a social reality, it was only natural that wealthy fathers should worry about their daughters' honor and the substantial property they had brought with them as a dowry. Various means were used, including communal edicts, to preclude any possibility of second marriages on the part of their sons-in-law, even if this possibility was remote and rare. Society as a whole was willing to adjust itself and to accept edicts of this type, thanks to the improvement in the status of the woman and her place in society, and because of her part in the support of the family, in the education of the children, and other responsibilities.

It is no coincidence that the one Jewish Diaspora in which an attempt was made to prohibit the husband from marrying an additional wife was Egypt, where there were many wealthy merchants. These were guided by concern for their daughters and for the substantial dowries they brought with them. Similarly, the partial attempts in Muslim Spain to limit polygamy, as shall be discussed below, are in my opinion directly connected with the large number of business trips of husbands to faraway places for commercial purposes, the taking of a second wife in the new place, and the abandonment of the first wife.

Evidently the other decree of Rabbenu Gershom, that which prohibits divorcing a woman against her will, is also connected with the above-mentioned reality.[21] In practice, a husband who finds himself far away on trade could bypass the edict against bigamy, which threatened him with ostracism by the entire community upon his return, by sending a divorce to his first wife. Perhaps this phenomenon was more common when the couple did not yet have any children. In practice, in light of the first edict and the strong position of the woman, it was only natural to complement it by a second edict not allowing a man to divorce his wife without her consent. It is clear that in this case too the edict cannot be dissociated from the socio-economic reality mentioned, which led to a general improvement in the status of the woman in German Jewish society.

Was Rabbenu Gershom's Ban for Only a Limited Period?

Did Rabbenu Gershom limit the validity of his ban on bigamy to the end of the fifth millennium alone—that is, until the year 1240? The earliest tradition regarding this comes to us specifically from a Spanish sage, R. Solomon Ibn Adret (Rashba), who was asked about a woman who suffered from a mental disease and whose husband requested permission to take a second wife. In his responsum, Rashba allowed him to do so, writing, among other reasons, that: "We have heard that Rabbenu Gershom only issued his edict for a certain limited time period, namely, until the end of the fifth millennium."[22] Rashba did not state the source of his tradition. It seems likely that he heard it from a Provençal or French sage, as he was in close contact with the sages of those places. In his day, there were also sages from Ashkenaz, from France, and from Provence in Spain. In any event, one of the French sages who settled in Provence—perhaps after the expulsion of French Jewry in 1306—told Rashba that there was a tradition among his colleagues who came with him from France to Provence that the edict of Rabbenu Gershom had been enacted for only a limited period of time: "There is a tradition in our hands that the time stipulated for his edicts has already passed" and therefore they accept this edict anew "upon every man at the time of his marriage."

Halakhic authorities extensively debated the reliability of this tradition. Some accepted it and others rejected it, arguing that it was inconceivable that it was preserved specifically among the Spanish sages while not being mentioned at all in the words of the Ashkenazic sages during the eleventh through fifteenth centuries. The latter sages were not only closer in place to the source of the ban, but had also received many oral and written traditions from their teachers; how then was it that none of these mentioned it? In any event, the doubt regarding the attribution of these words to Rashba has meanwhile been refuted with the publication of Rashba's responsa by S. Z. Havlin. R. Joseph Caro, who also received this tradition, raised the possibility that the Ashkenazic sages knew it, but deliberately concealed it because of their wish to continue the *herem* after the turn of the fifth millennium. But this conjecture is difficult to accept. They could easily have extended the applicability of the *herem,* just as they did regarding other edicts. Their absolute silence calls for explanation, and so long as we do not find in the manuscripts any testimony to the existence of this tradition in Ashkenaz in the eleventh to fourteenth centuries, one must doubt it.

In fact, it was easy for this tradition to flourish and to spread. The sages of Germany and France did not have a precise written text of this or other edicts of Rabbenu Gershom, a fact that should not be surprising. Communal edicts changed in accordance with the reality and the circumstances. The sages took ancient sources, including customs and edicts, and altered them. The ability to identify earlier layers is difficult because of the additions and changes over the course of time.

3. Polygamy in Spain

The question of polygamy in Spanish Jewry is a very complex one, about which there is considerable disagreement among scholars. All agree that important changes in this matter occurred in keeping with the political and social developments, and especially the political split in Spain and the ascent of a class of wealthy and influential Jewish courtiers, as shall be discussed below. The courtiers imitated the way of life of Muslim and Christian courtiers, which in turn left its impression upon other classes in society who strove to emulate this permissive and opulent way of life. But, in my opinion, the main factor contributing to polygamy in Jewish society in Muslim Spain was economic, as we shall see below.

Spanish Jewry between Christianity and Islam

The great political transformations that took place in Spain during the Reconquista, the renewed and gradual conquest of Spain by the Christians, left its clear marks on the social and spiritual life of the Jews in that country. Even after the Christian conquest, which occurred mostly during the twelfth century and the first half of the thirteenth, substantial Muslim cultural influence remained. Thus, the Jewry of Spain continued to live under the influence of both Muslim and Christian culture.

This social and cultural situation left a deep impression upon Jewish family life in the Iberian peninsula generally, and upon issues of personal status in particular. The Jews adopted for themselves several of the habits of the Muslims and Christians with their wives. This was caused by the migration of Jews from Muslim countries to Christian countries during the period of the Reconquista, the gradual dominance by the Christians over the cities of Spain, the deep relation of Spanish Jewry since the earliest generations to the teaching of the Babylonian Geonim and, above all else, their deep respect for the impressive Muslim culture, which profoundly influenced the culture, and mentality of Spanish Jewry during its "Golden Age."

The question of polygamy in the Jewish family in Christian Spain has been the subject of relatively extensive discussion. By contrast, only relatively little attention has been given to the situation in Muslim Spain. This derives primarily from the paucity of sources. In the absence of archival sources from this period, the responsa literature of the early Spanish sages—primarily from the eleventh and twelfth centuries—must serve as the primary source for studying polygamy in Muslim Spain.

The basic structure of the Jewish family in Muslim Spain was monogamous, but it is clear that there were also cases of polygamy, including some "not in a case of *mitzvah*"—that is, even when the first wife was not barren. The responsa of R. Yitzhak Alfasi (the Rif) and of R. Joseph Ibn Migash preserve testimonies of polygamy in Spain, alongside relatively numerous testimonies of the holding of concubines by Jewish men. However, the nature of these sources does not allow us to determine the number of polygamous families, although it seems clear that they do not refer to rare incidents alone. The responsa literature of the sages of Muslim Spain refers to the marriage of a second wife as an accepted event in society, which does not give the first wife any cause for suit.

One of the main factors causing polygamy was the intensive involvement of Spanish Jewry in commerce and the lengthy journeys this involved. The prolonged absence of husbands and the widespread polygamy of the neighboring

Muslim society had their anticipated affect. Most of the testimonies relating to the marriage of a second wife in the eleventh and twelfth centuries are connected with journeys of the husband to other places for commercial purposes. We may also learn of the commonness of polygamy from the use by husbands of the threat to marry a second wife, when in their opinion the first wife did not behave properly. For example:

Concerning Reuben who has a wife and a small child of a year and a half, and he has sworn that he will leave his country and marry a woman in another country, and thereafter he regretted this because he was very poor.[23]

Rabbenu Alfasi opposed his marriage to a second wife due to the indigence of the person in question. Were this not the case, he could have married other wives on the basis of the ruling of Rabba in the Talmud.

Did the sages and community leaders in Muslim Spain attempt to wage war against the phenomenon of bigamy—if only in a partial way—as we have seen done during this same period in Ashkenaz and in Egypt, or did they accept it as a self-evident phenomenon, in accordance with the conclusion of the Babylonian Talmud and the reality of the surrounding Muslim society? The main source for this discussion is preserved in several of Alfasi's responsa, which have not yet been properly discussed. He was asked about a man who had given *qiddushin* to [i.e. betrothed] a certain woman, and in the course of his commercial activity moved to another place where he married a second wife:

Reuven, from the city of Gian, engaged in trade in his own place and made his living from a shop, and he betrothed Rachel, and he went to eastern Spain and lived there for ten years, and there he married another woman and left Rachel abandoned ("chained"). And when she heard that he had married another woman, she sued him *for the penalty customary in Spain since earliest days,* which is two hundred dinars.[24]

What is the source of this early communal edict? On what grounds was the heavy monetary penalty, customary in Spain since the "earliest days," imposed? It seems clear that this refers to an edict accepted no later than the beginning of the eleventh century, making it one of the earliest communal edicts known to us from Spain, or perhaps the earliest of all.[25] A. H. Freiman, the editor of Maimonides' responsa, and Z. Leiter, the editor of Alfasi's responsa, both thought that the penalty was imposed upon Reuven because he married a second wife, as seemingly follows from the formulation of the query ("and when his wife heard that he had married another woman, she sued him for the penalty"). If they are right, then this is important evidence of a highly significant transformation in the status of Jewish women in Muslim Spain. But this interpretation seems to me to be erroneous. From the continuation of the query and the answer given by Alfasi, it is implied that the penalty was imposed upon the husband because of his abandonment of his wife and his extended stay away from home—

possibly after their betrothal and before solemnizing the marriage—and not because of his marrying a second wife per se.

And if this Reuben said, I will take her to the place where I married a second wife, or stay with one for a certain period and with that one for a certain period, is he allowed by law to do so?

Answer: This Reuben, if he earned his living in Gian, is not allowed to take his wife to another city. And since he had previously earned his livelihood in his own province and was not in the habit of travelling, he cannot go to another province for trade until he receives her permission, and all the more so that he is not permitted to take a wife in some other place . . . And all the more so that [he may not] go to another place and marry a woman, and go to this one for a certain period and to that one for a certain period. Therefore, if this Reuven does not return to his wife and live with her in her place, he must pay her the fine.

If the fine in question was imposed because of the very fact of his marrying a second wife, there would be no point to the husband's suggestion that he take his first wife to the new location, or that he live alternately with his two wives in the two places. What difference would it make if he changed his place of residence, so long as his second wife remains with him? Nor would there be any point to Alfasi's ultimate ruling, requiring the husband to return to his original place or to pay a fine: If he did not divorce his second wife, than the penalty should apply to him in all events!

In sources from this period, the verb *qidesh* ("sanctified") generally refers to the stage at which the betrothal contract had been written, but they were not yet actually "married," in the sense that they had not yet held the marriage ceremony (*huppah*) nor begun to live together as husband and wife. Between these two stages, there was a certain period of waiting, which was on occasion quite protracted. The early Spanish sages worried that this period might prove too long, and that meanwhile the husband might abandon his wife. The main reason for such abandonment and non-consummation of the marriage derived from the husband's absence due to the economic factor.

Offhand, one might challenge our interpretation of the fine, as having been imposed in Spain "since the days of the early ones" due to the fear of desertion of the woman and protracted absence of the husband, from the fact that the woman demanded the fine only after ten years. If it was because of abandonment, why wait such a lengthy period? But this objection is groundless. So long as the husband had not taken a second wife, the former was prepared to forego the penalty, on the assumption that he would eventually return to her once his business was established. Only after he married a second wife did she decide to utilize this sanction, which had long been available to her.

We do not find any evidence of clear-cut opposition to polygamy in eleventh-century Spain such as existed during that same time in Christian Europe or in

Egypt. However, it may have existed in some communities. On the other hand, the struggle against abandonment of wives in any event made marrying a second wife more difficult.

The Struggle against Abandonment of Wives and Postponement of Wedding Dates

Despite the fact that the above-mentioned source in Alfasi's responsum does not, in my opinion, relate to the struggle against polygamy, it is of great importance for the status of Jewish women in Muslim Spain. It preserves evidence of an early edict of the communities in Spain—whether all of it or some part of it—whose purpose was to combat the phenomenon of abandonment of women by their husbands, whether those who were married or those who were only "betrothed." A general edict of this type, especially one imposing a high financial penalty upon the husband, is only enacted in the case of dire need.[26]

What was the historical background for this? Examination of the responsa of the early Spanish sages indicates that we are dealing here with a rather widespread phenomenon that troubled Jewish society in the Muslim countries and in Christian Europe during the tenth and eleventh centuries. The extensive involvement in international and local commerce and trade led to frequent journeys and changes in place of residence. The husband or bridegroom first tried his luck in the new place, with the assumption and hope that within a short time he would become established in his business and that his fiancée or wife would come to join him. But frequently, this attempt continued for a number of years. The merchants, some of whom were still quite young, did not always enjoy success. At times, the "betrothal" was also made when the bride was still extremely young, as we discussed above, and this too led to the postponement of marriage and common dwelling. During the waiting period, the husband sometimes married a second wife from the place where he was staying. The substantial discussion of the influence of these trips upon the family unit indicates the concrete nature of the problem. Of course, the responsa literature only preserves exceptional cases, which required the intervention of the highest rabbinic authority. Many other incidents were doubtless resolved between the members of the couple or by the local *dayan*, without being mentioned in literature.

We already noted above the edict issued by Maimonides and his court against desertion of wives. This edict, with its various sections, reflects the severity of the problem. It mentions an edict from Spain that whoever sanctifies a woman makes an explicit condition at the time of *qiddushin* that, should he be absent from the place for more than one year, the *qiddushin* will be nullified.[27] As mentioned, one generation earlier, Rabbenu Tam had issued a similar edict in France. These edicts reflect the attempts by the merchants to circumvent them and to nevertheless engage in extended travels. The problem of desertion of wives presented itself at that time in full severity to the sages in Egypt, Germany, and France. In the historical research literature, Spain is not mentioned together with them. From Alfasi's responsa, we learn that during the eleventh century the Jews of Spain also combatted this phenomenon. The heavy fines imposed in Spain upon husbands who deserted their fiancées or wives is explicit testimony to this.

The sources preserved also contain numerous questions concerning the divorce of a woman from "betrothal," from which it follows that the phenomenon continued unabated into the first half of the twelfth century. Various sources from the eleventh and early twelfth century refer to a "fine" that was imposed in Spain upon husbands who failed to honor their obligations towards their fiancees or wives. Most of these cases do not explicitly state for what the fine was imposed. Examination of the sources indicates that the term includes various payments that the husband obligated himself to pay his wife in the betrothal or marriage document, in the event that he should fail to carry out his commitments. But, generally speaking, these specified a payment on the part of one who had betrothed or "sanctified" a woman and failed to formalize the marriage at the time he was obligated to do so in the document.

In one of his responsa, Alfasi refers to "the fine customary in that place," from which we may infer that the size of the penalty varied from one community to another. The two hundred dinar mentioned, imposed in the city of Gian according to the ancient practice in Spain, is to be seen as the accepted fine in those places where the local community did not impose any other penalty. This practice continued to be in effect in the first half of the twelfth century. Such fines are also mentioned several times in the responsa of R. Joseph Ibn Migash.[28]

The main purpose of this struggle was to prevent the abandonment of women; retroactively, it also served to reduce polygamy. One may assume that, were it not for these fines, polygamy in Spain would have been more widespread. Commercial activity, with all it involved, encouraged the marriage of an additional wife.

The close connection between this commercial activity and the structure of and relations within the family cell involved manifold aspects. We have already noted the problem of desertion of wives and the partial reduction in polygamous marriages. This activity also created a difficult problem of women who were unable to marry because of natural disasters and other mishaps on the roads, of which numerous testimonies are preserved in the sources of those days. On the other hand, it also brought many benefits to the woman because it increased her independence, her involvement in commerce, her economic power, and gave her a more active role in the education of her children and in the shaping of family life. In families of merchants, the woman also brought into the marriage a reasonable dowry that was legally defined as her personal property, thereby substantially reducing her degree of dependence upon her husband.

The Situation in Christian Spain

The Jewish center in Christian Spain—the largest in Europe during the twelfth to fifteenth centuries—is the only one in the Jewish world in the Middle Ages in which there was not a uniform practice regarding the issue of polygamy. The main factors causing this were the political split in the wake of the Reconquista, the differing attitudes among the various states of the Iberian peninsula to the Muslim cultural heritage and to other Jewish Diasporas in Europe, and the social polarization. The reality of the situation and the transformations that took place therein were also greatly influenced by the position taken by the rabbis and by the way of life of the Jewish courtiers. The question of polygamy in Christian Spain has been the subject of a relatively extensive discussion. I will mention in particular the important studies by Havlin and Assis.[29] Havlin published new sources from manuscripts that are of great value for understanding both Rashba's stance on this subject and the influence of Rabbenu Gershom's *herem* in Spain. Assis also studied the world view implied by the state archives in Aragon.

Scholars disagree among themselves on the question of the extent of polygamy in the Christian states of the Iberian peninsula. According to some, polygamy was not accepted among the Jewish communities in Christian Spain, except under certain extraordinary circumstances, because of three main factors: the official prohibition of the Crown against marrying a second wife; the influence of Rabbenu Gershom's edict; and local custom.

The royal prohibition was a direct continuation of the Roman-Byzantine tradition. In the state of Aragon, the death penalty was imposed upon anyone who married a second wife without permission of the king.

As against that, Havlin and Assis think that bigamy was not such an unusual phenomenon in Spain, and brought convincing proofs for this. According to Havlin, it was restricted primarily to the borders of Catalonia and Aragon, and was more accepted in other districts. Among other things, he cites the testimony of R. Nissim of Gerona (Ran) that in Castille it was customary to marry two wives. This should not be surprising, as in Castille the influence of Islam was greater than in Aragon. But in practice, there was no uniform practice among the Jewish communities in Christian Spain with regard to this issue. Some communities issued local ordinances against polygamy and others ignored it. Clarification of the situation in the various communities is not simple, particularly not in Aragon. The sources preserve vague and at times even contradictory testimonies. Thus, for example, Rashba testified in one of his responsa that in his city of Barcelona the phenomenon was common and many people took a second wife:

That edict [i.e., of Rabbenu Gershom] did not take hold in all our boundaries. Nor have we heard that it took root even in Provence, adjacent to France. And there have been cases in our place where Talmudic scholars married a second wife, as did many others, and no person has ever been concerned about this matter.[30]

On the face of it, this seems to be explicit evidence that many people in Barcelona, including learned men, took a second wife. However, in another of his responsa, he testified that in his place only a few isolated individuals married a second wife, and then only when their first wife was unable to bear children. Nevertheless, the second marriages were unsuccessful:

And there were two or three people in this city who married a second wife because they did not have children from them . . . Yet nevertheless we have not seen in any of these cases that the match was successful.

According to the first responsum, "many" people in Barcelona married a second additional wife. According to the second responsum—"two or three people" did so. The difference between these two sources lies not only in the description of reality, but also in Rashba's attitude to polygamy. The second implies a clearly negative attitude toward marrying an additional wife. His emphasis on the fact that not a single one of the marriages of those that took a second wife was successful, conveys a clear message to the interlocutor and to his environment.

According to Epstein, Baer, and Assis, these two responsa, and others, express a certain development in Rashba's attitude toward bigamy. Initially he permitted it, on the basis of the widespread practice in several communities in Spain. The first responsum belongs to this period. Later, he came to see it in an entirely negative light, as expressed in the second responsum. While this may have been so, there is no indication in the responsa themselves or in the other sources of the time sequence suggested or of a change that occurred in Rashba's position. In any event, the contradiction in his testimony regarding the *reality* in his place and time has not been resolved. The difference between these two responsa may relate more to the background of the inquirers and of their questions. In the first, Rashba was addressed by people from Provence with a question regarding a man who had been married for ten years and his wife had not yet borne children. The questioner wondered whether he was permitted to marry a second wife or whether the ban of Rabbenu Gershom was applicable to him. In this case, Rashba permitted him to marry; indeed, in his opinion he was even *required* to marry a second wife so as to fulfill the commandment to "be fruitful and multiply," as Rabbenu Gershom's edict did not apply to a case involving a *mitzvah*. He adds that in his locale many people married a second wife without any misgivings. All this was intended to calm the questioner and to remove any doubt from his heart that he might be violating Rabbenu Gershom's *herem*. His purpose there was clear—namely, to convince the questioner to take a second wife.

By contrast, in the second question, in which Rashba took exception to marrying a second wife and said that there were only isolated individuals who did so, his interlocutor was a married man who had had intimate relations with his household servant, whom he then released, married, and preferred to his first wife. Rashba was shocked by this incident, invoked the ban of Rabbenu Ger-shom, and noted that, while there were a few people in his city who had mar-ried a second wife, these marriages were all unsuccessful. All this, as a rebuke to the husband and to encourage the community leaders to take measures to protect women. In light of the utterly different circumstances of the two cases and the nature of the interlocutor's involvement in the event, and its clear ten-dentiousness, it is doubtful whether we can infer anything from it regarding any change in his principled stance. Frequently the rabbis writing the responsa saw themselves as educators and admonishers, their general remarks being related to the specific case about which they were asked in a methodic way. It is very difficult to build an entire theoretical doctrine on the basis of a respon-sum by a sage that was written with a deep emotional connection and out of a powerful wish to convince his interlocutors.

On the basis of the above-mentioned responsa of Rashba and their back-grounds, it would seem that the phenomenon of bigamy was common in Barcelona, and that there were even learned people who married an additional wife. Whereas in Ashkenaz a man whose wife was barren needed to divorce her in order to marry another woman, the men in Spain were accustomed not to divorce the first wife but to marry a second one in addition, of which there is additional evidence.

Assis, who examined archival sources from the royal archives of Aragon, concluded:

Jews in Northeastern Spain continued to marry two wives as they did previously, based upon the explicit claim that Jewish law allowed this. Between 1318 and 1338 at least fif-teen cases of bigamy are listed in the Chancellor's registry . . . The sages of Aragon did not accept the *herem* upon themselves in an unequivocal way, albeit they attempted to prevent or to limit incidents of polygamy as much as possible. We clearly find that these attempts were not successful. . . In the days of the Ribash [fourteenth century] Jews were accustomed to marry a second wife even against the will of the first who had not borne children, and this despite an [explicit] condition in the *ketubah* that prevented them from doing so.[31]

He noted some fifty cases of bigamy that were preserved in these archives and in the responsa literature. This is quite a considerable number, similar to the findings of Friedman in the documents of the Cairo Genizah. One is dealing here with a period during which there were official restrictions imposed by the royal rule in Aragon on marrying a second wife, from which it follows that the findings of Havlin and Assis are of great importance as testimony to the exis-tence of the phenomenon in the communities of Christian Spain, and especially in Aragon. These archives also contain certificates of legitimacy issued by the crown to children born from a second wife. It is highly likely that there were also many marriages with a second wife that were conducted in secret, without the knowledge of the authorities. It follows that the incidence of bigamy was in fact greater than that recorded in the documents found in the royal archives, confuting the view of those researchers who thought that, because of the royal prohibition against marrying a second wife, the phenomenon was rare in Spain. One of the important findings testified to by Assis is that almost all of the non-Hebrew sources dealing with bigamy relate to the upper classes in Jewish society. This is not surprising. As mentioned, maintaining two wives involved substantial financial expenditure. In addition to the payment to the crown for permission to marry a second wife, the husband needed to provide separate living accommodations for the two women. Wealthier members of the community could receive the royal permission in exchange for a high financial payment to the royal treasury, but it is clear that the very fact of the prohibition and the financial payment also limited the phenomenon. Assis examined the findings with respect to different areas of Jewish settlement in Spain, particularly in Catalonia and Aragon. The official documents of the crown indicate bigamous marriages in dozens of communities, which Assis enumerated and counted. The overall conclusion was that there were no substantive differences in relation to polygamy among the different districts of the kingdoms of Catalonia and Aragon.[32]

The Situation in Provence

Certain parts of Provence belonged to the royal crown of Aragon, so that there too the prohibition against marrying a second wife was in force. Thus, a document from 1259 explicitly states that King Jaime I of Aragon had granted permission to a certain Jew in Montpellier to marry a second wife, notwithstanding that the community was opposed to it. And indeed, in several of these communities there were local edicts prohibiting husbands from taking a second wife.

Epstein, who thought that in Montpellier they had accepted the ban of Rabbenu Gershom, bases this upon the opposition of the leaders of this community to the permission given by King Jaime I to a Jew to marry a second wife. But there is no proof that their opposition was based upon the acceptance of Rabbenu Gershom's edicts. It likewise follows from the query sent by the Provençal community of Villa Franca to Rashba that, on the face of it, the *herem* was accepted there. That question related to a woman, about whom there was severe suspicion that she had been unfaithful to her husband. The woman denied these suspicions, but her husband gave no credence to her denials and therefore refrained from sexual relations with her. The interlocutors stated that, as the edicts of Rabbenu Gershom were accepted in their town, he could neither divorce her against her will nor take a second wife.

Even though the inquirers clearly saw themselves as subject to Rabbenu Gershom's edict, one cannot infer from this that the *herem* was accepted generally in the Montpellier community. The possibility suggested by Havlin and Assis, that those inquiring were people from northern France who had migrated to Provence, seems to me a definite option. These migrations increased after the expulsion order issued against the Jews in certain regions of France, particularly in 1289, 1291, and following the general expulsion order in 1306.

Testimonies concerning local edicts in some Provençal communities against the involuntary divorce of a woman have been preserved in the responsa of R. Mordecai ben Yitzhak Kimhi, one of the sages of Provence at the time of Rashba. He mentions there the edict of the sages "that a person may not divorce his wife without her agreement, that of her relatives and that of the seven leaders of the city . . . and these edicts spread in several of our lands, and they were confirmed by the great sages of the generation. Also, they were recently renewed by Rabbi Moshe Nasi *in twenty-seven communities* in our lands."[33] These edicts are likewise mentioned in the responsa of another Provençal sage as having been made "by the great ones."[34] It follows from this that in many communities in Provence local edicts were introduced against polygamy and against divorcing a woman against her will. One is speaking here, not of accepting the edicts of Rabbenu Gershom as such, but of their clear influence. Support for this view also appears in one of Rashba's responsa. He tells of "an Ashkenazic scholar whose wife had a blemish," evidently referring to a severe mental disease. Because of his wish to raise a family, "this scholar" left his home in Germany and migrated to the community of Montpellier in Provence, in the hope that he would be permitted there to take a second wife. Rashba allowed him to marry a second wife because, in his opinion, Rabbenu Gershom's ban did not apply to cases of this type. If Rabbenu Gershom's edicts were observed in full in Provence as well, what would the scholar in question have gained by migrating from Germany to Provence? Moreover, in his responsum, Rashba testified that Rabbenu Gershom's edicts had not been accepted as such either in Spain or Provence.

In brief, many of the communities of Provence had local edicts that were intended to prevent—or at least make more difficult—the marriage of a second wife, even if these ordinances were not as strict or comprehensive as that of Rabbenu Gershom, especially as it had developed in Germany and France in the thirteenth century.

4. The Atmosphere in the Polygamous Family

The abundant sources in the various branches of halakhic literature—particularly the responsa literature—deal for the most part with the legal-halakhic aspects of the polygamous family, and hardly relate to description of the atmosphere within this family. The picture that emerges from the Bible is a harsh one: The polygamous family was filled with tension, disputes and hostility. On the other hand, one might have conjectured that the ubiquity of polygamy in the surrounding Muslim society, which allowed its believers to marry as many as four women, might ease the feelings of bitterness within the Jewish family in Muslim countries. Indeed, anthropological studies indicate the acceptance of polygamy in a variety of different societies.

A very few sources do afford us a glimpse, however slight, of the mental world of the "rival" wives within the polygamous Jewish family. Among these are the documents of the Cairo Genizah.[35] These sources, though few in number, are of great importance. The husbands who married a second wife committed themselves to provide each of their wives with a separate house and to relate to them with full equality. There were those who were meticulous in honoring these promises, and relations within the family were tolerable. However, it is clear that these promises were often honored more in the breach than in the observance. Tension was particularly high in those families where the second wife had been married due to the barrenness of the first. After the second wife became pregnant, jealousy in the home grew and the relationships became even more tense. Some of the women who had initially agreed to their husband marrying a second wife—usually because of their own infertility—thereafter recanted and asked for a divorce.

A document of great value for concretizing the depth of hostility regnant in the polygamous Jewish family was written by a youth whose father, Yehudah, had immigrated from Spain to Egypt. The father engaged in trade and, on one of his trips to Yemen he married his first wife, from whom was born Shlomo, the author of this letter. Several years later, the father married a second wife, who bore him three children. Shlomo greatly loved his father and did not hold any grudge against him because of the second marriage. However, he felt intense hatred toward the second wife and her children. The three children of the second wife—a brother and two sisters—died one after another. The author sees this as a miracle performed for his sake, and he is full of thanks and praises to God for the death of his step-siblings ("when my brother and sisters died, and there did not remain an adversary against me among the creatures").[36] But he was not satisfied with the death of his brother and sisters, but prayed that their mother should also die as soon as possible. Young Shlomo said nothing about his own mother, and sufficed with a hint that the second wife taunted her. It is difficult to imagine that the author's intense hatred toward the second wife did not derive from the general atmosphere in the home, and specifically from his mother's attitude towards her. This letter of a young boy is the strongest evidence of the intensity of animosity and jealousy that ruled in the polygamous household. The prevalence of marriage of a second wife in both Jewish and Muslim society could not blunt the edge of this animosity. The harsh picture of the polygamous family that appears in the Bible, in the home of the patriarchs and in those of Elkanah and David, returns here in full force. There are no parallel documents regarding the situation of polygamous Jewish families in Spain, but it is difficult to imagine that the picture was different in any substantive way.

Jewish sages in Europe and in the Muslim countries during the Middle Ages were well aware of the harsh atmosphere in the polygamous family. We already noted above the words of Rashba: that he does not know of a single family in which such marriages succeeded. One generation later, interlocutors from Aragon described such families to the Rosh as filled with "arguments, resentment and divorce."[37] One generation later, at the end of the fourteenth century, the Rib-ash warned that "there is no one who brings dispute into his home like one who takes another wife into his home."[38] In the sixteenth century, the sages of Eretz Yisrael repeated this approach. One of the sages even stated that a second wife in a family "is certainly more difficult for the wives than is beating."

R. Nissim of Gerona (Ran) even suggested the possibility that Rabbenu Ger-shom's concern in imposing the *herem* was not only the welfare of the women, but also that of the men, so as to assure them domestic harmony: "for per-haps this ban was intended, not only for the benefit of the women, but also for that of the men, so that they not bring conflict into their homes."[39]

However, not all the rabbis were as aware as he of the suffering of the women in a polygamous household, and especially that of the first wife, who felt aban-doned and betrayed. The second wife was usually younger and more attractive; all the more so if the former was barren and the second became pregnant. There were those sages who noted the halakhah permitting a man to marry two wives, the reality in their Muslim environment, and the economic wealth of those women living within prosperous families, and ignored the women's feelings.

One may conjecture that this phenomenon also existed in Spain in earlier generations. Assis, in the above-mentioned article about polygamy in Spain, and Lamdan, noted many examples of women who were prepared to tolerate the "rival" wife, either because of the favorable economic situation they enjoyed or because of their wish to remain within a family and not to be left alone.

The suffering of children in a polygamous household was also considerable. This was the result, not only of the sense of psychological oppressiveness in light of the arguments between the two women, but also of the fear of damage to their rights of inheritance. In Spain, a certain doubt was sometimes cast over their legitimacy and the legality of their status which, in Aragon, involved not only the rabbis, but also the king himself.[40]

5. Levirate Marriage and Bigamy

Yibbum or Halizah?

Yibbum, or levirate marriage—in which the brother-in-law marries his brother's childless widow so as to "to raise seed to his brother"—was practiced among both the Israelites and other nations before the giving of the Torah, as implied by the incident of Tamar and the sons of Judah (Genesis 38), and is understood in the Bible as a positive act intended to perpetuate the memory of the deceased brother. An element of shame is attached to failure to perform this *mitzvah*, to the extent that the man who does so is called "the house of him whose shoe was removed" (Deut. 25:10). Anthropologists have enumerated additional conjectures in explanation of this practice. The Torah speaks of a procedure of removing the shoe (*halizah*) which is performed when a brother refuses to perform levirate marriage with his dead brother's wife. And what about a woman who refuses to enter such a marriage? The Bible makes no reference to such a case. It may be assumed that in biblical times such an event was rare indeed. *Yibbum* was understood as one of the obligations of the woman in the institution of marriage, and it was assumed that she preferred to undergo *yibbum* rather than to remain a widow her entire life—a presumption strengthened by the biblical story of Tamar (Gen. 38). The woman was also interested in perpetuating her deceased husband's name, and for this reason as well she preferred to remarry under these circumstances. In the Middle Ages, many sages ruled that a woman who refused to undergo *yibbum* was considered as a "rebellious" wife, with all that entails (i.e., loss of *ketubah* and other financial benefits), unless there was a convincing reason for her refusal.

From the viewpoint of the woman, there were many advantages to *yibbum*. As a rule, it assured her an economic basis, a place to live, a supportive family, and an opportunity to leave behind her mourning and isolation. Moreover, frequently she, together with her deceased husband, had been supported by his parents within the framework of the extended family. *Yibbum* was also a moving and satisfying act for her, as it helped to perpetuate the memory of her husband and to provide him with offspring, particularly according to the world view of the Kabbalists, as will be discussed below. Moreover, some tannaitic and amoraitic sources suggest the possibility that the woman was responsible for her husband's death. A woman, two of whose husbands had died (or, according to some views, three) was considered a "murderous wife." Her bad luck or some medical reason had caused the death of her husbands, and therefore it was forbidden for her to marry a third time. One may assume, with a fair degree of plausibility, that there were those who already in their first widowhood began to fear that a given woman was "murderous," particularly if the husband had died a short time after marriage; this was frequently true in the case of women in need of levirate marriage, who had not yet borne her husband children. Perhaps she may have herself felt fears of this type. A rapid marriage to the levir (Hebrew: *yabam*), her late husband's brother, not only relieved the sense of oppressiveness, loss and loneliness, but to a certain extent put to rest the fear that it might be difficult for her to marry a second time. On the other hand, neither she, nor her parents, nor the members of her family, had any voice in the selection of her destined bridegroom—her brother-in-law, who had suddenly become a real candidate for marriage. Ordinarily, a prospective bridegroom was chosen by the girl's parents according to his family lineage, his status, his wealth, his character, and his suitability, and at least on the formal level it was necessary to receive the young woman's agreement to the marriage. In the case of *yibbum,* all of these factors went by the wayside. Neither his external appearance, nor his character traits or his degree of suitability were taken into account. His consanguinity was all that mattered.

It is true that the halakhah did provide a certain protection to the woman when there was extreme incompatibility between herself and the levirate brother, particularly if there was a great age difference between them. In such a case, the Court advised him to perform the ritual of *halizah* rather than to marry her: "One says to him: what have you to do with an old woman? Go marry one like yourself and do not introduce quarrels into your home."[41] But this afforded only partial protection; in the final analysis, all depended upon the agreement and decision of the brother. Concerning this, R. Joseph Ibn Migash already commented:

"One says to him: What have you to do with an old woman? What have you to do with a young girl? Go to one like yourself, and do not introduce dispute into your home." If he accepted this from them [i.e., the rabbis advising him], well and good; but if he preferred to perform *yibbum* he does so, and we cannot prevent him from doing so or impose upon him *halizah,* so long as he is able to support two women, and he is not yet so old as to be impotent.[42]

Rabbenu Asher wrote in a similar vein: "You should know that this is no more than good counsel that the Court is required to give him . . . but if he does not listen to their advice, he may do as his heart wishes."[43] The right of decision also left in his hands the option of pressuring the widow to forego some of the money that was due her according to her *ketubah* and some of her jewelry in exchange for *halizah*—and this, with the covert agreement of some of the sages. Medieval sources preserve many testimonies relating to cases of blackmail of this type, some of which will be discussed below.

The tannaim were in disagreement as to which was preferable: *yibbum* or *halizah.* Jewish sages in each generation likewise disagreed as to which of the two opinions was preferable. Although, generally speaking, the halakhah stated that one ought to perform *yibbum,* many authorities had compunctions about this and preferred to influence the levir to give *halizah.*

The great division in customs in this area existed, not only between the different Diasporas, but within the Diasporas themselves. Thus, for example, during the Geonic period in Babylonia, it was customary in the Sura yeshiva to perform *yibbum,* while in Pumbedita they performed *halizah.*

The historian Jacob Katz devoted a detailed and carefully documented discussion to the issue of *yibbum* and *halizah,* showing that the split among the opinions of the various sages was greater than what can be seen on the surface and as described in the research literature, and that one cannot speak of a single view in any given Diaspora.[44] He noted the transformations and historical factors that created these differences. It is not our aim here to examine this subject at length, but only to observe its influence upon bigamy. So as not to let the discussion get out of hand, I will suffice with citing the principal opinions of several of the leading sages and describing the situation in the different Diasporas, especially the question of the relation between levirate marriage and bigamy, which in my view is somewhat different from that drawn by Katz.

Yibbum and *Halizah* in Ashkenaz

There was no uniform custom regarding this matter in Germany and France. There were those who permitted *yibbum,* and such was the practice of most of the sages in Germany during the eleventh and twelfth centuries. There were those who preferred *halizah,* and such was the ruling of many sages in northern France following the decision of Rabbenu Tam. R. Judah Ha-cohen, a disciple of Rabbenu Gershom Meor Hagolah and spiritual leader of the community of Mainz following Rabbenu Gershom's death, ruled that *yibbum* was permitted, but that it is not to be imposed upon the woman against her wish. He also criticized those who used delay in granting *halizah* in order to blackmail the woman and advised misleading the levir in this case, but also opposed forcing him to give *halizah,* as *halizah* must be performed out of the individual's free will. It follows from his words that this was not only his personal stance, but that "thus have I received from my teachers."[45] His main teacher was Rabbenu Gershom, and these words almost certainly preserve a record of the custom in early Ashkenaz from the first half of the eleventh century. Rashi, in France, ruled like R. Judah Ha-cohen that, if both partners wish to perform *yibbum,* they are allowed to do so. However, Rashi granted considerable leeway in the case where the woman refuses to marry the levir, stating that one may even mislead the recalcitrant *yabam* who refuses to give *halizah* by offering him a financial reward that afterwards need not be realized. If he persists in his refusal, he is forced to give *halizah.* In this ruling, Rashi explicitly dissented from the practice of early Ashkenaz, which he knew from the period of his studies in Germany. The words of the tanna R. Eleazar ben Azariah, that if the woman "fell to one who was afflicted with boils one does not force her to undergo *yibbum,*" was greatly expanded by Rashi, who stated that "afflicted with boils" is merely an example, which applies not only to people with physical deformities, but to "whatever reason she might give." Whatever the reason may be, if the woman refuses to undergo levirate marriage, the levir is forced to give her *halizah* and to pay her the value of her *ketubah.*[46] Rashi's main innovation lies in a double recognition: of the woman's right to force the levir to give *halizah,* and simultaneously to receive her *ketubah* money.

Rashi's position here is a great innovation, and it was not for naught that there were many among the Jewish sages who raised a cry against it in both medieval and modern times. According to the literal sense of the passage, it is not mere chance that Rav Sheshet specifically mentions the ailment of boils as grounds for imposing *halizah*. This is a harsh, possibly contagious, disease, a kind of leprosy or other severe skin disease, which serves as a classic example of a severe defect that is liable to upset family life. It is very difficult to see this merely as an example for any sort of claim that a woman might raise to justify her refusal to undergo *yibbum* and to impose *halizah* upon the husband.[47]

What moved Rashi to propose this sort of interpretation and halakhic ruling? All of Rashi's comments in his commentary to the Talmud are carefully worded and precise, so that one cannot imagine that this is merely a routine use of language. Rashi was fully aware of the serious practical implications of his decision, and preferred to find a basis for it in the words of the Talmud, thereby providing it some grounding in the sources. Moreover, he was not in the habit of bringing halakhic rulings in his Talmud commentary, doing so primarily regarding those matters that were of practical relevance in his day and concerning which the sages' opinions were divided.

R. Levi ben Yaakov Ibn Habib (Ralbah), among the Jews expelled from Spain and the leading rabbi in Jerusalem during the early sixteenth century, explained that Rashi proposed this interpretation, indicating the great importance of women, due to a personal reason: his being a father only of daughters.[48] But, as has already been observed by Jacob Katz, it is difficult to attribute a ruling of this type to a biographical detail connected with Rashi's private life. In his opinion, what led Rashi to this ruling was the overall improvement in the status of women in Ashkenaz during that period. While this explanation is plausible, in my opinion it ought to be seen in a broader perspective. The sources indicate the difficult lot of Ashkenazic women who were subject to *yibbum*. Receiving *halizah* often involved numerous difficulties and blackmail. The weakness of the public leadership in Germany and France during the tenth and eleventh centuries, which found it difficult to impose its authority, made the situation even more difficult. Levirs refused to listen to the ruling of the community rabbis and delayed *halizah* for years in the hopes of extracting further financial concessions from the hapless widows. Rashi was well aware of this harsh reality and came to the aid of the widows by means of his ruling that any explanation she might offer for her refusal justified the imposition of *halizah* and her receiving her *ketubah* money in full.

To my mind, another weighty consideration needs to be added to this. Rashi's concern for the woman and for her status in family and in society follows clearly from all of his teachings, in which he also attempted to educate others to adopt his path and to influence the leaders of the community to exercise concern for the women. A number of examples of this have been brought in the present work.

One of the striking aspects of Rashi's character was his great sensitivity to the suffering of others, his respect for people, and his love of peace and harmony. A person imbued with such characteristics would find it difficult to stand aside upon seeing the oppression of women in general, and that of widows in particular.[49] The ruling here, allowing the woman to enter a levirate marriage if she so wishes, and forcing her levir to give her *halizah* if she refuses *yibbum* (while retaining all of her financial rights stipulated in the *ketubah*), is the best possible decision from the woman's viewpoint. As stated above, the woman often found it preferable from the personal, social, and economic standpoint to undergo *yibbum*. But while levirate marriage was understood as an act of kindness with the dead, one that served to preserve his memory, it is inappropriate to achieve this kindness at the expense of hurting the feelings of the woman.

Unlike Jacob Katz, who treated Germany and France as one, it seems to me that there was a substantial difference between the two. In France, most rabbis from the time of Rabbenu Tam on prohibited *yibbum* and preferred *halizah*. As against that, in Germany it was still customary to perform *yibbum* in the eleventh century, as we have seen from the testimony of R. Judah Ha-cohen. The leading Ashkenazic sages of the twelfth century continued in this path.

Today, we have further important information about the practice of *yibbum* in early Ashkenaz, which was preserved in the Genizah in Italy. R. Yosef Kara— colleague and disciple of Rashi—related the custom of the Jews of Worms and Mainz to name the son who was born after *yibbum* after the deceased brother, even though according to Talmudic halakhah there is no obligation to do so.[50] He even offered a "rational " explanation for the *mitzvot* of *yibbum* and *halizah*. In his opinion, just as the act of *yibbum* has the purpose of not allowing the name of the dead brother to be obliterated, similarly by the act of *halizah*, which is widely publicized, the name of the deceased will be remembered. We may therefore infer that during the latter half of the eleventh century in Ashkenaz it was customary to perform *yibbum*. It is difficult to imagine that this custom was only observed in the two communities mentioned above; rather, R. Yosef Kara testified about what he himself saw in the two communities where he studied.

Not only did many authorities in Ashkenaz permit *yibbum*, but there were married men who exploited this practice in order to blackmail widows, notwithstanding the *herem* of Rabbenu Gershom against marrying two wives. One of the important records indicating the extent to which *yibbum* was rooted in the social reality of twelfth-century Germany relates to the Origia Affair that agitated the Ashkenazic sages during that period, record of which was preserved in several sources. R. Eliezer ben Yoel Halevi (Rabyah) recounts that when he was young, he witnessed a case in which a woman named Origia was forced to pay a large sum of money to her late husband's brothers who wished to give her *yibbum*, even though they were themselves married. However, it turned out that the brothers' demand to perform *yibbum* was purely theoretical. As Rabbenu Gershom's edict was unable in principle to negate or override *yibbum*, they thought that they had the right to demand part of the property of the deceased brother.

Further testimony concerning the practice of the Jews of Ashkenaz is preserved in an account relating to R. Simhah of Speyer, who suggested to a certain woman an unconventional way of escaping forced *yibbum*. The halakhah states that, if the levir had sexual relations with the woman even without her consent, this act constitutes *yibbum* and she becomes his wife. A certain Ashkenazic man, who was anxious to marry his sister-in-law because of her prestigious lineage and wealth, tried to rape her and thereby affect *yibbum*. R. Simhah advised that she spit in his face and thereby utilize the halakha stating that if the woman spat at the man before the act of *yibbum*, she is thereby disqualified for *yibbum*:

A certain levir wished to forcibly perform *yibbum* with his sister-in-law because she was of prominent family and wealthy, but she did not wish it. And he lay in wait for her several times, until she came to Rabbi Simhah and asked him what to do. And he said to her: spit in his face. And she did so, and R. Simhah disqualified her from receiving *yibbum*.[51]

If *yibbum* had been prohibited in Germany and they had preferred *halizah*, as was generally speaking the case in France at that time (late twelfth and early thirteenth century), there would have been no need for this forced solution. Rabbenu Tam's influence was greater in France than it was in Ashkenaz, as may be seen from the teaching of the sages of France in the second half of the twelfth century. A careful reading of the detailed discussion of the issue of *yibbum* and *halizah* by R. Yitzhak ben Moses of Vienna in his book *Or Zaru'a* immediately senses the difference in approach between the Ashkenazic and French sages. In later generations, once the influence of the French Tosaphists grew in Germany, the phenomenon of *yibbum* greatly declined there as well. *Teshuvot Maharam* (by R. Meir of Rothenburg) relates a change that took place in the stance of the Ashkenazic sages, evidently during the thirteenth century, that made the possibility of blackmail more difficult:

In conclusion, at this time the communities imposed a *herem* upon a *yabam* who already has a wife, that he cannot fulfill the commandment of *yibbum* because of the Ban of Rabbenu Gershom, but he must perform *halizah* without money. And if he does not wish to do so they force him. And if she fell to a *yabam* and he is not married and he wishes to perform levirate marriage, and she does not wish, and he has no deformities, he may leave her in this state forever, or she gives him money so that he may give her *halizah*.[52]

This process, whereby the influence of the French sages within Germany became strengthened in the thirteenth century, received a great boost from R. Yitzhak of Vienna, the *Or Zaru'a*, and from R. Meir of Rothenburg. The great respect felt in Ashkenaz for the teaching of Rabbenu Tam played a decisive part in this development. However, even in the thirteenth century and later, there were those who continued to perform *yibbum* so long as the two sides agreed.

Yibbum and *Halizah* in Italy and Provence

In Italy, it was usually customary to perform *yibbum*. As late as the thirteenth century, R. Isaiah of Trani—one of the greatest medieval Italian rabbis—ruled that *yibbum* enjoys precedence. From his statement, it follows that there were even those who thought it permissible to impose *yibbum* upon the woman. But under the influence of R. Joseph Colon, who migrated from France to Italy in the fifteenth century, there were those in Italy who preferred *halizah*. However, R. Judah Leon of Modena testified that even in his day, in the seventeenth century, some in Italy continued to perform *yibbum*.[53]

Likewise in Provence, many people performed levirate marriages, but there was no uniform opinion on this topic. R. Abraham ben David of Posquières—the greatest Provençal sage of the twelfth century—preferred *halizah*. On the other hand, the great Provençal sages of the thirteenth and fourteenth century—including R. Menahem Hameiri—ruled that *yibbum* was preferable.[54]

Yibbum and *Halizah* in Spain

The great Spanish authorities, including Alfasi, Maimonides, Nahmanides, and Rashba, ruled that *yibbum* was to be preferred. It clearly follows from the sources that many medieval Spanish Jews did in fact practice *yibbum*, and that such was, in effect, the custom of most Jews in Muslim countries. *Yibbum* was understood by them as an important imperative, and anyone who neglected it was seen as desecrating the memory of the deceased husband/brother. This was the case even if the levir was already married. Moreover, in the twelfth century, one of the sages stated his view that *yibbum* even supercedes an explicit condition in the *ketubah* in which the husband promises not to marry a second wife. The great value ascribed to the practice of *yibbum* may be learned from the fact that, in the case where a married brother was unable to do *yibbum* and to live with two wives due to the objections of the first wife, who preferred to be divorced, the possibility was raised that he divorce his first wife and marry his brother's widow, all so that he might perform the *mitzvah* of *yibbum*.[55] However, when such a case was brought before Ribash, he opposed it because of the words of the rabbis that, if one divorces his first wife, even the altar sheds tears because of it; hence, in this case he preferred that the man do *halizah* rather than *yibbum*.[56]

But even in Spain, there were those rabbis who preferred *halizah* to *yibbum*, although they were a small minority. Beginning in the thirteenth century, when the influence of French sages began to grow within Spain, the number of those who opposed *yibbum* also began to grow, but they were still in a minority.

The combination of early marriage, a high mortality rate, and attempts at blackmail, created complex problems whose solution weighed upon Jewish society and which it was not easy to combat, especially when the "blackmailing" brothers sought various arguments to justify their refusal to give *halizah*. The most common way of combatting such extortion related to *halizah* was to promise money to the brother doing *halizah* and then not to fulfill the promise. Rashba exempted the woman from paying the money promised, ruling that even without giving notice "one may trick him and tell him, give *halizah* so that she may give you such-and-such," and then not fulfill the promise. But once this approach became known to the public it lost its effectiveness, as the extorting levir would then require real guarantees before agreeing to perform *halizah*. It is no accident that, in thirteenth century Spanish communities in which the local leadership generally speaking had great power, they followed Rashba's ruling forcing the extorting brother to perform either *yibbum* or *halizah* immediately.[57]

In Spain, a woman who wished to refuse levirate marriage with a man whom she did not want confronted considerable difficulties. While Maimonides had said that any woman who states that she finds her husband disgusting to her is entitled to receive a *get,* this opinion was not accepted by most Spanish authorities. Moreover, he likewise ruled that in the case of *yibbum,* if the prospective levir does not suffer from an actual deformity, the woman is required to marry him, as otherwise she is considered a *moredet* (rebellious wife) and loses her *ketubah.* Rashba was asked about such a case (in which the woman said she did not want to marry the *yabam,* because he is disgusting in her eyes or unsuitable), and he wrote that she is required to submit to *yibbum* ("certainly one forces her").[58]

It therefore should not be surprising that the responsa literature preserves numerous accounts relating to the various means used by widows in Spain to avoid *yibbum* with brothers-in-law whom they did not want. One of these was to receive fictive *qiddushin* from a strange man and to be divorced from him immediately, and thereby be relieved of *yibbum* and free to marry whomever she wishes. The ubiquity of the phenomenon may also be inferred from the public announcement given by the *yabam* immediately after the death of his brother, stating that the widow may not be married to any other person: "And Shimon was fearful lest she become betrothed and marry another man, and he stood in the synagogue . . . and prohibited his above-mentioned sister-in-law to the entire world. And the court ordered that she not leave the city and not receive *qiddushin* from any other person. But she went and left the city and received *qiddushin* from Judah, and immediately thereafter received from him a *get.*"[59] At times the members of the family took upon themselves the task that was rightfully that of the court, applying physical pressure upon the levir so as to force him to give *halizah*.

Yibbum and Polygamy

Yibbum was an important factor in the growth of the phenomenon of bigamy, as has already been observed by S. D. Goitein, referring to sources from the Cairo Genizah.[60] By contrast, Jacob Katz thought that it was almost always customary to perform *halizah* rather than *yibbum* when the brother-in-law was married, and that such was the case even in Spain.[61] This view seems to me rather doubtful. There is no doubt that the fact of the levir being married made *yibbum* more difficult and at times led to its nullification, but not to the extent described by Katz. It clearly emerges from the sources that *yibbum* was often performed even when the levir was married, and that this may have been the case even in Ashkenaz in the early generations—all the more in the Muslim countries and in Spain, in which *yibbum* was more widely accepted. An explicit example of this is to be found in a case debated by the sages in Egypt and beyond in the twelfth century. The husband had made an explicit condition in his *ketubah* that he would not marry another woman, and that should he do so his wife would be entitled to receive the divorce writ and *ketubah* payment. The husband's brother died without issue and the widow came for *yibbum* to the self-same husband. The levir's wife argued that he was violating an explicit promise made in the *ketubah,* and therefore she was entitled to a *get* and *ketubah* payment. The husband responded that one was dealing here with a case of "duress," which he had not imagined at the time of drawing up the *ketubah,* and that in practice this was not at all dependent upon his own will but that from heaven he had been "given" a second wife. The case aroused great controversy and various scholars, including Maimonides, took part in its discussion. He ruled that the husband did not owe his wife anything "and everyone agrees that the levirate wife is one that has fallen to him from heaven."[62] This ruling enjoyed the approval of several other rabbis.

The question that arose did not result from the fact that the levir was married, but from an explicit obligation he had undertaken in the *ketubah* not to marry another woman. If there had not been an explicit condition of this sort, the issue would not have become a subject for controversy and everyone would have agreed that the husband was allowed to enter into the levirate marriage despite being married. Not only does this source not confute this view but, on the contrary, it is a powerful proof of the ubiquity of *yibbum* in the Mediterranean basin even when the levir was married. Due to the conditions of the time (early marriage and relatively high death rate), such cases were quite common and they increased the incidence of bigamy among Jewish families. However, not all of the sages agreed with this decision. Some sages, who were in any event hesitant on the principled level whether they were in their day to prefer *yibbum* over *halizah,* tended in this case to prefer *halizah* and even to force it.

In one of the interesting documents that has been preserved in the Cairo Genizah, a woman subject to *yibbum* writes that she adamantly refuses to be married to the eldest of the brothers because he is already married: "and even if you cut my flesh into pieces, I will not agree to accept your view and will not listen to your voice that I be brought in to live together with a second wife. He has unmarried brothers."[63] It is clear from this that she was pressured to marry the oldest brother, as is prescribed by the halakhah, despite the fact that he was married and the woman asked to be married to one of the unattached brothers.

Another source from the Cairo Genizah tells of a *yibbum* that occurred in the family of the Nagid (the leading official of the Jewish community) as late as the fifteenth century, even though the levir was married. The levir explicitly promised that he would not show preference to his first wife: "and they arrived at an agreement that he would marry her and she also agreed to this. And they made a condition between them that he would treat the two women equally, one night with this one and one night with the other."[64]

A question addressed to Rashba tells of a fifty-year-old woman who "fell" before a married brother-in-law. Rashba advised that one attempt to convince the levir to give *halizah* "and not bring dispute into his house, since he has another wife," but if he refuses and is insistent, then he may carry out *yibbum*.[65] This was a principled ruling of the greatest rabbi in Spain at the end of the thirteenth and beginning of the fourteenth century, even though one was dealing with a woman aged fifty about whom it was doubtful whether she could still bear children. It is difficult to imagine that his decision was without public repercussions and that it did not reflect reality.

The conclusion that follows from this discussion is that in Spain too married brothers were accustomed to performing *yibbum,* and that *yibbum* increased the incidence of bigamy in Jewish society. Another factor that influenced matters was the strong position of several sages, and more than that of *Sefer ha-Zohar,* in support of *yibbum.* The commandment of being fruitful and multiplying in general is strongly emphasized in *Sefer ha-Zohar.* We have already noted in our discussion of the image of the woman in chapter 1, that according to the Kabbalists a man is not considered complete so long as he has not united with his partner in harmony and joy and she has borne him a son and a daughter. If he does so "then the supreme holy name is called upon him." By contrast, if a man dies without children, "he dies in this world and in the next" and "the Shekhinah does not rest upon him at all." He has not completed the Divine image in the world, and therefore needs to be reborn through metempsychosis so as to correct that which he left incomplete. A preferable form of *tikkun* (of mystical "correction") is to be reborn through *yibbum.* In this manner, the soul of the dead husband is so to speak reborn in the body of the infant created by the union of the dead man's wife with his brother. In the absence of *yibbum,* his soul must transmigrate through another union: "and it goes about and wanders in the world until it finds a redeemer to return him."[66] The act of *yibbum* can thus save the dead brother from getting lost.

According to this viewpoint, it is not at all surprising that there were brothers who chose to undertake levirate marriage with their sisters-in-law out of concern for the destiny of their dead brother's soul, even if this meant marrying a second wife, undergoing a serious economic burden, and bringing conflict into their homes. How could they allow their brother's soul to wander about the world?

The influence of *Sefer ha-Zohar* upon this subject, as on others, was particularly great after the expulsion of the Jews from Spain. Shaul Regev has examined the reasons for the commandment of *yibbum* offered by Spanish rabbis during the Late Middle Ages, particularly of those who were numbered among the rationalist philosophers, and of those whose thought was influenced by Kabbalah. As these sages are outside of the chronological framework set for this study, we cannot enter into a discussion of their stances. However, we can say in brief that the *Zohar* exerted a decisive influence on their explanations of the purpose of *yibbum*. The majority associated this *mitzvah* with the belief in transmigration of souls, which plays a central role in the *Zohar*'s outlook regarding the purpose of *yibbum*.[67] From an historical perspective, it is important to emphasize the probable influence of the fact that so many sages supported the above-mentioned outlook of the *Zohar* regarding the special value of the *mitzvah* of *yibbum* on people's attitude toward *yibbum*.

CHAPTER FIVE

Feminine Modesty and Women's Role in Supporting the Family

1. *The Talmudic Tradition*

The standards of modesty expected of women, their right to leave their homes freely, and their role in supporting the family, exerted a significant influence upon the image of Jewish women both in their own eyes and in those of the surrounding society. The Talmudic heritage concerning this issue is not unequivocal. While the sages spoke extensively in praise of modesty generally and of feminine modesty in particular, seeing a woman's remaining in her own home in a positive light, there are no clearcut prohibitions against the free movement of women. Rather, the sages' remarks concerning this subject usually bear the character of ethical exhortation. The story of Dinah, daughter of Jacob, who went out "to see the daughters of the land" and ended up being raped, served as a paradigm for numerous homilies in praise of modesty and critical of women who behave in immodest ways. "A breach beckons to a thief": If Dinah had not left her home to "see the daughters of the land," then Shechem, son of Hamor, would not have abducted her and assaulted her. Numerous homilies represent her as the guilty party, so much so that at the end of the eleventh century R. Toviah son of R. Eliezer wrote in his book *Leqah Tov* that it would have been better for Jacob had Dinah never been born.[1] The midrashic literature contains homilies related to this event denouncing women who go out in public bedecked in finery. The demand that a woman ornament herself only within her home, but not go out thus in public, is also common in ethical tracts written during the Middle Ages.

The basic etymological sense of a woman who is modest (*zenu'ah*) is of one who is to be found in her own home. The halakhah even allowed a husband to divorce his wife because she is immodest and "violates Jewish practice" without requiring him to pay her *ketubah* money: "And what is Jewish practice? That she goes out in public and her head is uncovered, and she spins in the marketplace and speaks with every person."[2] The sages of the Middle Ages and particularly during the modern period deliberated over the practical application of this halakhah.

Notwithstanding these and many similar statements in rabbinic literature in praise of feminine modesty and in condemnation of their "frivolity" or "lightness of mind," there were also sages that criticized husbands who were excessively strict with their wives and prevented them from going out, portraying this as an exceptional act.

In many of the Islamic countries in the Middle Ages, this was the accepted norm; what caused it was not the Talmudic tradition, but the reality of the surrounding Muslim society. Rashi saw fit to comment in his Talmud commentary that not only was the act of Papus ben Yehudah, who locked his wife in the house, exceptional, but that there was also a danger in following such a path: "'And when he left his house to go to the market place he locked the door behind her, so that she might not speak with any person.' And this is an improper trait, for through this hostility enters between them, and she will be unfaithful to him."[3] Not only is there nothing to be gained from shutting the woman in the house but, on the contrary, it upsets their relations and may lead to unfaithfulness. Trust and fairness in relations between the couple, rather than suspicion and excessive caution, are the best assurances of mutual loyalty. But we seek in vain for general support of this view. Many Jews in Islamic countries were influenced by the Muslims' strict attitude toward feminine modesty, who saw women leaving their homes and going about in public in a negative light, unless out of dire necessity.

2. Modesty in Muslim Society

The Muslims were very strict about feminine modesty and recognized the husband's right to restrict the woman's mobility. According to the Quran, Muhammed himself ordered his wives to remain at home and to be extremely careful about not speaking with strange men, lest the latter desire them. An interesting testimony of the extremes applied by medieval Muslims to feminine modesty is preserved in a *hadith* that relates of a husband who went on a journey and ordered his wife not to leave the house at all in his absence. The woman's parents lived in the first story of the same house. Her father took sick and she sent to Muhammed to ask whether it was permissible for her to go downstairs to visit him. Muhammed forbade her to do so, and commanded her to obey the orders of her husband. This order was repeated when the father was dying and the daughter wanted to visit him before he died. After the father's death, she sent a messenger to Muhammed a third time, this time to request permission to go to the funeral, and again the answer was negative. After the funeral, Muhammed sent her a message stating that, in reward for her obedience to her husband's orders, all her father's sins had been forgiven. Another *hadith* tells in the name of Muhammed's daughter, Fatima, that it is best that a woman not see or be seen by strange men at all.[4]

Yahya Ibn Amar, a Muslim sage who lived in Kairouan in the ninth century, instructed women not to take part in funerals, even of close relatives, nor to visit the cemetery, not even to visit the grave of her own husband. He also ruled that it was forbidden for a woman to wear shoes that draw the attention of men, either because of their beauty or the sound that they make, and that women who do not follow this rule are to be punished.[5]

Many other examples may be adduced to these. But all these traditions and rulings have one goal: to train women to be exceptionally careful about their modesty, to influence them as much as possible to remain in their homes, and to teach the community that woman's place is in the home. When they leave their home to go out in public, they need to cover their faces with a veil.

However, theory was one thing and practice another, and theory did not always correspond with reality. Legal rulings, ethical exhortations, and world views do not always testify to reality. Due to this difficulty, Boydena R. Wilson utilized another kind of source: the *Hizba,* the books of instruction used by the supervisor of public order to help maintain morality and modesty in Muslim cities during the classical period of Islam. These supervisors acted in the public realm on behalf of the Halifate or his representative, and had the right to inquire into the behavior and way of life of people.[6] It was their task to assure that the inhabitants of the cities—both Muslim and non-Muslim—would follow Muslim law. While most of the extant Hizba books are from North Africa and Spain, one may assume that they reflect the situation in other Muslim countries during this same period as well.

One of the striking findings that emerges from the Hizba literature is that not all of the women were meticulous about observing the stringent rules of modesty preached by the Islamic sages. Among them were even women who went to the meeting places of foreign merchants in the hopes of finding lovers and thereby earning their bread. The repeated exhortations that women refrain from visits to places frequented by foreign merchants indicates the commonness of this phenomenon and the concern that it elicited among the Muslim rulers.

According to Wilson, the conventional image derived from research concerning women in Muslim lands during the classic period, according to which they were enclosed within their homes, is simply not true. The *Hisba* books indicate that urban Muslim women frequently ignored the imprecations and efforts to keep them in their homes, silent and invisible.[7] But notwithstanding the importance of these testimonies concerning women who deviated from the general framework, they must be seen in their proper proportions, as relating to only a small group of women.

Further testimony as to the ignoring of the strict limitations upon women out of concern for their modesty is preserved in the phenomenon of Muslim women who received traditions from the sages and transmitted them to others. These include oral traditions (*hadith*) originating in Muhammed, which were transmitted from generation to generation by reliable men and women. As we shall see below in the discussion of women's education (chapter 7), Muslim women played an important role in this chain of tradition, and the names of many of them are preserved in the biographical dictionaries.

In any event, by all accounts, the insistence upon feminine modesty in Islam had a great impact upon the status of women, their place in society, and their role in the support of the family, even if there were exceptions.

3. Modesty in Jewish Society in Muslim Countries

The reality of Muslim society influenced the attitude toward female modesty in Jewish society in Muslim countries as well. The woman's right to come and go from her home as she wished was not recognized or accepted by all. At times, leaving one's home was perceived as an immodest act. Even when women did leave their homes, in some places they were required to cover their face with a veil, as was the custom of Muslim women, and to arrange for members of their family to accompany them so that they would not walk alone. Otherwise, there was a fear that they would be considered loose women, and this would damage their honor.

Maimonides explicitly states in his *Mishneh Torah* that a woman does not have freedom of movement:

It is shameful for a woman to be constantly going out, out of doors or in the streets. And a husband should prevent his wife from doing this, and not allow her to go out, except once a month or a few times a month, as is needed, as it is not comely to a woman but that she sit in the corner of her house.[8]

We search in vain for a source in Talmudic literature for his admonition that women should have permission to go out only once or twice a month. The attempts of several of Maimonides' commentaries ("armor bearers") to seek support for this in midrashic literature are not convincing. The remarks there in praise of female modesty and of women remaining at home are general and do not correspond to Maimonides' words, which have a specific practical application. It seems clear that what led him to this position was the influence of Muslim society. Such a view is supported by his remarks further on, in which he states that women in the land of Edom are not required to cover their faces in like manner.

Two sages, who describe the situation in Muslim countries during the second half of the twelfth century, indicate the extent to which restrictions upon women going out and the insistence upon covering their faces was accepted in Jewish society, and that Maimonides' words are not to be seen as purely theoretical. R. Shlomo Ibn Parhon (mid-twelfth century) writes:

It is the custom in the Land of Israel and Babylonia and Spain that all of the women cover their faces with a cloth. And when they wrap it around their faces they leave a hole opposite one eye at the edge of the cloth, with which to see, for it is forbidden to look at women... And only in the land of Edom [i.e., Christian countries] do women go out with uncovered faces.[9]

Similar things were written by R. Petahya of Regensburg, who visited Babylonia in the 1170s:

And no one sees any women there, and nobody visits his neighbor's home, lest he should see his neighbor's wife; [and if he were to come] they would immediately say to him: "Go away! Why have you come?"[10]

These comments by R. Shlomo and R. Petahya seem reliable. There is no logical interest that would cause them to invent such things out of whole cloth. Moreover, their descriptions are detailed and carry the mark of truth. This reality weighed upon those women who wished to work outside of their homes, although they could assist in the support of the family by labor that they performed within the home, such as spinning and weaving, and it seems quite probable, on the basis of the testimonies preserved in the sources, that they did so.

But the Genizah sources also indicate that some Jewish women went out of their homes, including some who went out to work. In his book, *A Mediterranean Society,* Goitein cites various examples of women who left their homes to work or for other needs. However, this was a departure from the accepted norm in Jewish society in Muslim countries.[11] When the husband opposed this and argued that it was not modest, the rabbis usually accepted his position. Explicit testimony to that effect is preserved in one of the questions addressed to Maimonides and in his response. The question tells of a husband who returned from a journey after an absence of three years and found his wife "teaching Bible to small children." He objected on the grounds that it deviated from the norm and harmed the family's honor: "Stay in your house like all the other people." Maimonides accepted this position and ruled that "a husband may prevent his wife from teaching a craft or reading."[12] Nor did the woman's claim that she and her children were on the verge of starvation because of the husband's difficulties in supporting the family change matters. The conclusion that follows from this is that, even if in practice women could go out to work outside of the home, this was perceived as a questionable activity that the husband could forbid if he so wished. We may reasonably assume that many women refrained from doing so in order to avoid damaging their family's honor.

A woman's appearance in court likewise constituted a problem, and generally speaking women refrained from appearing in court so as not to damage their honor. In the Talmud, the appearance of women in court is depicted as harming their modesty and dignity. But there were also exceptional cases, and during the Geonic period, by the end of the tenth century, some sages required women to come to court in certain cases.

There were women who were accustomed to "go out to bargain and buy and sell" even in Muslim countries. In the bourgeois or petit-bourgeois society to which many of the Jews in the Mediterranean society depicted in the Cairo Genizah belonged, it was difficult to isolate the woman. Nevertheless, appearance in court was perceived as an affront to the woman's dignity.[13]

Further testimony of the insistence upon modesty in Jewish society in Muslim countries follows from the fact that sages and poets refrained from mentioning the names of women in official letters or in halakhic literature. We do not find the names of women mentioned in the works of Babylonian Geonim or the sages from Muslim Spain, neither in their responsa, in folk literature, nor in poetry. We are speaking here of a period that extended over five hundred years, during which mention of a woman's first name was seen as an insult to her modesty. Even in eulogies recited over a woman after she died, they were careful about this matter. The greatest Jewish poet in Babylonia at the end of the twelfth and beginning of the thirteenth century, R. Eleazar ben Yaakov the Babylonian, wrote a heartfelt elegy upon the death of the only daughter of the Babylonian gaon R. Shmuel ben Eli, in which he describes her as a woman noted for rare virtues and rare wisdom—but he does not once mention her name. True, we do find the names of women in some Genizah documents, but these are in the context of private letters written by family members to one another, presumably on the assumption that they would not become known to the public. It was only the discovery of the Genizah that led to the publication of their names. And indeed, when strangers addressed someone in the Genizah society and wished to ask after his wife's health, he would only do so allusively and without mentioning her by name.[14]

Jewish sages in Muslim Spain continued this behavior, and it is only in the responsa literature of the rabbis in Christian Spain in the thirteenth century and thereafter that the names of women are mentioned, although still in a lesser degree than in the responsa literature of the Ashkenazic sages.

As against this, the sages of Germany and France often mention women's names in their halakhic works, in elegies, in chronicles of the pogroms, and in other works, without any concern of affronting their modesty. Women who contributed money to charitable projects, such as the building of a synagogue, often assured that their names would be commemorated in a prominent place. This was seen as adding to their honor rather than causing it damage. Bellette, sister of R. Yitzhak b. Menahem, who lived in Orléans in the mid-eleventh century, is described in a halakhic work as she who "guided the women of her city" in observing the customs of immersion in *miqveh*.

Rashi's disciples mention his daughters, Yocheved, Miriam, and Rachel, and his granddaughter, Hannah, by name. R. Eleazar of Worms mentioned his wife, Dulca, and their two daughters, Bellette and Hannah, in an emotional elegy upon their martyr's death at the end of the twelfth century.[15] Many similar examples could be adduced. Extant headstones for women in Ashkenaz from the eleventh to thirteenth centuries contain various terms of honor and admiration for women—and even more so in the thirteenth to fourteenth centuries—but the subject of modesty is only infrequently mentioned and does not occupy a central place.

Many other testimonies from halakhic literature and other works could be brought to indicate the great punctiliousness upon female modesty in Muslim countries, as opposed to the freedom they enjoyed in Christian Europe.[16] However, the sources mentioned are sufficient to indicate that the woman's freedom of movement and her role in supporting the family were quite limited. There was also a certain injury to her image: to wit, the extreme insistence upon female modesty in Jewish society in Muslim countries created an image of the woman as a person who was easily seduced and whose steps needed to be watched closely, a motif that was quite widespread also in the literature of Spanish Jewry. The husband needs to hide his wife from the gaze of an alien man, to limit her right to leave the house, and when she does go out she needs to cover her face, so that she won't be seen by other men. Moreover, it is reasonable to assume that this also damaged her self-image. We have already seen how, according to Rashi, excessive strictness regarding woman's "modesty" is liable to upset the relations of camaraderie in the home.

But one must not exaggerate regarding this matter of modesty. As mentioned, the Genizah sources indicate that women were active in the family, in society, and in the economy. In various stories brought by R. Nissim ben Yaakov in his book, *Ḥibbur Yafeh meha-Yeshu'ah* (Kairouan, eleventh century), women are portrayed as making efforts to support the family and working so as to help their husbands. In Spain, too, women played a role in supporting the family, a point to which we shall return below. Wilson's finding concerning the distinction between theory and practice regarding Muslim women in the city holds true regarding Jewish women as well. Another important testimony, to which proper attention has not been given in research literature, appears in one of the ordinances of Maimonides concerning women's immersion in the *miqveh* (ritual bath). This document bears witness, not only to women's freedom of movement, but also to their self-awareness.

4. The "Miqveh *Rebellion*" in Egypt

Many of the Jewish women in Egypt at the end of the twelfth century refused to perform the monthly ritual immersion in the *miqveh* or ritual bath. Instead, they followed the practice of the Karaite women and sufficed with pouring water over their bodies at home or in the public bath house. This "rebellion" seems to have derived from two factors: personal convenience and comfort—i.e., the greater cleanliness and availability of hot water in the Muslim bath houses *(hamam)*; and the considerable religio-ideological influence of Karaitism, which constituted a significant rival to Rabbinic Judaism during that period. This "rebellion" against the *miqveh* continued for several years. The stringent efforts taken by Maimonides and other Rabbinic leaders in Egypt in waging battle against this phenomenon indicates the social cohesion among the Jewish women, who appear as a united group:

We have therefore warned in the synagogues and study houses and taught them all of these matters . . . And after we publicized this matter in public *over the course of years,* we saw that the contamination remained as it was *and they did not return to the good except for one in a thousand.* And that this stumbling block involved the majority of the women, because they had taken hold of heresy [i.e., the Karaite path] and that immersion was difficult for them.[17]

The Jewish community in Egypt at that time numbered several tens of thousands. The refusal to immerse thus encompassed a very large number of Jewish women. Given that only "one in a thousand" resumed immersing—even if this figure involved a degree of rhetorical exaggeration that was not meant to be taken literally—notwithstanding the efforts of Maimonides and his colleagues, and the extensive period of time that the "rebellion" continued, it follows that this was a well-organized and cohesive rebellion of the women. The rabbis' lack of success in battling this phenomenon follows, not only from the repeated attempts to change it, but also from the reliance upon extreme edicts, including threatening the women that they would lose their right to *ketubah* money and forcing them to take an oath that they had immersed in *miqveh* before being allowed to receive their *ketubah*—all these are indicative of the women's self-confidence. They were prepared to battle for their position, and only the extreme steps taken by Maimonides and his colleagues led to the suppression of the "rebellion." The wording of the edict suggests not only the harshness of the conflict, but also the fears that a Rabbinic court might arise in the future that would be too lenient with the women due to their power and influence.

One may assume that there were leaders of the *miqveh* "rebellion"—for if not, it could not have maintained itself for a number of years nor encompassed so many women—but their names are not preserved. One may assume that the classical meeting places for the women were the synagogue, the *miqvehs* (before the "rebellion"), and possibly also the bath houses (*hamam*), which were universally popular in Muslim society.

A similar phenomenon—albeit not of the same intensity—occurred in Byzantium. R. Isaiah of Trani related that most Jewish women in his day (thirteenth century) were not particular about immersing in a kosher *miqveh*. His attempts to change this practice were only partly successful, and many women refused to listen to him.[18]

One of the interesting issues that emerges from this discussion is that of the reason for the great strictness in the issue of modesty. What is its source? Who is the "villain" in this story, the man or the woman? Is she light-minded and easily seduced, to the extent of needing to limit her freedom and describing her as one who is most fit to sit in the corner of her house? Or did these extra stringencies originate in the men's lustfulness and their inability to control themselves? Their "Evil Urge" became aroused whenever they saw a woman—even if the latter were strangers, and married—and therefore the women are required, ipso facto, to shut themselves up in their homes and to cover their faces when they go out in public. It is not they who are responsible for this, but the concupiscent men. These questions apply, of course, to both Jewish and Muslim society. The affront to the image of woman is far worse if they are understood as the cause for these strictures. The answer is not a simple one. Generally speaking, the authors, in their statements in praise of modesty, incorporated remarks directed against the weakness of both men and of women. In the Quran, Muhammed justified his demand of his wives that they be extremely careful in speaking with strange men on the grounds of man's weakness. It is the man within whom there dwell lustful thoughts, even if the subject of his conversation with women does not at all relate to sexual matters. R. Shmuel Hanaggid told women to close themselves up in their homes because of the weakness of the men ("men in the world go astray").[19]

Rabbinic midrashim place the blame for sexual promiscuity upon both sides; however, the woman is frequently depicted as the one bearing the primary responsibility: "a breach calls forth to the thief." While men's evil urge is the ultimate cause of the seduction of the woman, had the woman been insistent upon her modesty and closed the breach, she would not "call' to the "thief"— that is, to lust-filled men wishing to carry out their desires. R. Jonah of Gerona, in his *Iggeret ha-Teshuvah*, likewise indirectly places the blame on the women, who did not distance themselves sufficiently from the company of lustful men: "and she is punished for the sin of both of them, for she caused them to sin and did not behave modestly."

Some Jewish writers and poets in the Middle Ages portrayed women as hypocrites, who behave seemingly modestly, but in fact seduce the man and intend to arouse his lust. This motif also appears in Jewish folklore literature, just as it does in the folklore literature of other peoples in the Middle Ages and thereafter, and particularly in the *Fabliaux* literature that was widespread in Europe in the thirteenth century—as we have already noted in chapter 1 in the discussion of the woman's image. If only part of the guilt was imposed directly on the woman, this would suffice to damage her image.

5. The Situation in Jewish Society in Spain

The situation in Spain during the Muslim period and thereafter is of special interest. Even after the Christian conquest, the Reconquista, Jewish culture continued to be influenced by Muslim culture. The Jews in Spain were connected to the rich Arab culture in the depths of their souls. Did the impact of the Muslim attitude toward modesty continue to leave an impression even during the Christian period?

Medieval Spanish responsa literature refers to women who worked outside of their home, even though their number is small in comparison to the number of men engaged in trade mentioned in these sources. As responsa literature faithfully reflects the way of life and events occurring within Jewish society, one may conclude that Jewish women in Spain generally did not leave their homes to work, but that there were those who deviated from this rule. The same holds true for the area of Perpignan in Provence, which during the twelfth century was connected with the crown of Aragon.

A similar picture emerges from other sources of a different nature. Yom Tov Assis and Ramon Magdalena examined Hebrew financial ledgers preserved in the general archives of Navarra (Archivo General de Navarre), relating to the end of the thirteenth and primarily to the first half of the fourteenth century, in which are recorded loans that Jews made to others, and lists of the property of Jews. Two of the ledgers belonged to women, and include lists of loans and properties belonging to these two women. True, they appear as widows engaged in managing the extensive business dealings of their deceased husbands, but the very fact that they managed substantial financial estates indicates that this was an accepted phenomenon, and speaks of their own status. There were also women who loaned money at interest—in most cases, the woman continued her husband's business after she was widowed.

These same ledgers also refer to other women who engaged in trade, in handicrafts, and in money-lending. Two of the four large Jewish merchants who engaged in the footware trade were assisted by their wives. They engaged in manufacture, in repair, and in marketing shoes, and their customers were both Jews and Christians. Three women are mentioned in connection with trade involving various kinds of foodstuffs. The sources indicate the role of women in the manufacture and sale of furs, an important branch in which the Jews of Navarra had expertise. Three major tradeswomen are mentioned in these documents.[20] Nor is this phenomenon unique to Navarre; it was also widespread in the other Iberian kingdoms, Castille and Aragon. Notary documents from the community of Santa Coloma de Queralt, near Barcelona, are also indicative of women who engaged in trade and in lending at interest at the end of the thirteenth century.[21] While one is dealing there with a small community, the data are characteristic and significant for the discussion of the status of the woman. Nevertheless, in this community too the number of women active in the economy was clearly small in comparison to the number of men.

While most of the women mentioned in these documents were ones whose husbands had died and who continued their commercial activity, this does not detract from the fact that they served as significant property owners and conducted extensive commercial activity. One may assume that their weight in Jewish society grew alongside the growth in their economic power. True, in the case of some of those women who engaged in handicrafts (particularly spinning, weaving, and leather crafts), one may assume that their work was done inside their own homes and there is no indication that they left their homes to go to work, but one cannot say this is the case of those women who conducted varied and extensive commercial activity.

In the responsa literature as well, we find clear allusion to the role played by women in commerce, and the existence of wealthy and renowned women. Some of these women attained their position by virtue of the large dowry they brought into the marriage, and enjoyed a position of partnership in the property already in their husband's lifetime. Thus, the responsa of R. Yom Tov Ibn Ishbili (Ritba) mentions an extremely wealthy woman whose husband served as a courtier in the royal court by virtue of her great wealth ("for were it not for her money, he would not have been named assistant to the king").[22] Another woman owned money "over which her husband has no right."[23] It also follows from this work that there were women who appeared before the Rabbinic court, but "a modest woman whose way it is not to go out before important people" appoints a representative who argues on her behalf in court.[24] While most of these testimonies are from the fourteenth century and only a few from the thirteenth century, one may assume that they reflect the situation in the thirteenth century as well. There is no reason to be surprised at the important role played by widows in commerce, in loaning on interest, and in managing the estates left by their husbands, nor on the willingness of the sons to allow them to continue in managing the affairs of their fathers. The wives were active in these businesses during their husbands' lifetime, knew their commercial secrets, and in effect there was no substitute for them in terms of continuity of activity and their ability to collect money from debtors, especially non-Jews.

It is clear that the wealth and involvement in business of some women in Spain helped to enhance their public image and their status within the family. Hints of this are preserved in the responsa as well. Thus, for example, *Teshuvot ha-Rosh* (13. §11) tells of "a woman who conducted a business within her home and viewed to give charity or to hire a teacher" against her husband's will ("and the master of the house was opposed"). Rabbenu Asher ruled that there is no efficacy to her actions as they were done against her husband's wishes. However, the very fact that a woman decided to choose a teacher by herself, for herself or for her sons or daughters, and did not abandon her position even after her husband had expressed firm and explicit opposition, is a clear indication of the self-confidence that she acquired thanks to her role in supporting the family. The dispute was so severe that they were required to turn to the leading sage of the generation, Rabbenu Asher, to decide between them. The woman considered herself sovereign over the money she had earned by her own efforts, and therefore as having the right to give charity as she saw fit, even against her husband's wishes and above his protests.

The picture portrayed by these varied sources—halakhic and ethical literature and archival sources—is of women who assisted their husbands in supporting the family and who in some cases conducted extensive businesses by themselves, although in comparison to their counterparts in Ashkenaz their number was not great.

These wealthy women were much sought after and courted, and many men wanted to marry them. Testimony of this is preserved in the responsa literature. Some of the women considered themselves as heads of their families and as those who hold the initiative in their hand. Thus, for example, *Teshuvot ha-Rosh* (43. §14) tells of a person who "married an elderly rich woman . . . and afterwards she regretted it and turned her husband out of her house." The husband objected and sued her in Rabbinic court that she should live with him, "and she said, 'he is disgusting to me and I do not wish to live with him.'" The expulsion of the husband from the home even before their dispute was adjudicated in court, derived from her power and authority. And not for naught did the interlocutors note that one was speaking of a wealthy woman, a fact that was of importance in terms of the legal discussion itself.

Several times, responsa literature mentions the phenomenon of husbands who left all of their property to their wives rather than to their sons, an act that led to disputes between the widow and the other heirs after her husband's death. It is likely that only in a situation where the woman was responsible and involved in the business in an active way, or had received a large dowry and inheritance, would the husband leave her all his property and ignore his sons and daughters, as he knew that his property would remain in experienced and trustworthy hands.

It was customary in various communities in Spain for the woman to receive half of her husband's property after his death. This represented a change from the Talmudic halakhah, according to which the woman had far lesser rights in the money of the inheritance, a point to which we shall return in the next chapter, in our discussion of the economic status of the widow. This custom strengthens the feeling that relatively many women took a part in the management of the family business and its support, even if this was frequently done within the home. An additional factor underlying this custom was, evidently, the substantial dowry that many women brought with them at the time of their marriage, or wealth that they inherited thereafter. But one must not exaggerate on this point and see wealthy and influential women as characterizing Jewish society in general. As mentioned, both in the ledgers from the archives in Navarre and in the responsa literature from Christian Spain, they constitute a minority relative to the number of wealthy men engaged in commerce.

Nevertheless, this was a significant development in comparison to the reality of Jewish society in Muslim Spain. In the responsa and halakhic literature of the early first Spanish sages, we find no testimony to economic or social activity of wealthy women similar to that found in Jewish society in Christian Europe (including Spain). Even though an argument from silence is not conclusive, it seems very likely that their number was smaller, and one may assume that there were many women who assisted in their family's livelihood *from within the home,* engaging in such activities as weaving, spinning, leather work, and even petty commerce. It was difficult for Jews in Muslim Spain, as it was for their Muslim neighbors, to see women active in public as merchants and property owners.

6. Feminine Modesty and Women's Work in Christian Europe

In European Christian society during the medieval period, it was not considered immodest for women to go out to work, nor was there any objection to women taking part in economic life. Admittedly, some Jewish and Christian authors and thinkers portrayed them as light-headed and easily seduced, as we have already noted above in the discussion of the woman's image. However, this did not have any concrete impact on their right to leave their homes. Indeed, within the aristocratic classes, women enjoyed great authority and influence. A woman who had inherited a *feodum* enjoyed considerable power and authority. In practice, such women did not lose many of their powers even after marriage. Only in England did a woman lose her rights as heir to a *feodum* if she married, when they were transferred to her husband. In France and the low countries, by contrast, women exercised far-reaching governmental rights before they married, during their marriage, and after they were widowed. The same held true for southern France, in Catalonia, and in Tuscany. They even supervised the construction and maintenance of fortresses, textile plants and prisons, and held judicial rights. Most of the aristocratic women in the Middle Ages brought their husbands a dowry. As is known, during the Middle Ages noblemen were often absent from their homes for extensive periods, and during these periods their wives fulfilled most of their functions: from administering the rule over the *feodum,* through overseeing matters connected with the estate and supervising the peasants who worked its lands.[25] As we shall see below, there were clear parallels to this phenomenon in Jewish society in Germany and France, and the absence of Jewish merchants from their homes had a positive impact upon the woman's status.

Within the home, too, the noblewoman performed many functions. First and foremost, she supervised the servants and a good part of the household and the economic functioning of the estate. Women are frequently portrayed in the literature of the period as responsible for the economic matters of the family. In a book of guidance for women composed by Christine de Pisan (fourteenth and early fifteenth century), she offers the women suggestions how to conduct the household budget and advises them to acquaint themselves with property law as well.

The daughters of the nobility were educated to ride on horses, to participate in the hunt, to play chess, to sing, to dance, to read literature and poetry, to spin, and to weave. Women made pilgrimages to holy places and were spectators at chivalrous competitions. Some of them owned libraries, including sacred literature, philosophy, history, law, literature, and poetry. Some of them served as muses of artists and writers and as patrons of religious and cultural institutions. There seems to have been no difference between the education of men and women of the aristocracy until about the thirteenth century. According to Wemple and McNamara and other scholars, the position of women of the nobility began to decline during the twelfth and thirteenth centuries but, as we have shown above in our introduction, this view has recently been questioned by Theodore Evergates and others.

The rights of women were more restricted in the urban sphere, and they had no role in the rule or leadership of the city. They did not have the right to vote nor to be elected to the municipal councils, and therefore did not hold governmental positions, although some of them, if they were not spinsters or widows, did participate in municipal councils. On the other hand, they did play an important role in the municipal economy, be it in commerce or in manufacture and handicrafts. For this reason, they were even given a certain place in the guilds, that is, in the unions of craftsmen and small merchants. The daughters of the wealthy were much sought after and courted, both because of the large dowries they brought with them, and because of the help their fathers could give their husbands to enter into the commercial guilds.

Women played a significant role in crafts and in manufacture, there even being certain professions that were accepted as women's professions. The husband often taught his wife and daughters to take part in the work of the family enterprise. Many widows continued to engage in the work of their husbands and to conduct their businesses after their death, as was the case in Jewish society, including Christian Spain. At times, Christian widows in the city were allowed

Jewish couples (evidently husbands with their wives) dancing together at a wedding to the accompaniment of musical instruments. The women's heads are covered, while those of the men are uncovered. Italy, ca. 1470. MS. Rothschild 24, fol. 246b, from the collection of the Israel Museum, Jerusalem.

to join the guilds of the men, a privilege they were not allowed during their husband's lifetime. Separate guilds were likewise set up for women, which were particularly prominent in the making of woven goods, embroidery, jewelry, crystal vases, and book binding, but they also took part in many other professions, including medicine.

Women also played an important part in trade, primarily that in food stuffs, including in the markets and large fairs. Nevertheless, certain guilds did not accept women into their ranks through concern for their modesty, particularly because of the apprentices who stayed in the guild houses into maturity. Many women also served as servants, who constituted the lowest strata among the workers in the city. These included girls aged fifteen to twenty, and there was considerable fear of affront to their modesty; service was nevertheless one of the specifically female professions in medieval Europe.

Women also played an active part in the life of religion and society. They went to church, participated in religious processions, heard the exhortations of the monks in the streets of the city, and participated in various social ceremonies, and at times in popular games. There were also those who participated in parties and imbibed to the point of drunkenness. Nevertheless, some men— especially the wealthier ones—ordered their wives not to go out alone, but only in the company of a chaperone. Some preachers criticized those women who dressed overly elegantly, and in some places there were even ordinances against overly sumptuous dress.

The village women took part in all the labors of the field and farm, but the status of the village women is hardly relevant to the discussion of the status of the Jewish woman in the High Middle Ages. Jewish society was greatly influenced by the milieu of the Gentile city, but not that of the village. Most of the Jews in Europe during the period under discussion lived in cities, and only a small minority in villages. Hence I shall not discuss here the economic activity of village women.

7. The Situation in Ashkenazic Jewish Society

The attitude toward modesty in Ashkenazic Jewish society differed from that in the Muslim world. Beginning with the earliest responsa literature in Germany and France at the beginning of the eleventh century and through that of the twelfth and thirteenth centuries, women are shown as leaving their homes without any restriction or suspicion and as playing an important role in the support of the family. This picture emerges from other sources as well, both internal and external. The phenomenon is seen as natural and self-evident, eliciting neither surprise nor discussion among either the Rabbinic sages or the ordinary people. The reality of the surrounding Christian society, whose insistence upon female modesty was immeasurably lesser than that in Muslim society during the same period, certainly contributed to this. But internal factors within Jewish society, both social and economic, also played a role. Women took an important part in the support of the family, both in commerce and in loaning on interest. When husbands were away from home, the main burden of business fell on the wife, a situation that was quite common in early Ashkenaz due to the lengthy commercial trips of the husbands. Sources indicate women bargaining with both Jewish and Gentile men, suing them and being sued, appointing emissaries, travelling to the courts of feudal lords and negotiating with them. There is not the slightest hint in any of these sources that these things were seen as entailing any immodesty. Numerous examples of such activities are preserved in the responsa literature of the sages of Germany and France. We shall cite a characteristic example from the eleventh century from Germany, which relates to the First Crusade in the year 1096:

There was an important woman whose name was Minna . . . and they did not wish to kill her, for her name was known far and near, for all the great ones of her city and the princes of the land used her services.[26]

The "great ones of her city" and "princes of the land" refer to the feudal rulers. The term "important woman" *(ishah hashuvah)* also appears in other sources from this period. It does not refer to a woman who is great in Torah knowledge and good works, but one who enjoys great renown because of her economic and social connections with Gentiles. The description seems reliable, but even if it originated in the author's imagination, it is clear that he is drawing a picture that is familiar to him from his immediate environment. The women owned private property that they had received as gifts or as inheritance from their parents. Some of them engaged in business dealings with this property without even involving the husband. One of the women in Germany during the first half of the eleventh century justified making her own private partnership with Jewish merchants who journeyed to the Muslim countries, rather than with her husband, who also travelled overseas, due to the superior trade connections of the former.[27] We find here a wealthy married woman who has private property and feels free to do with it as she wishes without consulting her husband how to invest her money in order to make profit. She is even expert in the nature of trade over great distances and chooses her partners for business, while ignoring her husband who also engages in trade.

This situation left clear traces in the various branches of halakhic literature of the sages of Germany and northern France, particularly in the responsa. One of the most impressive testimonies is preserved in a discussion of the Talmudic law concerning the question of modesty. The Mishnah states that it is forbidden for a Jewish woman to be left alone with Gentile men due to the fear that they might assault her sexually: "because they are suspected of licentiousness." Thus, Maimonides rules that it is forbidden for a Jewish woman to be alone with a Gentile, even if his wife is with him, because "they are shameless" and he is likely to assault the Jewish woman even in the presence of his own wife.[28] On the other hand, the *Tosafot* question this same ruling, for "*it is impossible that a woman not be left alone with a non-Jew at some time . . .*" A number of suggestions are then offered to resolve the contradiction between this halakhah and the reality in Ashkenaz. Thus, it is explained that the prohibition only exists in a case where the woman was "conquered" by a Gentile ruler and he holds her by force against her will. In such a case there is ground to suspect that he may rape her; however, if she is alone with a Gentile under other circumstances the thing is permitted.[29] In this decision, the *Tosafot* preserved the "spirit of the halakhah," but it is clear that they did not interpret the words of the Talmud in their original sense. Particularly striking is the unequivocal statement that "*it is impossible*" for a Jewish woman to avoid being alone with a Gentile at some time or other. Why is such a thing impossible, if it is stated explicitly in the Talmud and the sages in the Muslim countries ruled thus?! It is clear that underlying this ruling is the above-mentioned economic situation of Jewish women in Ashkenaz, who played an extremely important role in commerce and money-lending. This formulation is a powerful one, and offers the strongest proof of the power of the phenomenon mentioned and the change that occurred in the sages' approach to the status of the woman and the question of her modesty in general. It is clearly impossible to separate this law from the above-described reality of society in Christian Europe, in which women went to work outside of their homes and their appearance in public was accepted by all.

This reality, in which women took a decisive role in business and in supporting the Jewish family, left its clear mark in the halakhah, as follows from the above-cited sources. Another interesting example is preserved in an incident that was elucidated by the outstanding sages of Germany at the end of the twelfth century, R. Simhah of Speyer and R. Eliezer ben Yoel Halevi. This involved a married woman who set out on a business trip with a strange man and stopped to rest in a forest together with two Jewish men, who proceeded to assault her sexually.[30]

The act performed by the woman, of setting forth on a journey through the forest with one strange man, clearly entailed the prohibition of *yihud* (being alone with strange men), which is totally opposed to halakhah. Hence, it is not surprising that there were some rabbis who wanted to forbid her to return to her husband—viewing this act as tantamount to consent to premeditated adultery. Despite that, the Rabyah testified that not only were such acts common in his day, but that the rabbis ignored them, to the extent that the act had became accepted and agreed by all, making the woman permitted to her husband. It is difficult to imagine such an incident being acceptable, except within the sort of economic reality described above. The power of this reality was so great, that it led in practice to the ignoring of laws that were accepted and well known to all, that were rooted in the Talmud. A new practice came into being, drawing upon the economic and social reality in Germany and France, while attempting to preserve the "spirit of the law."

A similar picture emerges from other sources. The sages explicitly testified that they decided not to protest, because they understood that the people would not listen to them. Economic reality was more powerful.

Two other important areas in which women were active were medicine and midwifery. As a rule, medieval women dealt extensively in healing, and even Jewish women took part in this activity and were integrated within the general reality in Europe, as has been shown recently by Elisheva Baumgarten. Midwifery was an explicitly female occupation; there were various remedies and techniques used by midwives during childbirth that were common to both Jewish and Christian midwives. Within Christian society, this profession was often passed down from mother to daughter, but there is no evidence that this was the case in Jewish society.[31]

During the Late Middle Ages, the rabbis in Germany attempted to find an explanation for the extensive ignoring of the laws of *yihud* with a Gentile, and some attempted to find a halakhic justification for this. One of the major German rabbis of the seventeenth century, R. Yair Bachrach, rejected this and stated explicitly that the source for the leniency lies in economic reality:

Because our main livelihood is from them [i.e., the Gentiles] and we need to negotiate with them, and because our women also engage in business negotiations, and we are much preoccupied with our livelihood and it is very difficult to make a livelihood . . . and the sages of past generations did not see fit to protest, because they realized that it is impossible to stand up this edict, and perhaps they protested but it did not help. And it may be that because of their desire to make money through business the women disobeyed their husband's orders concerning this.[32]

At the conclusion of his remarks, Bachrach attempted to place the blame upon the women who were not prepared to forego the considerable monetary profit, but it is difficult to assume that in practice the husbands were not also happy about their economic activity. The "craving of money" characterized not only the women, but also their husbands.

Particular importance is to be attached to the involvement of the women in the business of lending money at interest to Gentiles. William C. Jordan has shown that in northern France of the thirteenth-century, Jewish women loaned money to Gentile women for purposes of their business and their households. These were usually small loans, not intended for large transactions. Jewish women were the main source of these loans to Christian women, but these Jewish women loaned not only to non-Jewish women, but also to non -Jewish men.[33] The phenomenon also found expression in art. Paintings made by Christians in the Middle Ages show a Christian tradesman standing before a Jewish woman, giving her a pledge and borrowing money from her at interest.

Sefer Ḥasidim likewise portrays a milieu of Jewish women who loaned money at interest to Gentiles. R. Eleazar of Worms—one of the leaders of this pietist group—relates that his wife Dulca also engaged in loaning money to Gentiles. The ignoring by the Ashkenazic hasidim of the prohibition against being alone with Gentiles is deserving of special mention, as this group strongly emphasized the importance of modesty and the book contains exhortations to be especially careful regarding it. On the other hand, they generally preferred to ignore the dealings of women who loaned money to Gentiles, being aware of its great economic importance. At the basis of the approach of the sages of Ashkenaz and France to this entire issue lay a sense of deep respect for the women and their loyalty to the values of Judaism. We shall return to this point below, in chapter 11, in our discussion of the role of women in Jewish martyrdom (Kiddush Hashem).

This situation was not unique to Jewish women in Ashkenaz, but also characterized Jewish women in other countries of Europe, including England, Provence, Italy, and Sicily. Both married women and widows played an important role in the economic activity performed in their place, particularly in trade and in money-lending. In documents of notaries from Perpignan alone, Richard W. Emery found twenty-five women who engaged in loans, most of them widows, out of sixty-one loans by Jews that are documented in official documents.[34]

In Ashkenaz, we likewise find men who left all their property to their wives upon their death. The extent to which husbands and wives anticipated objections to the validity of such wills by the other heirs (primarily sons) may be seen by extant documents from that period, in which the husbands sought every legal means possible to leave all their property to their wives.

8. Changes in the Legal Status of Women

The changes in the economic status of women left their mark upon their legal status as well. One of the laws widely accepted by the early medieval sages in the wake of the Talmudic discussion is that one does not administer an oath to a woman even when she is required to swear by law, due to the fear that one will thereby cause affront to her dignity and shame her by standing before the court. Many of the medieval sages during the Geonic period and later deliberated concerning this question. A summary of the opinions of several of the Babylonian Geonim and the early Spanish sages appears in the book *Or Zaru'a*, alongside the change that occurred in the understanding of the legal status of the woman in Christian Europe. R. Yitzhak ben Moshe [of Vienna] first enumerates the opinions of the Babylonian Geonim and of R. Moses ben Hanokh of Spain, who stated that, generally speaking, one ought not to administer an oath to a woman. As against these views is brought that of Rabbenu Kalonymus of Italy (mid-tenth century), who was in close contact with the sages of Ashkenaz, and may even have spent some time there. He ruled that if another person is in partnership with the husband, one requires both the husband and his wife to swear that they did not take anything from the partnership.[35] Rabbenu Kalonymus's reasoning clearly indicates that he reached his conclusion in light of the widespread reality in his day in the communities of Christian Europe, in which the woman played an active part in business. Her concrete involvement in partnerships made by other people with her husband was what forced Rabbenu Kalonymus to require her to take an oath. Her exemption from oath was liable to undermine the economic arrangements of Jewish society in those days.

An additional change, likewise connected with the above economic reality, is the statement that the woman who engages in business negotiations is to be seen as her husband's representative, with all the obligations that implies. The Mishnah explicitly states that a woman is exempt from paying for any damages or bodily injury she might cause another person, because she has no property of her own, but they are all subjugated to her husband. Only after some time, should she be divorced, is she required to pay.[36] A case of this type was brought before Raban (R. Eliezer ben Nathan), one of the rabbis of Mainz in the first half of the twelfth century. He stated that the husband must pay the damages of his wife and to enter into judgment with those suing her in court, because of the important role of women in the economy and in the family property. In his responsum, Raban emphasized the varied activity of the wife in economic life in his day:

In these days, that the women are bailiffs and money changers and negotiate and loan and borrow and repay and receive payment and make and take deposits, it is to their benefit to require them to take an oath, for otherwise people will refrain from doing business with them."[37]

The important role played by the woman in supporting the family had a decisive impact upon the improvement of her status in a number of areas, as described throughout this book. As mentioned, no other factor exerted such a decisive influence upon the status of the woman during the period in question as did this one. It brought with it great equality, not only in privileges, but also in obligations.

Women's freedom of movement in Ashkenaz and their important role in supporting the family in the Middle Ages, which brought them into such close contact with the elite of Christian society, did not alter the basic attitude of the rabbis toward her modesty. They thought that Jewish women in Ashkenaz ought to do everything within their power to protect their modesty and privacy, even under difficult conditions, should they fall into captivity in the hands of Gentiles. This attitude left a clear mark on the legal status of captive and forcibly converted women, a subject to which we shall return in chapter 9, in our discussion of the role of women in Kiddush Hashem.

CHAPTER SIX

Woman as Wife and Mother and Her Economic Status

1. The Woman within Her Home

In the following discussion, we shall examine the inner world of the woman, her interrelationships within the family, and her economic status. Her economic status was connected to and greatly affected her relationships, and hence is also directly connected to the world of the woman. As the voices of Jewish women as such were recorded only rarely during the Middle Ages, it is difficult to describe in detail their feelings toward their husbands and children and their place within the family. While this difficulty exists regarding other subjects as well, it is particularly critical for our understanding of the emotional and mental world of the woman and her function as wife and mother.[1]

The tasks imposed upon Jewish women in Christian Europe, and to a certain extent also in Muslim Spain, in Egypt, and in North Africa, were particularly great during the period discussed here. Due to the menfolk's constant commercial journeys to distant places and their consequent absence from the home for extended periods, the women were forced to assume an active role in the family business—trading or money-lending—and were involved in their smallest details. They were thus an inseparable part of the petit-bourgeois Jewish society that emerged during this period. The yoke of child care and education also frequently fell upon them. In archival sources, in Rabbinic responsa, in the Codes literature, in ethical works, and in Christian sources, Jewish women are portrayed as partners in the conduct of business alongside their husbands—a point already noted in our discussion of the role of women in supporting the family (above, chapter 5). The question here is: In what way did this reality affect the woman's inner world and her status within the family, and was it sufficient to counteract the widespread stereotypes found in society, which had a basis in Talmudic tradition?

The Submissive Wife—Ideal or Reality?

The halakhic sources and those found in ethical and homiletic literature describe the woman as inferior to the man. Sages and ethical preachers implored the women to honor their husbands and treat him as the master and ruler of the home. If we were to describe the actual role of the woman within the family and her relation with her husband according to these words, the result would be a rather miserable picture. In Jewish literature from the Middle Ages and at the beginning of the modern period, writers typically describe the ideal woman as submissive and as performing her husband's will, as taking care not to dominate him, to treat him with royal honor, and to be a paragon of shyness and innocence. Dozens of such texts are preserved in the sources. But do these in fact reflect reality? This question is of the utmost importance, not only for determining the role of woman in the family and society, but also for understanding her inner world, both emotional and mental.

Many medieval Jewish sages spoke in praise of the "submissive" woman who honors her husband and does his bidding. Maimonides even enumerated this in his *Mishneh Torah* among the woman's obligations. After speaking of the husband's duty to honor his wife more than his own body and not to be moody or temperamental in the home, he adds: "And they also commanded the wife to greatly honor her husband, and that his awe be upon her, and that she conduct all of her acts according to his wish, and that he be in her eyes like a prince or a king."[2]

One of the Babylonian sages expressed this idea with great force. He called upon the wife to honor her husband, to treat him with devotion, to stand up when he enters the house, and even to accept his blows with humility and silence:

And wives are required to honor their husbands . . . and when the husband enters from the outside, the wife is required to stand up and is not permitted to sit until the husband sits. And she is not permitted to raise her voice to him, and even if he strikes her she should be silent, as such is the way of modest women.[3]

These things appear in a manuscript attributed, evidently erroneously, to Rav Yehudai Gaon, one of the greatest and most important of the Babylonian Geonim (eighth century).[4] But even if these words originated with another sage, they reflect a definite mood within certain circles of Jewish society, evidently under the influence of Islam. Even if the author did not use the term "king," in practice he saw the husband in this light. The call to the woman to stand up when the husband enters the house, and to receive with silence and understanding his screams and blows, does not appear in the classical halakhic sources, the Talmud or the Midrash.

R. Shmuel Hanaggid several times called upon the woman to refrain from "lifting up her head" before her husband, and to accept his superiority and his "dominion" in the family with understanding, chastising those husbands who allow their wives to behave as if they were the head of the family. The ideal, "innocent" wife, is one who listens silently without argument.

Even in *Sefer ha-Zohar*—which takes a partially egalitarian approach between man and woman—the male is depicted as the one who dominates the female and gives her power, and only when the men are "guilty" do the women rule over them. In several passages, it is stressed that the man is the decisive factor in family life, similar in status to a reigning ruler, "And neither the female nor her representative are allowed to do any thing without the permission of the husband. Likewise in receiving guests, it is not proper that the woman receive a guest without her husband's permission. The blessings that rest upon a woman are given to her through her husband, who receives extra blessing on her behalf."[5] The husband's obligation to rule over his home and the ideal of the submissive woman were universally accepted. At most, we find appeals to the husband not to dominate in an exaggerated way. For example: "If the wife behaves properly, it is incumbent upon the husband to honor her and to make her happy and not to subjugate her too much."[6] We have already taken extensive note of these theories in our above discussion of the woman's image in chapter 1.

How great is the gap between the ideal of the submissive wife and reality! Anyone reading the Genizah documents, the responsa literature of Maimonides and his contemporaries, that of the sages of Spain and Ashkenaz, and other sources, receives a completely different picture. The women struggle courageously for what seems right to them, and are as far from the submissive image allotted them by the men as is East from West.

Examples of this from every genre of literature are so numerous and so convincing that there is neither reason nor space to enumerate them all. I will only mention here three particularly powerful examples to which research literature has not yet devoted the necessary attention, relating to the rebellion of Jewish women in Egypt at the end of the twelfth century, and in Italy and Germany during the thirteenth century. In Egypt, this rebellion related to the refusal of Jewish women to immerse themselves in the *mikveh*, as discussed above in chapter 5. Only a person enjoying high self-image and a well-established social position could have withstood for so many years the harsh pressures of Maimonides.

A similar phenomenon developed in one of the Diasporas in Byzantium during the thirteenth century, although its impact was smaller. R. Isaiah of Trani, the leading Italian sage of the thirteenth century, recounted the limited success he had in persuading the women of "Romania," who were not particular about the laws of immersion and adamantly refused to accept his opinion. Some communities refused to listen to him: "And I was in other communities and everything that I asked, they refused to accept, and I could not prevent them. And those violating this prohibition became ever greater, and this sin became as if permitted to all those in all the communities of Romania."[7]

While it is not specifically stated here that it was the women who challenged him and refused to accept his rulings, it seems unlikely that they did not take an active part in this opposition, and it is no accident that in his sermon in the synagogue he took care that women also be present.

Even more interesting was the "rebellion" in the Ashkenazic communities during the thirteenth century, which continued thereafter as well. A large number of women "rebelled" against their husbands, refused to have marital relations with them, and asked to be divorced. The high rate of divorce "astonished" the sages, first and foremost R. Meir of Rothenburg (Maharam), the leading Ashkenazic authority of the age, who attempted to halt this phenomenon through unconventional means and while waging "war" against the power of the women. The terms used by the rabbis of the time to describe the women ("arrogant," "loose," etc.) also indicate their power and the profound gap between reality and the image of the submissive wife that was set aside for them. This subject will be discussed in detail below, in chapter 11, where we shall also present the social and environmental background that fostered this development.

Between the lines, echoes the voice of powerful women, very different from the ideal of the submissive and shy figure depicted by thinkers during the Middle Ages and the early modern period. These were moralistic exhortations and wishes. The reality was usually very different.

Between Husband and Wife

The sources from the Cairo Genizah provide an instructive example of the difference between theory and practice. Many of the women mentioned in these sources and in Maimonides' responsa insisted upon their rights and were at times the dominant force in their homes. In *Megillat Ahima'az*—a family chronicle that reflects the *mentalité* of Jewish society in southern Italy during the mid-eleventh century—the woman is portrayed as being able to postpone her daughter's planned marriage against her husband's will, and as being the one to investigate prospective candidates for her daughter's hand. The author even places within the husband's mouth a sharp complaint against his wife because she had forced him to delay their daughter's wedding for so long. The same scroll relates that, while the men were arguing among themselves, the woman left their work in the kitchen and went aside and beat them.[8] While one is speaking here of a literary creation in which imagination and reality are intermingled, the image of the woman is similar to that found in many other sources and that which the author saw in his environment. An imaginary world is constructed according to the concepts familiar to the author and common in his environment. In dozens of responsa from Muslim and Christian Spain, women are shown as standing up firmly against their husbands and as not being prepared to renege on their rights. There were those who objected to the husband's marriage with a second wife even though the halakha permitted this and the phenomenon was accepted in their time and place, presenting the husband with the choice between themselves and the second wife. Many other women struggled for their economic rights. These sources in the responsa literature were most often addressed to the rabbis in the wake of some family dispute, and these naturally portray disputes between the partners; however, in many of them one also finds depicted relations of love and camaraderie between husband and wife. One should note that the "positive" sources and "positive" reality were generally speaking not documented or preserved at all. By its nature, responsa literature generally dealt with the negative side of reality, preserving disputes and disagreements. An impressive testimony of the woman's power within the family is preserved in one of the responsa dealing with laws of inheritance. According to halakhah, the sons inherit the property of their deceased father, while the mother/widow receives housing and a living stipend so long as she remains a widow. In order to bypass this practice, many husbands wrote wills stipulating that all or most of their property would be given to their wives as a present and that they could do with it as they see fit. This was a widespread phenomenon, impressive in its power, which we have already discussed in extenso in the preceding chapter.

Even in those wills leaving sums of money to the *heqdesh* (communal funds for sacred or charitable purposes), the husbands often preferred to designate their wives as responsible for the use to be made of the money they contributed, rather than relying upon the officials appointed by the communities. The equality of the two partners in the initial building up the property and wealth of the young couple led, by the nature of things, to greater equality in its division in the event of the husband's death. It seems quite likely that, in addition to the love felt for his wife and the consideration of the wealth that she had brought from her parent's home, there was also great respect for her talents and her ability to manage the property in an effective manner so that it would continue to bear profits. Husbands also relied upon the wife's willingness to care for the children. In several cases, the sons saw this as an affront to their prerogatives and asked assistance from the rabbis, relying upon traditional Jewish law. The rabbis even worried that those women who were wealthy and influential in their homes would feel that they had complete control over the property and would take it for themselves after their husbands' death.

It would seem that some of the rabbis' exhortations in praise of the superiority of the male and his dominance within the family were in reaction to the concrete power of the woman. Thus, for example, R. Shmuel Hanaggid importuned a husband not to let his wife rule over him. He did not even find it necessary to explain why such a situation was improper, on the assumption that everyone understood it.

The important role of women in conducting the everyday matters of the household and in helping the husband, not only in economic matters but also in other areas, follows both from the sources of the Cairo Genizah and from those sources relating to the Jewish family in Christian Europe. R. Eleazar of Worms enumerated the activities of his wife Dulca on behalf of the family and on behalf of the yeshiva students, which were numerous and varied: "She made books with her effort . . . she sewed some forty Torah scrolls . . . With her own hands she sewed clothes for the students . . . she bought milk for the students and hired tutors through her own efforts," and other similar activities on behalf of her household and her husband's yeshiva.[9]

An impressive testimony to the strong position enjoyed by the woman in family and society due to her important role in supporting the family is preserved in the text of Grace After Meals in a Siddur (prayer book) that has not yet been published. This version contains the blessing of the householder recited by the guest, taken from the Talmud, which is primarily a blessing for economic success. The mistress of the house, who worked hard to prepare the meal, is not mentioned in the Talmudic version. We may assume that the main reason for this was that she (and her property) were conceived as being subjugated to her husband, the master of the house, and that she was automatically included within his blessing. In MS. Bodleian 1103 (fol. 8b), written in the fourteenth century, which among other things preserves customs and instruction from the school of the medieval German Pietists (*Hasidei Ashkenaz*), we find a variation of the above-mentioned blessing that includes a blessing for the woman: "May it be the will of our Father in Heaven that the master of this house never be ashamed and the mistress of this house never be embarrassed . . ." In the Grace for a Wedding Feast (ibid. 20a), the formula reads: "May it be the will of our Father in Heaven, that this bridegroom never be ashamed and this bride never be embarrassed . . . *and that they be very successful with all their property.*" This addition presumably originated in the economic transformation: the role of the woman in supporting the family, the generous dowry that she brought with her at the time of marriage, her portion in the estate of her parents, and her independent property rights, as we shall discuss below at the end of this chapter.

Only rarely do we find detailed descriptions in the responsa literature of disputes between husband and wife of a specifically sexual nature—that is, sexual demands on the part of the husband that the wife was unwilling to fulfill or vice versa. Generally speaking, such disputes were alluded to in general terms such as mentions of "rebelliousness" of the wife. The small number of disputes of such a type is surprising. It is difficult to imagine that this factor was not present in those days, just as it is a perennial problem between marital partners in all places and at all times. One could argue that the Talmudic statement that gave the husband greater rights in this area completely reduced the opposition of the women to their demands. But the halakhah also recognizes the legitimacy of the sexual needs of the wife within the framework of the family. Such recognition appears in the Mishnah, in the Talmud, and among the medieval rabbinic sages. It even established a certain order in terms of the frequency of sexual relations between the couple in accordance with the husband's occupation.[10] The sages also imposed certain limitations upon the husband regarding relations with his wife: He was not allowed to have relations with her against her will, nor when he was drunk, nor when depressed or moody, nor if he felt hatred toward his wife, nor if he had decided that he wished to divorce her. It was likewise forbidden for him to have relations with his wife while fantasizing about another woman. The statement by the rabbis in the Talmud that "a man must love his wife like his own body and honor her more than his body," is repeated numerous times in the words of the medieval sages.[11]

R. Abraham ben David (Rabad of Posquières), the greatest Provençal sage of the twelfth century, devoted an entire work to this topic, which he derived from the statements of the sages in the Talmud and midrashim. He called upon the husband to "appease" his wife before performing sexual relations, to take account of her wishes, to refrain from doing things that she did not like, and from thoughts about another woman. One who has relations with his wife against her will harms the offspring to be born. If his wife is hateful to him, relations with her are considered "like harlotry and not marital relations." The same holds true when the wife tells her husband that she does not want him or if there is a quarrel between them, "and he nevertheless has relations with her, she is to him like a harlot." "And if she gives birth and he had thought about another woman, or is she was forced at the time of relations . . . he harms the fetus and harms himself, for he is called a rebel and a transgressor."[12]

The woman's rights in this area are even more strongly emphasized in *Sefer ha-Zohar,* with the value of love in married life being accentuated. Tishby wrote of this:

But in marital life per se, particularly regarding the actual time of coition, the *Zohar* gives preference to the woman and requires greater consideration of her wishes and rights. . . . The man must approach the place the woman has prepared for them to lie together, and even if his bed is comfortable and nicer than that, he must forego it. Even if he has a bed of gold . . . and she has prepared her bed with stones, on the ground, and with a covering of straw, he must abandon his own and lie down there so as to please her . . . Before coition the man must please his wife with pleasant words, to draw her to him with affection and to awaken her desire and arouse her love . . . But if he cannot behave thus, he should not lie with her. . . The author of the *Zohar* repeatedly emphasizes the importance of feelings of love in sexual life.[13]

The birth of a son and daughter as the result of sexual relations that were performed in unity and joy give a person wholeness, and God's name is called upon him. The need for sanctification at the time of coition is incumbent upon both partners.

It would seem that the absence of discussion of sexually related disputes in the responsa literature does not derive from the non-existence of the phenomenon.

Disagreements of this type were most often not addressed to the major responsa authors, who were the leading rabbis of the generation, but were resolved within the family circle or in front of local judges. Thus, only a relatively small number of such cases are preserved in the responsa literature. As against that, "major" disputes such as those deriving from travels of the husband, violence in the family, impotence, and the like are mentioned more frequently. In MS. Bodleian 692, we find a query concerning the rape of a wife by her husband who was ill with leprosy and forced his wife to remain with him, even having children with her by force: "and his wife refuses to be with him, and he forces her to remain with him, and she became pregnant from him. And since he is a violent person, she fears for her life, yet she needs to be with him."[14]

The exhortations of the rabbis concerning the need to restrain and to limit sexual lust even within the family cannot by themselves be taken to indicate the reality. Such was the desired ideal, but it would seem that there was nevertheless a great distance between it and reality. The harsh words of R. Zalman of Bingen concerning men and women who sought lovers even before they had completed the process of divorce sheds a certain light upon this interesting question in relation to the situation in Ashkenaz in the fourteenth and fifteenth centuries. He is speaking words of moralizing, which often involve exaggeration, but there is nevertheless a certain element of truth in his words, as follows from the large number of divorces. The relatively numerous accounts of concubines and of prostitution in Spain and other centers, to be discussed below, also support this.

Several sources concerning family crises in wake of pogroms, preserved by chance, indicate the relations of closeness, love, cooperation, and friendship between marriage partners. In his emotional elegy upon the murder of his wife, R. Eleazar of Worms describes her not only as a modest, energetic, understanding, God-fearing, and kindly woman, but also alludes to the feelings of love and understanding that existed between them, noting that she never angered him.

Even though one is speaking here of an elegy, both the introduction and every line in the poem indicate his intense feelings, and it is difficult to see what he wrote as mere hyperbole. Similar testimony from tenth-century Spain is preserved in the poetic epistles evidently exchanged between Dunash ben Labrat and his wife when he was forced to leave his home because of a dispute with Hasdai Ibn Shaprut. The wife longingly describes the background of the separation while holding their only son in her arms and exchanging gifts with her husband as a memento. Dunash's response, in which he expresses his astonishment at her fear lest he forget her, allude to the feelings of closeness between them, even though his words are not as emotionally expressive as those of his wife.[15]

R. Yitzhak ben Yehudah, Rashi's teacher and head of the yeshiva at Mainz during the second half of the eleventh century, commanded his son, R. Yehudah, to treat his mother, Rabbenu Yitzhak's wife, with special respect at the time of her funeral, and to walk barefoot to the cemetery even before the funeral, even though according to Jewish law the obligation to walk barefoot only applies after the burial, upon returning from the cemetery.[16] It is likewise related that the respect shown to his wife by Maharil, the leading Ashkenazic sage at the end of the fourteenth and beginning of the fifteenth century, even extended to his manner of speaking with her, habitually addressing her in the more formal third person.[17]

It follows from these things, that others were also in the habit of honoring their wives in their manner of address. In this respect, Jews behaved in the manner accepted in Gentile society, in the relations of knights to their ladies. Several of the great Tosaphists behaved in like manner. An interesting illustration of this is preserved in the words of R. Yitzhak ben Shmuel (the Ri), the greatest Tosaphist of the last quarter of the twelfth century, who told how the sages relied upon the testimony of women from the family of Rashi in certain cases of doubt regarding halakhic rulings. The style of his words likewise indicates the great veneration and respect that he showed toward them. He concludes his words with the statement that "we rely upon our logic and upon the testimony of the daughters of the leading lights of the generation."[18] These women also played an important role in family ceremonies (see below, chapter 8).

The Woman as Mother

The woman assumed a decisive role in the raising and educating of the children. Such is the picture that emerges both from the Cairo Genizah sources and from those dealing with Jewish women in Christian Europe. This is true, not only of the periods during which the husband was absent from the home, when the main burden of child care fell upon the wife, but even when he was at home. The grandmother also assisted extensively in the raising of her grandchildren. Marriage and childbirth at a relatively young age were also contributory factors to this situation. The young mother was lacking in life experience and needed the advice and guidance of her mother or mother-in-law.

The frequently found conflict between divorced partners concerning custody rights over their children often led to harsh disputes. The halakhah recognized the mother's right to custody so long as the children were small, and of her daughters after that. In Maimonides' words: "If the divorced woman wishes her son to be with her, he is not separated from her until he reaches the age of six full years, and the father is compelled to support him while he is with his mother. After the age of six years the father may say: If he is with me I shall support him, but if he is with his mother I will not support him. But the daughter always remains with her mother, even after six years."[19] Rashba (R. Solomon Ibn Adret) stated that even relatives of the deceased father have the right to take the son under their custody, on the assumption that the education they would give him would be preferable to that he might receive from his mother.[20] Likewise, R. Joseph Ibn

Migash, in the first half of the eleventh century, noted the psychological connection between mother and daughter and the guidance the mother could give her daughter to prepare her for everyday life, as justification for the right of the divorced mother to receive custody of the daughter.[21]

Such a dispute concerning the custody of children arose in full force when one of the parents, especially the mother, decided to remarry. The father feared that his daughters might move over to another family and would no longer be under his supervision. Evidence of harsh disputes against such background have been preserved in the sources, and they already occupied an important place in the Geonic literature. The parents' words bear testimony to the stormy emotions experienced by the former partners and by the relatives generally.

At times, the grandparents from both sides also participated in these disputes, demanding custody of their grandchildren after the death of their son or daughter. Such disputes frequently broke out when the surviving partner wished to leave the place where he or she had lived and go to live near his or her parents. The grandparents feared being cut off from their small grandchildren. Rav Sherira Gaon (tenth century) established the following rule:

> The law is with the father . . . even if the mother [of the child] were still alive and she says, I will raise him, once he has reached the age of six he is given to his father to raise . . . and all the more so after the death of the mother, that he is not given to his maternal grandmother, but rather to his father who will teach him Torah and teach him a profession . . . For what do women know of the study of Torah or of teaching a trade that they can teach their grandsons?[22]

Rabbenu Asher ben Yehiel (Rosh) invoked a similar argument—namely, that the daughter is influenced more by her mother than by her father, and it is therefore preferable that she should grow up with her. On the other hand, the obligation to teach his son Torah is incumbent upon the father, hence it is preferable that he should be educated with him. Against that, Rashba states that: "One must always behave regarding these things according to what the court sees." That is, these are not unequivocal, hard and fast rules, but the court must examine the particulars of each case on its own merits and arrive at a decision on the basis of the welfare of the orphans.

Even though Jewish law imposed the obligation of teaching sons Torah upon the father and not upon the mother, the women also played an important part in their children's education. As mentioned, in Ashkenaz and France many children studied in their homes, and it is clear that the women also served as overseers of this study.

The Genizah documents tell of women who came into harsh conflict with their husbands over the issue of their children's education, feeling that the father did not devote sufficient attention to this education and turning to the Jewish authorities for assistance. One woman requested in her will that her daughter's education be seen to following her death. Another Genizah source tells of a woman who "raised her children and taught them Torah," and even of a woman who was separated from her husband and moved her place of residence in order to provide her small son with better education.

Other testimonies emerge from those sources indicating that many women remained widows, refusing to remarry out of fear that this might harm their children. According to R. Judah son of the Rosh (Spain, fourteenth century), the majority of women did so: "For most of the widows who have sons or daughters do not marry and a stranger shall not pass among them."[23] The fear of harm coming to their children sometimes led widowers to marry a relative of their deceased wife: "Reuben married a certain woman and she bore him children and died while the children were still small, and if he were to marry a woman who is not related to his children she will not raise them well; therefore he wished to marry Leah, the sister of Shimon, who was a relative of the children."[24] In the chronicle about the acts of martyrdom of 1096, the women are depicted as exerting the greatest influence on their sons and daughters and husbands, a point to which we shall return in chapter 9.

During the Late Middle Ages in Italy, women are portrayed as fulfilling a very important function in teaching generally, and in the education of children in particular. Many testimonies have been preserved of this, but as the period in question is beyond the scope of the present discussion, we shall not deal with it here. It is nevertheless worth commenting on the great influence exerted by the Renaissance culture on the spiritual and social world of the women and on their way of life.

2. Prostitution and Concubinage

In Christian Europe

The role of the woman in the family and in Jewish society was greatly influenced by the institution of concubinage, which was particularly widespread in the circles of the Jewish courtiers in Spain. Sexual relations outside of marriage and other deviations from the religious and social norms were common in the Middle Ages, in both Christian Europe and in the Muslim countries. The gap between the ethical and religious ideals and reality was great.[25] The attitude toward prostitution in medieval Christian society was influenced by the position of the Church fathers, particularly by that of Augustine (354–430), one of the greatest of the Church fathers. Augustine stated that the practice of prostitution is shameful because it caters to carnal lusts (*luxuria*); however, from a social viewpoint it also fulfills a positive function. He compared it to a sewerage canal that removes the filthy water from the palace, without which the palace would become filthy. Prostitutes circumscribe the occurrence of adultery and licentiousness within society. Without it, married men, addicted to carnal lusts, would try to seduce virgins and other men's wives.[26]

In wake of Augustine's statement and those of other thinkers, medieval Christian society permitted prostitution to exist legally even though they saw it as a contemptible profession. During the twelfth and thirteenth century, established brothels existed in most of the countries of Christian Europe: Italy, France, Germany, England, and Spain. Social and economic factors greatly increased the demand for prostitutes. Many men did not marry at all, while others did so at a relatively advanced age. Students in the university towns and churchmen were among the regular customers of prostitutes, while merchants away from home on commercial journeys, especially those who traveled great distances, made use of their services. The prostitutes knew the places where the merchants stayed, and many of them went there to offer their services.

The authorities appointed supervisors over the brothels, who also collected taxes from them. Generally speaking, the brothels were officially restricted to certain streets in the lower sections of the city, so as to separate them from the homes of "respectable" citizens but in practice many prostitutes also operated elsewhere, especially in those places where foreign merchants were concentrated.

Some women turned to prostitution due to economic pressure, while others did so for personal reasons. In general, the moral behavior in Christian Europe in those days was rather low. The sources preserve record of numerous cases of rape, adultery, concubinage, and homosexual relations. The sublime words about ethical values found in the writings of various churchmen and other thinkers were on the order of theory alone. The same holds true for various laws intended to implement these views, whose distance from reality was very great. Nor may we forget that literature primarily reflects the way of life of elite circles within society; regarding the more marginal groups we have very little information.

This situation directly influenced the Jews, and not only because of the direct relationship between the two societies in all areas of life. From one of the questions addressed to R. Judah Mintz, it follows that brothels were established in the Jewish neighborhoods as well, at the order of the authorities, so as to protect married women from harm. He even tells that attempts to abolish them were unsuccessful because "it seems to the Gentiles that it is a good thing to place prostitutes in the marketplaces and town squares and in all the corners of their houses, so as to save them from a graver sin, that is, from relations with married women."[27] Rabbenu Mintz continues there that, due to this unfortunate situation, he was forced to allow a nursing mother to marry because the Christians insistently demanded that she be given over to prostitution, and had she not married she would have been forced to obey them.

R. Isaac Arama, one of the Spanish sages of the second half of the fifteenth century, cited in his book *Aqedat Yizhaq* a harsh debate that he had with the leaders of the community in Spain, who not only allowed the establishment of brothels in the Jewish community, but even subsidized this measure financially.[28]

It is difficult to determine the scope of prostitution and concubinage and other deviations from the accepted norms of sexual behavior within Jewish society. The rabbis attempted to avoid public discussion of this subject in its particulars for reasons of modesty. The accepted assumption was that one was dealing with material that was better kept silent, and that as far as possible it ought to be discussed with discretion within the family circle or verbally before local rabbis. Even when they were dealing with a complex case and there was need to take counsel with a well-known and recognized scholar, they attempted not to spell out the details of the sexual liaison but to suffice with hints and general remarks.

Prostitution and deviations from the religious and ethical norms in this area within medieval Jewish society may be divided into three groups: sexual relations with Gentile servant girls or with Jewish women who were defined as "concubines"; sexual relations between two unmarried people; and adultery and infidelity of one of the marriage partners. We shall not go into a detailed discussion of these subjects, but limit our remarks to those points related to the status of women.

In Spain

The sexual behavior of Jews in Spain has been discussed in detail by Yom-Tov Assis.[29] His research is based upon a variety of sources, both internal and external: responsa, homiletic literature, halakhah, poetry, and archival sources. His findings indicate a permissive way of life accepted primarily among the elite circles, first and foremost the court Jews whose influence upon the rest of society was great.

Many Jews had sexual relations with Christian and Muslim women, notwithstanding the legislation that prohibited sexual contact between members of different religions. The official punishment for such contact was death; however, most Jews placed on trial for this offense were acquitted, often thanks to a timely bribe to the royal coffers. Even those found guilty were usually subjected to heavy monetary fines rather than being executed as required by the law. Assis did not deal with the question that is the subject of our own present study, but not of his: What was the impact of this situation upon Jewish family life and upon the status and world of Jewish women? How did the women of those elite circles, whose husbands allowed themselves to take maidservants and concubines and to have sexual relations outside of the family framework, feel? The voice of the women is not heard, and we are thus unable to give a full answer to this question. Despite their importance, the few hints found in responsa literature do not allow us to give a clear answer to this question. It may be that the ubiquity of the phenomenon in Muslim and Christian society in Spain "eased" the feelings of disappointment and frustration on the part of the Jewish woman. Moreover, in Spain the man was allowed to take a second wife. One nevertheless can imagine the misery of these women, whose servants and concubines began to behave arrogantly towards them, the supposed mistress of the house. As mentioned, it follows from the Genizah sources and from Maimonides' responsa that in Egypt the women had the right to choose the maidservants for their household and that the husband could not hold a maidservant who was hated by his wife. This fact indicates the extent to which relations with maidservants served as a burden upon family life.

Another important finding brought by Assis is the large number of deviations from the religious norm in other areas as well, such as relations with unmarried Jewish women, adultery, unfaithfulness of women toward their husbands, the existence of Jewish prostitutes, and homosexual relations. Even though the sources do not allow us to determine the exact scope of these phenomena, they suffice to indicate that they were not seen as extraordinary or unusual. I will not enter here into a discussion of these sources, but only to the question of Jewish prostitutes, which relates directly to the subject of our research. The other sources, despite their importance, go beyond the issue of the status of women in Jewish society. Nevertheless, it is worth emphasizing that Assis's findings hold true for both Muslim and Christian Spain.

The responsa literature of the Spanish sages contains extensive discussion of these questions, particularly that of concubinage and adultery, and less so regarding premarital relations. The *Digest of Responsa Literature of the Medieval Spanish Sages,* published by the Institute of Jewish Law at the Hebrew University of Jerusalem, contains more than one hundred cases involving deviations from the religious and social norms in this area, including all three groups mentioned (concubinage, adultery, premarital relations). However, the men and women involved quite frequently denied the accusations leveled against them, claiming that these were false accusations made by interested parties or by estranged spouses. As a rule, we have no way of ascertaining the truth, and in any event there is some doubt whether the statistical data reflect reality. One of the most important phenomena in this area, which greatly impacted upon the status of Jewish married women, is the place of female servants in family life, which we shall discuss next.

Maidservants and Concubines in the Muslim Countries

Slavery was commonly accepted in both Christian Europe and in Muslim society. Maidservants were necessary for the running of the household, but for centuries they presented a serious problem to the Jewish family. Many of the Jews in the Middle Ages belonged to the elite classes and kept non-Jewish maidservants in their homes. At times, particularly in the Muslim countries and in Christian Spain, these servants also served as mistresses. The extensive references in responsa literature to the question of Gentile maidservants who served as mistresses to their masters—both married and single—indicate the wide extent of the phenomenon. The use of the servant as mistress was well-known and accepted in Islam and, notwithstanding the fact that Jewish law forbade the master having sexual relations with his servant girl, the custom greatly influenced all levels of Jewish society. The power of reality was greater than that of the Law. Moreover, the master could free his servant and then marry her as a second wife. Genizah sources preserve numerous testimonies to the scope of this phenomenon, which attained dimensions unimagined in the time of the Mishnah or the Talmud. The responsa literature—including the responsa of the Geonim and those of Maimonides—likewise contains accounts of maidservants who were freed after becoming pregnant from their masters, of their marriage, and their entering into Jewish society. In one of the questions addressed to R. Natronai Gaon in the mid-ninth century, it explicitly states:

... there were many people from various places who purchased beautiful servant girls. And they say that they are buying them as servants, but we suspect that they are buying them for something else ... and there are even those who say of their maidservant, "I have already freed her and she is with me as a kind of concubine."[30]

The best testimony of the power of this phenomenon is the explicit change in the halakhah made by Maimonides regarding the permissibility of marrying a Gentile maidservant-concubine as a wife. The Mishnah states that a man suspected of having had sexual relations with a non-Jewish servant is forbidden to marry her even after she was freed; if, however, he nevertheless married her, the court does not require him to divorce her. Maimonides was asked about "a youth who bought a beautiful [Christian] maidservant," and who thereafter freed her and lived with her. He rules that the master is allowed to marry her immediately, and explicitly comments that he ruled thus in opposition to the written halakhah, due to the situation in his place.[31]

Maimonides remarks there that he had already ruled a number of times that a man may marry his freed maidservant, from which it follows that one is not speaking here of an isolated case. The reason given indicates that he assumed that, were he to prohibit this practice as dictated by Mishnaic law, they would in any event not obey him. According to Maimonides, it is better to attempt to resolve the problem in a decent manner, even if it departs somewhat from the parameters of the halakhic norms. It is preferable that they commit one sin and marry their concubines rather than to constantly have forbidden relations with them, any children who might be born to them being a problem to both the parents and to Jewish society.

And indeed, the children born to maidservants did constitute a burden to Jewish society. Some masters acknowledged their paternity of these children, raised them, and concerned themselves with their education. Others were ashamed of them and attempted to conceal their connection with the children of the maidservants. The extent to which the phenomenon of concubinage burdened the Jewish family may be seen from the fact that a general ordinance was introduced in Egypt, added to the ketubah, stipulating that the wife was allowed to choose the maidservant according to her judgment, and not that of her husband. Presumably, she would refrain from choosing an attractive servant to avoid causing temptation to her husband. Only an unfortunate reality that weighed greatly upon Jewish family life can explain the existence of such an ordinance. A similar condition may be found in some Muslim marriage contracts drawn up in Egypt at the end of the ninth century, stating that the wife is entitled to demand the divorce of any second wife that the husband might take, and to choose his household maidservant. But in the eleventh century, such conditions are no longer found in Muslim Egypt, although they are found in North Africa.[32]

In Spain as well many maidservants doubled as mistresses. This phenomenon was common in the circles of the Spanish aristocracy, and the Jewish courtiers imitated their way of life. After many of the customs of the community were prohibited in 1281, R. Todros Abulafia called upon the members of the community to repent, so as to awaken Divine mercy. He proposed certain ordinances so as to assure that this repentance would be accepted and fulfilled by all the members of the community. These ordinances emphatically reiterated the subject of prostitution and the sin of keeping Gentile maidservants as concubines, from which we may infer that he saw this as the main "stumbling block" in the way of life of the members of the community.

Further indication of the power of this phenomenon may be seen in the remarks of R. Moses of Coucy, who tells how, during his visit to Spain in 1236, he chastised the Jews there for their carelessness in observing the *mitzvot*. According to him, his admonitions made a great impression, as at the same time there were supernatural phenomena (earthquake and the like) that were interpreted by the people as a sign from Heaven of the need to return to God. He related that one of the results of his sermons was the "sending away of many Gentile women," a clear reference to concubines.[33]

Similarly, the harsh admonitions of R. Jonah Gerondi against sexual relations with Gentile servants and the comparison he draws between this act and those sins for which one is subject to the judicial death penalty may be understood in light of the ubiquity of this practice in Spain, and may help to explain the harsh threats chosen by Rabbenu Jonah to rebuke the people.[34]

The words of other Spainish sages of the thirteenth and fourteenth centuries, including those of Nahmanides and other Kabbalists, also contain admonitions against sexual relations with Gentile maidservants.

Prostitution

During the first half of the fourteenth century, the rabbi of the community of Toledo, R. Judah son of the Rosh, was asked by his nephew, R. Shlomo, concerning the lot of the prostitutes in his community. These Jewish prostitutes did not immerse in the *miqveh*, so that sexual relations with them was considered a severe transgression according to the halakhah. The inquirer was debating whether to expel them from the city, in which case their place would be taken by Christian women, or to leave them in their place. His concern was that the replacement of Jewish prostitutes by Christian ones would elicit the wrath of the authorities and possibly even of Christian society generally, bringing in its wake danger to the community as a whole. The authorities prohibited sexual relations between Christian women and members of other faiths, or indeed between members of any different faiths, imposing a severe punishment upon the act. The questioner and the respondent spoke in an allusive manner, so as not to bring the matter to the attention of the authorities, but the allusions are transparent enough and speak for themselves. R. Judah was aware of the danger, but nevertheless ruled that the Jewish prostitutes should be expelled, as the danger to the "soul" entailed in sexual relations with a Jewish woman who had not performed ritual immersion was more severe, in his view, than the danger "to man's body"—that is, the punishment likely to be imposed by the authorities for relations with Christian women.[35]

One might have expected the respondent to have lambasted the entire phenomenon and to have asked his interlocutor, his own nephew, to abolish the phenomenon entirely, and not allow either Jewish or Christian prostitutes to ply their trade. He did not do so, because he was well aware of the social reality in Jewish communities on Spain during that period: namely, the widespread nature of sexual licentiousness, particularly among the higher levels of society. He knew that any attempt to take on the practice head on and attempt to abolish it would meet severe opposition and not be crowned with success. Moreover, the authorities viewed the existence of brothels in a positive light, so as to prevent adultery with married women, as explained above.

This source preserves clear testimony as to the existence of Jewish prostitutes, and there is additional evidence as well. It seems to have been fostered by the existence of prostitution in Gentile society and the encouragement of the authorities, as well as by the permissive atmosphere accepted among the elite social circles of Spanish Jewry since earliest times.

What was the social and economic status of the Jewish prostitutes? I have not found any sources enabling us to give a well-grounded answer to this question. Study of the phenomenon of prostitution in Jewish society during the period under discussion is greatly lacking due to the poor state of the sources, in contrast to the relatively extensive evidence about the attitude toward prostitutes in Christian society and their economic standing.[36]

The sources preserve accounts about men who had sexual relations with Jewish women without either marrying them lawfully or their being defined as concubines. As a rule, these liaisons only became known after these women became pregnant and bore children, and inquiries were addressed to the rabbis as to the obligation of the father toward his children. However, the number of questions dealing with this is smaller than those involving adultery (defined in Jewish law as relations with a married woman) or one who has relations with his Gentile maidservant.

Reason would suggest that relations between unmarried people were more common than acts of adultery, but since as a rule they did not present any halakhic problem that needed to be addressed to a known rabbinic authority, there are few references to them. Only if the girl became pregnant and the man refused to marry her, or if there was a dispute concerning the economic compensation due for raising the child or the like, were things recorded for posterity. The halakhic problems involved in the case of relations with a servant girl or adultery are greater, and hence their memory is more often preserved.

In Muslim society, there also existed the phenomenon of concubinage and of prostitutes who hired themselves to wealthy traders visiting the city. In Wilson's study of the tasks imposed upon the supervisor of morals, the *Muhtasib,* we find that there was serious concern about breaches of morality in the Muslim cities due to the large number of cases in which women came to the inns where merchants stayed so as to serve them as mistresses.[37]

A relatively large group of responsa dealing with the subjects of prostitution, adultery, unfaithfulness, and suspicions of licentiousness, appears in the responsa of R. Asher (*Teshuvot ha-Rosh,* Sect. 32), reflecting the social reality in Spain at the beginning of the fourteenth century. These are of great importance from the methodological viewpoint, indicating as they do that only those problems that were unusual from the halakhic respect were discussed. Incidents of licentiousness and infidelity that did not involve halakhic difficulties are not mentioned there at all. Thus, for example, the Rosh was asked about a *kohen* (member of the hereditary priestly clan) who had relations with an unmarried widow who bore him a son, regarding the latter's status as to the priesthood. What caused the interlocutors to turn to the Rosh was the issue of the child's fitness for the priesthood; hence their words were preserved. If one would have been dealing with a regular Jew and not a *kohen,* or of relations between a *kohen* and the same woman without any children being born (or only daughters), the subject would not have been recorded at all. Another question deals with a Jewish woman who had been Reuben's concubine, and there were subsequent rumors but no evidence that he had sanctified her as his wife; thereafter the woman married Reuben's nephew. The Rosh validated the marriage ("the mistress of his father's brother is permitted to him"), as there was no explicit corroboration of the fact that Reuben had given her *qiddushin.* If the act of concubinage alone had taken place, without the rumors of *qiddushin* and without the woman's subsequent marriage to another, the whole story would not have appeared in *Teshuvot ha-Rosh*. Further examples of this kind may be found there. The common denominator of them all, as mentioned, is the presence of some unusual element from the halakhic aspect that accompanied the event, and caused the query to be sent. It follows from this that we cannot evaluate the phenomenon of prostitution and adultery on the basis of their preservation in responsa literature, as only unusual cases received such mention.

Prostitution and Concubinage in Ashkenaz

The situation in Spain should not be surprising. The great closeness between the Jews and their environment, including close social and cultural connections and the involvement of Jews in the Gentile courtier culture—all these served as suitable background for the reality described above. The connection of the Jews in Franco-Germany to the surrounding culture and society was less intense. Hence the phenomena of prostitution and concubinage were far smaller, but they existed there too.

R. Judah ha-Cohen, who lived and was active in Mainz during the first half of the eleventh century, was asked about a Jew who had a Gentile maidservant who also served as his mistress and who had fled him with the assistance of another Jew. It is possible that the latter desired her for himself, or he may have thought it was incumbent upon him to uproot the "evil act" of another Jew.[38]

Sefer Ḥasidim deals extensively with the incidence of permissiveness and harlotry among Jews. Its numerous references to this subject and its manner of relating to the incidents discussed suggest that one is dealing with a reality of which the pietists were acutely conscious, and not merely a theoretical discussion. This book serves as the best testimony to the commonness of the phenomenon in Ashkenaz and the fact that it constituted a problem even for Jewish pietistic society. We shall cite here a number of examples that indicate not only the existence of the phenomenon, but also its intensity.

One of the striking features of the figure of the Hasid is his refraining from looking at women; even if everyone mocks him for his excessive piety, he is to ignore them. The high spiritual levels that are promised to one who "brakes his impulse to look at women" indicate how common this phenomenon was and how difficult it was to refrain from it. The author wishes to convince his readers, and hence makes extensive use of stories and examples from the sexual life. While many of these are imaginary, the author's use of this motif calls for explanation.

Some of the cases tell of men who suspected their wives of having been unfaithful, and came to take counsel with the sage how to behave with them. For example: "A certain man had a wife who did not behave properly and was suspected of licentiousness, and her husband knew, and he also knew that she was not careful about the laws of menstrual separation." "A certain person came before the sages, and said to them: Tell me what to do, that I may have desire for my wife. And they did not wish to tell him, because the sages knew that she was a harlot." A man who knows that his daughter is a "harlot" is not allowed to marry her to a *hasid* while concealing the truth from him. On the other hand, he may allow her to marry whom she wishes, as otherwise she will be unfaithful after she marries.[39] Almost certainly, the use of the word *zonah* ("prostitute") here and in other cases in *Sefer Ḥasidim* does not refer to a woman who practices prostitution in the commercial sense, but one who was known on occasion to have sexual relations with strange men.

Sefer Ḥasidim objects to a man divorcing his wife, unless there are grave reasons for doing do. Among these circumstances the author includes the woman being a "harlot," and he appeals to the sage not to consider the pressure of the relatives, but to assure in this case that she be divorced.[40] A father who knows that his son is committing adultery must chastise him, even if the son threatens to convert to Christianity. On the other hand, the father must take account of his son's wishes and character and allow him to choose a wife who seems appropriate to him: "One whose son is wild, if he takes a wife whom he does not desire, he will lie with other women. Therefore he should allow him his desire."[41] It is difficult to separate these warnings from the reality familiar to the author from his own locale and to see it as a purely theoretical discussion. Nevertheless, such incidents must be seen in their correct proportion and not as characteristic of Ashkenazic Jewish society in the thirteenth century as a whole.

Sexual relations outside of the framework of marriage, and particularly acts of adultery, were understood by Jewish society in general, and that of the Hasidim in particular, as a very serious act, from which there follows the great attention given to them. *Sefer Ḥasidim* contains detailed instructions concerning the desired way of repentance "for one who had relations with a married woman." The author also refers several times to the question of repentance for one who had sexual relations with a Gentile woman. Other sources from Franco-Germany from this period bear testimony to Jews having sexual relations with Gentile women. The author was likewise aware of the answers offered by people to justify these acts, such as the precedents of Samson and Esther, and attempts to rebut these.

R. Judah ha-Hasid, R. Eleazar, and their fellow pietists were not naive. They knew the power of the sexual drive and hence did not suffice with general advice, but sought concrete ways to influence their disciples to accept their words. The detailed advice offered to a man as to how to avoid and restrain the sexual impulse reflects a profound psychological perception and understanding of the human soul, and above all the willingness to discuss these subjects openly.

The numerous admonitions are all addressed to the Hasidim themselves. The ignoring of the woman's side is striking. The authors hardly addressed at all the question of how to keep women from looking at men and being drawn toward them, and did not offer them far-reaching promises concerning the reward they might expect in Paradise if they kept themselves from the society of men. Offhand, this would seem to reflect admiration of women for not being so easily drawn after their impulses, but in truth the reason is something else. This is a further indication of the extent to which male society did not devote attention to women similar to that devoted to the man. The authors of *Sefer Ḥasidim* dealt in great detail, far more so than any other group in medieval Jewish society, with every aspect of human life, because they saw their book as a comprehensive life guide for the Jew. Because of this tendency, one might expect that they would devote a place to the spiritual and emotional world of women equivalent to or similar to that devoted to men—but one's hopes are disappointed. One may assume that in principle the picture is balanced, and that the caution to be exercised to avoid approaching the opposite sex, and the reward promised to one who refrained from doing so, would be identical—but they did not state this explicitly. Elsewhere, the author advised a person who had had sexual relations with a certain woman not to publicize the matter:

If he sinned in secret and it was not known to other people except to that same woman with whom he sinned, when he repents he would be wise to make it known to that woman that he has repented, but not to others, and he should not speak with her again.[42]

And what of the woman's repentance? Why is it sufficient for her to be informed of the man's repentance and not to suggest to her suitable ways for her to repent as well? In contrast to the extensive and detailed discussions presented by the authors concerning the man's soul-searching, his feelings, his impulses, the temptations that confront him, and the means of dealing with it, there are very few direct references to women and their own moral and spiritual world. Nor is the almost complete ignoring by *Sefer Ḥasidim* of the emotional world of the woman in its discussion of sexual life to be compared to its similar ignoring of the woman's place in Torah study, forms of prayer, festival observance, and the like. The latter, in the context of the reality of that time, were in fact closer to the world of the men, and it was natural that they would concentrate more on them. But this argument does not apply to the discussion of people's sexual lives. Regarding this topic, one might have expected an identical place to be devoted to the two sexes, or that at least considerable space would be devoted to the world of women.

In brief, the extensive space devoted by *Sefer Ḥasidim* to questions of licentiousness and deviations in sexual life indicates the extent to which the leaders of the Hasidim were aware of the tremendous power of the sexual impulse and its important place in both family and social life. Their discussions of these issues include many and varied aspects. They utilize passages from the Bible, from rabbinic legend, from folk stories, and above all, their sharp powers of observation, in order to try to persuade the Hasidim to distance themselves from "involvement with women" entirely.

R. Alexander Zuslin (Germany, first half of the 14th century) acknowledged a woman's complaint against her husband that he had had sexual relations with a Gentile woman as sufficient grounds for divorce. Later on it became known to him, in his words, that R. Meir of Rothenburg had already ruled thus. He also testified that he had seen Jews who were executed for having relations with Christian women.[43]

Latin documents from the principality of Savoy preserve testimonies concerning Jews who were accused of sexual assault of Christian women, and of those who made use of the services of Christian prostitutes. In a document from 1404, a German-speaking Jew was accused of visiting a Christian prostitute on the Sabbath and refusing to pay her fee on the grounds that this would involve a desecration of his Sabbath. He vehemently denied the accusation. In 1387, another Jew was accused of raping a Christian woman and a monetary fine was imposed upon him. A document from 1386 details a weighty accusation lodged against a Torah scholar, R. Samson of Savoy, for sexually attacking a Christian woman.[44] As a result of this accusation, a large monetary penalty was imposed upon R. Samson, which was later reduced after he promised to secure a loan for the Duchess of Savoy from another Jew.

The small number of Jewish rapists mentioned in the halakhic literature is striking. A large number of acts or suspicion of rape involve Jewish women who were "captive" among the Gentiles. Does the absence of discussion of acts of rape reflect the reality, and was the phenomenon in fact so rare? This seems to me very doubtful. True, one may assume that the existence of brothels in Christian Europe, as mentioned above, to some extent reduced the incidence of rape, but it seems more likely that this literary situation was the result of halakhic factors. Acts of rape against the Jewish woman's will did not engender a halakhic problem to be preserved in the responsa literature, unless one was speaking of the wife of a *kohen*. An ordinary Jew's wife was, generally speaking, permitted to him after rape. Only "borderline" cases of this type are mentioned. On the other hand, rape of a Jewish woman by a Gentile, or even the suspicion or presumption of rape when she was in captivity, raised other halakhic difficulties, as we shall see below in chapter 9. Nevertheless, this explanation, with all its importance, is not a full answer. One may assume that events that were "unusual" from a halakhic viewpoint tended to accompany the act of rape, and that it would have been necessary to relate to them. In our discussion below concerning the permissive way of life that spread in Italy during the period of the Renaissance, we shall again deal with the Jewry of Ashkenaz, many of whom migrated to northern Italy.

In Italy

The age of the Renaissance in Italy was characterized by a permissiveness that permeated various circles of Jewish society. Already in the *Maqamot* of Immanuel of Rome (b. ca. 1260), one can see the traces of the new cultural world of Jews who were greatly influenced by the Renaissance culture and the way of life of their neighbors. Immanuel writes of lovers who steal women from their "stupid and fat" husbands, and of adulteries of women. Immanuel's new style has been summarized by Dvora Bregman:

In marked contrast to the sweet style of the refined love sonnet, there is the low sonnet . . . that depicts sensual love and sin, with an anti-establishment tone and coarse language. In the low sonnet one finds a variety of earthy and instinctual figures who carry out a philosophy of permissive pleasure-seeking in refreshing and vital situations . . . Due to their realistic nature and their avowed intention of provoking anger, the spicy eroticism with which they are filled cannot be concealed as an allegory, or as a poetic conceit . . . The love in these sonnets is nourished by sin and gives pleasure to its heroes, as it does to those hearing the poem, like "stolen waters that are sweet."[45]

A rabbinic ordinance from Italy from the year 1418 states: "Also, as we have seen that this generation is susceptible to transgressions and false oaths and forbidden sexual relations, even with married women . . . and Gentile women are permitted in their eyes." Hence, the heads of the communities decided to appoint in every city and in every region a person whose task would be to be concerned about rectifying this situation. According to Bonfil, one should not exaggerate the significance of this ordinance and see it as characteristic of Jewish society in Italy generally, but only as relating to unusual cases:

This fact well explains why there are actually very few testimonies of sexual relations between Jews and Christians . . . Out of 2,286 documents pertaining to the Jews in the Duchy of Milano during the course of the fifteenth century . . . we find only slightly more than forty cases of this type, including accusations made by zealous functionaries whose purpose seems to be blackmail . . . These were considered deviations from the norm, and the society did not display any tolerance towards them. This being so, the rare cases of sexual relations between Jews and Christians are far from indicating a dynamic of integration; to the contrary—they specifically illustrate how strict and unyielding were the social barriers between the two groups.[46]

Bonfil is not concerned, as he says there, to examine the way of life and the mental world of the women, but the interaction between the Jewish and Christian societies. It is quite possible that he is correct regarding his conclusion that one should not exaggerate the significance of the occasional sexual liaisons between members of these two societies. However, as for the influence of the Renaissance upon permissiveness in Jewish society, it is difficult not to attach weight to the sentence that mentions "we have seen that this generation is susceptible to transgressions . . . and forbidden sexual relations, even with married women." Even if this relates to only a small minority, these things bear considerable weight. One must not forget that the important numerical data cited by Bonfil (forty cases in which Jews were accused of sexual relations with Christian women, out of 2,286 documents) relate to sexual relations outside of Jewish society, which were forbidden by law and punishable by death.[47]

An impressive testimony of the transformation that took place in Italy and of the influence of Renaissance culture on all levels of Jewish society is preserved in the ordinances enacted in 1507 by R. Judah Mintz and other sages for the communities in the area of Venice, most of whose Jewish residents were immigrants from Germany. While one is speaking here of the late Middle Ages, this was nevertheless the culmination of a process that had already begun at the end of the thirteenth and beginning of the fourteenth century, as implied by the above-mentioned poem of Immanuel of Rome, and other sources.

Among other things, R. Judah Mintz and his colleagues opposed those phenomena characteristic of Renaissance culture that had taken root among the Jews in the Venice region as well, and they wrote:

No woman should be washed by a Gentile man in the bath house, but only by a Jewish or Gentile woman, and no male should be allowed to enter the place where the women go about nude in the bath house. We have also made an edict that the men should not dance with the married women, no man with any married woman, except on the days of Purim; but they may dance with the unmarried women.[48]

The details of this regulation were explained by Robert Bonfil, who noted the relation of the phenomena described here to the norms of behavior accepted in Christian society during the Renaissance period, a discussion that we shall not repeat here. This source provides explicit testimony of the permissive way of life that had spread among the Ashkenazic Jews who migrated to Italy in the late Middle Ages. What is striking here is the permission for men and women to dance mixed, including married women with other men on Purim, and men with single women all the other days of the year. One may assume that the Ashkenazic pietists, the ancestors of these Jews, would have been astonished to hear of the way of life of their descendants and of the ordinance made by the rabbis five generations later.

This finding about the Ashkenazic Jews who lived in northern Italy in the fifteenth and sixteenth centuries forcibly raises the question: Did these Jews adopt a completely new way of life after their migration, or were some of these elements already practiced in their country of origin, in Germany? Had this question been raised in the past, one may assume with a large degree of probability that the researchers would have adopted the former possibility, namely, that this was a "revolution" in the way of life of the German Jews in their new home. However, a recently published finding by Israel Yuval concerning the large number of divorces in Germany in the fifteenth century and the accusations of R. Seligman of Bingen that husbands and wives conducted love affairs with others even before they were divorced, raises the possibility that one is dealing here with a more deeply rooted phenomenon, even if it only involved isolated individuals—an issue to which we shall return below (see chapter 11).[49] All these factors affected both the relations within the Jewish family and the status of women in society generally.

The responsa literature preserves testimonies of adultery and prostitution in Provence as well. Here, too, we see a milieu of profligacy and frivolity that typified the way of life of some of the Jewish youth:

> Concerning a matter that occurred in Carpentras involving a certain harlot woman, who was available to all comers, and a certain group of loose people went there and they were eating and drinking with her.[50]

It tells there of a youth who, in this flighty atmosphere, gave a coin to that prostitute "for the sake of *qiddushin.*" R. Yitzhak ben Mordecai, one of the Provençal sages of the second half of the thirteenth century, was called upon to decide the question of the validity of such *qiddushin.* Not only did the community allow the girl to engage regularly in prostitution, but, according to the description, wild parties took place in her house, in which Jewish youths also participated. Other such testimonies exist from Provence as well.

3. The Woman's Economic Status

We have seen that the important role played by the woman in supporting the family and the petit-bourgeois nature of Jewish society greatly influenced not only the status of the woman in society, but also her place within the family and her relationship with her husband. In the following discussion, we shall examine the impact of this situation upon the woman's economic status. In the previous chapter, we noted the nature of women's economic activity and the important role they played in making economic decisions within the family. We shall not reiterate these points here, but rather take note of several important areas that were not discussed above.

By its very nature, marriage involves an explicitly economic side. Generally speaking, the parents of the young couple supported their children, helping them to become established and to make their first steps as an economically productive unit. Indeed, the young couple frequently lived with one or another set of parents, particularly during the first years of marriage, and ate at their table. The commonness of marriage at an early age, which we noted in extenso in chapter 2, was a main factor in this. However, the young couple quickly became a social unit of economic importance in its own right. In twelfth century Germany, many Jews made their living from money lending, and by and large the young couples did so as well, receiving an initial sum of money from their parents with which to begin their life as an independent economic unit.

We already noted previously the transformation that occurred in Christian society at the end of the twelfth century, and particularly thereafter, in which there was a significant increase in the size of the dowry the bride was expected to bring into the marriage. According to Herlihy, the main factor contributing to this was the greater number of women available for marriage as against the number of men. While not all of the factors that led to this were relevant to Jewish society, as is the way of social phenomena of this type, it exerted influence upon society as a whole. Anyone reading *Sefer Ḥasidim* can easily see the importance of the family's wealth as a factor in making matches, and how difficult it was for poor parents to find husbands for their daughters.

Just as the sizes of dowries increased in Christian society, so too did they in Jewish society and, as we shall see below, in both societies there was a certain setback in the economic rights of the women in the thirteenth century, although it is doubtful whether there was any direct connection between them.

Women's Jewelry

The firm economic position of many Jewish families during this period created a reality that was characteristic of petit-bourgeois families, including conspicuous ceremonialism and showy clothing, intended to emphasize their wealth. The family's wealth directly affected the world of the women. One of its most striking expressions was the large number of jewels worn by the women and the place they occupied in their world and in family life generally. The elaborate clothing and ceremonialism of men and women alike displeased a number of sages and communal leaders. One of the outstanding Italian rabbis of the thirteenth century, Rabbenu Benjamin, who belonged to a pedigreed, and ancient family (Delli Mansi), sarcastically described this externalized culture, in which every detail of dress and ornamentation was the object of excessive attention.

The Jewish woman held an important place in this externalized culture. Generally speaking, the discussions of the rabbis bore a halakhic character (e.g., whether it was permitted to go out into the public domain on Shabbat wearing these jewels), but between the lines one can see the large number and great value of these jewels in the women's eyes. Thus, for example, R. Eleazar of Worms commented at the beginning of the thirteenth century:

It is the custom of our women to go out wearing beautiful ornaments . . . and rings of silver and gold and gold chains and earrings gilded and inlaid with silver.[51]

The context of these remarks is important. The Talmudic halakhah states that it is forbidden for women to go out into the public domain on Shabbat wearing jewelry because they might remove them to show to other women and to take pride in them. However, this law does not apply to wealthy women, as their wealth is well known and they don't need to show off their jewelry or remove them from their bodies. R. Eleazar of Worms characterized the women in his time and place as belonging to the category of "important women." The sources preserve many testimonies about the large number of jewels and their important place in the world of women. These were also subject to sarcastic criticism.

Likewise in the words of Rabbenu Tam, from the mid-twelfth century, we find indications of the attachment of women to their jewelry, to the extent that it was feared that they would violate the halakhah and not obey the instructions of the rabbis: "Rabbenu Tam wrote that we do not prohibit the women from wearing their rings, as they will not listen to us, and 'Leave Israel alone; it is better that they violate the law through error and not do so deliberately.'" Were the rabbis to forbid the women to wear their rings on Shabbat when they go out in public, there is a fear that they might not accept the ruling. These jewels also performed an economic function. At times women preferred to invest their own money in them: On the one hand, they were made of silver and gold and preserved their economic value and, on the other, were easily carried about when necessary.

The high monetary value of the jewels may also be inferred from the regulations of Rabbenu Tam and those of the communities in Spain (beginning of thirteenth century), stating that, if a woman died during the first year of her marriage, her husband must return to the members of her family not only her dowry—as shall be discussed below—but also her jewelry. The specific mention of jewels indicates their great financial value, as otherwise they would not find it necessary to enumerate them.

The Financial Arrangements of Marriage

In Ashkenaz and Spain, certain financial arrangements were fixed regarding marriage and the rights of divorced or widowed women to inherit the family property. These arrangements were extremely comprehensive, clearly affecting the woman's status, and one can see a clear development therein. We shall suffice here with citing the essential points of these arrangements.

The changes in financial arrangements between the couple—and especially the size of the dowry and the important role of the woman in supporting the family—led to a more egalitarian approach to the customs of inheritance as well. According to Talmudic law, the husband inherits all of his wife's property, even if she died immediately after marriage. In medieval Jewish society, there was a gradual demurral from this halakhah, particularly in the countries of Christian Europe. As the wealth and economic assets brought by the wife into marriage grew, regulations intended to ensure her rights and those of her birth family and direct heirs grew accordingly. The equality in the initial investment and support customarily provided by both sets of parents brought in its wake corresponding equality in the rights of inheritance.

During the Talmudic period, there was no fixed value to the dowry brought by the woman nor to the "addition" to her *ketubah* (*tosefet ketubah*). These were fixed on the basis of the economic ability of the family and the parents' willingness to help their children. In Ashkenaz, a uniform amount was fixed for the *ketubah*. A *taqqanah* from 1381 fixed the amount at six hundred gulden, which was a very high sum.[52] This suggests that one was not dealing with a concrete obligation, as many of the families were unable to pay such an amount. In practice, the husband was not in fact required to pay this sum in the event of divorce. The main purpose of the high amount recorded in the *ketubah* was to assure the woman control over a significant portion of her husband's resources after his death. Her experience, talents, and knowledge of the scope of her husband's business served as surety of the proper managing of the family's business even thereafter. The high amount written in the *ketubah* transferred a large part of the husband's estate to the control of the woman, in practice. On the other hand, in the event of divorce, the woman was not actually paid the high sum of six hundred gulden but only a part thereof, as the financial rights of both parties in the event of divorce were determined by mutual agreement. The financial commitment in the *ketubah* was, in practice, a kind of formal declaration whose purpose was to honor the bride and the family as a whole, rather than to establish a firm contractual obligation. R. Meir of Rothenburg wrote in one of his responsa: "In this country it is customary to write the dowry as a standard sum—the rich man does not add, so as not to embarrass one who does not have it."[53]

The practice of providing the daughter with a large dowry may be inferred from the regulation made by Rabbenu Jacob Tam and his colleagues in the mid-twelfth century, concerning the return of the full or partial value of the dowry to the girl's parents in the event that she died within a year of marriage. This *taqqanah* was also accepted by the Provençal communities, and is discussed extensively in research literature.[54]

The transfer of the parents' property to their children at the time of their marriage brought in its wake a change in the order of inheritance. According to Torah law, the daughters do not inherit from their parents, but in Ashkenaz it was determined that daughters would receive a certain portion of the inheritance. To this end, the parents gave them a *shetar yerushah* ("document of inheritance"), whose nominal value was in fact higher than their proportional share in the inheritance. This document stated that, if the sons agree to give them half of their share in the inheritance, the document will be null and void. Thus, at the time of her marriage the daughter was in practice given an additional financial commitment over and beyond her dowry, and her right to receive a part of the inheritance was assured in practice.

The *shetar yerushah* thus became one of the obligations the bride's family took upon itself at the time of marriage. R. Moshe Mintz, a mid-fifteenth century figure, described the giving of the *shetar yerushah* to the bridegroom by the bride's father "as is the custom in this country."[55] He even justified the giving of these documents as a means of increasing the daughters' attractiveness and as a way of making it easier for them to find suitable husbands. The bridegroom's solemn commitment to write large fictitious sums due to their wives in the *ketubah,* so as to increase the woman's honor at the time of her marriage, led to cases in which the bridegrooms asked their wives to write them a counter-document in which they agreed to forego a portion of the *ketubah* money that the husband was obligated to give her in the event of divorce or death.

A change of great significance occurred in Spain around 1200. The development there was described in detail by Simhah Assaf, whose main points we shall bring here:

In Spain, which for centuries was under the influence of the Babylonian center, and which for a long time had been divided into different kingdoms and principalities, there was no fixed custom for all of the communities. There were places in which the husband inherited all of his wife's property, whether or not she had children, in accordance with Talmudic law; there were other places in which it was customary that, if the woman left a son, he inherited all of his mother's property immediately after her death, while if the son was still a minor, a guardian would be appointed; and there were yet other places, in which the husband and the sons divided the woman's inheritance equally. This situation, in which each community determined its own special regulations regarding the inheritance of the husband and wife, continued as late as the days of Rashba (end of the thirteenth century).[56]

Great importance was attached to the regulations accepted in Toledo during the first half of the thirteenth century. They were very influential, and were accepted in other centers of Spanish Jewry as well. The essence of these regulations was that, in the case that the wife died during her husband's lifetime and she was survived by children, the husband divided her estate, including real property, with her sons or daughters equally. In other words, the husband inherited only half the property to which he was entitled under Talmudic law. If the woman had no surviving children, her estate was divided between her husband and her heirs from her father's family. However, if the woman's mother was still alive and there was evidence that she assisted in providing the dowry, she was entitled to half of the dowry, even though according to Talmudic law the mother does not inherit from her daughter.

This final detail, that under certain circumstances the mother and not other members of her family (including her own brothers) inherited her daughter's property, is very significant. This is a clear deviation from Talmudic law, and is conclusive proof of the important role played by women in both economic and family life and in the running of the household in Christian Spain as well. In practice, the woman or her heirs were assured half of the family's property. The sages even disagreed as to the question, whether the woman was allowed to sell one or another portion or to give it as a gift to whom she wishes during her husband's lifetime.

These "*Taqqanot* of Toledo" were accepted in most but not all of the Spanish communities; in practice, numerous local customs related to this point. In an overall historical perspective, it is worth turning our attention to the fact that, in terms of their concern for equality in the woman's status, the regulations from Spain are more far-reaching than those of Rabbenu Tam. According to the edicts of Toledo, the husband is not allowed to inherit all of his wife's property if he has children from her, but is required to divide his inheritance with these sons or daughters. On the other hand, according to the ordinance of Rabbenu Tam and various other German communities, in this case the husband is allowed to inherit everything, in accordance with Torah law, and not to give anything to his wife's children. According to Assaf, two factors contributed to this difference. First, it was the custom in the Land of Israel to make the husband's rights to benefit from his wife's property dependent upon her dying without children. Italy and France were influenced by the Palestinean practice, as they were in other areas. Secondly, the practice of monogamy that was prevalent in most European countries—particularly after the edict of Rabbenu Gershom—assured the woman that if she had sons they would inherit her property and that of her husband, unlike the case in Muslim countries and in Spain, where there were husbands who took a second wife, so that there automatically arose the need to protect the woman's property so that it not pass into "strange hands."

The reasons adduced by Assaf, particularly the second one, are convincing. Nevertheless, one might add here the background of what was accepted in the Gentile environment. There was greater awareness in Christian Europe of the woman's right to inherit from her parents and her husband. It was well-established custom in Christian society of the High Middle Ages that every woman brought certain property into her marriage, just as every man made a certain economic contribution to the new family. In a number of European countries the couple's property became common property for the duration of the marriage. The practice in Jewish society was in principle similar to this. Nonetheless, a certain retrenchment in the economic rights of the woman, particularly those of the widow, occurred in Christian society during the thirteenth century.

We have already noted the transformation that took place in Christian society at the end of the twelfth century, when the number of women seeking husbands exceeded the number of men who sought wives, as a result of which—together with other factors—the size of the dowries the women were expected to bring with them into marriage increased. This phenomenon existed in Jewish society as well, but with a significant difference. Whereas the dowry and inheritance received by the woman from her parents were in the final analysis available to her and to her children, in Christian society, notwithstanding the increase in the size of the dowries, the woman's rights of inheritance were harmed.

Explicit and detailed evidence of this has been preserved for Italy, and hints of this exist for other areas of Europe. Until the middle of the twelfth century, the great majority of marriage agreements from Italy reflect equality between the partners. From that time on, legislation in the Italian cities began to restrict the woman's rights to her husband's inheritance. Thus, in 1143 in Genoa the woman's right to a third (*tertia*) of her husband's property after his death was abolished.[57] There are many hints that a deterioration in the economic status of women began in Christian Europe already at the end of the twelfth century.

CHAPTER SEVEN

Women's Culture and Education

One of the major areas of discrimination against Jewish women in the Middle Ages was that of education and culture. Many of the women were illiterate, and they were even deliberately denied the opportunity for formal study of a number of areas of "sacred studies." The deprivation involved was not only one against the talents and potential erudition of women. As the study of Torah was one of the essential and most important values of Jewish culture, greatly extolled in all of the holy writings, women's exemption from the obligation to perform this *mitzvah*, and even, according to some sages, the explicit prohibition against their studying Torah, seriously damaged both their public and self-image. Three main factors led to discrimination against women in the area of education: the Talmudic tradition, excessive insistence upon feminine modesty, and the situation in the neighboring non-Jewish society. Nevertheless, some women did enjoy the good fortune to succeed in acquiring knowledge and erudition, including Torah knowledge, notwithstanding the theoretical limitations imposed upon women in this area.[1]

1. The Talmudic Heritage

The obligation to study Torah was not seen as incumbent upon women, nor were women formally obligated to teach their sons Torah. The Mishnah and the Palestinean Talmud even contain a harsh statement of the tannaitic sage, R. Eliezer ben Hyrcanus, against teaching Torah to women; one which exerted considerable influence in the Middle Ages and whose impact is discernable in certain circles even in our own time: "R. Eliezer said: Whoever teaches his daughter Torah is as if he teaches her *tiflut*." The term *tiflut* refers to licentiousness, lewdness, or immodesty, and was interpreted thus in the Babylonian Talmud, ad loc.

The explanation of the amoraitic sage R. Abahu harmed the image of women further. According to him, R. Eliezer opposed teaching Torah to women because by studying she will not only enhance her wisdom, but also her deviousness, which she may exploit for evil purposes, such as to deceive her husband and to conceal illicit activities.[2] An ignorant woman will find it more difficult to conduct her affairs in secret and to hide them from her husband. A similar reason for denying women education was also suggested in other cultures, such as by the Roman thinker Seneca, who relates that his father withheld education from his sisters so that they might retain their innocence, or in medieval Christian society by Philippe de Novare, who consistently argued that one ought to deny all education to women, even if they belonged to the aristocratic class. If a woman knows how to read she can receive letters from lovers, and if she knows how to write she can write to them, thereby bringing shame upon her family and upon the society as a whole.[3]

The pessimistic reasoning of Philippe de Novare and others helped to shape the image of women as light-minded and unfaithful, as noted above in our discussion of the image of woman (chapter 1). There is no explicit testimony to a similar influence of R. Abahu's words regarding Jewish society, but it seems quite clear that they too harmed women's image. R. Abahu did not explicitly discuss the question implied by his words: Why is there no analogous suspicion of this sort regarding men, and why are they permitted to study Torah? For, according to this approach, it will also teach them how to behave deviously. One obviously may answer in a formalistic manner by stating that the obligation to study Torah was imposed upon men alone, but this answer is inadequate. R. Abahu seems to have been more fearful of the misuse of wisdom and craftiness specifically by women, who are "flighty" or "light-headed." In any event, R. Eliezer's words enjoyed much attention in the Middle Ages, being accepted by the majority of the rabbis, rather than the position of R. Eleazar ben Azariah and of Ben Azzai, who allowed women to study Torah, even if only in a partial manner.

R. Eliezer ben Hyrcanus was extreme, consistent, and decisive in his opposition to the study of Torah by women. How negative his approach was may be seen by the story in the Jerusalem Talmud concerning a wealthy woman who asked him why, even though the people involved in the sin of the golden calf all committed the same sin, they were not all punished in the same manner, some being killed by the sword and others by the plague. R. Eliezer refused to answer her and commented cynically that she should engage in weaving rather than in the study of Torah, adding, "May the words of Torah be burned and not given to women."[4]

R. Eliezer unconditionally refused to answer her, even regarding a question that involved neither halakha nor *pilpul*, but an explanation of an incident brought in the Torah. Medieval Jews, even if they accepted R. Eliezer's words in principle, greatly departed from them in practice, as we shall see below. However, his above-mentioned remarks in Mishnah *Sotah* ("Whoever teaches his daughter is as if he teaches her *tiflut*") and their discussion in the Babylonian Talmud made a significant impression.[5] True, Eleazar ben Azariah—one of the greatest of the tannaim—disagreed with R. Eliezer, noting that women come to the occasion of the *hakhel* in Jerusalem [the septennial reading of the Torah to the entire people by the king; see Deut. 31:10–13] in order to hear words of Torah, from which it follows that it is permitted to teach words of Torah to women. However, his position was hardly ever cited in the works of the medieval sages. Moreover, R. Eliezer's words were seen as a directive deriving from religious considerations. Torah study for women was understood, as least in broad circles within Judaism during the Middle Ages and thereafter, as problematic from the religious viewpoint. In this respect, the position of the Jewish woman was worse than that of the Christian or Muslim woman. Even when Christian or Muslim scholars opposed study by women, they did not do so on the basis of religious considerations. The fact that ways were found within Judaism to bypass R. Eliezer's words did not fully counteract the negative influence of his position in principle.

Moreover, from the reasoning given by R. Abahu in the Talmud, it follows that there was a fear, not only of teaching Torah to women, but of any kind of discipline that makes a person wiser, as the fear described here was that the acquisition of *wisdom* as such would lead to craftiness. The philosophical and scientific speculation widespread in the Muslim countries and in Provence, particularly during the eleventh to thirteenth centuries, was seen in principle as a kind of "danger," as it explicitly increases wisdom.

The amoraim also disagreed regarding the acquisition of general knowledge and culture by women. The Jerusalem Talmud cites the opinion of R. Abahu in the name of R. Yohanan that "it is permitted for a person to teach his daughter Greek, because it is an ornament to her."[6] But alongside this there was also another opinion. The opposition did not leave an impression upon medieval Jewish society, and in many places we find testimony of women who acquired general education for purposes of their economic activity as well.

On the other hand, the Talmud brings various stories about Beruriah, the wife of R. Meir, daughter of R. Hananiah ben Teradyon, the only woman in the Talmud who enjoyed known and accepted halakhic authority. In several cases, she is even described as one whose traditions and teachings were preferable to those of male scholars. These stories served as proof to the medieval scholars, that one cannot speak of an absolute prohibition of Torah study to women, and that there are women who are also outstanding in their knowledge of Torah. Indeed, in the Middle Ages, learned and educated women were to be found both in the Muslim countries and in Christian Europe. The attempt of several scholars to see the bizarre legend cited by Rashi concerning the alleged suicide of Beruriah in wake of her infidelity as intended to convey a negative message regarding women's Torah study, is remote from its literal sense and opposed to the view held by R. Nissim of Kairouan. According to his tradition, Beruriah was not unfaithful and did not take her own life, but fled to Babylonia with her husband, R. Meir.[7] And indeed, we did not find any agitation in the Middle Ages against Torah study by women based upon this story of Rashi.

2. The Situation in Muslim Society

In Islam, there is no opposition in principle to the acquiring of education by women, such as that found among several of the Jewish sages in the Mishnah, in the Talmud, and even in the Middle Ages. Before the appearance of Muhammed, there were learned women in Arabian society, including well-known poetesses. A famous saying of Muhammed calls upon every Muslim man and woman to acquire knowledge. The composers of biographical dictionaries extensively describe the travels of men and women to centers of learning in order to receive knowledge and traditions from famous teachers. Religious traditions had been transferred from generation to generation verbally from the days of Muhammed, including by women, although later on this practice became more restricted. The main factor underlying this was the fear that the acquisition of learning by women and the reading of their poems in mixed society would be an affront to their modesty. However, learned Muslim women continue to appear in the sources throughout the Middle Ages. Hundreds of women are mentioned as preserving an oral tradition whose source is in Muhammed. It is clear that there were literate Muslim women even in later periods and that some of these also engaged in writing poetry, albeit one is speaking of only a very small minority.[8] Study activities of Muslim women in the elite families took place primarily in their own homes. In general, informal education was extremely widespread during the first centuries of Islam, during which those who sought knowledge travelled to seek out famous teachers. Study was conducted within the mosques, in the home of Sufi mystics, or in schools. In any event, it was already possible to acquire erudition in schools during the Ummaya period. The vast majority of the students were youths, but at times there were also schools for young women, and in some of them the girls studied together with the youths. From the tenth century on, the *midrasa* began to develop, in which more advanced education was acquired, but women did not officially study in these institutions, and only men served there as teachers. Even after the *midrasa* was set up, many people, including women, continued to study in their own homes.

An important source on the education of women and their position in Muslim religious life may be found in a unique literary genre: biographical collections of men and women who verbally transmitted the *hadith*—the oral traditions attributed to Muhammed. Those scholars who sought out select teachers so as to receive these traditions included among them women.

Ruth Roded, who examined some forty of these biographical collections composed from the ninth century on, wrote several studies concerning this literary genre and the role played therein by women.[9] Her findings are significant, not only for the study of the education of Muslim women in the Middle Ages, but also for that of their place in society. Some women were not only learned, but also enjoyed renown as repositories of knowledge. Many of these women had studied with the great scholars of their age. In later generations, learned women were scholars and served as teachers, and also enjoyed great social prestige. During the fourteenth century, there was a great increase in the number of learned women. During this period, many of them began their studies at a tender age, continuing them even as mature women and in the presence of their teachers. But during the sixteenth century, the number of learned and erudite women began to decline, and by the beginning of the seventeenth century, they ceased to appear in the biographical collections. It would seem that the testimony of men was considered preferable.

There were also Muslim women who engaged in mysticism, and those who were celebrated for their piety and who served as an example for later generations. However, these learned women were only a small minority, and the decisive majority of Muslim women were illiterate. An additional point worthy of mention is the important role played by the family in the education of women, as was also the case in Jewish society. The grandmothers served as a source of ready knowledge for the education of women, and in this too there are parallels in the Jewish society.

How can one reconcile the important place taken by women in acquiring knowledge and education and in transmitting traditions, with the strict standards of modesty that were customary in Muslim society? Scholars have suggested several possible solutions. Possibly society insisted upon modesty on the part of the women who gave over the traditions, who covered their face with a veil or were hidden behind a curtain. However, several biographies emphasize that there was need for direct contact between the one giving the tradition and the one receiving, and that it was essential that the one receiving see the face of the one giving it. Members of the family may have accompanied the woman when she went to receive or to give over traditions, so as to protect her modesty. The learned women were usually older, reducing the fear that she would be seen as a sexual object. Finally the phenomenon of women giving over traditions was rare, and therefore they may have been willing to overlook the problem.[10]

3. The Situation in Christian Society

The situation in Christian Europe was similar, but the number of women who knew how to read and write was greater. Most of the women were ignorant, but among the circles of the nobility and the wealthier bourgeoisie, in the nunner-ies, and among the Beguines, many women were literate. Many churchmen advo-cated giving elementary education to women generally, and to those of the nobility in particular, so as to enable them to read prayer books and to learn the rudi-ments of the faith. Women of the nobility required more education so as to ful-fill their functions and to control their territory suitably when they headed a territorial seigniory. Only a few churchmen encouraged broad general educa-tion to women, so as to enrich their spiritual world and to serve as a source of edification and pleasure. Christine de Pisan complained that she was not given an education in her childhood, because the custom at that time was not to give education to girls. Her complaint was based upon the privilege, the ability, and the willingness of women to learn and to acquire knowledge, and the conscious-ness that this privilege is not the exclusive prerogative of men.

The noblewomen who learned to read and to write read prayer books, sto-ries and poetry. Some of them studied in their homes with private tutors (male or female), while others attended schools adjacent to the monasteries or those for children of the urban aristocracy. We do not have exact numerical data, but it is possible that the proportion of educated Christian women was higher than that in Jewish society.

A small number of women acquired a comprehensive education. Hildegard of Bingen, and Heloise and Christine de Pisan are outstanding examples. They knew various languages, including classical languages. There were also noble-women who had extensive libraries in their homes, while others assisted in the establishment of institutions of higher education and in building churches, and encouraged artistic creativity. Many of these served as patrons for authors, poets, and artists.

In Europe, some women owned books (in manuscript) that they had acquired or inherited from their parents. Susan G. Bell studied this subject, relying upon catalogues of libraries, wills, and lists of family property. She found 242 women, not including those of church circles, who had books in their possession between the years 800 and 1500. The number of these women grew in the fourteenth century and doubled in the fifteenth century. Most of these books came to the women by inheritance, but some women bought books despite their high price. These women spent a significant part of their time in reading books, and these books were also important in the cultural life of their day. This reality was perpetuated in art as well: in a number of paintings one sees women shown reading books. Some women from the elite levels of society brought books as part of their dowry at the time of their marriage. Some of these married noble-men and knights from far-off places, and in this way served as a channel for transmitting culture. There were also some among them who contributed money for the copying and lending of books, a step to which they were moved by the high price of manuscripts. As we shall see in the next section, *Sefer Ḥasidim* describes Jewish women who took similar steps, coercing their husbands to con-tribute money for the purpose of copying books and lending them out.[11]

Christian women displayed a particular interest in "belles-lettres." The courtly literature that flourished in the High Middle Ages was directed specifically toward women. However, one should not exaggerate the significance or weight of this group of noblewomen. It was extremely limited, and one cannot derive from it conclusions about the whole. The same holds true for the value of courtly literature. This literature was of no interest to women of other social classes, while the nobility was an extremely small group. However, it was this class specifically that influenced Jewish society. The traces of courtly literature can be clearly seen also in *Sefer Ḥasidim*.

Members of the lower classes, of both sexes, received no education, and the great majority were illiterate. On the other hand, among the urban women who belonged to both the high and petit bourgeoisie, there were those who did enjoy education. Some of the boys who served as apprentices were sent by craftsmen to school to learn reading and writing for purposes of their work. There were also girls who received vocational training. The latter studied together with the boys in co-ed schools, and only in 1375 were the first ordinances issued in Paris to separate boys and girls in school. Testimonies concerning schools for boys and for girls are extant for various places in Europe, including Italy, England, and Germany.

No detailed or reliable accounts have been preserved regarding the conditions of study. One may assume that, apart from reading and writing the vernacular, they also studied the rudiments of religion and of prayer. Institutions for higher education were closed to women—not only the universities, but also the special schools in which they studied law or preparation to engage in business and com-merce. This discrimination led to a gap within the urban upper class between the education of men and that of women. This reality, in both the higher and petit bourgeoisie classes, likewise affected the situation in Jewish society.

4. The Stance of the Jewish Sages in the Middle Ages

Medieval Jewish sages related extensively to the statement of the *tanna* R. Eliezer that one ought not to teach Torah to women. However, their influence was only partial, and in practice there was a substantive retrenchment from them. Even those who accepted R. Eliezer's position in principle attempted to interpret it narrowly. Among these were Maimonides, whose words reflect a definite demur-ral from the opinion of R. Eliezer. His words left a definite impression upon members of the following generations:

Our Sages commanded that a person should not teach his daughter Torah, because most women's minds are not focused toward studying . . . Our Sages said: Whoever teaches his daughter Torah is as if he taught her *tiflut*. To what do these things refer? To Oral Torah. But regarding written Torah, a person should not teach them to a woman *ab initio*, but if he taught them it is not as if he taught her *tiflut*.[12]

There are two leniencies in this ruling as compared to the words of R. Eliezer: He writes "most women's minds are not focused toward studying," rather than "all women," and his prohibition against study does not apply retroactively to written Torah. It would appear that both the historical situation and Maimonides' philosophical training strongly influenced his willingness to dissent, if only even in part, from the positions of R. Eliezer and R. Abahu.[13]

The Ashkenazic Hasidim demurred more definitively from the position of R. Eliezer, ruling that a man is *obligated* to teach his daughter halakhic rulings in codified form. R. Eliezer's remarks about *tiflut* were interpreted by them as referring only to deep study of Talmud (*pilpul*) or to the "secrets of Torah" (i.e., mystical or esoteric subjects). Any other study is not only permitted, but is also suitable and desirable. They emphasized that a father is required to teach his daughter all the mitzvot so that she may observe them properly, thereby opening to women wider opportunities for Torah study. This permission was even expanded further to infer from Scripture (Deut. 1:1) that women can study other aspects of Torah.[14] R. Yitzhak of Corbeil (France) followed a similar path, calling upon women to study those *mitzvot* that they are required to fulfill, and his remarks were widely known.

But in practice, the Hasidim were not even insistent upon this limitation. The fact that women listened to the sermon on Shabbat is one indication of this, a point to which we shall return below. They did not offer an explicit explanation for the distinction drawn among different kinds of Torah, but it is clear. In light of R. Abahu's explanation of R. Eliezer's approach, they may be divided as follows: those types of study that involve greater depth, that develop "craftiness" in the heart of the one studying and allow him to abuse his knowledge of Torah, are prohibited, whereas that type of study based primarily upon repetition and knowledge does not evoke the same concern. This reasoning is evidently that which underlies the profound study of Torah and of Talmud on the part of certain women from families of rabbis and of Hasidei Ashkenaz. These same women proved that they are outstanding, not only in their knowledge of Torah, but also in their character, and hence there was no fear that they would be corrupted by acquiring "craftiness."

During the late Middle Ages, the sages of France and Germany accepted the basic distinction drawn by Maimonides between written Torah and oral Torah. Among these was R. Jacob Moellin (Maharil), the leading Ashkenazic sage at the end of the fourteenth and beginning of the fifteenth century. Indeed, he accepted the basic statement that there is a fear that the teaching to women of "*pilpul* and reasoning" would help them to acquire deviousness and perform forbidden acts "in a hidden and concealed manner."

Another way of "getting around" R. Eliezer's statement was proposed by another Italian sage at the end of the Middle Ages, R. Samuel Archivolti, rabbi of Padua during the sixteenth century. Even though he stands outside of the chronological framework of this work, his words deserve mention because of their unique nature. In his opinion, not only is a woman of suitable intellectual capacity allowed to study Torah and philosophy, but she is even obligated to do so. The Mishnaic prohibition applies *ab initio* only to young girls. In his opinion, refraining from acquiring wisdom will in fact hurt the woman who is deserving by her talents "to receive the fulness abundance of wisdom."[15] In his opinion, the sages spoke regarding the most common situation, because the decisive majority of women do not study Torah, and their merit lies entirely in training their children in Torah and in helping their husbands, but in his opinion they did not intend to negate the great virtue of a woman who does study. However, his ruling in affirmation of the study of Torah by educated women cannot cover his negative opinion regarding the abilities of most women.

5. Learned Women

In various different sources, testimonies have been preserved concerning medieval Jewish women who acquired both Torah and general knowledge, and even of some who took part in public life. Even though they are not great in number, the phenomenon is very important. They indicate that R. Eliezer's opinion that one does not teach Torah to women was not accepted as such and that various ways were found to circumvent it. Those women who were learned, learned Torah from their fathers or in other ways. Independent study can explain only some of these cases, but not all of them. One may assume that the presence in some families of private teachers also allowed the daughters to join the studies held at times within the circle of the immediate family.

Deserving of special mention is the presence of learned women in Jewish society in the Muslim countries where, at least in theory, there was insistence upon stricter norms of modesty. The best known of these was the daughter of the Babylonian Gaon, R. Samuel ben Ali. R. Petahyah of Regensburg, who visited Baghdad during the 1170s, described her work as a teacher of Bible in the famous yeshiva of her father as follows:

And he [R. Samuel] has no sons, but one own daughter, and she is expert in scripture and Talmud and teaches Bible to the youths. And she is enclosed within the building, [in a room] with one window, and the students are outside and below and do not see her.[16]

However, according to some researchers this story is of a legendary character and is not to be seen as a trustworthy historical source. It is difficult to agree with them. R. Petahya knew R. Samuel well and stayed in his mansion. The precise details that he gives regarding him and the decorations in his home clearly indicate this. Moreover, R. Eleazer ben Yaakov, the greatest Babylonian poet of the period, wrote an elegy concerning the death of this daughter in which he described her as an outstanding scholar whose unusual wisdom was widely known.

While it was customary in dirges or eulogies to praise the deceased and to extol them rather freely, nevertheless the excessive praise with which she is described must be indicative of broad learning, and not only in the area of Bible, and her great renown. It is not surprising that R. Eliezer did not mention her name despite her greatness. In those days, in the Muslim countries, this was considered an affront to the honor and modesty of a woman, and therefore he refrained from mentioning her name.

At the end of the Middle Ages, a woman, the Rabbanit Asenath Barzani, headed a yeshiva in Kurdistan. She was not only a scholar, but also a poetess. As her activity goes beyond the chronological framework of our book, we cannot discuss her here, notwithstanding the great interest in this figure.[17]

Another educated woman who belonged to the elite of Jewish society in Muslim Spain and mastered the mysteries of Hebrew poetry was the wife of Dunash Ibn Labrat (Spain, second half of the tenth century). The poem of farewell that she wrote to her husband when he was forced to leave her and her small son and to flee for his life, reveals not only an extraordinary writing ability and poetic beauty, but also mastery of the intricacies of the Hebrew language and of the use of biblical language, all of which indicate that she was a woman of broad culture and erudition in many areas. Another learned woman was Qasmuna, evidently the daughter of R. Samuel Hanaggid. She was also outstanding in this area and wrote poems in Arabic, as was also done by Muslim women who belonged to the Islamic courtly society. It follows, that she evidently learned the art of poetry from her father.[18]

Samau'al ben Judah Ibn Abbas (al-Magribi), the twelfth-century convert to Islam, related that his mother, who was born in Bazrah, and her two sisters, delved deeply into study of Torah and were in the habit of writing Hebrew. During the second half of the eleventh century Bellette, daughter of R. Menahem and the sister of R. Elijah the Elder and R. Yitzhak from Le Mans, was active in France. These sages (father and sons) led the communities of northern France throughout the eleventh century. Bellette is described as a woman of authority and a spiritual leader of the women in the city where she lived. Again, R. Eleazar of Worms described his wife Dulca—who died a martyr's death in 1196—as a "pious" and "righteous" woman who taught other women and was expert in halakhah and who regularly came to the synagogue on Shabbat to hear her husband's sermon.

It follows, both from the Genizah sources and from Maimonides' responsa, that there were learned women in Mediterranean Jewish society who knew how to read and write and taught Torah, even if they did not reach the level of the above-mentioned learned women. There were some who served as teachers. One of Maimonides' responsa tells of a woman who served as a teacher for many years. In one of the documents preserved in the Cairo Genizah, a dying woman orders her sister to care for her daughter's education, referring in passing to their mother, who was a learned woman. These sources were preserved by chance, and it is very likely that there were many other women like them. Similarly, there were many female teachers in Italy at the end of the Middle Ages.

One should not force an interpretation of all of the above-mentioned cases as referring to women who studied Torah by themselves without any framework either in the circle of their own immediate family or from Talmudic scholars. If such were the case, it would be impossible to describe them as *talmidot hakhamim,* scholarly women whose Torah was also listened to by rabbis. Moreover, explicit testimonies have been preserved of women who studied with learned teachers. Thus, for example, R. Joseph ben Moses testified that the daughter-in-law of R. Israel Isserlein learned Torah from an outstanding scholar, while scrupulously maintaining the rules of modesty:

And I remember that his daughter-in-law Reidel studied before an elder named R. Yudel Sofer, in the home of the Gaon, in the place where most of the members of the household were present, and the elder in question was married.

Women also engaged in copying Hebrew books. At times, one may infer from their words that one is not speaking here of simple copying, indicative of technical knowledge of reading and writing in Hebrew, but of understanding the halakhic matters discussed and of a certain expertise therein. Without understanding the context of things, it is difficult to copy them precisely, particularly when one is dealing with manuscripts. One of the most famous copiests was Paula, a descendant of R. Nathan, author of the *Arukh,* who was active in Italy at the end of the thirteenth century. Her knowledge in the Hebrew language and her expertise in halakhic literature may be inferred from her colophons.

Thus, she concluded MS. Bodleian Or. 80 with a prayer on behalf of all Israel: "He will in His mercies allow me to see His glory and our glory and to take us out of the great darkness in which we are today and which has aroused in our time." Very few writings by women themselves are extant from the Middle Ages, particularly in Christian Europe. There follows from this the importance to be attributed to Paula's words. Another work is a copy she made for herself and for the members of her household, which she concluded with a similar prayer:

Thus is concluded this work, the Commentary on the Prophets, copied by Paula daughter of R. Abraham the Scribe . . . in the city of Rome. . . . May the Omnipresent allow us to read it, me and my seed and my seed's seed to the end of all generations.

Another female book copiest was Miriam daughter of Benaiah the scribe. At the end conclusion of copying a manuscript, she wrote: "Do not hold me guilty if you find errors therein, for I am a nursing woman." One may assume that she learned the profession of copying from her father. The pious men of Ashkenaz were also familiar with a situation in which women knew how to write holy books. While they opposed the writing of Torah scrolls by women, because they are exempt from learning Torah, they did not object to their writing Torah.

Maharil, the leading Ashkenazic sage of the fifteenth century, had an ambivalent stance toward Torah study by women. He objected to the writing of halakhic literature for women, just as he opposed writing halakhic handbooks in German and Yiddish for the ignorant masses, out of a fear of popularization of halakhic literature. He preferred that women learn those laws that they needed verbally rather than from written sources. On the other hand, he did allow women to recite the blessings over the Torah recited prior to study, and thought that the prohibition against teaching Torah to women applies to the father, but that the woman is permitted to study Torah by herself, and that she receives a reward for this, like a person "who is not commanded but does it." Maharil's wife, Schondlein, even wrote a halakhic responsum to a woman who asked her a question concerning the laws of menstruation—evidently in her husband's name.[19]

Toward the end of the Middle Ages and at the beginning of the modern period, there were learned Jewish women in Italy as well. But this subject takes us beyond the chronological framework of the present work. One may nevertheless assume that the increased literacy in European Christian society during the thirteenth and fourteenth centuries also affected the situation in Jewish society, including an increase in the number of women who knew how to read.

6. Education of Women in Jewish Society

What was the situation in Jewish society in Muslim countries? R. Pethahiah of Regensburg described the widespread religious knowledge of Babylonian Jewry on the basis of what he observed during the second half of the twelfth century, and related that he did not encounter a single ignorant Jew "throughout the land of Babylonia, and in the land of Assyria and in the land of Media and Persia."[20]

Pethahiah did not refer here to the level of education of Jewish women in Babylonia, and it is doubtful whether they received one similar to that of the men, as next to the above description he speaks of the great insistence upon feminine modesty in Jewish society, so much so that "one does not see any women there." Under such strict conditions, it would be difficult for women to go out to study, although they could still study within their own homes with a relative or a learned woman—analogous to the practice among the elite families of Muslim society, as we saw above.

The Cairo Genizah preserves testimonies about small boys and girls who studied together in elementary primary schools. There were public schools and private schools, in which both male and female teachers taught. Nevertheless, as the goal of such elementary school education was to prepare those studying there to assume an active part in public worship, generally speaking only boys attended regularly. From the letters of women found in the Genizah, we learn that some of the women who received letters did not know to read them themselves and had need of others. However, the Genizah sources also preserve other testimonies of young girls and maidens who studied in school, and this also held true for the Alexandria community. One of them describes a class of young girls who studied with a blind teacher. The wealthy and elite families often insisted upon giving an advanced Jewish education to their daughters as well, usually by means of private teachers. However, the most impressive phenomenon is the mention of women among those poor who were literate, and often more than that. The woman mentioned in Maimonides' responsum who served as a teacher also came from the poorest sector of Jewish society. One of the letters of the Genizah contains the will of a dying woman, who asked her sister to make sure that her daughter would continue her studies and be learned, as their mother had been. The sick woman is also not from a wealthy family:

My greatest charge to you is to take care of my youngest daughter and make an effort that she should learn. I know that I am imposing a great burden upon you, as we do not even have enough money to support her, all the more so for the expense of study.[21]

Women participated in synagogue worship. The Genizah fragments mention pious women who were meticulous about fulfilling *mitzvot* and making contributions to the synagogue. All these citations further support the assumption that there were those among them who were able to read Hebrew and to pray. According to Goitein, most of the women from all levels of society knew the basic prayers. Regarding orphan girls as well, care was taken that they should at least know the prayers.

On the other hand, among all the tens of thousands of remnants of the Cairo Genizah, there has not been found—not even in private letters—a single work, whether poetry or words of thought, written by an Egyptian woman, whereas regarding Muslim Spain there are allusions to Jewish women who wrote poetry, as described above. In light of the large quantity of fragments in the Genizah and their comprehensive nature, this is a very interesting finding.[22] In my opinion, the fear that such a work would affect the modesty of the woman, was the main reason for their refraining from writing.

But one should not be misled by these examples from the Genizah sources. Even if many Jewish girls did receive a rudimentary education, only a handful received higher education as well. This was the result, not only of the prohibition against teaching Torah to women, but also to a large extent of concern for their modesty. Study with male teachers and leaving the home were perceived as immodest behavior, particularly in the case of married women, as we already noted above in our discussion of female modesty and their working outside of the home. Marriages at a relatively young age, which were very common, also curtailed women's ability to study.

7. Girls' Education and Erudition in Ashkenaz

Moshe (Moritz) Güdemann arrived at the conclusion that the vast majority of Jewish women in Ashkenaz did not know how to read or write. In his opinion, their level of education was even lower than that of the Christian women who lived in the same region. An even larger number did not have mastery of the Hebrew language. From the remarks of the rabbis concerning Grace After Meals, one arrives at the conclusion that many women did not at all understand "the holy language." Support for this may be found also in *Sefer Ḥasidim:*

And if someone comes to you who does not understand the Hebrew language and is God-fearing . . . or if a woman comes to you, instruct them to learn the prayers in a language that they understand, for prayer is only in the understanding of the heart. And if the heart does not understand that which comes out of the mouth, what does it help? Hence, it is good that one prays in a language that he understands.[23]

The basic assumption here is that the woman does not understand the language of prayer, but it is very doubtful whether one may conclude from this that one is speaking here of the totality of Jewish women in Germany. It seems more likely that one is speaking here of most but not all of them, as was the case in Christian society as well. A clear distinction needs to be drawn between the ability to understand "simple" Hebrew and the flowery language used in the *piyyutim* (liturgical poems) and prayers. Even men sometimes found it difficult to understand this language. Thus, for example, R. Mordecai ben Yitzhak Kimhi testified that in southern France during the thirteenth century: "At this time, due to our great sins, most of our sons and daughters speak . . . Arabic and Greek and the language of each people, and even most of the men do not know how to speak Hebrew, so how can we expect the women to understand the language used in the Talmud?"[24] We cannot infer from this that they were illiterate in the vernacular, as that was essential for their business. From other sources as well, one derives a picture of women who do not understand Hebrew, making it difficult for them to fulfill such *mitzvot* as Prayer and Grace After Meals. Closer examination reveals that most of them had technical knowledge of reading Hebrew, but did not understand the meaning of blessings and prayers. The same held true for Muslim countries as well.

Various testimonies have been preserved concerning women who prayed in the vernacular rather than in Hebrew. A similar problem arose regarding the reading of the Haggadah on Passover night. There were those women who did not understand what was being read; hence, a number of sages were in the habit of reading some sections from the beginning of the Haggadah in the local vernacular.

One of Maharil's responsa tells of a certain rabbi who had planned to write a book about the laws of menstruation "in the German language" because the women and some of the men did not know Hebrew. This elicited the ire of Maharil, who tried to dissuade the author from carrying out his plan.[25] These sources indicate how far removed the Hebrew language, and particularly the language of the prayers, was from the women and from some of the men; however, under no circumstance is one to draw such a conclusion about everyone. Many knew how to read Hebrew and understood the language of the prayers. The assumption that this does not hold true for all Jewish women finds support in other sources, indicating that Jewish women in Christian Europe were literate. First and foremost, one should mention the words of one of the disciples of Pierre Abélard, one of the great scholastic thinkers of the twelfth century. This author noted that those Christians who educate their children do so, not for the sake of heaven, but out of the desire for profit. They hope that one of the brothers might become a priest, so as to assist the rest of his family. They likewise take into consideration that a priest has no heirs, and needs only his clothes and his vestments, so that whatever he acquires ultimately reverts back to his parents or his brothers. The Jews, by contrast, send all of their sons to study, out of zeal for their God and love of His Torah, and in order that they might understand the Law of God. No matter how poor a Jew may be, and even if he has ten sons, he will send all of them to study—not for any material benefit, as the Christians do, but simply in order to understand God's teaching. And, he concludes, this includes not only the sons, but also the daughters.[26]

True, this author's aim was to chastise the Christians because they are not as devoted to the education of their children as are the Jews, for which reason one must relate to his words in praise of the Jews with some caution. However, it is difficult to imagine that he would have invented things that had no basis in reality, when his readers could easily refute his words, as they knew personally the way of life of the Jews who lived with them and with whom they came into close economic and social contact. It is likely that he did exaggerate somewhat in his praise of the Jews, as it is difficult to assume that all of the Jews gave an education to their daughters, but there must be a kernel of historical truth in his words. Evidently, some girls learned reading and writing so that they could pray and participate in religious life, as well as help to support their families. In brief, some of the Jewish women also understood Hebrew, while many others worshipped in the synagogue or at home in the vernacular.

In *Sefer Ḥasidim*, we find an explicit exhortation to teach halakhic rulings to girls, and from the context there it seems that the young girls studied with teachers, evidently in their homes. The author criticizes studying with a teacher who is a "young man," from which it is clear that if the teacher is married or older or a woman, it was acceptable. Among other things, he writes: "but those mitzvot which they are commanded to perform, they must learn in a language which they understand. But the man is commanded to study in the Holy Tongue."[27]

The conclusion, that girls should study "in a language which they understand," seems to be the solution to the seeming contradiction that emerges from the sources. Most of the women did not know how to read or write in Hebrew and learned "the commandments" in the vernacular, usually German or French. They were not ignorant, but only some of them knew Hebrew. This is the explanation for what we stated earlier with regard to the idea that women could not understand Grace after Meals in the holy tongue. I do not see any way of determining exactly what percentage of Jewish women knew Hebrew, nor to compare this figure with the literacy rate among Christian women. In any event, if we add to this the number of Jewish women who were literate in the vernacular, one would arrive at quite a respectable number.

Knowledge of the vernacular allowed Jewish women to assist their husbands in supporting the family, particularly in the trade of money-lending. There is no doubt that the important role played by women in the family economy encouraged many of them to acquire the ability to read and write that would help them in their businesses. R. Eleazar of Worms told of a hasid who taught his daughters to write, because if they would not know how to write they would need to ask others to write for them "letters of bond on the security pledges taken when they loaned out their money, and thus they would be alone with the scribes and might sin . . . or acquire a bad name."[28]

As mentioned, R. Eleazar of Worms, one of the leaders of the Hasidei Ashkenaz, related that his wife Dulca regularly came to hear his Shabbat sermon in the synagogue.[29] It is clear that this refers to a sermon, a condition of whose understanding was substantial knowledge of Torah. Nor does it seem likely that she was alone in doing so. Such phenomena influence the surrounding society, and it seems quite likely that other women also came to listen, at least those whose husbands were numbered among the pietists.

In general, the sources mention the names of women from Germany and France who were noted for their knowledge of Torah, all of whom came from families of noted scholars. Some women served as cantors for other women. They evidently worshiped out loud and with song in the women's section, and those women who did not know how to read Hebrew prayed after them. The list of women killed as martyrs at Nürnberg includes "Richenza, the prayer leader of women."[30] On the gravestone of Urania in Worms, who died in 1275, it states that she was the daughter of Abraham, "the leader of the singers" and that she also "sang the *piyyutim* for the women with a melodious voice."[31]

Society did not perceive the woman as a person, one of whose goals in life was to study Torah. Fulfilling *mitzvot* and good deeds—yes; but Torah study—

no. This follows from the wishes that a father gave himself on the birth of a daughter: "May it be God's will that I may raise her to sew, to spin, and to do good deeds." By contrast, the blessing upon the birth of a son was that, "May it be God's will that I may raise him to Torah, to the marriage canopy, and to good deeds." The preferred occupation of women was weaving and sewing. While this was the common occupation of women everywhere in the ancient world and in the Middle Ages, the felicitations mentioned indicate that this involvement was seen as something of value. As it is brought in the Mishnah (*Ketubot* 5.5) as a symbol of the occupation of women, even the leading sages saw this in a similar light. Thus, for example, R. Eliezer ben Samuel ha-Levi of Mainz in the fourteenth century wrote in his will that his daughters "should not sit idle without labor, for idleness leads to boredom and to licentiousness: they should either spin or cook or sew."[32] In the words of praise written by R. Eleazar of Worms upon the death of his wife and two daughters, he saw fit to mention the involvement of the daughters in weaving as a proof of their modesty: "she serves her Creator and spins and sews and embroiders / filled with fear and love of her Maker without fault." In medieval Christian society, sewing and embroidery were also seen as one of the central occupations in the life of a woman, memorialized not only in prose but in works of art as well.

8. The Situation in Spain

What was the level of knowledge and method of education of Jewish women in Spain? This is a great riddle. The little we know about this subject is even less than what can be gleaned from the Cairo Genizah and from the sages of Ashkenaz and France about their respective communities. If there do remain at least some isolated indications of learned women regarding the Muslim period, such as those cited above, regarding Christian Spain these are not available. It follows from this, that any attempt to describe their education and manner of education is mere speculation. It seems likely that there were no substantial differences between them and what we have seen as to other Jewish diasporas and in the sources of the Cairo Genizah, and that in wealthy and pedigreed families women did in fact acquire some sort of education. The existence of educated women in the circles of elite families, including those of R. Yehudah Halevi and Dunash Ibn Labrat, also supports this assumption.

An interesting source has been preserved in the words of R. Jonah of Gerona, one of the important Spanish sages of the thirteenth century, who was greatly influenced by the teachings of German Pietism. In his work, *Iggeret ha-Teshuvah,* an extensive discussion is devoted to the tasks imposed in his day upon women. He emphasized the important role played by their concern for the Torah study of the head of the family and their sons. He spoke of the merit they enjoy "because they send their sons to the school, and take care that their sons will engage in Torah, and have compassion upon them when they come home from school, and draw their hearts with kindly words that they should desire to be involved in Torah, and watch over them that they not neglect the Torah ..."[33]

R. Jonah also implored the women to take care to pray three times a day, and that their main prayer be "supplications on behalf of their sons and daughters that they be God-fearing, and that their sons should succeed in learning the Torah, for a woman's principle merit in the World to Come is that her sons serve God and do His will and fear Him." In this, he distinguished between the daughters, who should be God-fearing, and the sons, who should also "succeed in learning Torah." He likewise emphasized that a woman's main merit derives from her sons, who serve God and study Torah. True, these words are based upon a rabbinic homily, but had he known a reality in which women also study Torah, one may assume that in his numerous imprecations to women he would have referred to this as well. The assumption, that he did not encourage women to study Torah themselves, gains further support from his remarks concerning the ability of women to acquire merit by encouraging their husbands to study Torah:

> The modest women may save their souls and those of their husbands, when their husbands come home from their labors, and they are tired and weary and do not remember to turn some part of their effort and the thoughts of their hearts to Torah, the women should remind them to open one of the holy books and to engage in words of Torah, and not to engage in vain things.[34]

In this discussion as well, concerning the manner in which "modest" women may merit in *mitzvot*, there is not the slightest hint that they should themselves study Torah. This position of R. Jonah is surprising. He was greatly influenced by the approach and teachings of Hasidei Ashkenaz, among whom attention was specifically given, as mentioned earlier, to the study of Torah by women, at least in reference to those commandments that they are required to fulfill. Why did R. Jonah so completely ignore this, and not even mention in a hint women's involvement in study, even though he spoke extensively of women's merits and their ability to shape the life of the family as a whole? This may possibly be connected to the intense struggle against the decadent lifestyle that had taken root among the circles of Jewish courtiers in Spain. It was this struggle that drove R. Jonah to play a decisive role in the polemic against Maimonides' writings and to be one of the leaders in the struggle against philosophy. During this period, there was widespread permissiveness among the circles of the Jewish aristocracy regarding sexual life, including relations with maidservants. R. Jonah seems to have tried with all his might to educate his contemporaries to greater insistence on the modesty of women, and it may be that he associated this with their not going out to study, even for purposes related to Torah study. But this is no more than speculation.

In any event, he makes interesting use of the rabbinic homily regarding the way in which the things were said to Moses at Sinai: "'Thus shall you say to the house of Jacob and tell the sons of Israel.' 'The house of Jacob' refers to the women." R. Jonah interpreted this dictum as follows: "At the time the Torah was given, Moses our Teacher, peace upon him, was commanded to speak first to the House of Jacob, namely, the women, in order to teach them succinct chapter headings [of the laws], that they might succeed in understanding."[35] The limitation implied by his words—that is, limited words in accordance with the "limited" understanding of women—indicates that he did not ascribe great value to the intellectual talents of women, in this respect following Maimonides.

9. Education of Jewish Women in Italy and Sicily

Information concerning the education of Jewish women in Italy until the period of the Renaissance is very scarce. Nevertheless, one should take note of R. Isaiah of Trani's ruling stating that a father is permitted to teach his daughter Torah, and the activity of the scribes Paula and Miriam (mentioned above), who copied holy books, as indicating the existence of educated women in Jewish society in Italy. One may assume that they belonged to the higher class within Jewish society. The poems of Immanuel of Rome, around 1300, support this assumption. True, the author was a man, but he places in the mouths of the women who serve as the subject of his poems intense expressions of their longing for greater freedom and liberty from the domination of their husbands. Nor did Immanuel hesitate to describe women who demonstrated the heat of passion. We thus have here one of the few sources in which there is heard during this period—albeit indirectly—an echo of women's voices. Here one is no longer speaking of love as related to kindness and compassion, but of a description of love as sin, in which women bewail their bitter lot that their husbands do not satisfy them and they even await lovers to bring pleasure to their lives. As Devora Bregman has already correctly noted, "the lack of social caution in Emmanuel's love sonnets is unique. Emmanuel . . . perhaps relied upon the free atmosphere that was dominant to be felt in his day in certain Jewish circles."[36]

The desire for freedom from the dominance of husbands usually accompanies higher self awareness and a certain level of education. However, substantive proof for the quality and nature of women's education is not found in these sources. Further support for the assumption, that during the period of the Renaissance a certain improvement took place in the level of education of Jewish women and that some of them even knew how to read Hebrew, may be found in the fact that at the end of the Middle Ages there were learned women in Italian Jewish society, including some who served as teachers. It may be that they thereby continued an older tradition.[37]

In Sicily, the entire family participated in the ceremony of kissing the Torah scroll in the synagogue on Yom Kippur night and on Hoshana Rabba, similar to that which was customary in certain places in the Muslim countries. This follows from the following description by R. Obadiah of Bertinoro:

I also saw that on Yom Kippur night and on the night of Hoshana Rabba, after they con-cluded the Evening Prayer . . . the women came together with their families to bow down and to kiss the Torah scrolls . . . All night long one group came and another went.[38]

R. Obadiah portrays the Jewish women in Sicily as attached to their religion. He does not describe woman as being learned or as reciting the prayers according to the fixed order. Many of them were marked by intense religious experience and emotion. He also alludes to the influence of the Gentile environ-ment on several of their customs. It follows from his remarks that these women were not learned. Zeldes, who examined various sources pertaining to the cul-tural world of Jewish women in Sicily, arrived at the conclusion that almost all of them were uneducated: "The Sicilian documentation speaks a good deal about Jewish schools and teachers, but these always refer to young men, and there is no mention of study by girls or instruction of female teachers; unlike the Jew-ish men, whose signatures at times appear in notarized documents, there have thus far not been found any signatures of women."[39] He also cited the testimony of a Sicilian Jewish woman from 1376, who sought license to engage in medicine. Her late husband had also been a physician. The license was given after she was tested by expert doctors, but there is no testimony of her medical studies. Zeldes conjectures that she may have acquired her education as an apprentice with a noted physician, or perhaps with her husband. On the other hand, her license explicitly states that she was renowned for her talents and great experience, and therefore she was given the desired license. Zeldes also notes there that a nota-rized document from 1455 mentions a widow from Palermo who testifies of her-self that she does not know how to read or write (*ignara litterarum*), but one cannot tell to what extent this case reflects the general situation.

The picture that emerges from the description by R. Obadiah in the fifteenth century and from other sources concerning the conflict between the slight for-mal education enjoyed by Jewish women as against their intense religious devo-tion, reappears in other sources. As we shall see in the next two chapters, in the discussion of the role of Jewish women in religious life and in martyrdom, there was no correspondence between the level of education of Jewish women and the intense religious feelings that pulsed within them. Indeed, it would seem that their participation in religious ceremonies at home and in the community to a large extent shaped their spiritual and emotional world.

CHAPTER EIGHT

The Role of Women in Religious Life and in Family Ceremonies

edieval Jewish society saw the fulfillment of the *mitzvot* as the highest religious value. The community was understood as a "holy congregation," with all that implies for the public and private life. In such a society, the participation of members of the community in religious life, whether at home or in the synagogue, was of great significance. Moreover, the synagogue became the most important institution, not only for the community's religious life, but also of its social life in general, serving as it did as the meeting place of members of the community for discussion of matters of common concern. In practice, the synagogue served as that institution of the Jewish community that gave expression to Jewish existence and partial independence within the framework of its exilic existence. The active participation of women in religious life, particularly in the synagogue, would raise their image in the eyes of society and in their own eyes. On the other hand, their removal from this aspect of life would damage that image.

1. The Biblical and Talmudic Heritage

In the Bible, women did not play any official role in the functions that accompanied the holy service in the Sanctuary, the Temple, or outside them. Even the daughters of the priestly families did not participate in this service. Nevertheless, there were women prophetesses and they came to pray in the sanctuary and the temple.

The Talmudic tradition regarding this point is more complex. In the Talmud, women are frequently grouped together, in a not particularly flattering way, with "servants and minors"—that is, non-Jewish slaves and children. The most important Talmudic ruling on this subject is: "Regarding all time-bound positive commandments, women are exempt [from performing them]" (*b. Berakhot* 20b; *Qiddushin* 29a). This rule excluded women from the performance of many positive precepts, and in practice led to their exclusion from the circle of those who were obligated in many commandments that gave a special flavor to religious life, such as wearing tefillin, reciting the *Shema* morning and evening, dwelling in the Sukkah, hearing the shofar on Rosh Hashana, and many others. Another ruling, that a woman may not read the Torah due to "the dignity of the public" (*b. Megillah* 23a), removed women from a major focus of religious activity in the synagogue. One who believes in the holiness of the Torah but is not allowed to bless over it or to read it is likely to feel cut off from one of the most moving moments in the entire service.

Not only were women not obligated in the fulfillment of many *mitzvot*, but they were included in the same category as servants and minors, a fact that likewise affected their image. The relationship between this exemption and the prohibition against teaching Torah to women, discussed in the previous chapter, led some of the medieval sages to utilize negative terms vis-a-vis women (see our discussion of the image of woman; above, chapter 1). However, examination of the halakhic underpinnings of the exemption from time-linked positive commandments, and the rabbis' own testimony concerning those women who did fulfill these commandments on a voluntary basis, serves to somewhat soften their sting. Indeed, in the halakhic literature itself, the exemption of women is rooted in halakhic principles that are based upon biblical language. But the public as a whole, both men and women, were not conscious of these detailed discussions and not all of them understood that this was the reason for women's exemption. Non-observance of the *mitzvot* thus placed women, in the eyes of many, on a lower level than the man.

The central subject to be discussed here is those changes that occurred during the period under consideration in the religious life of the Jewish woman. In various points in this work, we have observed the considerable changes that occurred in the economic and social status of women, particularly in Christian Europe. The question that needs to be asked is this: To what extent did these changes, which measurably improved the status of women, also impact upon her role in religious life? We shall begin by noting the religious status of women in Christian society, due to the close relation between the situation in Jewish society and that which prevailed in the neighboring non-Jewish society. The status of the Muslim woman vis-a-vis prayer in the mosques was a limited one, and therefore one that we shall not address here.

2. The Role of Women in Religious Life in Christian Europe

The Christian woman did not fulfill any official role in the religious cult. She was not allowed to serve as a priest or preacher; all women, including nuns, were forbidden from touching the sanctified vessels or vestments or approaching the altar during worship. Women were not allowed to serve in the sacred service—whether daughters of the aristocracy or those from the cities or villages. This situation was based upon the words of Paul that women are to be subservient and silent when in church, "If there is anything they desire to know, let them ask their husbands at home. For it is shameful for a woman to speak in church."[1] The Church even gave a rationale for this suppression of women: Man was created first and only thereafter was woman created from his rib. She sinned in the Garden of Eden and was seduced by the serpent.[2] The Church fathers portrayed women as the heirs of Eve, who cooperated with Satan and caused her husband to sin. Medieval thinkers described her as subjugated by her very nature to man, because the man is blessed with greater reason and analytic power than is the woman.

During the twelfth century, a certain change took place in the Christian world in terms of the role of woman in religious life. On the one hand, the cult of Mary was greatly strengthened, and she was depicted as the holy mother who intervenes between the believer and God, serving as a conduit of Divine grace to the human race. On the other hand, there spread throughout Europe the cult of Mary Magdalene, symbolizing the sinful woman who had undergone full repentance. She too was portrayed as intervening or mediating between God and man, a function already attributed to her by Anselm of Canterbury (1033–1109).

These two women became symbols of feminine loyalty, of intense faith, of self-sacrifice and help to others—a process that also influenced the understanding of the institution of marriage.[3] The religious revival that began in Europe in the eleventh century and continued through the twelfth century swept women in its wake as well. The number of nuns increased, as did that of the Beguines— women who were influenced by the religious awakening but did not go to live in special institutions, devoting themselves to the service of God while living in group homes. Even though the nuns were described as following in the footsteps of Mary and were considered as brides of Christ, they could not receive the sacrament of ordination, nor were they allowed to serve in any sacerdotal function in the ritual conducted in the church.

During the twelfth and thirteenth centuries, the religious revival in Europe increased and greatly influenced women as well. From the twelfth century on, new monastic houses were established for both men and women as part of the activity of the new orders that were established in Europe. Many women joined these new nunneries. At the beginning of the thirteenth century, the Franciscan and Dominican orders were established, including a special order for Dominican sisters. Many women entered these monasteries out of a deep religious sentiment and in a quest for a way of life that would give them fuller emotional satisfaction. Within the monasteries, the women engaged in prayer, in work, in reading, and in copying sacred manuscripts, but the hours of the day were devoted mostly to prayer. From the thirteenth century on, the number of nuns who cared for the sick also grew. Most of those accepted to the monasteries belonged to the higher classes of society, the nobility and the high bourgeoisie—classes that had a closer connection to the Jews than did the middle or lower classes.

Particularly important for the relationship between Jewish women and their environment was the movement of the Beguines. While this movement was not part of the church establishment, it was an important religious movement, and in 1180 assumed the form of a semi-monastic order. It was set up in the framework of a movement whose members sought a religious life having significance. In this movement, more so than in the monasteries, there was room for free activity on the part of the women and for free expression of their spiritual and emotional world. Initially, the movement consisted of women from the upper classes of society, but it gradually came to encompass a wider spectrum. Many continued to live in their own homes, including women who were widows or had separated from their husbands. In 1233, Pope Gregory IX recognized the Beguine movement, but during the latter half of the thirteenth century the Church began to persecute this order. At the beginning of the fourteenth century, in 1311, it was decided to disband the Beguine orders and the persecutions became harsher. This great religious awakening of women went beyond the framework that the Church was willing to accept, hence it decided to wage intense battle against it. The monastic orders and municipal authorities were at times against them and at times tried to defend them.

An impressive phenomenon, indicative of the deep religious enthusiasm that took hold of many women in Europe at that time, was their willingness to fast, out of the belief that fasting atones for sins, purifies the soul, and brings man closer to his Creator. As the women were those who prepared food and were responsible for it, it assumed a central role in their religious world. Caroline Bynum, who devoted a special study to this subject, noted the broad scope of this practice and its religious and social significance.[4] Among the Beguines, a number of women mystics or women who were considered holy emerged . Generally speaking, Christian women played an important role in the development of religious activity during the Middle Ages, among them those who enjoyed veneration also on the part of the church leaders. Many women mystics were also active in society and did not isolate themselves and shut themselves in.

As we shall see below, there were explicit parallels in the religious life of Jewish women in Europe to a number of these phenomena. Even though we do not have evidence of any concrete and direct connection between the two groups, it is difficult to separate them from one another, taking shape as they did against the background of the prevalent cultural and spiritual atmosphere in Christian Europe.

3. The Performance of Time-Linked Positive Commandments

We do not have a clear picture of the role of Jewish women in religious life in Germany and France from the extant sources. However, various hints indicate that changes in this area already began to take place at the end of the eleventh century, and more so in the twelfth and thirteenth centuries. One of the important sources relating to this is associated with Rashi's teacher, R. Isaac Halevi, who served as head of the yeshiva in Worms during the latter half of the eleventh century:

R. Isaac Halevi also taught that one does not prevent women from reciting the blessing over lulav and sukkah . . . But if they wish to undertake the yoke of mitzvot they are permitted to do so, and one does not object . . . and since she performs mitzvot, she cannot do so without a blessing.[5]

The phrase, "one does not prevent the women from reciting the blessing" is unusual. It seems significant that the wording used is not, " . . . that women are permitted to recite the blessing," or that they must do so, but only that one does not prevent them from doing so. It may be that this language reflects a situation in which women demanded this right for themselves and began to recite the blessing. As a result, the sages deliberated this issue, and R. Isaac Halevi ruled that one does not prevent them from doing so. This was a kind of "concession" to reality, to a new norm that began to spread in those days.

The deliberations on this question on the part of sages active at the end of the eleventh and beginning of the twelfth century clearly indicate that they did not have a single early and clear-cut tradition on this question. Hence, they do not rely upon the behavior of the earlier rabbis but upon their own understanding of the relevant Talmudic discussions of the subject.[6]

From the testimony of R. Eliezer ben Nathan (Raban), who was active in Mainz during the first half of the twelfth century, it would indeed seem that it was the Ashkenazic women who took the initiative and began to recite blessings over time-bound *mitzvot*, and the sages reconciled themselves to their behavior and sought a halakhic basis for it. From the words of Rabbenu Tam, one might also say that he saw this as a custom that developed in Germany that he agreed to accept and to support.[7] This ruling was opposed to the situation in the Talmudic period and to the opinion of the Babylonian Geonim and the early Spanish authorities.

The change in Ashkenaz in the second half of the eleventh century heralded a further significant change in the twelfth century and in the first half of the thirteenth. Not only did the sages allow women to recite blessings over time-bound positive *mitzvot*, but they also granted them a more significant place in religious worship as a whole. In principle, the Ashkenazic sages could rely upon what is related in the Babylonian Talmud: namely, that the sages attempted "to pacify the women," and behaved beyond the letter of the law.[8] It was not for naught that the Tosaphists appended to these sources their own ruling permitting women to recite blessings over time-bound positive *mitzvot*. It is possible that the demand of women to assume a greater part in religious worship also may have been connected with the religious revival taking place in Europe during that period, as we have seen above. Christian women also played a role in the shaping of prayers and religious worship in the church.

From a historical viewpoint, two larger questions emerge from these sources: a) What was the number of Jewish women who sought to fulfill the *mitzvot* in question and to recite the blessing over them? Does this refer to a small number of isolated women or to a broader phenomenon? b) What was the motivation for this development in the eleventh century? It is very tempting to relate the entire phenomenon to the situation in the surrounding Christian society, in which a major religious awakening occurred during the eleventh and twelfth centuries, one that did not pass over the women, even if in smaller numbers. Indeed, there does seem to be a connection between the phenomena in the two societies and they did draw upon a common cultural atmosphere. However, in my opinion, the main factor underlying this change was the general improvement in the status of Jewish women in Ashkenaz during the period in question. The intensive involvement of women in economic and social life and the improvement in their image and in their self-image led to demands for greater participation in religious life as well. The fact that a similar phenomenon occurred in certain circles of the elite class in Christian society merely reinforced the parallel phenomenon in the Jewish world.

It seems to me that the phenomenon in Ashkenazic Jewish society was a broad and significant one and that one is not dealing here with isolated women alone. The extensive discussion of the sages concerning women's recitation of blessings suggests that one is speaking of a widespread phenomenon and not of a marginal issue. The best proof of this follows from the words of Rabbenu Tam quoted earlier. He justified his ruling that women may say the blessing over time-bound positive *mitzvot* by saying that, "they were accustomed to do so and to fulfill them." An explanation of this sort is suitable to a widespread practice that became a custom. Had this been a custom of a handful of women only, it is difficult to imagine that he would have described it as a custom from the halakhic viewpoint. The practice of isolated individuals cannot become a halakhic norm and achieve standing as a "custom." One may assume that the first to struggle for the right to say these blessings were women from the elite classes of Jewish society, who in their wake gradually brought women from other classes.

Rabbenu Tam wrote his words in the middle of the twelfth century. The custom gained further momentum after his ruling, which was also supported by his nephew, R. Yitzhak ben Samuel (ha-Ri), the leading Tosaphist during the last quarter of the twelfth century. The statement by R. Mordecai ben Hillel, at the end of the thirteenth century, that all women are required to recline at the Passover Seder, which will be discussed below, also indicates a widespread phenomenon that encompassed many women in Jewish society. There was hence no simple parallelism between the developments in Jewish society and that in Christian society. However, one must not forget the numerical differences. The Jewish population was small, and the wish of the general public to imitate the elite groups was great.

The vast majority of the Spanish sages objected, as mentioned, to allowing women to recite the blessing over time-bound positive *mitzvot*. Some of them even explained the basis for the exemption of women from these commandments on the grounds that they are preoccupied with raising children and in serving their husbands. Thus, for example, did R. David Abudarham (Spain, thirteenth century) explain it, as did R. Elijah Capsali of Candia (sixteenth century), who studied in Italy, who feared that women's voluntary assumption of these mitzvot would harm domestic harmony. The spiritual world of the woman and her religious feelings do not play any role in his considerations, which are determined exclusively by the needs of the man.

4. Women in the Synagogue

Women's Role in Prayer

In the chronicle concerning the persecutions of 1096 (i.e., the First Crusade), it is told that women were the predominant force in arousing the men to activity—a subject to be discussed at length in the next chapter. The titles given them—"pious women," "holy ones," "pure ones" (*hasidot, qedoshot, tehorot*)— are also of great significance for our discussion here. They are even described as participating in prayer in the synagogue in a fixed manner.[9] The author may have had a reliable tradition, or perhaps the stories are only the result of his imagination. But even in the latter case, a person imagines things according to the reality that is familiar to him. Nevertheless, we cannot tell whether these anecdotes reflect the actual position of women in the synagogue at the end of the eleventh century, or at the time of their writing, somewhat later.

The accounts relating to the end of the twelfth century and the beginning of the thirteenth century are more concrete. R. Eleazar of Worms relates that his wife Dulca was among those who assisted in providing supplies for the synagogue, and that she visited the synagogue frequently, taking care to arrive early for prayer and to leave the synagogue late, so as not to make her prayer appear as if it were a burden. In the heartfelt elegy he wrote after she was killed by Christian rioters, he described her as taking care to pray daily, morning and evening, and regularly attending the synagogue. She taught other women how to pray and to embellish the prayer with music. These sources use the term "women's synagogue." Does this refer to separate groups of women or to a separate prayer framework for women? There may have been different kinds of synagogues: There were those in which the women's section was built within the synagogue, as a raised gallery or separated from the men's section by some other means. But there were also those in which the women's section was not directly attached to it, but located in a separate building, adjacent to the synagogue, without any passage communicating directly between them. An additional type may have been a mixture of these two types, in which the women's section was a structure unto itself, but a small and narrow opening connected it to the men's section. The women's prayer leader stood near that small window, following the prayer of the men's cantor, and repeated the prayer aloud in a musical voice, so that the women could hear and take an active part in the prayer. Evidence for this is to be found in the laws for the prayers of Tisha b'Av in the *Kol Bo*:

And thereafter they extinguish all the lamps and the cantor begins to recite the lamentations to sadden the souls and to break the hearts. And they recite dirges there for about a quarter of the night, the men in their synagogue and the women in their synagogue. And likewise during the day the men recite dirges by themselves and the women by themselves, until about a third of the day has passed.[10]

It is difficult to interpret the term, "their synagogue," as referring to the women's section; the description of the separate reading of dirges during the day suggests that this refers to separate buildings. This conjecture may possibly be strengthened by means of remnants from synagogues in Europe. From the remnants it would seem that the women's section was not part of the main synagogue structure, but a separate, adjacent structure. In the women's synagogue in Worms, an inscription appears indicating that the structure was built in 1213 as synagogue for women, meaning that it was completed later than the men's synagogue and adjacent to it.[11]

The worship arrangements in the women's synagogue indicate that the women felt the need to express their religious feelings. Confirmation of this may be found in those women who served as cantors. Two of these, Richenza and Urania, were mentioned in the previous chapter. On the grave of Urania, who died in Worms in 1275, there appears among other things the inscription: "who sang the *piyyutim* for the women with musical voice." If this referred only to a passive listening by the women to the singing of the *piyyutim* by the men, this could have been done in the women's section of the synagogue during the prayer. However, she "sang for the women with a musical voice"; hence, they took an active part in this singing. As the halakhah as understood at that time forbade men and women singing together, this was done separately. If we might have thought that R. Eleazar of Worms was praising the singing of his wife and daughters as part of the milieu of Hasidei Ashkenaz, the inscription on Urania's grave indicates that other women did so as well. This may have been the manner of worship of all the women in Franco-Germany. The title given to Richenza in the Nürnberg memorial book, "prayer leader of the women," makes it clear that this refers to a woman who served as cantor for the women.

Sefer Ḥasidim describes the atmosphere among those women who regularly came to worship in the synagogue—not only on the Sabbath but also on week-days. One is speaking here of a comment made in passing, and hence more valid as historical testimony. A woman's leaving the synagogue to go home before the end of the service is described as a serious transgression.[12] In another pas-sage, the author describes a situation in which young women left for the syna-gogue early in the morning, before daybreak. If one wished to disseminate information that would reach the women, this was done in the synagogue. The value of women's prayer, according to Sefer Ḥasidim, is very great, and there-fore a woman who does not understand Hebrew prays in the language with which she is familiar.

At the beginning of the fifteenth century, R. Jacob Moellin (Maharil) empha-sized that all of the women, both married and single, need to be in the syna-gogue for the prayers of Rosh Hashana from beginning to end:

> They must make haste to prepare all of their needs, both jewelry and food preparation, so as to be free to go to the synagogue and be there to hear the shofar, and not trouble the public to wait for them . . . And they should all prepare themselves to be in the syn-agogue, both women and maidens, to hear the prayer and the shofar blasts from begin-ning to end, and thus are we accustomed today.[13]

The will of R. Eliezer ben Samuel ha-Levi, who was active in Mainz during the first half of the fourteenth century, preserves a testimony about women's prayer in the synagogue also on weekdays: "These are the things that I request my sons and daughters to do: they should go morning and evening to the House of Prayer, and they should be punctilious about saying Prayer and reciting the Shema."[14] The phase, "they should go morning and evening to the House of Prayer" indicates that women attended synagogue regularly on weekdays as well.

From the halakhic discussions of R. Asher ben Yehiel (Rosh), of R. Jonah of Gerona, and of other Spanish sages in Spain regarding women's prayer being recited in the vernacular and not in Hebrew, it follows that one is speaking of prayers recited in the synagogue. The permission they granted to pray in the vernacular was based upon the fact of public prayer, which was recited in Hebrew and through which the obligation of all those present in the synagogue was dis-charged. Since many women did not understand Hebrew, one may assume that, in order for their prayers to be acceptable, they made special efforts to attend public prayer in the synagogue. The statements by R. Jonah of Gerona describe a similar situation in Spain. He attached great value to the prayer of women, as follows from his explicit appeal to them in Iggeret ha-Teshuvah:

The woman should take care to pray evening, morning and noon. And at the end of her prayer she should make her main supplications on behalf of her sons and daughters, that they be God-fearing, and that her sons be successful in their study of Torah, for a woman's primary merit in the World to Come is that her sons serve God, may He be blessed, and do His will and fear Him.

The place of women in the synagogue in Sicily, as described by R. Obadiah of Bertinoro, is quite interesting. On Yom Kippur night and on Hoshana Rabba, "the women came together with their families to bow down and to kiss the Torah scrolls . . . All night long one group came and another went." R. Obadiah emphasized the women's devotion to religious ceremonies and their attempt to imitate customs that were accepted in the Gentile environment. This description fits in well with the devotion of the Jewish women in Sicily and their readiness not to abandon their religion, as their husbands often did in the generation of the expulsion from Spain. Many preferred to be cut off from their husbands and children and not to leave their faith, as we shall see in the next chapter.

In Renaissance Italy, the wives of Talmud scholars enjoyed a special status in society and within the synagogue. In certain communities, the wife of the rabbi of the community had a special place on the eastern wall of the women's section, just as the position on the eastern wall of the men's section next to the ark was considered the most honored place.

But despite the presence of many women at synagogue worship, it would seem that their involvement in liturgical activity was hampered by their lack of knowledge of Hebrew. While we cannot state the extent of the phenomenon, it appears from the sources that it was quite widespread. It may be that the majority of Jewish women were unable to understand the contents of Grace after Meals or of the prayers generally due to their ignorance of the Hebrew language. Another factor that weighed upon women's participation in synagogue worship was the increased strictness regarding the laws of menstruation, as a result of which many women did not come to the synagogue, as explained above in chapter 1.

This issue is indicative of the deep religious sensibilities of the women and their strong connection to the synagogue, on the one hand, and the injury done to their image as people who were kept away from holy things and prohibited from entering the synagogue at certain times, on the other. Yedidiah Dinari has examined these facts thoroughly and shown how folk customs led to strictures over and beyond the basic halakhic approach regarding distancing at time of menstruation, particularly in Franco-Germany. He also showed that these new strictures were introduced at the end of the twelfth century, during a period when the influence of Hasidei Ashkenaz was growing. There was a tendency to be particularly strict regarding these matters in mystical circles, among those circles that had deep roots in Hekhalot literature and in early Italy, which influenced the spiritual world of Hasidei Ashkenaz. We will not deal with this issue here, and will suffice with emphasizing the role of the women themselves in distancing themselves from the synagogue. It was largely their own "fear of the holy" that led them to be so strict in distancing themselves from holy things. Among the strictures upon which they insisted were prohibitions against the menstruant reciting blessings, praying, entering the synagogue, and touching the Torah scrolls, and according to some authorities even looking at them. While one is speaking here of ancient customs that have hoary roots in Palestinian times, the strictures observed in Ashkenaz nevertheless speak for themselves. Several of the Ashkenazic sages specifically noted the decisive role played by the women themselves in adopting these customs. We shall suffice with the words of R. Eliezer ben Joel ha-Levi(Rabyah), one of the leading sages of Germany at the end of the twelfth century: "And the women were strict with themselves, and separated themselves at the time of their menstruation, that they do not enter the synagogue and that even when they pray they did not stand in front of others."

A similar process occurred in other Jewish centers. As noted above in chapter 1 in our discussion of the image of women, most of the Babylonian sages objected to these strictures, although some traces of them already can be found in their time and place, and thereafter in Spain. They reached their height in Ashkenaz; paradoxically, the increase in the status of women and their role in religious life specifically strengthened these strictures. However, in the fifteenth century, things turned around and the women began to feel affronted by these limitations. R. Israel Isserlein permitted them to enter the synagogue on the High Holy Days, "because it saddened their spirits and sickened their hearts that all are gathered together and they must stand outside."[15]

Women contributed money for the construction of synagogues—for both their orderly running and for other charitable goals. In 1034, a synagogue was built in Worms with the contributions of Yaakov ben David and his wife Rachel. The memorial book of the community of Nürnberg mentions women who, along with their husbands, contributed to charitable purposes. These women are mentioned with their full names, including their patronym, a further indication of their status. The same book mentions other women who contributed to a variety of charitable purposes, as did various women in Spain who also gave of their own money to charitable causes.

R. Jonah of Gerona's words likewise imply that women gave money to charity. He called upon the women to appoint one among their number who would be responsible for collecting funds "to clothe the poor and to help many people." In medieval Spain, there were "mitzvah societies" that played an important role in caring for the needy. Rabbenu Jonah called upon the women to involve themselves in this activity, and did not find any contradiction between this and insistence upon modesty. Not only did he see no difficulty in women's involvement in public acts of charity, but he saw this as complementing their other good deeds. Numerous other examples may be adduced.

Woman as Godmother

Another subject indicative of the role of women in rituals conducted in the synagogue is the function of the woman as godmother (*sandaq* or, in the feminine, *sandeqa'it;* the person who holds the infant during the *Brit*) at the circumcision of her grandson or son. While the testimonies to this custom originate from the thirteenth century, it appears that one is speaking of a much older custom. R. Meir of Rothenburg attempted to abolish this practice and waged war against it with great intensity. What troubled him was not so much the fact of a woman acting as godmother per se, but that she sat in the synagogue during the course of the circumcision ceremony, adorned in her finest jewelry and perfumed while surrounded by men participating in the celebration. In his opinion, this was definitely immodest. It is difficult to imagine such a thing taking place in a synagogue in one of the Muslim countries in the Middle Ages. But Rabbenu Meir and his disciples were only partly successful in struggling against this phenomenon, a fact that bears explicit witness to the power of women and their central place in the religious life of the community and the family:

That which is done in most places, that the woman sits in the synagogue among the men, and the infant is circumcised while held in her bosom, does not seem to me at all a proper custom, even if her husband or her father or her son is the *mohel.* For it is improper for a woman to come in, elaborately adorned, among the men and in the presence of the Shekhinah.[16]

One of Rabbenu Meir's disciples stated how difficult it was to do battle with the phenomenon of "godmothers" ("and there is no one who takes heed") and it is clear that the women objected to its abolition. There is even record of a dispute between two grandmothers who fought over this privilege, and came to the rabbi to settle their quarrel, the rabbi ruling that the paternal grandmother took precedence over the maternal one (MS Bodelian 692). The custom continued to exist in some communities until the beginning of the fifteenth century. R. Jacob Moellin (Maharil) also opposed it, from which it follows that in at least some families or places there were those who continued to observe the practice.[17] There may also be some connection between this custom and the important place played by Christian women in the baptism ceremony of newly born infants.[18]

R. Meir of Rothenburg's insistent objections nevertheless made an impression, and the number of women who served as godmothers gradually decreased. As we have not found any parallel to this custom in any Jewish diasporas outside of Germany, this may also be viewed as a sign of the dramatic rise in the position of women in Ashkenaz during the twelfth and thirteenth centuries.

Unfortunately, the sources do not enable us to state when this new custom started nor how it became part of a religious ceremony. It appears to have already been practiced in the twelfth century, at the impetus of the women themselves. It is difficult to assume that the men would have abolished the earlier custom, in which a man served as *sandaq,* merely out of respect for their wives. It seems more likely that the women demanded this privilege for themselves. It is also possible that this custom originated at a time when men were often absent from their homes on account of business, as noted in several places in this book. Under such circumstances, the woman saw herself as the head of the family and asked to fill the role of the godfather, and gradually the custom spread to most of the Jewish communities in Ashkenaz. One may assume that the fact of the woman drinking the wine in the synagogue at the time of the *Brit,* and at times her functioning as godmother, also contributed to her being perceived, in both the eyes of society and in her own eyes, as a person who took part in religious activity.

MS. Montefiore 129 (fol. 66b) relates that on the night before the circumcision women gathered around the infant's crib to pray for his welfare, as a kind of charm for his health: "And the women were accustomed to be awake the entire night to guard the child." The fact that it was women who guarded the newborn infant likewise indicates their role in religious activity and their recognition by society in general. It may be that women were specifically chosen for this task due to the belief that women had greater powers to chase away evils spirits liable to harm the newborn.

Inclusion of Women in Invitation to Grace and to the Reading of the Torah

The Mishnah (Berakhot 7.2) states that women are not included in the group of three or ten people required for the Invitation to Grace (*zimmun*): "One does not recite the *zimmun* with women and slaves and minors." The Talmud does, however, cite a *baraita* stating that woman may recite the Invitation when they are by themselves, without men: "Women recite *zimmun* by themselves and slaves recite *zimmun* by themselves." The Talmud explains the prohibition against women and slaves reciting *zimmun* together as due to the fear of licentiousness. Maimonides cited this ruling, and evidently understood women's reciting *zimmun* by themselves as an obligation and not merely as an option, but added the limitation: "Women recite *zimmun* by themselves or slaves by themselves, but they do not recite it with God's Name."[19] He refers here to the invitation with ten people, in which God's Name is mentioned ("Let us bless our God of Whose bounty we have partaken"), which he did not allow women to do. He did not cite a reason for this restriction, but it should seem, as explained ad loc. in R. Joseph Caro's *Kesef Mishneh:* "Every 'thing of holiness' is not recited by less than ten, [who are] adults and free men," and a woman is not perceived as a free person because "the fear of her husband is upon her." This is an interesting example of the manner in which the woman's image influenced her halakhic status. Not surprisingly, some Ashkenazic sages did include women in the *zimmun* for ten, including the mention of the Divine Name; not all of them were prepared to define the woman as one "the fear of whose husband is upon her," whether from a social or halakhic viewpoint.

The lack of knowledge of Hebrew on the part of the majority of the women, as clearly implied by the sources, seems to have been one of the main factors in their refraining from *zimmun*. How could they recite the invitation by themselves if they were unable to read Grace After Meals or understand what is written? Indeed, there were daughters of learned people who were accustomed to reciting the *zimmun* and whose fathers concurred in this.

There may also have been sages who included women in the recitation of Grace with ten, alongside men, so that they could mention God's name in the *zimmun*. It is related of R. Simhah of Speyer, one of the outstanding Ashkenazic authorities at the end of the twelfth century, that "he would include a woman [in the quorum of ten] for *zimmun*."[20] If the use of the verb "to include" (*lezaref*) is deliberate here, and its use is similar to that in rabbinic sources, it is clear that Rabbenu Simhah included them together with the men. However, one might conceivably read this as implying that the women formed their own minyan of ten for Grace, without men. However, the simple sense of the language suggests the former view (particularly the phrase, "to include a woman" and not "women"). If R. Simhah in fact did include women in the *zimmun* with men, he presumably relied upon the reason given in the Talmud against a combined *zimmun* of women and slaves, specifically—namely, to prevent licentiousness. Such a suspicion does not exist within a family gathering. Indeed, it seems difficult to isolate this ruling from the relatively strong status of women in Ashkenaz in all areas of life. This may also have bearing upon R. Simhah's positive attitude toward women in other areas, especially his great strictness toward husbands who behaved violently toward their wives.

R. Meir of Rothenburg's ruling about women's being called to the reading of the Torah is of great significance for the discussion of the status of the woman. He ruled that, in a community where there are only *kohanim* (members of the hereditary priestly family), women may receive *aliyot* to the Torah in the synagogue, recite the blessing, and read the Torah themselves. True, he was speaking there of a rare case of a community consisting of only a few families, all of whom were from the caste of *kohanim*. However, this ruling is important in principle for the status of women, their place in the synagogue, and their self-image.

An additional change took place in the twelfth century, when women were obligated in additional mitzvot or volunteered to perform them. We shall discuss several examples.

5. Women in the Celebration of Passover

Reclining at the Seder

The obligation to eat and drink matzah and wine in a reclining posture on Passover night is one of the main features of the Seder, whose purpose is to symbolize freedom: "in the manner that kings and great people eat." The Jerusalem Talmud deliberated the question as to whether women also ought to recline. By contrast, the Babylonian Talmud rules that women are exempt from reclining on the Seder night, apart from "an important woman," who must recline.[21] The woman's exemption derives from the fact that she is subjugated to her husband, so that her reclining would in any event not indicate that she is truly free. In addition, there may have been some concern about the lack of modesty involved in sitting in reclining fashion. But the fact that the sages required an "important woman" to recline supports the former view— namely, that the exemption is related to a woman's subjugated status vis-à-vis her husband. If the reason for the prohibition were related to modesty, there would be no justification for drawing the distinction between an important woman and any other woman.

The definition of an "important woman" in the words of the medieval Jewish sages bears directly upon the historical situation in their time in various centers. The rabbis in the Muslim countries and even in Christian Spain did not devote much attention to this halakhah and hardly addressed themselves to the meaning of the expression, "an important woman." The Ashkenazic sages, by contrast, dwelt upon the meaning of this term at length.

It is difficult to assume that there is no connection between the intensive involvement with this issue of the scholars of Provence, Germany, and France and the historical reality, as opposed to the relative silence of the sages in the Muslim countries and Spain in relation to this. The reality as observed by the Talmudic commentators and *posqim* in Germany, France, and Provence led most of them to the conclusion that women must recline. They knew many women in their time and place who fulfilled important economic functions, brought with them a respectable dowry and inheritance rights, and participated in the support of their families. It was difficult to perceive them as figures subjected to "the fear of their husbands," a point that we have already noted at length in our discussion of the role of women in supporting the family. They were thus easily identified with the Talmudic concept of an "important woman."

Not only is the extensive involvement in this issue impressive, but also the decision of the rabbis. Many of the Tosaphists ruled that all of the women in their place, in Germany and France, are to be considered important women, and such was also the opinion of leading Provençal sages.[22] There can be no doubt that the socio-economic reality served as background for this ruling, and is clear testimony to the great transformation in the status of the Jewish woman in Germany and France and the important part she played in religious life.

Searching for *Hamez* on Passover Eve

The Babylonian Talmud states that women are "trustworthy" for inspecting their house for *hamez* (leaven products): "All are trustworthy for removing the *hamez*: even women, slaves, even children."[23] What is meant by the term "trustworthy" (*neamanim*)? Are women trusted to carry out the search independently, or does their trustworthiness only extend to their testimony that the men carried out the inspection? Earlier and later sages debated this question. Rashi states in his Talmudic commentary that the woman is not trusted to conduct the search, but only "to testify that her husband searched." As against this, Maimonides allowed women to search for the *hamez* herself: "All are fit for the inspection, even women, slaves and minors."[24] The uncertainty does not derive from the vagueness of the language in the Talmud alone, but also from the words of the Jerusalem Talmud on this same issue, which are important for the image of women generally. It states there, that women are relied upon, because they are "lazy" and they inspect slowly.[25]

What is the meaning of this phrase? Offhand, it seems to be a negative commentary on the women, who because of their laziness do not search thoroughly—and so it was understood by many scholars. On the other hand, other sages, such as those of Provence, interpreted the words of the Jerusalem Talmud as being in praise of the women. In their opinion, the phrase *azlanut* does not carry the connotation of laziness and lackadaisical behavior, but a positive one: The women's search is slow and thorough. Therefore, not only is it praiseworthy, but is preferable to that of the men. Thus, for example, one of the leading sages of Provence, R. Menahem Hameiri, explained that: "since they are *azelot* they examine everything—that is: they perform their task slowly and are not preoccupied with other concerns, but 'examine everything'—that is, with all their strength, very well."[26] According to Saul Lieberman, the Meiri's interpretation and that of other sages who read like him is the literal sense of the text—a thesis supported by the context in the Yerushalmi.

Many of the Provençal sages dealt with this passage, some reading it in a positive manner and others in a negative light i.e., that women are lazy about inspecting for *hamez*. However, all of them agreed that women are allowed to inspect for *hamez*. It should be added that one is not speaking here about a merely theoretical dispute. The words of the sages clearly imply that this is how the women in their locale behaved: they inspected *hamez*, just as they checked to make sure that there were no worms in the vegetables, removed veins from the meat, and the like. This is in fact implied by the words of the Ashkenazic sages: they allowed women to inspect the *hamez*, as was accepted in their place.

It is very likely that the economic reality also influenced the approach of Provençal sages and the custom of allowing women to inspect the *hamez* in Christian Europe, and evidently in Spain as well. The husbands were frequently absent from their homes for extended periods of time. Thus, just as the women took an active role in supporting the family and in educating the children, so it was natural that they would take care to the religious commandments, such as Kiddush, Havdalah, inspecting for *hamez,* and so on. The sages could prove from their experience that women in their place were not at all lazy, as they made great efforts in supporting the family and raising the children.

6. Women Circumcisers

The Talmudic sages disagreed as to whether or not a woman may perform a circumcision: Rav prohibits it and R. Johanan allows it, the halakhah being decided in accordance with the view of R. Johanan.[27]

Among the medieval posqim there were three approaches to this issue: (a) allowing a woman to circumcise; (b) allowing a woman to circumcise only post factum, in the absence of a qualified male *mohel* (circumciser); (c) disqualifying women from performing circumcision altogether. Nearly all the authorities in Germany until the thirteenth century permitted a woman to serve as *mohel.* By contrast, nearly all the Spanish sages allowed a woman to circumcise only in the absence of male *mohel.* Most of the sages in northern France and Provence allowed a woman to perform circumcision, but there were those who forbade it. The Ashkenazic sages who explicitly allowed a woman to circumcise included several of the outstanding figures of the period. In fact, until the thirteenth century, there was not a single Ashkenazic authority who prohibited it, with the exception of Rabbi Asher ben Yehiel, who was active in Spain.

Anyone examining the discussion of the Ashkenazic sages will arrive at the conclusion that this was not a purely theoretical debate, but a discussion of an actual, concrete, live issue. It is possible that some small Jewish communities did not have a qualified male *mohel,* but only a female *mohelet.* But it is also possible that the permission given women to circumcise in Ashkenaz also derived from their generally high status in various areas of life.

7. Women as Ritual Slaughterers

The Mishnah (*Hullin* 1.1) states that: "All are allowed slaughter and their slaughtering is kosher, with the exception of a deaf man, one who is mentally defective, and a minor." *Zevahim* 3.1 explicitly states that even the sacrificial offerings in the Temple may be slaughtered by a woman. The permission for women to slaughter is stated explicitly in the halakhic codes written in the Middle Ages. Maimonides emphasized that their slaughtering is acceptable even if they slaughtered "by themselves, without the presence of learned scholars, provided only that they are competent in the laws of slaughtering."

Was this observed in practice in the Middle Ages? Did women serve as ritual slaughterers for members of their family and for others? The answer is positive: Female ritual slaughterers were to be found in most of the Jewish diasporas. Thus, the Tosaphists testified that: "It is an everyday matter for us to rely upon a woman or a servant for slaughtering and removing the veins."[28] In Renaissance Italy, the phenomenon of *shohatot* (women slaughterers) was very common.

Various explanations have been offered for this. Some historians think that it related to the high status of women, to the extent that they were given a certain degree of equality. Others conjecture that this practice derived from Italian Jewish families moving to the mountains during the summer time, while the men remained in the city to work. Due to the intense heat, it was difficult to send kosher meat to the mountains out of town without spoiling, and therefore the young girls learned the laws of *shehitah* (slaughtering) and served as slaughterers for their families in their mountain vacation spots. Bonfil thinks that the main cause of this practice was the demographic structure of Italian Jewry during the Renaissance. Many Jews lived in small communities, some of which were composed of a very small number of Jewish families. Isolated families of Jewish money-lenders settled in hundreds of remote towns and villages. These families were unable to support a professional *shohet*, and therefore trained their daughters to serve as slaughterers. Bonfil also brought evidence of the granting of licenses to slaughter even to very young boys, around bar mitzvah age, for the same reason.[29]

Toward the Late Middle Ages, a certain retreat from the permission granted women to slaughter occurred. R. Jacob Landau, one of the Ashkenazic sages who was active in Italy at the end of the fifteenth century, wrote that:

Even though the opinion of the *posqim* was thus [i.e., that slaughtering by women is allowed], the custom throughout the Jewish exile is for them not to slaughter, and I never saw them slaughtering; therefore one is not to allow them to slaughter, for custom overrules halakhah, and the custom of our fathers is Torah.[30]

Similarly R. Moses Isserles wrote that: "There are those who say one is not to allow women to slaughter, as the custom has already been established that they do not slaughter, and thus the custom is that women do not do so."[31]

To summarize, the reality that emerges from the sources is that Jewish women in the High Middle Ages served as ritual slaughterers, in both Muslim countries and in Christian Europe, but that the practice was limited primarily to small communities.

8. Fast Days and Acts of Charity by Women

Of special interest are the fast days that women took upon themselves in order to atone for their sins and to strengthen the effect of their prayers. R. Meir of Rothenburg was asked about a certain woman who took upon herself to fast every Monday and Thursday until Rosh Hashanah. From the accompanying halakhic discussion, it is clear that this referred to a lengthy period that extended for nearly half a year, from after Passover until Rosh Hashanah. It was customary to hold a series of three fasts (Monday, Thursday, and the next Monday) after Pesah and after Sukkot. The justification was that, as a result of the rejoicing and hilarity that accompanied the festivals, people may have sinned, and the fast comes to atone for this. The woman in question was strict with herself and decided to continue this fast for half a year, until Rosh Hashanah.

R. Yitzhak Or Zaru'a testified that in his country, Bohemia, women were in the practice of fasting if they touched a wax candle on Shabbat.[32] Several times, in passing, *Sefer Ḥasidim* mentions various fasts that women were accustomed to perform. It follows that this was a widespread and accepted phenomenon, which did not at all surprise people. Another rabbi stated that a woman who angered her husband must fast for three days—a ruling that may have been influenced by the ubiquity of fasting among Jewish women.

This custom is of particular interest, because the practice of fasting was widely accepted in the Christian world at that time. Women took fasting upon themselves as part of a process of repentance and purification, as has been discussed in detail by Caroline Bynum.[33] There may be a relationship between these two phenomena, and the spiritual atmosphere in Germany and in France influenced both societies.

Sefer Ḥasidim describes women who engaged in charitable acts, some of whom even attained a higher level than their husbands:

One woman was charitable but had a husband who was stingy, who did not wish to buy books or to give charity. And when her time came to perform her [monthly] immersion she did not wish to do so. He asked her, Why do you not immerse yourself? She said: I will not immerse myself unless you agree to buy books and give money to charity. And he did not want to do so, and she refused to immerse until he would agree to buy books and give charity. He complained to the sage about her, who told the man: May your wife be blessed that she forced you to do a mitzvah.[34]

The books referred to here were ordered from scribes who copied them by hand, and were intended to be loaned to students who needed them, who could not buy them themselves due to their high price. Elsewhere, *Sefer Ḥasidim* tells of a woman who received money from her husband as a gift in order to buy a coat, who instead used the same money to buy books to loan out to students.[35] Whether these specific incidents actually occurred or whether they are the imagination of the author, who preferred to portray his ideas in the form of a story, they reflect the milieu that was familiar to the *hasid*. This phenomenon is common in *Sefer Ḥasidim* and, as we have already seen in the previous chapter, women in Christian society also owned books that they took care to have copied and to loan out.

In Spain, as well, the sages mentioned a situation in which women encouraged their husbands to perform *mitzvot*, as mentioned in the previous chapter. In his *Iggeret ha-Teshuvah*, R. Jonah of Gerona preached to women who worked and earned money to give to charity. He advised them to work more than usual and to give charity from the extra profit, so as not to be dependent upon their husband's agreement and not to be pressured to give money that is in practice their husband's property. Other acts of charity of women in Spain and Germany, related to contributions to the synagogue, are mentioned in the sources.

9. Refraining from Eating Meat During the Season of Mourning

Some women in Ashkenaz were strict upon themselves and were in the habit of refraining from eating meat during the period of "*Bein ha-Mezarim*," the mournful period in commemoration of the destruction of the Temple between the fast days of the seventeenth of Tammuz and the ninth of Av. This was a supererogatory stricture, because the accepted, well-established custom in Ashkenaz was to refrain from eating meat only from the beginning of the month of Av, or even only during the week in which Tisha b'Av fell. *Sefer Kol-Bo* quotes in the name of Rabbenu Asher: "And I saw cherished women who refrain from eating meat and from drinking wine from the seventeenth of Tamuz until the tenth of Av, and they say that they received the custom thus from their mothers, generation after generation . . . and there are some men who also behave thus."[36] This was a very strict custom, far beyond the usual one or the letter of the law. R. Samson of Sens testified (ca. 1200) that this custom was observed only by "the great ones of the generation." The fact that there were women who behaved thus indicates something about their self-image and place in the society. Moreover, the literal sense of what is recorded indicates that the women were more insistent about this custom than were the men.

We noted above that women in Sicily participated in the prayers and dirges of Tisha b'Av in the synagogue. Elsewhere as well, the women were involved in the acts of commemoration held on this traumatic day, but not only then. An interesting testimony is preserved in *Sefer Kol-Bo* (ibid.) concerning the involvement of women in the hopes for redemption involved in this day:

Any kind of washing for pleasurable purpose is forbidden the entire day . . . But it is ancient custom that women wash their heads from the time of the Afternoon Prayer on Tisha b'Av, and the first elders, of blessed memory, introduced this custom for a good purpose. And they based it upon what is written in the aggadah, that the Messiah was born on Tisha b'Av, and that just as we make a commemoration of the destruction and the mourning, so does one need to make a commemoration of the coming redeemer and comforter, so that they not despair of redemption. And this sign was only needed for women and those who are weak, but we all believe and are certain in the consolations that are written and repeated in the books of the prophets—but the women who are unlettered need strengthening.

10. Women as Bearers of Halakhic Traditions

Halakhic sources from Ashkenaz mention women from prominent families who performed an important task in guiding other women in fulfilling the *mitzvot*. Rashi was asked concerning a certain detail in the making of ritual fringes (*zizit*), and relies upon the account of a certain woman (Bellette) and her tradition. Other women, including Dulca, the wife of R. Eleazar of Worms, also played an active role in preparing *zizit*. He related that she participated in the preparation of various sacred ritual articles. From the Maharil's disciples we learn, that not only were there women in Ashkenaz who saw themselves as obligated to wear *zizit*, but there were those who were accustomed to wearing a *tallit qatan* under their clothing on a regular basis:

And he [Maharil] said that it is not clear to him why there are certain women who place themselves under the obligation to wear *zizit*. And they asked him, why does he not protest against the Rabbanit Bruna, who lived in his city, who always wore a *tallit qatan*. And he answered: Perhaps she will not listen to me. . . Even though I have seen women who wore four fringed corners, and today too there is one in our neighborhood, it seems to me that this is a bizarre thing, and is considered arrogance.[37]

It follows from this source that one was not speaking of only one woman, but of others as well, and specifically from the elite class of Jewish society. Maharil's fear that "Rabbanit" Bruna might not accept his admonitions indicates that he was familiar with her character and knew that this was an act that had been done after much consideration. He does not state whether Bruna and the other women recited the blessing for wearing *zizit*. In any event, this source is of importance for the self-image of women in Germany at the end of the fourteenth and beginning of the fifteenth century. R. Avigdor Kara, a thirteenth-century French sage, wrote of "some righteous women who were accustomed to wearing tefillin with a blessing and to enwrap themselves in *zizit*."[38]

At a later period as well, mention is made of women who related customs of sages from their families. These were seen as reliable precedents, and major halakhic authorities accepted them and relied upon them. Among these women one should mention Yocheved, the daughter of Rashi and the wife of R. Samuel of Ramerupt, and Hannah, the sister of Rabbenu Tam.

The woman as mistress of the house. The husband and sons are shown
standing before the mother, who is seated as head of the family upon an
elaborate chair. They speak of her merits and "praise her." Illumination for
the Book of Proverbs ("a Woman of Vallor"), near 31:28. Note the dress of the
woman and of the men. Italy, ca. 1470. MS. Rothschild 24, fol. 78b, from the collection of the Israel Museum, Jerusalem.

11. The Role of Women in Family Ceremonies

Women played a major role in family ceremonies in Ashkenaz. The only partial insistence on separation between men and women made this easier and
increased women's place in these ceremonies, particularly at the circumcision
ceremony, at the initiation of children to study Torah, at weddings, funerals,
and burials. They likewise played an active part in family ceremonies on sab-
baths and festivals.

We noted above the function of the women as *sandeqa'it* at the circumcision
ceremony in many German communities, while adorned in her best attire. The
attempts of R. Meir of Rothenburg and his disciples to combat this practice,
which were not always successful, show clearly the readiness of society to see
the woman as an inseparable part of the circumcision ceremony. This ceremony
was not exclusively "male territory." Even after the phenomenon of women serving as *sandeqa'it* had greatly declined or was not practiced at all, women continued to play an active part in the celebration of the *Brit.* Thus, they carried
the young infant to be circumcised to the entrance to the synagogue. The mother
even drank the wine upon which the blessing was said at the *Brit Milah.*

Women also had a central place in the wedding ceremony. In paintings from the fifteenth century, they are shown standing at the *huppah* (wedding canopy) during the ceremony together with the men. Detailed descriptions of weddings are extant only from sources for the late Middle Ages; however, it is difficult to imagine that great changes occurred in these ceremonies. First, because institutions and ceremonies of this type are characterized by an atmosphere of conservatism in other societies as well. Second, the detailed descriptions in the sources are from the period during which a certain decline had taken place in the status of the Jewish woman in Ashkenaz relative to her status in the High Middle Ages, including greater strictures with regard to modesty, from which one may infer that they must have played at least as great a role during the period under discussion. Third, in neighboring Christian society, women took a great role in family ceremonies. However, all this remains in the realm of speculation, and we have no hard evidence for the period in question.

In *Sefer ha-Minhagim* of Yuspa Shamash (Worms, seventeenth century), women are mentioned in various different stages of the wedding ceremony. "The men who are there go to the home of the bridegroom and wish him Mazal Tov, and if they wish they also go to the home of the bride to say Mazal Tov to her. And the bride's mother goes, accompanied by neighboring women and relatives, to the home of the bridegroom and wishes the bridegroom Mazal Tov."[39] All of the members of the community were invited to the festive ceremony on the Friday night before the wedding. However, out of modesty, the bride and her maidens did not eat in public. The married women and young girls played a more active role in the celebration that took place the next day, on the Sabbath. This celebration is described as follows:

Then the women come, led by the *Rabbanit,* wife of the head Rabbinic Judge, to the home of the bride, and the bride sits there on a special chair and they dress her in festive clothes ... and they sing songs and poems of the bridegroom and bride ... And the bride goes first with her two maidens on her right and left, and all the maidens after her, and the entertainers before them with musical instruments ... and the bride dances with her maidens and with the other maidens.[40]

The women sing and dance like the men. Even though it is hinted in several places in this detailed source that they tried to maintain certain rules of modesty, the encounter between the two sexes took place throughout the entire ceremony. It is clear that we cannot learn directly from this text regarding the situation in the High Middle Ages, but it is entirely possible that the ceremonies in early Ashkenaz were similar to those we have seen from the seventeenth century. Nevertheless, this is not real proof.

The *piyyutim* written for weddings emphasize that the wedding is an important event for the community as a whole. The national, "communal" aspect is emphasized in many *piyyutim* that were composed for the Sabbath adjacent to the wedding. All of the Sabbath prayers, in both *Shaharit* and *Musaf,* were altered for the occasion, the wedding being strongly emphasized in the accompanying liturgical poems. If great importance were not attributed to the wedding, as the creation of a new unit of Jewish existence in the Diaspora, it is difficult to imagine that leading sages from the early years of Ashkenazic Jewry would have composed *piyyutim* for this occasion. In MS. Bodleian 1103 we find testimony concerning several components of the ceremony in the synagogue (*Shabbat Hatan*), which again provides clear evidence of the great importance attached to the event by the community and the tendency toward communal cohesion that characterized its various parts. It relates there of the participation of all the members of the community in the celebration, of the changes in the order of prayers, and of the oaths and commitments that the bridegroom took upon himself, both toward his wife and toward the community.

In North Africa, the women also took an active part in the wedding ceremony. At the beginning of the eleventh century, a sage from the community of Kabbes addressed Rav Hai Gaon and told him : "It is customary in our place that, in the homes of the bridegroom and of the bride, the women play on drums and dance and bring Gentiles who play on instruments, on harp and violin and flute." Rav Hai was very surprised to hear these things, and stated that "such a thing is unseemly and forbidden, even if the women do so by themselves."[41] From his remarks we may infer that in Babylonia, under the watchful eyes of the Geonim, women were not allowed to participate in the wedding celebration with men, but in distant North Africa they did do so.

CHAPTER NINE

Women's Role in Jewish Martyrdom in Europe in the Eleventh to Thirteenth Centuries

1. The Descriptions of Women in Chronicles about the Pogroms

Jewish women occupied a distinguished place in Jewish martyrology in the various European diasporas, particularly in Germany and northern France during the eleventh through thirteenth centuries. There is no other genre in the medieval Jewish world in which women occupy such an important and central place, and are portrayed in such a sympathetic and admiring manner, as in these stories.[1] The authors of the chronicles granted them honorifics, the like of which is unknown regarding Jewish women in Muslim countries: "holy," "pure," "righteous," "pious," "daughters of kings," and the like. These chronicles describe extensively the active role played by women in death for the Sanctification of the Name and their heroic acts. According to what is told therein, the first victim of the persecutions that occurred during the First Crusade (1096) was a woman, who took her life with her own hands and served as a symbol for others. Not only did these women not object to the killing of their children by their husbands and not attempt to save them, but the authors saw in them the dominant factor that stimulated others to do the same.

The husbands are portrayed as being uncertain how to behave and how to react to the threat of conversion and murder, while the women are shown as passionately encouraging them to rise up and act. They particularly sought vengeance upon seeing the sacrilege committed by the Crusaders against the Torah scrolls:

And when the holy and pure ones, the daughters of kings, saw that the Torah scroll was ripped, they cried out in a great voice to their husbands: See, see the holy Torah, how the enemies have ripped it ... *And when the men heard the words of the holy ones,* they were filled with a great zeal for the Lord God and for His holy and precious Torah.[2]

In numerous places, the authors of the chronicles emphasize the role played by the women in the acts of slaughter for the sake of Kiddush Hashem (martyrdom). They emphasize their great devotion and willingness to die a martyr's death, to the point of cruelty to their own children, describing in great detail how the children fled and tried to hide themselves, while the mothers overcame their natural feelings and had no pity on their children:

And the woman took the lad and slaughtered him, and he was small and very pleasant . . . And when the lad Aaron saw that his brother was killed, he cried out: Mother, do not slaughter me! And he went and hid under a cabinet. . . But she pulled him by his feet from beneath the cabinet where he had hidden, and offered him up to the High and Supreme God.[3]

This woman is even described as relating to her children's blood as the blood of the sacrifices, thereby further emphasizing the aura of holiness surrounding this act and connecting it to similar motifs found in ancient literature discussing acts of martyrdom by women. It seems likely that the contemporary reader will see this as an act of cruelty, but the author's intention was totally different. He wished to show these women's great piety and rare devotion to the commandment of Kiddush Hashem, to the extent of ignoring the natural powerful feeling that beats in the heart of every mother toward her children. Their greatest fear was that the Christian rioters would kill the adult Jews, take their children, and raise them as Christians.

Young girls are likewise depicted as sacrificing their lives as martyrs and seeing themselves as being offered upon the altar. Girls asked their mothers to slaughter them after they themselves had sharpened the "slaughter knife," just as was done when offering sacrifices in the ancient Temple.

The author describes the women as having so great an abhorrence of the Christian sacraments, that they were unable to tolerate even the smells of the church. Thus, even those who had initially agreed to convert were unable to stand these odors and refused to enter the church to be baptized for Christianity. The power of this emotional abhorrence to Christian rite was very intense.

In all of the Jewish chronicles concerning the violence of 1096, the women are described as doing active battle with the Crusaders and attempting to prevent them from breaking into the places where Jews had taken shelter: "These righteous women would throw stones at their enemies through the windows and the enemies would stone them in return, and they would be hit by the stones until their flesh and faces were completely cut up into pieces."[4]

2. The Historical Reliability of the Descriptions in the Chronicles

The main question to be addressed by this discussion is that of the historical value of these chroniclers' descriptions. Did the women in fact perform the acts and say the things attributed to them? Did the twelfth-century authors of these chronicles have a tradition, whether verbal or written, that confirmed these things, or are they the product of the authors' imaginations? This is a weighty question, much debated by researchers of this period, one that is still subject to controversy. True, the authors mention numerous details, including the names of small children, but their writing must be seen as tendentious, intended to encourage others to follow this path and to imitate the acts of sacrifice. Moreover, it may easily be proven that the chronicles borrow motifs from the midrashic literature concerning the destruction of Jerusalem and the burning of the Temple, according to whose lights the authors describe what happened in Mainz at that time. This served a dual purpose: to emphasize the magnitude of the disaster that befell Ashkenazic Jewry, and to glorify the martyrs who behaved in the same way as did the young priests who offered their lives and were burned to death in the flames that consumed the Temple.

The great similarity among the various chronicles describing the pogroms of 1096, and on occasion even the similar or identical wording, indicates that the authors borrowed from an earlier source that sought to represent the martyrs of 1096 as an example for others. According to Yitzhak Baer, this earlier author wrote very close to the events. The detailed descriptions of the active part played by the women in Kiddush Hashem, repeated in these chronicles, indicates that these descriptions were taken from that same early source, supporting the assumption that they contain an historical core.

As mentioned, scholars are in disagreement concerning the historical reliability of the chronicles concerning the events of 1096. In my opinion, these doubts are even stronger with regard to the acts of the women, whose tendentious character here is very striking. The honorifics granted to the women, the comparison to the "righteous woman" of ancient legend who died with her seven children, and the allusion to the legends of the destruction in midrashic literature, all reinforce this assumption. Women enjoy an extensive role in these *aggadot*, particularly in *Midrash Eikhah Rabbati*. It is reasonable to assume that the authors were also familiar with the words praising righteous women and their virtues as martyrs of the Christian church over the course of generations. It would not be at all surprising, if these phenomenon also exerted influence upon them, in their emphasizing the virtues of Jewish women who did not fall short of their neighbors in this respect as well.[5]

In many places in these chronicles, the community of Mainz is compared to Jerusalem and Zion, at times by allusion and at times explicitly. One may thus understand why the authors had need for figures and descriptions that were widespread in the legends of the Destruction. Nor were the authors of these chronicles the first to do so. The *paytanim*, liturgical poets who lived and wrote at the time of the persecutions of 1096 or shortly thereafter, also followed this path. They compared the acts of the martyrs of 1096 to the binding of Isaac, not only in terms of the readiness of those "bound" to die for God's Name, but in terms of preserving their meritorious acts for future generations of the Jewish people. The authors compared those who died in 1096 to the Ten Martyrs of the Hadrianic persecutions, bewailing the destruction of Mainz with the same words with which Jeremiah bewailed the laying ruin of Jerusalem, often interjecting phrases from the Book of Lamentations in order to describe the magnitude of the catastrophe that had befallen the Ashkenazic communities of Germany in the events of 1096.

All these factors reinforce the doubts about the reliability of the detailed descriptions of the role played by women in the persecutions of 1096. One is almost certainly speaking of tendentious, highly exaggerated writing. It nevertheless seems likely that women did take an active part in Kiddush Hashem, whether in consenting to their husbands' actions or in slaughtering their children. This motif is repeatedly emphasized in the above-mentioned *piyyutim* written at the time or shortly thereafter. Their words seem more reliable than those of the chronicles, even though they also involve a definite tendentiousness.

Not all of the women are shown as dying as martyrs. Allusions to other kinds of behavior are also preserved in the chronicles, as in the story of the attempt to flee by one of the maidens who refused to sacrifice her life. One cannot determine for certain whether this description is the product of the author's imagination, or whether he had traditions about people who tried to escape and save themselves and were not allowed to do so. In any event, the attempt to embellish the entire event with a mantle of heroism is clear, a point to which we shall return in our discussion of the description of the beauty of the martyrs.

The great role played by women in acts of martyrdom in Ashkenaz is emphasized, not only in the chronicles concerning the persecutions of 1096, but also in the sources relating to other persecutions, both earlier and later. Thus, R. Ephraim of Bonn, in his elegy for those killed at Blois in 1171, returns to this motif. His brother, Hillel ben Yaakov, tells of seventeen women who died as martyrs in these riots. He emphasized their devotion and their prompt willingness to "sanctify the Name."

R. Eleazar of Worms, in his pathos-filled dirge upon the death in 1196 of his wife Dulca and his daughters, describes in detail not only his wife's numerous virtues, but also of her self-sacrifice to save his own life despite her injury. She left their house to cry for help, thereby drawing the attention of her two murderers and enabling her husband to lock the house and call for help.[6] From a historical viewpoint, the description of her death is reliable, even if R. Eleazar may have exaggerated his wife's praises in the elegy he wrote after her death.

To summarize, it is very difficult to determine the exact historical core in many of these descriptions. However, the very willingness to describe the women with such an aura of sanctity is very important for understanding their image and status in Jewish society.

3. The Role of Women in Jewish Martyrdom According to Christian Sources

The Christian sources relating to the death of the Jews in persecutions reinforce our assumption that a historical kernel of truth is concealed in the Jewish sources concerning the active role played by women in martyrdom. They clearly indicate that, in the eyes of Christian society, the women specifically were understood as a major factor in the refusal of Jews to convert to Christianity and in their willingness to die as martyrs. In chronicles written by Christians in Germany, the Jews are depicted as cruel people who did not even have mercy on their own children. In some of these chronicles, the slaughtering of the children is depicted as it was intended, to save the children from forced conversion to Christianity. But several of the authors saw this as further evidence of the cruelty and evil power that was latent, in their opinion, in the Jews.[7]

In these chronicles and in other sources written by Christians, the women are described as agreeing with their husbands to kill all the members of the family, including their children, while some of them killed themselves with their own hands. One account written around the year 1300, evidently by the head of the Dominican monastery in Schlettstatt, describes the persecution of the Jews in the city of Würzburg in 1298. One of the heroes of the story is a Jewish woman:

A young and beautiful Jewish woman was taken captive by her neighbors, who promised to save her if she would convert to Christianity ... "We will take care of you, [to find] a husband and property, and free you from all kinds of taxes and tariffs." And the woman replied: "Give me till tomorrow to answer you" ... The next day the woman returned and said to them with a happy countenance and a seeming note of joy: "You should know, gentlemen, that I have just slit the throats of my children" ... The hangmen took her to the place of execution and there she willingly died.[8]

Concerning other women, it is related in these same sources that they killed themselves with their own hands to sanctify the Name, so as not to fall into the hands of Christians who might to force them to convert. Thus, for example, in a source from the middle of the fifteenth century: "... among them was a Jewish woman who strangled herself with her dress ... They decided to kill themselves under the dark of night, using ropes and belts, as did the women in Mödling and in Perchtoldsdorf."[9]

While these sources are also tendentious and may not be accepted as reliable, the description of the women as heroic and stubborn was evidently derived from a known reality. It is difficult to imagine that these Christian authors had an interest to specifically describe the Jewish women as willing martyrs—but this is ultimately conjecture. Another important source is to be found in the writings of Jews who converted to Christianity, especially those of Victor von Karben, who had been a rabbi and converted in 1477, serving thereafter as a priest in the city of Köln. His wife and three children refused to join him and remained Jews. In his book, *Juden Büchlein*, he stressed the stubbornness of the

Jewish women who refused to convert and preferred to die as martyrs, while encouraging their husbands to do the same. His description is reminiscent of what is told in the chronicles about the edicts of 1096. Von Karben's remarks about Jewish women have been summarized by Havah Frankel-Goldschmidt:

Victor von Karben attributes a considerable share of the Jews' religious devotion to the women. They were often the ones to prevent their husbands from carrying out their decision, even when the latter had already decided to convert to Christianity. He explains that the women generally speaking refused to follow in the footsteps of their husbands— as happened to him as well—thereby preventing the husband from converting as well, out of love for them. There were persecutions in which Jews were confronted with the choice between baptism and death by fire; when the women saw that their husbands were hesitant, they grabbed their children and ran with them into the fire. Their husbands went after them by default . . . Von Karben connects the religious zeal of the women, paradoxically, to their inferior position among the Jews.[10]

4. The "Beauty" and "Purity" of the Women

The desire of the Jewish chroniclers to extol the martyrs from the communities of Germany and France may explain another rather interesting feature of their writing; namely, that these authors refer to the physical beauty of the martyrs, particularly that of the women. This is a widespread feature of the chronicles concerning the violence of 1096, but it appears not only there, but also in later chronicles.

On the face of it, this phenomenon is surprising. Is the external appearance of the martyrs of any importance? According to the sources, parents killed their children for Kiddush Hashem, so that they would not fall into the hands of the Christians and not be forced to abandon their religion. Is there any difference in this respect between a boy and a girl, or between beautiful children and plain-looking ones? Is this motif one deserving of emphasis in the heroic description of the devotion of the Jewish martyrs?

Evidently, here too the tendency of the authors to compare the disaster that befell the communities of Ashkenaz to the destruction of Jerusalem and the burning down of the Temple finds expression. In the Bible, and even more so in midrashic literature, the beauty of the sons of the people of Jerusalem is mentioned among their other virtues, in order to emphasize the magnitude of the disaster that befell the Jewish people.[11]

Another point worthy of attention is the lack of accusations toward the Christians of rape of the Jewish women and girls during the rioting. Such accusations do appear in the sources of the Cairo Genizah regarding Muslim soldiers and rioters in Palestine under Fatimid rule, and especially during the eleventh century. The Crusaders who attacked the German Jews are described in these chronicles in an extremely negative light and as filled with hatred toward the

Jews. Nevertheless, the authors and liturgical poets refrained from alluding to any acts of rape or affronts to the honor of the women, not even of those who were captured by them. This may have derived from the tendency, which permeates these sources, to portray the women as pious and pure. The image of the women as pious, as pure, as holy, and as giving their lives to sanctify God's name, would likely have been harmed if acts of rape and violation of their bodies had in any way been associated with them. On the other hand, the chronicles do record that the rioters stripped their victims and buried them naked. This may be an indirect allusion to abuse of their bodies, or it may be intended to say that the rioters coveted and stole their beautiful raiment. I prefer the first possibility. The plundering of their fine clothing is described in the context of fierce opposition to the rioters, and the stripping may have been an act of revenge. But it is impossible to ascertain the actual historical reality with any certainty.

5. Kiddush Hashem and the Cultural and Social Status of the Women

But even the exaggeration and tendentiousness found in the descriptions of the role of the women in acts of martyrdom in Germany and France does not refute the basic fact that the women took an active part in these events. This fact is very instructive, both regarding their ideational and mental world, and of their place in society. We cannot imagine that a woman would be capable of slaughtering her child with her own hands or allowing others to do so without being suffused with deep faith in the religious ideals shared by the community, with deep antipathy toward the Christian faith, and a deep feeling of fellowship and solidarity with all the members of the community. The identification with and sharing of the women in the ideals upon which the Ashkenaz Jewish community had been trained for generations, their behavior and reactions, clearly testify to their being part and parcel of the social fabric of the community as a whole.

This cohesion is no accident. Anyone examining the foundations of the Franco-German Jewish community and its ideals will gain the clear impression that the early Ashkenazic sages and community leaders invested great effort in strengthening the foundations of the community and its authority and in fostering the sense of unity among its members. The conversions to Christianity at the beginning of the eleventh century and the sages' serious concerns about the success of Christian agitation and the pressures exerted by the Church upon Jews to convert evidently contributed to this.

Various innuendoes preserved in the sources suggest that, at the beginning of the eleventh century, even the children of outstanding rabbis converted to Christianity, including the son of Rabbenu Gershom Meor Hagolah, one of the greatest medieval Ashkenazic sages, and possibly also the son of R. Simeon ben Isaac ben Abun, the greatest Ashkenazic *paytan* of the eleventh century.[12] The sages' intensive involvement with the question of the status of apostates shows that one is dealing with a widespread phenomenon. How is one to explain the transformation that occurred in Jewish society between the beginning of the century and its end, when even the simple people, including servants and proselytes, took an active part in Kiddush Hashem and killed themselves and their families with their own hands? The primary explanation for this is to be found in the intensive educational activity of the sages and community leaders during the course of the eleventh century, after they became cognizant of the crisis that befell their flock at the beginning of the century. From the chronicles concerning the persecutions of 1096, as well as from parallel sources, one learns that the women were also involved in this educational activity.

Further evidence of the spiritual world of women and their deep integration into the Jewish community in Ashkenaz and its values may be seen from the large number of cases in which husbands converted to Christianity and their wives refused to join them, even though they were thus left in a difficult personal situation as "chained wives." The prospect of obtaining a divorce writ from the apostate husband was not easy. At times these women were subject to a protracted period of being considered as *agunot* ("abandoned wives"), and it was not for naught that this subject occupied an important place in the responsa literature of the period.

The temptation to convert to Christianity was great. Christian religious propaganda, coupled with economic security and social pressures, bore fruit. The number of converts was quite significant, although the Jewish sources tend not to elaborate upon this phenomenon.

Various speculations may be suggested to explain the refusal of women to convert together with their husbands, but the basic picture remains: in these cases their loyalty to Judaism was greater than that to their husbands.[13] The same held true in other places—including Sicily—as follows from various sources and from the deliberations in the responsa concerning the validity of a *get* given by an apostate.

6. The Description in the Chronicles and the Public Image

It would be a serious error to assume that the exaggerations in the words of the Jewish chroniclers nullifies their historical value for exploring the status of Jewish women in Ashkenaz during the Middle Ages. Even if descriptions written in the twelfth and thirteenth centuries do not testify precisely to the actual role of women in martyrdom, and even if they do include a certain element of exaggeration, they are of great importance both for their portrayal of the public image of women in Jewish society and for the positive image of them that they convey. One may assume that the readers of these chronicles were numerous, as the subject attracted people's attention, and that they did not have the tools needed to enable them to determine the degree of reliability of the sources. The fact that they were written by some of the leading figures of Jewry, including R. Eliezer ben Nathan (Raban), the leading Ashkenazic authority during the twelfth century, and R. Ephraim of Bonn, gave them a good deal of authenticity and reliability in the popular eye. These chronicles contain detailed descriptions, including the names of fathers, mothers, sons and daughters, and specific and detailed words said by the female martyrs. All these certainly increased their trustworthiness in the eyes of their readers. They saw before them Jewish women who prodded their husbands to respond to the affront to the sancta of Judaism and to give their lives and those of their children for their faith. Their active role in Kiddush Hashem, with all the attendant details, raised their status in the eyes of society as a whole, even if this was not the authors' intention.

The chronicles' descriptions of the violence during the eleventh and twelfth centuries served the Jewish society as a tool for improving the image of the woman, similar to that served by the figure of Mary the mother of Jesus and the stories concerning her in Christian society. The quest for feminine elements on the Godhead and the role of Mary in Christian theology grew during the course of the twelfth century, among other things in wake of the religious and social reform within the Church brought about by Pope Gregory IX who, some time after his ascent to the papal throne in 1073, expanded the cult and functions of Mary in religious life. During the course of the twelfth century and later, new monastic centers were set up for women, in the framework of the religious reform that called for a return to a more "authentic and pure" Christian way of life. It seems reasonable to assume that these developments left their impression upon Jewish society as well.

Another factor that fostered the creation of a more positive image of women in Christian society—and may have to some extent influenced some of the Jewish authors—was the important role part played by women in the heretical movements of the eleventh through thirteenth centuries. A relatively large number of Christian women joined these heretical sects, which appeared in Europe from the eleventh century on. Historians still disagree regarding the complex of factors that encouraged these women to join the heretical sects, but all agree that the women enjoyed greater rights and a more respected position in the heretical movements than they did in Catholic society. They also adopted for themselves a more profound religious life than in the Catholic church. This was a weighty consideration for the large number of women joining these movements, in addition to providing a solution to their economic and personal problems. It is possible that this relative improvement in the image of the women among these circles in Christian society created a social and cultural atmosphere that encouraged the authors of the Jewish chronicles to emphasize the role of women in martyrology. But we have no real proof of this, and cannot go beyond conjecture.

An additional important fact relating to the image of women needs to be borne in mind in the present discussion—namely, that we do not find similar descriptions concerning the involvement of women in Kiddush Hashem in the Muslim countries or in Christian Spain, with the exception of a few scattered allusions to the martyrdom of women in the persecutions of 1391 in Spain, which lies outside of the framework of the present discussion. In fact, the nature of Jewish martyrdom in Muslim countries during the eleventh and twelfth centuries was rather different from what occurred in Germany and France. Many of the Jews of North Africa and Spain converted to Islam and to Christianity, at times in a temporary manner, without there developing a literary genre praising the virtues of martyrdom such as that in Germany. But even in the little that was written, the authors could have invoked the motifs of heroism and sacrifice of women had they seen fit to do so.[14] This is further testimony of the relatively good position of women in Ashkenazic Jewry society during the eleventh to thirteenth centuries. Women did take a more active and important role, specifically, in the society of Jewish conversos in Spain at the end of the Middle Ages. Hayyim Beinart noted the existence of a messianic movement headed by a woman; Renée Levine-Melammed discussed their critical role in transmitting Jewish traditions to their children.[15]

Nadia Zeldes, who investigated the behavior of Jewish women during this same time period in Sicily, when it was under the rule of the kingdom of Aragon, arrived at a similar conclusion. Her study, based upon documents from the central archive of Palermo (Archiv de Stato di Palermo), indicates that the women preferred keeping their Judaism to keeping their husbands, who converted. They frequently even gave up their children for this reason. While it is impossible to determine accurately the actual number of women who refused to convert, "there is reason to assume that their number was not negligible." The community demanded that the royal vizier force those Jews who converted to Christianity to give a divorce writ to their wives so that they not remain "chained."[16]

From an overall historical perspective, the brave stand of Jewish women in the face of persecution may be seen as testimony to the strength of their religious faith and to their inner world, while the literary portrayals of this stance written by men testify to their position in society. Clear confirmation of this view is found in the attitude of the rabbis of Ashkenaz and France to captive and apostate women. The Mishnah states that when a Jewish woman is held captive by non-Jews in order to extort money from her husband she is thereafter allowed to return to her husband, but if she was imprisoned under sentence of death, she is forbidden to him (*Ketubot* 2.9). The underlying psychological assumption is that, when a Gentile's aim is to collect ransom money for a Jewish woman he will not touch her, on the assumption that any harm caused her will affect his ability to collect money for her. On the other hand, if the woman has been condemned to death, he has no reason to restrain himself from indulging his desires and sexually violating her. Moreover, a woman in danger of her life will seek any possible means of saving her life: She will make herself attractive to her captors and voluntarily offer to have sexual relations with them so as to save her life. Such willful coitus converts the act to one of infidelity, and hence the woman becomes forbidden to her husband thereafter.

Medieval reality forced upon the rabbis a deep discussion of this issue. Persecutions, forcible and willing conversions, and the taking of women into captivity occurred in many Jewish communities. If a married woman converted to Christianity in order to save herself and thereafter returned to Judaism, and wished to return to her family, is she considered like a captive? And if her life was threatened so as to force her to convert, is she forbidden to her husband? Or is perhaps the very fact of her willingness to convert, even if only for appearance's sake and temporarily rather than dying as a martyr, in itself a harsh accusation against her?

These subjects were examined in detail by Yaakov Blidstein. The following are some of his conclusions relating to the place of Jewish women in Kiddush Hashem. The medieval Jewish sages deliberated and debated these questions and disagreed on them. However, the decisive majority of the sages of Germany and France—who dealt with these subjects more extensively than did the rabbis of other countries—tended to be lenient in the rules regarding captive and apostate women. R. Simhah of Speyer, one of the leading Ashkenazic authorities during the second half of the twelfth century, argued that the Talmudic prohibition, based upon the suspicion that the woman willingly submitted to relations with the Gentile, only applies in a case where she had no other hope of being saved—a situation that was not relevant to his time. Jewish women who fell into captivity or converted saw the disaster that had befallen them as a temporary one, and hoped somehow to come out of it whole. Hence, they may be relied upon to guard their own purity even under difficult conditions: Whereas the Talmud saw the woman's psychological state as pressing upon her until she allowed herself to have sexual relations with her captor, here the woman's psychological state was seen as strengthening her and enabling her to withstand every temptation. This clearly reflects the great respect in which the Ashkenazic sages held the character of their womenfolk.[17]

True, there were a few sages who thought differently; however, the majority followed the approach of Rabbenu Simhah. And indeed, in various cases brought before the sages, they tended towards leniency, and even forced Jews who were engaged to women who had been forced to convert and returned to their religion to marry them, even if in the interim they had become engaged to other girls.

Impressive testimony to the respect and trust in which the rabbis held their wives and daughters may be seen from a case that aroused fierce polemic in its day. An engaged maiden from the community of Würzburg in Germany was forced to convert and subsequently returned to Judaism. Her fiancé refused to marry her and took another woman instead. Almost all of the rabbis of Ashkenaz attacked him for this. One of them even described him as "unfaithful," and forced him under pain of *herem* to divorce his wife and return to his fiancée.[18]

A further indication of the positive attitude of the rabbis even toward those women who had been forced to convert may be seen from the wording used by the sages in the questions addressed to them and in their responses. They do not use harsh language toward these women, but address them with understanding, compassion, and mercy.

There is no doubt that the insistence by the Christian rulers upon law and order in the places under their rule, including punishment for rape, made it easier for the rabbis to adopt such an approach. Some of them even said as much. Thus, for example, R. Menahem Hameiri:

> It seems to me that wherever there is fear of the rulers, the woman is permitted . . . for these things were only said regarding these Gentile nations who are like brigands, making a law unto themselves. But one who is imprisoned in the compound of the courts—there is no worry. And I ruled thus in practice, and the great ones of the generation agreed with me.[19]

In brief, the great respect shown by the rabbis to their wives and daughters and their confidence that they would remain faithful to their husbands with all their strength, during this period specifically, was based upon their belief in the women's moral fiber. The above-mentioned view of R. Simhah of Speyer greatly influenced the position of other rabbis. It is difficult to assume that the rabbis themselves did not at times feel that the application of R. Simhah's approach was somewhat artificial. However, the image of their wives, as they knew them from everyday life, sustained them in time of troubles and difficulty.

7. Between the Chronicles of 1096 and Sefer Zekhirah

Susan Einbinder recently published an article about the transformations that took place in the image of the Jewish women who died as martyrs during the twelfth and thirteenth centuries, basing her analysis primarily upon a comparison between the image of women in the chronicles and *piyyutim* concerning the violence of 1096 and their image in R. Ephraim of Bonn's *Sefer Zekhirah* and in *piyyutim* that were written during the twelfth and thirteenth centuries. In this work, R. Ephraim of Bonn gathered together memories of what he had himself seen in the persecutions of Jews between the years 1146 and 1196 and what he had heard from others. Whereas in the sources relating to the persecutions of 1096 the women are seen as active and even dominant, in the later sources they are passive and the discussion of their acts is relatively slight. A

further difference relates to the locale of the events described. In 1096, the women
are shown outside of their homes, in the center of the city and in the courtyards
of the rulers, while in the twelfth and thirteenth centuries their main place is
in the home. Moreover, the tendency is no longer to depict them as actively
struggling against the Christian rioters, as initiators and leaders, but to limit
their presence in the public sphere and to emphasize their presence at home
and within the family circle. When they are outside of their homes, they are
attacked and endanger the entire community.

> The *Sefer Zekhirah* marks a real change in the use of female characters in martyrolog-
> ical pose. They no longer actively defy the Christian enemy, but are idealized for their
> passive responses to violence. They are not attacked at home but on the geographical
> fringes of the Jewish world or in the markets and courts beyond it . . . Women who ven-
> ture outside the limits of the Jewish community bring danger to themselves and to their
> communities.[20]

The women who are active in R. Ephraim's *Sefer Zekhirah* are not shown in the
context of the family, but stand on their own. As against that, in 1096 the family is in the center and the woman is active within its framework. Women's
voices are heard but little in *Sefer Zekhirah* and in the twelfth and thirteenth
century *piyyutim*.

According to Einbinder, these literary changes are not by chance but express
a decline in the status of women in Germany during the twelfth and thirteenth
centuries. The sages feared their going out in public. Even though the women
continued to play an active role in supporting their families, particularly in money-
lending, in her opinion there are other indications of a decline in their status, and
a tendency on the part of the rabbis to restrict women's role in society and to place
the home in the center. These literary changes indicate the dangers that awaited
the Jewish woman outside of her home. Whereas in 1096 the main danger was
from acts of violence, during the course of the twelfth and thirteenth centuries
the main danger was from persecution of the Jewish community and limitations
placed on them by legislation of the Church and the ruling authorities. In light
of these pressures, it was preferable to emphasize the place of the woman in the
family and the importance of the religious framework.

Her presentation of the problem is solid and the discussion is conducted
within a broad historical perspective. However, I question the solution offered
by Einbinder. Every author has his own style: R. Ephraim of Bonn was not graced
with the same desire to impress the reader that characterized the author of the
source from which the authors of the chronicles of 1096 drew their material. The
world of the *men* in *Sefer Zekhirah* is also quite limited and is not at all comparable to that of the chronicles mentioned. We search there in vain for the dec-
larations and admonitions placed in the mouths of the martyrs of 1096, or for
their initiatives. R. Ephraim usually sufficed with a brief description of the main

incidents, very different from the detailed and dramatic description found in the chronicles of 1096. The clearly didactic tendency that emerges from these same chronicles is also far weaker in R. Ephraim. And we must not forget that many of the authors of *piyyutim* on the events of 1096 also borrowed from these chronicles, just as the later authors of *piyyutim* took from R. Ephraim.

It is difficult to assume such a far-reaching sociological transformation on the basis of the writing of one man and of a handful of *piyyutim*. For this, we need to examine the approaches of additional sages. I do not wish to reject the question asked by Einbinder per se, but only to soften its force somewhat. The solution proposed by her seems to me more problematic. Only one or two generations separate R. Ephraim from the time of writing of the chronicles. It is difficult to assume that such a significant social change, leading to a major change in the attitude toward women, occurred in such a short period of time.

The main difficulty in her proposed solution lies in the fact that other, numerous and varied sources indicate that throughout the twelfth and the first half of the thirteenth century (and perhaps even later) Jewish women continued to be very dominant in society. One is not speaking here only of their involvement in money-lending in their own homes, but also of involvement in commerce that required travel and at times staying outside of their homes, as we have already noted in our discussion above, in chapter 5. From the sources brought there it follows that not only were the sages aware of the women's extensive activity outside of their homes, but that *they did not attempt to stop them*.

The attempts of Rabbenu Tam and other sages to take steps against the "rebellious" woman do not indicate a decline in her status, as suggested by Einbinder, but actually indicate a significant increase in her power and fear of an increase in the number of "rebellious wives." We shall see below, in chapter 11, how numerous these "rebellious" wives were in the thirteenth century. If there was indeed a change in relation to the women's martyrdom and a change in their image in *Sefer Zekhirah* and in the *piyyutim*, it seems to me that this may be attributed, not to the women's weakness, but specifically to their increased power, a fact for which we have brought abundant evidence in this book. It is possible that certain sages preferred not to celebrate and praise them excessively and refrained from describing women as playing an active and leading role in martyrdom, out of fear that they might "raise themselves up" over their husbands even more. During the second half of the thirteenth century, some sages complained that the women "lord it" over their husbands, that they were "arrogant" and the like, as we shall discuss below in chapter 11. However, as mentioned, the extant sources are insufficient to indicate a definite change in relation to the Kiddush Hashem of women in the twelfth and thirteenth centuries.

CHAPTER TEN

Violence Toward Women

H usbands' violence toward their wives is discussed in both the Genizah sources and in the halakhic literature, suggesting that the practice was a common one, which weighed upon the institution of marriage. The sources indicate that it existed in various circles within society, and not only in the lowest ones.[1] While the sages waged battle against it, they were only partially successful. We shall begin by examining the Talmudic tradition regarding this issue and the situation in the neighboring non-Jewish society, which greatly influenced the situation in medieval Jewish society.

1. *The Talmudic Tradition*

The Bible nowhere refers specifically to the case of a person who treated his wife violently. Even in the Talmud, an explicit discussion of this issue is absent. However, the *Tosefta* does state that if a person beat his wife, the court may confiscate a portion of his property to buy with it land, which then becomes the wife's personal property; nevertheless, the husband is permitted to enjoy the income derived from it ("and he eats its fruit").[2] This was a serious monetary penalty, one allowing the purchase of a plot of land. The fact that the husband is allowed to enjoy its income does not detract from the fact that a large monetary penalty was imposed upon him. Thus, the ruling indicates that wife-beating was perceived by the sages as a criminal act. Maimonides summarized the law regarding a husband who beat his wife as follows:

A husband who struck his wife is required to immediately pay her damages and [compensation for] the shame and the pain, and it all belongs to her, and the husband has no share in their fruits [i.e. income]. And if she wished to give the money to another person she may do so: thus ruled the Geonim. And the husband must heal her just as he heals all her illnesses.[3]

From the words, "and the husband has no share in their fruits, and if she wished to give the money to another person she may do so," we see that the Geonim were stricter regarding the case of a husband who hit his wife than was the *Tosefta*. The fact that the Talmud itself does not explicitly take up this issue, evidently indicates that its approach was that there was no distinction between a wife-beater and any other person who acts violently toward his fellow man.

The medieval Jewish sages relied upon another Talmudic source as well, from which they inferred that a husband who behaved violently toward his wife is required to compensate her. This source speaks of a husband who causes harm to his wife during the course of sexual relations, bringing an opinion that he is to be held accountable, from which the medieval sages drew an analogy to the case of a violent husband as well. If a husband who unintentionally harmed his wife during intimate relations is held responsible for damages to her, all the more so one who deliberately struck her and without her consent.[4] The medieval Jewish sages accepted in principle the view that the husband has no right to beat his wife, and that if he did so he is deserving of punishment. In principle, they deliberated three questions relating to this issue: (a) What is the punishment to be imposed upon the violent husband? (b) Is a husband permitted to hit his wife so as to force her to perform those household duties that she is required to do according to halakhah, or in order to educate her when her behavior is "improper"? (c) Is a husband's beating of his wife valid grounds for divorce, even against the husband's will? And what means may be used to force him to do so?

The rabbis held a variety of opinions on all these questions, and as a rule those in Christian Europe were stricter with the violent husband than they had been previously. Their discussions enable one to uncover, not only the underlying "theory" (i.e., attitude to wife-beating), but also between the lines to discern the social reality—and at times there was a considerable distance between the two.

2. The Situation in Christian and Muslim Society

Medieval people—whether Christians, Muslims, or Jews—considered the wife as subjugated to her husband and "under his hand." Feudal society in Europe was based upon the view that in principle there is no natural equality among human beings. Society was composed of classes, in which the lower class was subjected to that above it. At the top of the hierarchy stands the ruler, below him the nobility who are subject to him, and beneath them the lower classes. Those who belonged to the lower classes were subject to the domination of those who stood in a higher position within the social hierarchy, and were understood as being "beneath his staff" (*sub virga sui*). The resort to this sort of terminology (staff, rod) indicates that the right of the person enjoying a higher position to strike the one beneath him was understood in the Middle Ages as a justified and accepted one. This picture was duplicated in the Muslim world. In both societies, the woman was understood as inferior and as being under the rule of her husband, as we have already noted in the first chapter.

This approach exists in the teachings of the medieval Jewish sages as well. Even Hasidei Ashkenaz, who were generally sensitive to issues of equality between human beings and even among living creatures in general, saw the woman as subject to the rule and authority of her husband, as "given into his hand," and as his "servant." As noted in the discussion of the image of the woman (above, chapter 1), many Jewish sages thought that the verse "and he shall rule over you" implies the husband's right to impose his rule over his wife. There were even those who thought that he is obligated to do so, using terminology such as "slave" and "handmaiden" to explain this. Another important factor that needs to be taken into consideration in this discussion is the profound belief of medieval people that beating is an educational technique, whose use is both appropriate and necessary. The biblical statement that "he who spares the rod hates his son" was taken literally, as implying the obligation of parents and teachers to use blows as an educational tool.[5] We shall suffice with one illustration to indicate how widespread was the acceptance of this approach: In one of the letters preserved in the Cairo Genizah, a teacher apologized for not hitting sufficiently a problematic student because of his special situation, even though he knows that he ought to do so. He even advises the relatives of this student to threaten him with additional blows.

Christian Europe recognized the husband's right to hit his wife so as to educate her and to force her to accept his authority. The charters of various cities even granted him explicit permission to do so:

In the legal code of Aardenburg in Flanders in the fourteenth century it is stipulated that the husband may beat his wife, injure her, slash her body from head to foot and "warm his feet in her blood." If he succeeds in nursing her back to health afterwards he will not have transgressed against the law. The right of a husband to beat his wife "within limits" was generally recognized.[6]

While some churchmen and thinkers admonished husbands not to beat their wives more than the accepted degree, in practice the beating of wives by their husbands was an accepted social norm in Europe. Jewish sages were well aware of this reality and of its influence upon Jewish society. R. Meir of Rothenburg, who was a vigorous and outspoken opponent of violence toward women, commented in two separate responsa that "such is the way of the Gentiles." Nevertheless, there can be no doubt that the norm accepted in Christian Europe left its mark upon European Jewish society as well.

In Islam, too, it was accepted that the husband was allowed to beat his wife if she did not behave modestly or fulfill her duties toward him. It is stated in the Quran that the husband is allowed to beat his wife if she does not behave with the requisite modesty.[7] Not only is the husband allowed to strike his wife when it seems to him that she does not behave with the proper obsequiousness and modesty, but it even advised doing so under special circumstances, so as to train the woman and return her to the right path. But alongside this permission, the Quran also calls upon the husband not to misuse this license and to seek pretexts for hitting his wife unjustifiably when she has done no wrong and after she has already set right her ways. However, violent husbands could misuse this clause, claiming that the woman's behavior was improper, particularly in light of the strictness of Orthodox Islam concerning issues of modesty. It was for good reason that this was accompanied by a warning that God is supreme and great and examines the hearts. There is no doubt that the reality in Muslim society exerted a negative influence upon violent husbands in the neighboring Jewish society, and to a certain extent may have also left its mark upon the attitude toward wife-beating of Jewish sages in Muslim countries. According to S. D. Goitein, even so outstanding a sage as Maimonides was influenced by this.[8]

3. The Position of the Babylonian Geonim

The attitude toward wife-beating of Jewish sages everywhere, particularly in the Muslim countries, was greatly influenced by the position on this question of the Babylonian Geonim. These Geonim were active for a period of nearly five hundred years (seventh to twelfth centuries), and did not have a uniform stand on the issue of violence toward women. One can distinguish various outlooks in their extant responsa, even though in principle all of them denied the husband's right to beat his wife, except for those cases in which she refused to perform those household duties that were incumbent upon her, in which case the husband or the court were allowed to exert force. The exception to this was the ruling of one Babylonian sage, who called upon the woman to accept the beatings of her husband with understanding and silence:

And women are required to honor their husbands . . . And she is not permitted to raise her voice to him, and even if he strikes her she should be silent in the manner of modest women.[9]

This ruling is unprecedented in the teachings of any other medieval Jewish sage. It is extraordinary, not only in terms of the issue of violence toward women, but also in other statements found in the same document, such as the requirement for the wife to stand when her husband enters the house, as if he were a ruler or a king, and to feed him with her own hands, as one would a small child. These things seem to reflect the influence of the norms of Muslim society. Another sign of this is to be found in the identification of the woman's submissive behavior with modesty, similar to that found in Muslim sources from this period, despite the fact that there is no substantive connection between the demands made upon the woman in this source and modesty.

From whom did these statements originate? The manuscript in which they appear is described as part of a work attributed to Rav Yehudai Gaon, who was active during the middle of the eighth-century and was considered one of the greatest of the Babylonian Geonim. If this identification is correct, one could imagine that these rulings would exert a significant and harmful impact upon the status of the Jewish woman in her home, including issues of violence. Not only was Rav Yehudai considered one of the greatest sages of the Geonic age in Babylonia, but he also left a number of important disciples. However, this attribution is extremely doubtful. As mentioned, Rav Yehudai's ruling left a deep influence on his disciples and on their successors. How, then, can we explain that there is no trace of these directives in the teachings of subsequent generations, but were completely ignored by them? We do know that, because of his great renown, some medieval sages were in the habit of attributing various anonymous sources from the Geonic period to Rav Yehudai Gaon. Moreover, because he was blind, his disciples sometimes incorporated their own teaching within the teachings they transmitted in his name. All these factors raise serious doubt as to whether these words are in fact his. It seems more likely that this Babylonian source belongs to the non-normative halakhic literature that flourished in the Muslim countries during the ninth century, various remnants of which survive, that differ from accepted halakhah and custom. One important fact is deserving of mention: We have not found the slightest trace in any other Jewish source from the Middle Ages of the admonition to the woman to be completely subservient to her husband, such as is found in this source. True, Maimonides also called upon the woman to treat her husband as a king, but in his case the sense and context of the things is entirely different, as he likewise required the husband to behave toward his wife with the greatest respect, something of which there is no hint in the present source. He was told "not to impose upon her great fear, and that his speech with her be gentle, and that he not be impatient or angry."[10]

The Babylonian Geonim ruled that, if a husband strikes his wife, a monetary fine is to be imposed upon him in accordance with his economic status and the severity of his action, particularly when one is not speaking of a one-time occurrence. However, they disagreed among themselves as to whether the violent husband may be forced to give his wife a divorce.[11]

On the other hand, Rav Paltoi (Gaon of Pumbedita, 842–857) allowed the Court to coerce the violent husband to divorce his wife.[12] The permission to force a divorce is significant, not only in terms of the punishment imposed upon the violent husband, but also as indicative of the frequency of the phenomenon in the Jewish family. If the wife has the power to force her husband to grant her a divorce, including appropriate financial compensation, then the husband would be reluctant to treat her with violence. Such a punishment would greatly reduce such occurrences, especially as divorce in Jewish society was fairly common, and there was thus no fear of creating a social stigma for the divorcée that would deter her from threatening her violent husband, nor from carrying out this threat.

The considerable hesitation of the Babylonian Geonim regarding this issue derived from their fear lest the children of the divorcée from any second marriage would be considered illegitimate. This was so because, according to some rabbinic opinions, any divorce given under compulsion was considered invalid, hence any subsequent marriage was considered outright adultery. The Sephardic sages also deliberated concerning this question. On the other hand, there were those sages in Christian Europe, particularly in Germany, who explicitly advocated imposing a divorce upon the wife-beater with every possible means.

A question addressed to Rav Hananiah (Gaon of Pumbedita from 938–943) tells of a husband who argued with his wife "and grabbed her hair, and some of her hair came out in his hand."[13] He stated that, in principle, the husband is required to pay the fine fixed by the Talmud for any person who commits an act of this type, especially as it was done to his own wife: four hundred *zuz*. However, in Babylonia they did not impose monetary fines, for reasons explained in the Talmud, and hence he ruled that this sum was to be added to the amount he was obligated to pay in his wife's *ketubah*.

In another responsum of a Babylonian Gaon, such an arrangement was also proposed as a compensation. When a woman caused bodily harm to her husband, the sum of her *ketubah* was reduced, whereas if he harmed her he was punished. However, this act was not viewed with the same severity as that of a stranger beating the woman, as the husband has "proprietorship" over his wife:

But if others harmed his wife, their punishment is more severe than that of a husband who harmed his wife, for the latter has proprietorship over her, while another person has no proprietorship over her. Therefore, the court places him under the ban (*nidui*) until he makes peace with her and her husband, for one cannot compare one who harms an unmarried woman with one that harms a married woman.[14]

We shall see below that, in contrast with this ruling, the sages in Ashkenaz were stricter with a husband who hit his wife than they were with a stranger who hit her.

Another ruling that severely hurt the woman and provided violent husbands with an excuse to justify their acts, originated in a ruling accepted by at least some of the Babylonian Geonim—namely, that the husband was permitted to beat his wife (or to ask the court to beat her) if she refused to perform the domestic tasks that she is required to do by law. These tasks are listed in *Mishnah Ketubot*, but there is no indication there that the wife's refusal to perform them justifies beating her so as to change her mind. This ruling might provide a violent husband with justification for hitting his wife, based on the argument that she was unwilling to perform all the labors that she was required to do, and there were not always people in the house to testify that the husband was lying. Some of the Spanish sages accepted this ruling, as we shall discuss below, which may have been a tradition they received from the Babylonian Geonim. Even if the intention was that the court, and not the husband, was to administer physical coercion, there still remains a certain opening that weighed down upon the wife and which could be misused by a violent husband.

4. The Position of the Spanish Sages

R. Joseph ibn Avitur, one of the prominent sages in Spain at the end of the tenth and beginning of the eleventh century, discusses the question of a husband's violence toward his wife, taking a kind of intermediate position. On the one hand, he ruled that wife-beating is a valid ground for divorce and that one may even force the husband to give her the *get* against his own will; on the other hand, he restricted this to cases in which the husband beat his wife more than once, and the court and elders of the community had warned him in advance not to repeat the acts of violence against his wife. Only in a case where he ignored this warning and continued to hit his wife may one impose divorce upon him.[15]

These words express a recognition in principle of the right of the beaten wife to force her husband to divorce her, but the two conditions he imposed—the need for warning, and for the testimony of a reliable witness—might in practice hamper the realization of this right. It seems likely that the husband would refrain from acts of violence or threats while a "reliable" witness was present in the couple's home.

R. Samuel Ha-Naggid, who lived and was active during the first half of the eleventh century, in several places in his book *Ben Mishlei* deals with the issue of wife-beating. He refers harshly to a domineering wife and advises the husband to beat her in order to educate her. In his opinion, the woman needs to be submissive and to accept the authority of her husband. The husband was viewed as a kind of father whose obligation was to educate not only his children, but also his wife. Ha-Naggid portrays as the ideal wife one who accepts the chastisements of her husband with love and humility. By contrast, the woman who is argumentative and unwilling to accept the authority of her husband and to submit to his will is the explicit example of the bad wife—and there is nothing worse to a man than a bad wife.

True, it is difficult to rely upon metaphors used in a poem, which are not necessarily meant to be taken literally. However, the fact that Ha-Naggid repeats this motif several other times in his work supports the assumption that they express his world view and are not merely flowery language. Moreover, it is reasonable to assume that his words do not reflect his private view alone, but also a widespread mood among the circles of Jewish courtiers in Muslim Spain in his day. This circle, as is known, was greatly influenced in its culture and way of life by the environment of the Muslim courtiers.

Whether we interpret Ha-Naggid's words literally or take them merely as literary hyperbole, one may assume that they were displeasing to the Jewish women in Spain. Samuel Ha-Naggid was among the most highly admired figures in Spanish Jewry in his day and in the subsequent generations. Hence, his words in praise of the submissive woman and in support of the husband's right to beat a domineering wife could be understood literally, at least by some of his readers.

5. Maimonides' Position

Maimonides' opinion on this issue is of great importance. As we noted above, he ruled that a monetary fine is imposed upon a violent husband, from which he cannot derive any material benefit. In this respect, Maimonides followed the ruling of the Geonim, which was stricter than the tannaitic approach, according to which the husband is entitled to enjoy the income accruing from money that he had paid as penalty to his wife. While he attributed this stricture to the Geonim, the fact that in this case he nevertheless accepted their opinion indicates that this strict view was in fact acceptable to him. It is doubtful whether he would have been so strict in the case of beating that did not involve bodily harm, but it is difficult to state this with certainty. The verb *habal* (used by Maimonides in presenting this rule) is used in the Talmud and by medieval sages both in the sense of ordinary hitting and in that of beating that involves real bodily harm. Maimonides does not treat specifically the question of the woman's right to force her husband to divorce because of his violence toward her. Seeing as how he did not mention it, it would seem reasonable to assume that he did not acknowledge such a right. On the other hand, he did recognize the right of the woman to force her husband to give a divorce in a case where she found him repugnant (see below, chapter 11). Violence on the part of the husband could certainly arouse feelings of revulsion on her part.

Maimonides' most significant ruling on this issue concerns the recognition of the right of the court—and possibly of the husband—to beat his wife so as to force her to carry out those household tasks that the sages required her to do according to halakhah: "Every woman who refuses to perform one of the labors that she is required to do, may be coerced to do so, even with a whip."[16] The Mishnah enumerates the labors that a woman is required to do in her home:

These are the labors that a woman does for her husband: she mills, and bakes, and laun-
ders; cooks, and nurses her child; makes the bed, and weaves wool.[17]

Who is the subject of the permission to beat the wife so as to force her to perform household labors—the husband or the court? Opinions differ on this
point. Some interpreted Maimonides' words as saying that permission is granted
to the husband. However, most of those who dealt with his words interpreted
them to mean that the husband brings her to the court and that the court orders
her to be beaten until she agrees to perform the labors mentioned. The difference between the two views is very significant. If the woman is brought to the
court, she has the opportunity to present her own arguments, an investigation is conducted, the court requires witnesses, and only thereafter does it
give its ruling. Moreover, the wife has the opportunity to state that she foregoes
the right to be supported from her husband's property, in which case she is
exempt from doing any labors. Another possibility is that she may claim that
her husband is "repugnant" to her and she no longer wishes to live in his
company. In such a case the laws of *moredet* (the "rebellious wife") are applicable, and she is entitled to receive a divorce, but loses all her financial rights.

On the other hand, if the right to beat his wife is granted to the husband, she
is entirely subject to his arbitrary whim. A violent husband could justify the
harm done to his wife by claiming that she refused to carry out one of the labors
incumbent upon her, and the wife would find it difficult to defend herself or to
prove that what he says is false unless she could find witnesses to support her
claims. Maimonides was aware of this problem, and further on writes: "If he
claims that she did not do [the labors], and she says that she does not refrain
from doing them, one places a woman among them or neighbors. And this,
according to what seems reasonable to the judge." However, this too does not
entirely close the opening given here to the violent husband.

The use here of the phrase *kofin,* in the plural (i.e., "they force" and not "one
forces"), leads one to the conclusion that it was the court and not the husband that coerces the wife, but one cannot state this definitely. In any event,
R. Menahem Hameiri, one of the greatest Provençal sages, understood Maimonides' intention as to say that the husband himself beats his wife.

Concerning this ruling by Maimonides, R. Abraham ben David (Rabad) of
Posquières wrote: "I never heard of beating women with a whip."[18] The word
"never" means that Rabad, in his own locale, did not know of any halakhic tradition or legal precedent recognizing the right to beat a wife for refusal to
perform her duties. It is clear that he did not mean to say that one may not beat
a woman under no circumstance, for according to Jewish law a woman is subject to judicial punishment just like a man, including corporal punishment.
Hence, one cannot interpret Rabad's words as completely refuting any possibility of women being beaten, even by the court. Rather, he meant to say that

he never heard that a husband has the right to hit his wife, as in Maimonides' view (as understood by several sages), or that the court may order her beaten for refusal to perform her household tasks.

What was the motivation for this strict ruling of Maimonides? He did not make any comment about this. According to Goitein, Maimonides was influenced by the severe concern that a woman who sits idle will ultimately come to licentiousness, and that hence one may use any means, including violence, to force her to work. The fear of the woman sitting idle is already mentioned in the Mishnah. In his code *Mishneh Torah*, Maimonides gave serious weight to this consideration:

Even if she was very wealthy, and even if she had several handmaidens, she does not sit idle without work, for idleness leads to licentiousness.[19]

Maimonides was clearly very concerned about the woman sitting around with nothing to do; nevertheless, it is doubtful whether this was in fact what guided him in the above-mentioned ruling. Were this the case, he would have written explicitly that the woman is required to perform at least one of the labors enumerated so that she not be idle. This is in fact stated regarding a wealthy woman, as Maimonides mentions in his words. On the other hand, here he used the plural ("any one of the labors which she is required to do"), from which it follows that she is required to do all the labors, and if she refuses to do so he may force her "with a whip."

There may be those who would attempt to connect this ruling to Maimonides' contemptuous attitude toward women's intellectual abilities that is sometimes found in his writings, but such a view is difficult to accept. With regard to various subjects, one finds in his writing great consideration of the needs of the woman. Among other things, he allowed a woman who is considered a *katlanit* (a "murderous" wife, two of whose husbands had died—see below, chapter 12) to marry by means of a subterfuge, against Talmudic law, and he also stated that the rule of *moredet* is not imposed upon a woman who refuses to have relations with her husband because she finds him disgusting. It seems more likely that in this case Maimonides was influenced by the above-mentioned tradition of the Babylonian Geonim, that one may force the woman to perform all of the household tasks. One also needs to take into consideration the atmosphere in the surrounding Muslim society that, as mentioned, allowed the husband to beat his wife for "educational purposes."

One of the questions addressed to Maimonides refers to a woman whose husband beat her extensively so as to make her forego the financial rights to which she was entitled upon her divorce, and she was forced to agree to this because of his violence: "Reuben married Rachel and was with her for five years, and he pursued her and hurt her and beat her and insulted her."[20] Maimonides sufficed with a very brief responsum, only three lines long. He did not express shock at the case itself, nor did he admonish the husband for his violence, as did Rashi, R. Simhah of Speyer, R. Meir of Rothenburg, and other sages in Christian Europe who were asked about analogous cases. However, one cannot infer anything from this about Maimonides' attitude toward wife-beating, as he was in the habit of being laconic in his responsa, which he limited to the halakhic aspect alone.

Maimonides' ruling—namely, that under certain special circumstances it is permitted to beat one's wife—or the tradition of the Babylonian Geonim, left their mark upon the rulings of the sages in Christian Spain, including R. Ibn Adret (Rashba), who led the Barcelona community during the second half of the thirteenth century and who had great influence not only in Spain but also beyond it. From several of his statements it appears that, under certain circumstances, he did not demand the punishment of the wife-beater. Thus:

Rachel, Shimon's wife, left her husband's home because of quarrels and argument, that he constantly beat her . . . and cursed her parents in her presence and always told her in her presence that he would divorce her. And Shimon demanded that she return to his home, and she said . . . and do not hit me or insult me for no reason from now on, having done no wrong, and then I shall return to you.

Answer: That which Rachel demanded, that he not hit her nor insult her from now on, and if not then she will not return to him, the law is with her. For the more he beats her, which is not in accordance with the way of [treating] decent women who have done no wrong, as she argues, it is well known that she is not judged according to the law of *moredet* . . . For this is not "rebellion," but she is fleeing from his blows.[21]

While in this case Rashba supported the wife's claim, his statement that the husband beat her "having done no wrong," indirectly supports the argument that, if she had behaved wrongly, then the law would be different. We find support for this assumption in another of his responsum:

A husband who beats his wife every day until she needs to leave his home and to go to her father's home, tell me what is the law. Response: The husband may not beat his wife. . . . On the contrary, he must honor her more than his own body. And the Court asks and inquires who is responsible. And if he beat her and caused her pain unlawfully, and she fled, the law is with her, for a person cannot dwell with a serpent in one basket . . . And if she was responsible, in that she curses him for naught, the law is with him, for one who curses her husband in his presence goes out without *ketubah* money.[22]

Rashba was opposed to the husband's violence, but added that "if she was responsible, in that she curses him for naught, the law is with him." That is, one does not punish a husband who hit his wife under special circumstances, "for educational purposes." He was nevertheless aware of the danger in this ruling, as a violent husband can always explain away his actions as being in reaction to the inappropriate behavior of his wife. Therefore, he stated further on that:

And it seems correct to me, that if it is known that he beat her, which is not the way [to treat] proper Jewish women—that is, that he constantly beats her—then he is not believed when he claims that she caused it, by cursing him in his presence.

His "persistence" in beating his wife indicates that he is looking for an excuse for his behavior.

Rashba ruled in accordance with an early Sephardic tradition that originated among the Babylonian Geonim, namely, that only in the event of long-standing, continued violence, and only after a warning from the court, is the husband forced to grant a divorce.

To complete our picture of violence against women in the Oriental countries, let us briefly examine the situation in Egypt. The above-mentioned ruling of Maimonides regarding the right of the husband to force (whether himself or by means of the court) the woman to perform those household labors that she is required to perform by law, left its mark in Egypt, the main site of Maimonides' activity. Only a few extant documents in the Cairo Genizah sources deal with complaints of women about their husband's violence toward them. As already noted by S. D. Goitein, in these sources the complaint generally speaking was not about the act of hitting alone, as in such a case the things would not have been brought before Maimonides and the other judges. Rather, other complaints were involved in the center of the discussion; beating was only brought as an additional element in clarifying the complaint.[23]

This is very important from a methodological viewpoint. The fact that in most of these complaints the issue of violence was not the central subject but was additional to other disputes between partners, indicates that beatings were more common than in the few complaints extant in the documentation, but that by themselves they were not a sufficient reason for the woman's complaint. It may be that some of the women, who were used to this behavior from their Muslim environment, did not perceive beating as an act that affected their honor, and were therefore reconciled to it.

Violence toward women was particularly common among the lower classes. Economic pressure augmented the emotional tension and conflicts between the couple. In this miserable reality, the woman paid the price of her husband's frustration. But, as is the case in modern society as well, violence did not pass by the higher socio-economic classes. At times, women from established families abandoned their violent husbands to seek shelter with their parents or relatives. The husband needed to persuade them to return to their homes by promising that the violence would not repeat itself. Records of several such cases have been preserved in the Genizah.[24]

6. The Situation in France and Italy

The Jewish courts in France provided greater protection to battered wives than did those in Muslim countries. The Provençal sages did not accept the ruling of the Babylonian Geonim and Spanish sages, but followed in the footsteps of the sages in northern France and Germany, who were stricter with wife-beaters. Evidence of this is found, inter alia, in Rabad's stringent opposition to the latitude that Maimonides granted to the court or the husband to beat a woman who refused to perform her household duties. The opinion of Rabad, who was considered the greatest Provençal sage of the twelfth century, was very influential. His wording, "I never heard of permission to punish women with sticks," indicates that he never encountered such a tradition in his own locale. The same picture emerges from the rulings of R. Menahem Hameiri, a figure active in Provence in the late thirteenth and early fourteenth century, who was asked whether a husband is permitted to hit his wife with a stick at the time of her menstruation. The questioner was concerned about the ritual impurity of the menstruant, but not about his wife's dignity. In his response, Hameiri stated that there is no prohibition here in terms of the proscription against touching a *niddah*, but that the act of hitting as such is totally unacceptable under any circumstances.[25]

Many of the sages of northern France, including some of the leading Tosaphists, dealt with the question of wife-beating, ruling that a battered wife is to be viewed like any other person who has been harmed by another. This ruling is progressive relative to what is found among the Spanish sages and the Geonim. This follows from the following edict against wife-beating proposed by R. Peretz ben Elijah:

The cry of the daughters of our people has been heard concerning the sons of Israel who raise their hands to strike their wives. Yet who has given a husband the authority to beat his wife? Is he not rather forbidden to strike any person in Israel? Moreover, R. Isaac has written in a responsum that he has it on the authority of three great Sages . . . that one who beats his wife is in the same category as one who beats a stranger. Nevertheless we have heard of cases where Jewish women complained regarding their treatment before the Communities and no action was taken on their behalf.

We have therefore decreed that any Jew may be compelled on application of his wife or one of her near relatives to undertake by a *herem* not to beat his wife in anger or cruelty or so as to disgrace her, for that is against Jewish practice.

If anyone will stubbornly refuse to obey our words, the Court of the place to which the wife or her relatives will bring complaint, shall assign her maintenance according to her station and according to the custom of the place where she dwells. They shall fix her alimony as though her husband were away on a distant journey.

If they, our masters, the great sages of the land agree to this ordinance it shall be established.[26]

R. Peretz ben Elijah was active during the second half of the thirteenth century. The above words are extant in only one source (MS. Montefiore 130), and we do not know whether the proposed edict was in fact accepted by other sages and used in practice, or whether it was a purely theoretical proposal that was rejected by the sages. The suggested edict is far reaching: R. Peretz was willing to take measures against violent husbands even before they beat their wives, in the event where the wife felt that her husband was about to beat her. It was declared in advance that if a husband beat his wife, he would be subject to automatic excommunication (*herem*) from the community. The second half of the *taqqanah* stated that wife-beating would be considered as valid grounds for divorce. In any event, the testimony preserved therein concerning the position of the leading Tosaphists is very significant. Due to their high standing and great influence, one may assume that these words found a real echo in the rulings of other sages in France, in Germany, and in England. This source nevertheless indicates the difficulties encountered by the women in several communities in which their complaints were not properly handled. It would appear that the reality in the neighboring Christian society influenced things for the worse.

It is worth commenting on the words of R. Hayyim ben Barukh, who was also active in France during the thirteenth century. He does not directly treat the question of a husband who beats his wife, but rather that of a woman who hit her husband. His wording suggests, however, that he may not have responded with the same severity to the beating of a woman by her husband: "A woman who angered her husband must fast for three days. And a woman who beat her husband, you shall cut off her hand or else she must fast for forty days in one year."[27]

The command, "you shall cut off her hand" (from Deut. 25:12) is evidently meant to be interpreted as a purely literary flourish, not to be understood literally: namely, the act is so severe that the woman doing the beating deserves to have her hand cut off. We can interpret in like vein the words of R. Meir of Rothenburg, cited below, that one is to cut off the hand of the male wife-beater.

The position of R. Isaiah of Trani, the most prominent Italian sage of the thirteenth century, is similar to that of the French sages. He ruled that a husband who beats his wife must compensate her for the damage he caused her and, if he is in the habit of beating her and affronting her honor in this manner, may be forced to divorce her should the wife wish it, and must pay her *ketubah* money. It stands to reason that this stance was shared by other Italian sages of the same period in light of his preeminent position there, but we have no clear documentation of this.

7. The Situation in Germany

The Jewish sages in Germany were stricter with violent husbands than those of any other medieval diaspora. As we stated above, the French sages equated the husband who behaved violently toward his wife with one who struck a stranger. From the viewpoint of the woman, this statement was a positive step, in that she was granted full legal equality with the man. By contrast, the German sages—

R. Simhah of Speyer, R. Meir of Rothenburg, and others—ruled that one ought to be even stricter with a wife-beater than with one who attacked a stranger:

And his punishment is greater than that of one who beat his fellow man . . . He should be subject to a strict fine, whether in his body or in his money, for what he did, for he needs a great atonement . . . and if the husband does not persist in maintaining domestic peace, but continues to beat her and to insult her, we agree with you that he is subject to the ban in both the Upper [i.e., Heavenly] Court and in the Lower [i.e., earthly] Court, and he should be forced by means of Gentiles to give a divorce.[28]

For the first time, we find here Jewish sages ruling that a husband who beats his wife is to be subject to bodily punishment, in the sense of measure for measure. R. Simhah noted that this was also the opinion of his judicial colleagues in his own community. R. Meir of Rothenburg noted that this was a tradition that had been known to the German sages who preceded him: "And he who beats his wife, *I have received a tradition* that one is to be stricter with him than with one who beats his fellow, because one is not obligated to respect his fellow, but one is obligated to respect his wife."[29] R. Meir saw beating as a serious sin, and he too advocated the use of both corporal punishment and the ban against the violent husband: "For it is the way of the Gentiles to behave thus, but Heaven forfend that any Jew should do so. And one who beats his wife is to be excommunicated and banned and beaten. . . and even to cut off his hand if he is habituated to do so . . ." He adds that if the wife wants a divorce, the husband is forced to give her a divorce writ and to pay her *ketubah* money.

He repeated this view in another responsum and emphasized the woman's right to impose divorce upon her husband. Nevertheless, the question itself provides further evidence of the commonness of wife-beating, in that the husband refused to promise that he would never again beat his wife. One of R. Meir's disciples, R. Alexander Zuslin ha-Cohen, emphasized how strict they were in Germany with a husband who behaved violently towards his wife: "The great [sages] were very severe with a husband who beat his wife . . . and they went on at length and were very strict about this."[30]

R. Simhah of Speyer (ibid.) proposed, on the basis of his own opinion and that of his colleagues in the rabbinic court, that the *herem* be imposed upon a violent husband until he agreed to give a divorce to his wife, and even that force be used to do so, having him beaten by Gentile thugs until he agreed to grant her a *get*. All this notwithstanding the reluctance of the sages insofar as possible to impose a *get* by force. And indeed, other sages in Spain and among the Spanish exiles opposed R. Simhah's decision. R. David ben Zimra (Radbaz)—the leading sage in Egypt during the sixteenth century—virulently opposed this and argued that R. Simhah had "exaggerated" and that there was some doubt as to the legitimacy of any children who might be born subsequently to the woman, should she remarry: "and it seems likely to me that such a child will be a bastard."[31] By contrast, not a single sage in Germany or in France failed to acknowledge the right of the battered wife to demand a divorce and impose it upon her husband.

What led the Ashkenazic sages, more so than those in any other Jewish diasporas in the Middle Ages, to be so harsh with the wife-beater? Evidently, the relatively good position of Ashkenazic women in most areas of life during the eleventh to thirteenth centuries, as we have seen throughout this work, and the important role they played in Jewish martyrdom, influenced the sages' stance in this matter. However, they strongly emphasize not only the need to compensate the woman and to punish the husband, but also the "great atonement" the husband needs to make for his acts. The *herem* imposed upon the husband further contributed to their seeing the act of wife-beating in very strict terms.

The great strictness observed in Germany regarding this matter is to be attributed as well to the influence of German Hasidism at the end of the twelfth and thirteenth centuries. The leaders of these pietists saw in any affronts to human dignity, and particularly in the act of lifting a hand against another person, a very serious affront. On the one hand, the wife had been beaten and humiliated; on the other, the act of beating exerts a negative effect upon the soul of the errant husband. In order to atone for this, there is need in their opinion to behave toward him in the same way as he had behaved toward his wife, and to impose upon him corporal punishment.

The leaders of German Hasidism used various means to persuade husbands to refrain from violence toward their wives. Being aware of the great love between a father and his children—whom he tends to see as his very own flesh, unlike the case with his wife—they suggested a mental exercise, whereby the violent husband, at the moment of his anger, visualize to himself the image of his daughter. Would he want her husband, his son-in-law, to beat her? The anger that he would feel toward such a violent son-in-law is meant to lead him to understanding the severity of his own act and thereby prevent him from harming his wife, at the very moment he is about to raise his hand to her.[32]

The reliance upon this "personal" argument, the call to the husband to love his wife as he does his daughter, likewise indicates how difficult it was to uproot the plague of violence in the family merely by preaching about the respect due to the woman and the value of human beings in general—motifs that are widespread in *Sefer Ḥasidim*. Hence, the attempt to play upon a person's emotions and not to suffice with an appeal to his rational world. It is difficult to separate the great severity with which Hasidei Ashkenaz viewed wife-beating from their attitude toward the respect due living beings generally. One may not harm any living creature. Even beating an animal is forbidden: hence, it was not by chance that they placed the prohibition against beating an animal and that against beating one's wife next to one another. They added: "One should think to oneself, 'If I were in the hands of another person, how would I wish them to treat me?'; and he should behave in that way with those that are subject to him."[33]

The basic insight is that both the wife and the domestic animal are "given over" to the hands of the husband/owner, who is their master, and an appeal is addressed to him to stir his feelings of compassion toward them. We shall suffice with one more source from *Sefer Ḥasidim* to indicate, not only the great severity with which they saw the use of physical force, but also the use of terminology similar to that of R. Meir of Rothenburg, referring to cutting off of the hand of the one hitting:

And our Sages said, that whoever smites the cheek of his neighbor, as is as if he smote the cheek of the Shekhinah. That is, whoever slaps the cheek of a Jew . . . is as if he slapped the Shekhinah, and there is no way to correct this but to cut off his hand . . . Therefore, O man, be very careful and guard yourself not to lift your hand against any man or woman, child or adult, save when you need to discipline your son.[34]

It was not only the physical violence of beating that disturbed them. The injury to the other person's dignity and the sense of shame caused him were seen by them as an even more serious sin. Hence, from the viewpoint of the one doing the beating, it is not sufficient to make financial compensation for the psychological damage and pain inflicted; he requires further punishment to atone for his sin. A punishment of measure for measure will bring him full atonement for his sin. There follows from this the demand to beat the errant husband and the emphasis that he is in need of atonement.

This approach follows from another ruling of Hasidei Ashkenaz as well. They addressed the one beaten and asked him to forgive the one who hit him and to pray for mercy on his behalf, even if he did not express any regret at all and did not ask of him forgiveness for his acts.[35] This sin is so severe, that without forgiveness on the part of the battered man or woman and their prayers on his behalf he cannot be forgiven at all.

In light of the connections of the above-mentioned Ashkenazic sages with the teachings of Hasidei Ashkenaz, whose remarks on the subject of wife-beating were brought above, it seems likely that these teachings affected these sages.

8. Wife Beating for "Education"

The perception of the wife as being under the authority and responsibility of her husband led a number of medieval Jewish sages to the conclusion that he is permitted to beat her so as to educate her if she "sinned." The Babylonian Gaon Rav Zemah (head of the Pumbedita yeshiva, 872–890) ruled that if a woman struck another man or woman, her husband is allowed to hit her "so that she will not be accustomed to doing so."[36] From the context, it is clear that this refers to a woman who was in the habit of striking others, and therefore the Gaon permitted the husband to strike her.

R. Eliezer ben Samuel of Metz (1120–1200) likewise allowed the husband to strike his wife under special circumstances. He strongly opposed domestic violence, but added: "if his intention is to admonish her and guide her, or to admonish and guide his fellow man, it is permitted."[37] It follows from this, that just as a husband is permitted to strike his wife so as to correct her, so is one allowed to hit another person in general when the latter sins, for "all Israel are responsible for one another." The woman is treated here as part of society as a whole, and the same rules apply to her as to any other person—namely, that it is permitted to strike him or her for educational ends. But according to R. Solomon Luria (Maharshal), R. Eliezer addressed himself here to the community leaders and sages alone, who are allowed to hit a wrongdoer so as to educate him; otherwise, the entire social fabric would disintegrate.

R. Israel Isserlein, one of the leading German sages in the fifteenth century, was asked about the case of a woman who cursed her father and mother and whose husband's admonitions concerning this were ineffective. He permitted the husband to strike her so as to get her to stop committing such a serious sin. He saw in this an educational act, and described the woman as subject to her husband's authority: "Whosoever is under the hand [i.e., authority] of another person, and that person sees that he commits a transgression, he is allowed to hit him and to admonish him so as to cause him to cease the transgression, and there is no need to bring him to the court so as to make him stop."[38] His words suggest that he was familiar with the position of R. Simhah of Speyer, who saw wife-beating as a severe act deserving harsh punishment. But in his opinion, this does not apply in a case in which the woman behaves improperly. He did not raise the opposite case: Is a wife allowed to beat her husband so as to educate him and to make him desist from a forbidden act? But it is clear that he would not allow it, as the husband is not "under the hand" of his wife. On the other hand, it is also seems doubtful that R. Simhah of Speyer and the Hasidei Ashkenaz would agree with the ruling of R. Eliezer of Metz and R. Israel Isserlein permitting a husband to beat his wife in such a situation.

We have thus seen that some sages in Babylonia, in Spain, and in Ashkenaz allowed the husband to beat his wife for purposes of education, despite the fact that there is no explicit source for this in the Mishnah or the Talmud. What are the roots of this approach? It is true that the rabbis' fundamental assumption that the woman is subject to the authority of the husband is shared by many patriarchal societies in human culture, but it is hard to assume that it was this alone that guided the above-mentioned sages. In my opinion, they were influenced by the story of Eve's sin in the Garden of Eden and the punishment given her there, and especially the verse "and he shall rule over you" (Gen. 3:16), which they interpreted as granting the husband rule and control over his wife.

9. Summary: Between Theory and Reality

The activity of the Jewish sages in all the Diasporas against beating wives is of great significance, but a clear distinction needs to be drawn between the stance of these sages and reality. One should not be led astray by the rabbis' principled opposition to wife-beating into thinking that the phenomenon per se was rare in medieval Jewish society. A firmer position against violent husbands on the part of sages in a particular area is not in itself evidence of the rarity of the phenomenon. Their strictness may well have had its origin in the feeling that the prohibition against wife-beating was in itself insufficient to protect her, from which there followed the need to utilize harsher steps so as to limit the phenomenon or to abolish it. The above-mentioned words of R. Peretz ben Elijah of Corbeil and his appeal to other French sages to issue a joint *taqqanah* against violence against women is one indication of the distance between theory and reality. He explicitly mentions that there were communities in which battered wives did not receive any help. His suggestion to impose an automatic *herem* upon the husband in the event that he should beat his wife, also shows the miserable reality. One may conjecture that the strong position taken by the sages against violence toward women afforded the woman a certain protection while her complaint was being considered by the court. However, the sources indicate that violence against women was to be found in all Jewish communities. Four main factors hindered the struggle against this phenomenon: its ubiquity in the Gentile environment; the feudal nature of society, in which everyone was subject to the rule and domination of the person above them in the social hierarchy; the ubiquity of marriage at an early age; and the perception of corporal punishment as an integral and important part of education in the Middle Ages.

But even if the opposition of the Jewish sages to violence toward women could not abolish the phenomenon but only restrict it, it is difficult to assume that the harsh expressions directed by the sages toward violent husbands did not leave their impression upon both men and women. Their principled approach helped to improve the woman's image in society and certainly represented a significant change relative to the dominant norm of their environment.

CHAPTER ELEVEN

The Divorcée and the "Rebellious Wife"

THE DIVORCÉE

I t is a common assumption that the family unit in medieval Jewish society was strong and stable and that divorce was a rare phenomenon. However, this assumption, which even appears in research literature, is rather erroneous. Divorce was quite common, in some locales even more so than in contemporary Western society. During the course of the Middle Ages, discernable and significant changes took place regarding the Jewish woman's right to initiate divorce and to receive suitable financial compensation, changes that originated in political changes and in the altered social and economic status of women.

1. The Biblical and Talmudic Heritage

The Torah (Deut. 24:1) portrays the man as enjoying the exclusive prerogative of both establishing and dissolving the family unit. The decision and execution depend entirely upon the man's will: He is the one to marry the woman, he is the one who decides on divorce, and he is the one to execute it. This is a natural outcome of the basic approach that perceives the woman as the property of the man.

What was the attitude toward divorce as such? In the book of Malachi (2:15–16), one finds hints of a distinctly negative attitude: "So take care that no one break faith with the wife of his youth. For I hate divorce, says the Lord God of Israel." But the sense of these verses is ambiguous, and may also be interpreted to the detriment of the woman who, if she is hated by her husband, ought to be divorced. And indeed, the tannaim, amoraim, and even the medieval commentators disagreed regarding the interpretation of this verse.

The Mishnah (*m. Gittin* 9.11) presents three opinions regarding divorce, based upon the above-mentioned verse in Deuteronomy:

The School of Shammai said: A person should not divorce his wife unless he found in her some unseemly thing . . . The School of Hillel said: Even if she spoiled his food . . . Rabbi Akiva said: Even if he found another more attractive then she.

The Talmud includes aphorisms describing divorce in negative terms, but these do not prohibit divorce as such, but only state the pain they cause God. On the other hand, the Talmud advises one who is married to a "bad" wife to divorce her. We search in vain for any comments about a bad husband and the way to free oneself of him. The sages certainly knew such people, but there was no point in discussing it as, according to Talmudic law, the husband alone has the right to divorce his wife while she has no corresponding option of that sort.

In brief: The relevant biblical verses were open to varying interpretations; the biblical and Talmudic tradition placed few moral constraints upon the husband whose relations with his wife had soured and had begun to contemplate divorce, and no legal restraints upon him whatsoever. The ordinary Jew in the Middle Ages, his relatives, friends, and at times even the sages in his environment, could conclude from the biblical and Talmudic heritage that a husband is allowed to divorce his wife if she does not please him, even if she has done him no wrong. The large number of divorces in medieval Jewish society likewise drew upon this reality, even if other, economic and social factors, had far greater impact upon this.

2. The Attitude of Medieval Jewish Sages to Divorce

The attitude of the medieval sages toward divorce finds expression primarily in their exegesis of the Bible and the Talmud, in speculative literature (philosophy and ethics), and in the responsa literature.[1] Their views also had an impact upon the attitude of the society to divorce, as clearly follows from the sources referenced below. For the sake of brevity, we shall suffice with a discussion of the position of several of the leading sages, whose discussions focused upon the above-mentioned verses from Malachi and the controversy between Beit Hillel and Beit Shammai concerning the interpretation of the verses from Deuteronomy. The medieval exegetes also used these verses as they wished, interpreting them in praise or censure of woman, in accordance with their own understanding and the reality in their locale. Some of them include an explicitly didactic tendency, while ignoring the literal meaning of the verses and the rabbinic midrashim. As a rule, the verses in Malachi were interpreted in support of the woman, namely, that it is improper for a man to divorce a wife who has served him faithfully for many years and has meanwhile lost her beauty—but there is no consistency in this. We may exemplify this briefly in the words of several of the leading biblical exegetes of the Middle Ages. Rashi, in his commentary to Malachi (2:16), elaborated upon the sin of those who returned to Zion from Babylonia who had married Gentile wives in addition to their devoted wives, who had borne the harsh yoke of exile that caused their external appearance to deteriorate. He spoke movingly of the exploitation and betrayal of these woman.

R. David Kimhi (Radak), in his commentary to Malachi (ad loc.), spoke at length of the importance of love between husband and wife, stating that if there is no love between them it is better that the husband divorce his wife than that he remain married in a situation of hatred, because "this is a great betrayal."

In principle, great caution must be exercised in using exegetical literature to discover the personal stance of the sages. The medieval exegetes often remained close to the text at hand and its discussion in tannaitic and amoraitic literature, and their writing did not always reflect their personal attitude toward divorce.

Moreover, even those who saw divorce as a negative act that "saddens" the Almighty Himself expressed understanding for its existence and saw it as a special dispensation that was given to the Jewish people because of their unique standing. It was specifically the closeness of God to the people of Israel and their special level that allowed them to divorce their wives in the absence of love between the partners. This love is a basic condition for the existence of the Jewish family, among whom God allows his Shekhinah to dwell.

The elaborate discussion of this subject also derives from its polemic nature vis-à-vis Christianity, which prohibited divorce entirely and saw matrimony as a religious sacrament. Interestingly, these discussions speak of the husband's hatred for his wife as one of the grounds for divorce, but discuss very little regarding the wife's attitude toward him—this, in accordance with the basic approach that sees her as attached to the husband and dependent upon him.

Medieval Jewish mystics responded critically to the dissolution of the family unit. Hasidei Ashkenaz accepted the view of Beit Shammai, that a husband is only allowed to divorce his wife if he found in her "an unseemly thing"—that is, infidelity—and that otherwise he needs to "render account." They even forbade a man to serve as witness and to sign a *get* that was to be given to a woman "who had not transgressed": "A man who divorces his wife without cause, when she has not transgressed: no honorable person should sign upon it [his divorce writ] nor be a witness, and all the more so [not] be an emissary." Only if the husband is far away is it a *mitzvah* to bring a *get* from him. Likewise, "If she had been unfaithful and her relatives do not allow to give her a divorce because of shame, it is a mitzvah to assist her divorce."[2]

Giving a divorce to a woman without her "transgressing" is seen as an improper act. Although no reason is given for this statement, it seems clear that it is based upon a preference for the approach of Beit Shammai as against that of Beit Hillel. It may be that the author thought that Beit Hillel also opposed divorce that was not based upon "an unseemly thing," and that their permission to divorce "even if she spoiled his food" is only intended retroactively, so as to prevent quarrel and hatred between the partners. As we have seen, other medieval sages thought thus as well. In any event, it is difficult to separate the strong position taken by German Hasidism against unjustified divorce from their strong abhorrence of affronts against human dignity and causing shame to another person generally. No other circle in medieval Jewish society so firmly and emphatically advocated refraining from all actions or speech that might directly or indirectly hurt another person's feelings or insult him. They were concerned about the shame that might be caused to the divorcée, and were possibly worried as well that some people would think that she was divorced because of "an unseemly thing." The fact that divorce was common in thirteenth-century Ashkenaz did not entirely eliminate this suspicion. Just as cancellation of an engagement was understood by Hasidei Ashkenaz and by other Ashkenazic sages as a grave act that might embarrass or shame the girl, so too was the case with divorce.

The Spanish Kabbalists gave an explicitly sacral character to marital life. The husband is able to cleave to the Shekhinah by means of his union with his wife, which is accomplished by means of the holy letters with which the world was created. They described the connection between the people of Israel and its God, including the relation of the isolated individual who wishes to attach himself to the Shekhinah, by means of explicitly erotic symbols.[3] Divorce dissolves this state. The separation from the woman, who is the reflection and ward of the Shekhinah, is very difficult for the man and weakens his attachment to the Shekhinah, for "the Shekhinah does not leave his home because of his wife." It therefore should not be surprising if even the angels on high weep when a man divorces his wife.

The Kabbalists were nevertheless aware of reality, and stated that if there is no cure for a "bad woman," it is desirable that the husband divorce her and marry another woman. Moreover, at times divorce is the result of a predetermined decree concerning a given person's fate. God matches a particular man and woman according to their merits and deeds. Divorce (or widowhood) derive primarily from the predetermined decree concerning a person's match. This idea, too, appears in *Sefer Ḥasidim*.[4]

R. Isaac Abravanel devoted a lengthy discussion to the permission granted for divorce, displaying sympathy for the approach of Beit Hillel. As a proud Jewish courtier in Spain, he referred several times in that discussion to the husband's wish to protect the honor and status of his family, for which reason the divorcing husband is not even required to specify the "unseemly thing" that he found in his wife. In his opinion, it is preferable that they divorce rather than allow hatred and discord and quarrels between them to multiply. Nevertheless, due to concerns about the proliferation of divorce—in any event when the woman is simply no longer attractive to the husband—the halakhah makes the process of divorce difficult; thus Abravanel.

Even before him, Maimonides offered a similar explanation, although in his opinion the divorce procedure derives primarily from the suspicion that the woman who was disgusted with her husband might be unfaithful to him. Maimonides also sought to negate the practice in Islam, whereby the husband divorces his wife through speech alone.[5] R. Menahem Hameiri, the great Provençal sage of the early fourteenth century, followed the approach of Beit Shammai in his interpretation of the above *mishnah*: "That divorce is to be avoided and is repugnant when there is no reason for it. One who divorces his wife for no reason is hateful and abominable." He even used the phrase, "treachery and breaking his covenant" regarding the husband.[6]

The extent to which the sages' attitude toward divorce was influenced by the reality of their locale may be seen by the words of R. Seligman of Bingen, in Germany (mid-fifteenth century). He criticized the high divorce rate in Germany, to be discussed below, to this end even interpreting the above-mentioned dispute between Beit Hillel and Beit Shammai in a clearly tendentious way. In his opinion, Beit Hillel's permission to divorce a woman "even if she spoiled his food" only holds true when this was done deliberately to annoy her husband. Moreover, in his opinion these permissions were only stated after the fact, but *ab initio* a person should not divorce his wife at all, except under special circumstances. An additional restriction or limitation is that Beit Hillel's words were supposedly only said regarding a second marriage, "but in a first match, even if she sinned against him, he should not hasten to divorce her."[7]

3. Grounds for Divorce

In the responsa and halakhic literature of the eleventh through thirteenth centuries, ten main grounds or reasons for divorce are mentioned: (a) the husband's journeys and the wish to uproot the place of residence of the family; (b) the woman's claim of impotence on the part of the husband; (c) barrenness and childlessness; (d) violence and improper behavior of the husband toward the wife; (e) claims of "infidelity" on the part of one or another partner; (f) illness of the partner; (g) difficulties in earning a living; (h) the woman's claim that she finds her husband repugnant; (i) marital incompatibility; (j) religious apostasy.

1. The first factor, *the husband's travels to distant places,* is the main motivation for divorce in sources from the eleventh century, particularly in Muslim Spain. One of the striking features of medieval Jewish society was its great geographical mobility, including extensive migrations and travel to distant parts for commercial purposes. The young woman often confronted a difficult dilemma: to join her husband and thereby cut herself off from her parents, her relatives, and her surroundings, or to divorce her husband.

At times the couple confronted this dilemma when one set of parents decided to immigrate: that is, ought they to join the migrating parents, or remain with the parents of the other partner in the old place? Either decision meant extended separation from the parents of one of the young partners. This was a weighty and complex decision; moreover, under the conditions of the Middle Ages, it was very difficult to maintain contact with parents or other relatives who had migrated to another country. Most often, such moves meant separation for the rest of one's life. Hence, it is not surprising that at times the couple would prefer to break up their own family unit, at times even with the encouragement of the parents. The sources imply that there was often substantial parental intervention in these deliberations, particularly in the case of the girl's parents.

The protracted absences of husbands who went off on business and stayed away for lengthy periods in remote places appears extensively in the responsa literature of the sages of Spain, France, and Germany. One must remember that these things were usually recorded in those cases in which a dispute arose between the couple. Many other cases, in which the two sides arrived at a mutual decision to divorce, were not preserved in writing. The combination of marriage at a young age, frequent absences of the husbands for lengthy trips, and immigration of the parents, weighed heavily upon the Jewish family, and were the main explanation for the frequency of divorce to be found among them. At times it was even difficult to locate the husband, whose business took him from one place to another, so as to ask him for a divorce, and this too involved significant financial expense.

11. *Impotence* as grounds for divorce is mentioned frequently in medieval sources. However, one must approach this subject with caution, and it is difficult to determine its frequency on the basis of the discussions. In certain cases, it may not have been the real motive underlying the woman's desire for divorce, but she preferred using it because it made it easier for her to receive the *get* sought and to retain her financial rights, particularly from the beginning of the thirteenth century on. In discussing this subject, one needs to examine developments that occurred in the rights of the woman. According to the halakhah, if the husband admitted the validity of her claim he was required to divorce her and pay his wife her *ketubah* money. If he contested the claim, the woman was under certain circumstances considered more trustworthy than he, and she could even still receive her *ketubah* money along with the divorce writ. This was a complex issue, discussed at length by the medieval sages, in which opinions differed, and we cannot enter into the details here.[8]

Already in the Mishnah there are signs of a change regarding this matter. The original, ancient halakhah stated that a woman who claims that her husband cannot conduct sexual relations with her is believed and is entitled to the *ketubah* money. But later the tannaim changed their view, saying that perhaps the woman was interested in another man and fabricated this accusation against her husband. Hence they ruled that one must instead try to make peace between the partners, in the hopes that the woman would agree to remain with her husband.

The suspicion that a woman might have become interested in another man is repeated frequently in the discussions of the medieval sages. But counterpoised to this was another Talmudic principle: namely, that a woman "does not dare" to say an absolute falsehood in the presence of her husband because she has a certain sense of innate respect towards him, making it difficult for her to brazenly lie in his presence. Hence, if she claims that he is impotent, she is to be believed, as he knows whether her words are true or not. The deliberations of the medieval sages oscillated between these two opposing principles.

An interesting development took place regarding the issue of impotence. The Babylonian Geonim and the early European sages, up to the twelfth century, ruled that the woman's claim that her husband is impotent is not to be accepted when he denies it. At the end of the twelfth century, R. Yitzhak ben Abraham (Ritzba), one of the greatest disciples of Rabbenu Tam and himself an outstanding Tosaphist, stated that the woman is to be believed, on condition that she sues for divorce alone and does not press additional monetary claims. Her foregoing these claims reinforces the credibility of her claim, as it seems clear that what motivated her was not pecuniary greed but the wish to enjoy full family life and to bear children. The suspicion expressed in the Talmud, "lest she placed her eyes upon another," does not apply in this case, and he is forced to divorce her. By contrast, in that case where the woman demands *ketubah* money and does not suffice with divorce alone, her husband is not forced to divorce her. Ritzba's view was accepted by the sages of France and Germany, and was likewise accepted in Spain, beginning from the end of the thirteenth century.[9] Rashba, the greatest Spanish authority of the time, ruled that the woman is to be believed in that case where she does not demand her *ketubah,* and others followed in his wake. Later, many ignored the requirement that she forego her *ketubah* and believed the woman even without it.

A decisive majority of medieval Jewish sages ruled that divorce is to be imposed upon a husband who is required by law to divorce his wife because of impotence. This point is deserving of special mention, due to the rabbis' profound hesitations about imposed or forced divorce. In this case, the sages were concerned about a double harm to the woman: that she does not have sexual relations with her husband, and that she has no children. Nevertheless, there were those sages who ruled that the husband is forced to give a divorce in this case only if the woman based her suit for divorce, not only on the husband's impotence, but also on her wish for children to take care of her in her old age and to see to her burial. Her personal needs in themselves were not judged sufficient. Many of the sages even postponed the imposition of divorce until ten years had passed since the marriage. One of the causes of impotence, according to the sages and the simple people, was magical enchantment, which is at times invoked by husbands as justification for their inability to perform sexually with their wives. This fits in well with the belief in magic and in magical powers characteristic of medieval people generally. Its association with the reproductive process is not at all surprising, given that sex and childbirth have been associated with magic since hoary antiquity. We even find husbands who claimed that they have been enchanted and are unable to perform with their wives, and therefore asked to marry another wife to prove their potency.

III. *Barrenness* was another commonly cited reason for demanding divorce, on the part of both the husband and on that of the wife. The halakhah stated that barrenness was justifiable grounds for divorce after ten years of marriage, seeing that it weighed heavily upon the continuation of the family unit. According to many sages, the matter does not even depend upon the couple's wishes. There were those sages in the Middle Ages who forced the two partners to be divorced in such a case, unless the husband married another wife in the hope that she would bear him children. Maimonides summarized the law thus:

> If he married a woman and stayed with her for ten years and she did not give birth, he divorces her and pays her *ketubah,* or marries a woman capable of giving birth. And if he does not wish to divorce her he is compelled and beaten with a stick until he divorces her.[10]

The alternative of taking a second wife who would bear him children was not a live option in Germany, in France, or in England, where it was forbidden to marry a second wife. Earlier Spanish sages often expressed an opinion similar to that of Maimonides. Thus, this is an explicit example of the community's involvement in the life of the individual and of the family, based upon a view in which the family is a sanctified unit constituting the basic core of community life. At the center of life lie, not the rights of the individual, but the duty of the community as a whole to carry out the world of *mitzvot.* R. Asher ben Yehiel even inferred from Rav Alfasi's remarks on this issue that he was not only compelled to divorce his wife, but that he was also forced thereafter to take another wife. The same holds true, in his opinion, for a bachelor who had reached the age of twenty and was not yet married. On the other hand, as the woman is not formally obligated in the *mitzvah* of being fruitful and multiplying, she was not compelled to marry. The sages were divided on the issue of the rights of the barren woman who had been divorced. According to Maimonides, she is not entitled to receive her *ketubah* unless it is known that the hindrance to childbirth lay with her husband. Rabad of Posquières, in his glosses, disagrees with Maimonides, and states that, in the first or second marriage, the childless woman is entitled in all events to receive the *ketubah* money. This opinion is likewise expressed by the Tosaphists.

The early Spanish sages likewise deliberated this issue. Maimonides, specifically, who was considered in his day an expert physician, in the event of doubt attributed barrenness to the wife. The medical knowledge of his time did not enable him to know how frequently the cause of barrenness originates in the man. In various medical works, Jewish sages did deal with infertility and the means of curing it.[11]

This dispute is of great significance for the economic status of the woman after divorce. Economic fears often prevented women from realizing their desire to divorce. Without the *ketubah*, she was liable to be subject to real penury. The number of infertile women in those days was relatively large, due to the lack of proper medical care. The subject occupies an important place in the biblical stories, as it does in medieval halakhic literature and in both Jewish and Christian folk literature.

iv and v. *Violence* toward women as grounds for divorce is discussed elsewhere in this work (chapter 10), as is *infidelity,* which we noted in the context of prostitution and concubinage in Jewish society (chapter 6). Wife-beating is discussed extensively by the medieval sages, in contrast to charges of infidelity, which were raised but little as grounds for divorce—far less so than in modern society, and not surprisingly. The basic recognition by the halakhah of the husband's right to marry a second wife removed, from a psychological respect, the sting from his "infidelity" with another woman. This was particularly true of Jewish society in the Muslim countries, in which marrying a second wife was an accepted practice, and concubinage was also widely recognized. But although claim of a one-time infidelity on the part of the husband was not always recognized as a ground for divorce, if the wife asserted that her husband habitually enjoyed the favors of prostitutes, the Ashkenazic sages of the thirteenth century required him to divorce his wife and to pay her *ketubah.*[12]

vi. The husband's *illness* was not a simple matter from the woman's viewpoint. The *mishnah* in *Ketubot* enumerates five cases, including illness and physical defects of the husband, as valid grounds for divorce on the part of the woman. What about those severe diseases that do not appear on that list? Medieval Jewish sages disagreed on this point. Some were reluctant to add to them, even in the case of severe illnesses. We shall suffice with one example: A woman urgently sought a divorce on account of the mental illness of her husband, who was also violent:

Her husband was wild and his craziness increased from day to day. And she asked to divorce him before he goes completely crazy and she would be left chained to him forever [because under Jewish law a man who is *non compis mentus* cannot legally issue a divorce–AG]. For he is utterly mad and she is fearful that he may kill her in his anger, for when he is angry he hits and kills and throws and kicks and bites.

R. Asher (the Rosh), who adjudicated this case, ruled that he cannot be compelled to divorce her.[13]

vii. Surprisingly, the grounds of *repugnance,* which was widespread and commonly used during the early and High Middle Ages and to which the Geonim, Alfasi, Maimonides, and others gave decisive weight, allowing a woman to initiate divorce and receive a *get* on the claim that she found her husband repugnant, lost much of its force from the late thirteenth century on. We shall discuss this phenomenon below, in the section on the "rebellious wife" and the attempt to reduce the divorce rate in Germany at the end of the thirteenth century. Not only did the sages attempt to reduce the economic rights of the *moredet,* but even to eliminate the very possibility of her receiving a divorce. The same picture appears in Spain as well, possibly under the influence of the developments in Germany. The Rosh, who migrated to Spain, tried to gradually introduce the new rulings that he had received in Germany and in France among the various communities of Spain, particularly in Castille. In all of his discussions of women's claims that the husband was disgusting to her, he repeated his ruling that divorce may not be imposed upon the husband in such a case. It is doubtful whether he was completely successful in abolishing the rulings based upon Maimonides' approach, but it is clear that his stance made a considerable impression because of his prominent stature in Castille.

R. Asher expressed astonishment at the wish to impose the writing of the *get* on the husband. After all, the woman is not required by law to bear children; why not then leave her without a *get* until she submits to the husband's conditions? These remarks teach us a great deal about the personality of the Rosh and of his attitude toward women in his day. He seems to have ignored the fact that he was dealing with a human being with a personality of her own, and with feelings of love and of hatred, and that it was indeed possible that she was psychologically unable to tolerate relations with her husband.

VIII. *Incompatibility* was also a widespread cause of divorce, even if it was only infrequently mentioned as such. Its frequency derived from two main factors: early marriage, and lack of consideration by the parents of the childrens' wishes and feelings in choosing their intended partner. We have already referred to these two factors in various places throughout this work. Once the children matured, their wishes and feelings often changed, and the partners chosen for them in their youth were no longer suitable to them.

IX. *Religious apostasy* on the part of one of the partners, particularly that of the husband, was quite frequent. Husbands who converted were asked to divorce their wives, who refused to convert with them, so as to enable them to remarry. The act of conversion as such did not nullify the halakhic status of the converted husband as a Jew, and there was thus need for a valid Jewish divorce writ. Those who refused to do so raised serious problems of personal status for their wives— a point that we have already discussed above (chapter 9).

THE "REBELLIOUS WIFE"

The reason for divorce most frequently cited in the halakhic literature of the Middle Ages is the wife's "rebellion." The *moredet* ("rebellious wife") is defined as one who refuses to have sexual relations with her husband or, in another view, one who refuses to perform those household tasks that are incumbent upon a woman. The Mishnah and Talmud explicitly state that monetary sanctions are to be imposed upon a "rebellious" wife: the amount of her *ketubah* money is gradually reduced until she loses it completely and, at the end of one year, her husband is allowed to divorce her. Similar sanctions are imposed upon a "rebellious" husband: the amount due to his wife in the *ketubah* is gradually increased, until he finally is forced to divorce her.

Frequently, the purpose of the woman's "rebellion" was in fact to pressure her husband into giving her a divorce. The woman abstained from sexual relations or from housework in the hope that this would force him to accept her demand for a divorce, while preserving her financial rights. This was a common reason for "rebellion," and the sages' discussion of this issue must be examined in its light. In practice, the entire issue may be seen as a struggle of the woman for recognition of her right to undo the family unit and to receive a divorce from her husband. As mentioned, this right had been withheld from the woman for a long time, but during the Middle Ages important changes took place that substantially changed the woman's power in this area, which had implications for her social status as well.

1. The Change at the Beginning of the Geonic Period

A major change regarding the entire issue of the *moredet* occurred during the early Middle Ages, only a few years after the Muslim conquests and the entry of the decisive majority of the Jewish people under Muslim rule. The sages stated that any woman who wishes to receive a divorce from her husband may receive it immediately. A number of documents have been preserved regarding this change, which greatly influenced Jewish sages in the Middle Ages in various places. One of the most important of these involves a statement by Rav Sherira Gaon made at the end of the tenth century, who related that in 651 Jewish women turned to the Muslim courts so as to force their husbands to issue them a Jewish divorce. The sages were concerned that such a *get* would not be kosher, and refused to allow the Muslim authorities to interfere in internal Jewish matters. The Muslims may have done so in an effort to encourage Jewish women to convert to Islam as, according to Muslim law, the previous marriages of a Jewish woman who converted to Islam are not recognized, and she could thereby free herself of her husband without requiring his consent. In reaction to this, the sages issued a ruling that a woman who rebels against her husband may receive an immediate divorce, while retaining her financial rights.

Rav Sherira testified that in his time, namely, the second half of the tenth century, the same edict was still in effect in Babylonia, and he asked his interlocutors from North Africa to follow it as well. R. Samuel ben Ali Gaon confirmed that in his day, two centuries later, the same regulation was still in force in Babylonia. Sources from Ashkenaz indicate that, in the eleventh century this rule was accepted there as well, and that they acted accordingly. Nevertheless, the repeated questions raised about this issue suggest certain misgivings and uncertainties about it among the sages. This is hardly surprising, as that same regulation from the beginning of the Geonic period was explicitly opposed to what is implied in the Talmud. There was a clear feeling that the historical circumstances in the Muslim countries then were totally different from those in Christian Europe, and it was doubtful whether a *taqqanah* introduced four hundred year earlier was still valid.

The acceptance of the edict of the *moredet* by Rabbenu Gershom deserves special mention. Taken in conjunction with another regulation of Rabbenu Gershom, that which prohibits a husband from divorcing his wife against her will, an absurd situation was created in which things were turned completely upside down. The woman could force her husband to divorce her because of the ordinance of *moredet,* while he could not do so because of Rabbenu Gershom's new *taqqanah.* Rabbenu Gershom's decision to leave intact the *taqqanah* of the *moredet* may be explained, first and foremost, on the basis of the great respect he felt for the Babylonian Geonim and his perception of their ordinances as binding. Moreover, one was dealing here with a very early *taqqanah,* one that had already been observed for several centuries. But he may also have seen this Geonic ordinance as of value in its own right, because it allowed a woman who was suffering under the yoke of her husband to become freed of him.

The sources indicate that the *taqqanah* of *moredet* was observed by Jewish society in both the Muslim world and in Christian Europe for a period of nearly five hundred years, even though there was no uniform practices regarding the payment of the *ketubah* money. The "rebellious wife" received it in some places, while, in others she did not. In any event, this ordinance gave great power to the Jewish woman. It would be a mistake to see the issue of the *moredet* only through the narrow halakhic prism of grounds for divorce. It also had important implications for the status of women, both in her home and in society generally. If, during the period of the Mishnah and the Talmud, the husband was able to threaten his wife, whether explicitly or indirectly, that he would divorce her and nullify their marriage, similar power was now given to the woman, whose position vis-à-vis her husband now changed in a fundamental way. Even if one cannot speak of full equality between the two partners, there was a clear and significant measure of equality in this sphere.

2. The Retreat from the Taqqanah of Moredet during the Twelfth Century

A significant retreat from the ordinance facilitating divorce through the woman's becoming a *moredet* occurred in the twelfth century, in both Christian Europe and in some of the Muslim countries. The main architects of this change were the major French and German sages active during this century: R. Eliezer ben Nathan (Raban) in Germany, Rabbenu Tam in France, and R. Zerahiah Halevi in Provence, together with Maimonides in Egypt. Rabbenu Tam's position on this issue exerted decisive impact on the sages of Ashkenaz and France during subsequent generations. He strongly attacked the ordinance of *moredet*, in a manner unprecedented by any other sage before or since. In his words, the Geonim did not have the right to make a regulation of this type, forcing a husband to give a *get*, because in principle such coercion is improper and places in doubt the very validity of the document. All the more that this ordinance is not incumbent upon later generations.

These harsh words of Rabbenu Tam, the greatest of all the Tosaphists, written around the middle of the twelfth century, made a powerful impression. Anyone examining the position of the German and French sages in the twelfth and thirteenth centuries can see this clearly. Many of them were taken aback by his firm position and by the fear of illegitimacy of the children who would be born in the wake of such an imposed *get*, and retreated from the Geonic ordinance. One can also observe a certain withdrawal from the Geonic *taqqanah* among the Provençal sages. Thus, R. Zerahiah Halevi (Raza"h) argued that the ordinance of *moredet* was from the outset intended to be a temporary one only.

Maimonides discusses the issue of *moredet* in detail in his book *Mishneh Torah* and deals with it in his responsa as well. His position regarding the *moredet* had great impact, particularly upon the Jewish communities in Spain. He did not accept the Geonic ordinance on this subject; only in that case where the woman claimed that she found her husband repugnant did he issue a similar ruling:

A woman who withheld sexual relations from her husband is called a *moredet* . . . If she said: "I find him repugnant and I cannot have intercourse with him," he is forced to divorce her immediately, because she is not like a captive, to be subjected to intercourse with one who is hateful to her; and she is divorced without receiving her *ketubah*. . . . And if she rebelled against her husband so as to cause him anguish, and said: "I am causing him anguish by this, because he did to me such-and-such" . . . she loses her *ketubah* and does not receive *ketubah* money at all; and she does not receive her *get* until twelve months have passed . . . And the Geonim said that in Babylonia they have different customs regarding the *moredet; but these customs did not spread among most of Israel,* and many great people in most places disagreed with them.[14]

Maimonides does not require any explanation from the *moredet* as to why she finds her husband repugnant, nor does the court need to examine whether there is any substance to her words. The very claim that she cannot have sexual relations with her husband because he is repugnant to her is in itself sufficient to entitle her to an immediate *get*. The court even forces him to do so, even by means of brute physical force. Nevertheless, he denied her right to *ketubah* money.[15] One clearly sees Maimonides' rationalistic world view and medical erudition reflected in the explicit reason offered for this ruling: "because she is not like a captive, to be subjected to intercourse with one who is hateful to her."

Most of the medieval Jewish sages did not accept Maimonides' opinion: namely, that a *moredet* claiming that she found her husband repugnant is entitled to an immediate divorce, even under compulsion, without any attempt to make peace between the partners. Maimonides' opponents feared that giving so much power to the woman would be likely to weaken the family unit and increase the incidence of divorce. They also thought that such a quick forcing of divorce—without investigation, questioning, and warning—would turn it into a forced *get*, of doubtful validity. Such a ruling by Maimonides would quickly become known throughout the different Jewish communities, even reaching the ears of women and of their relatives who advised them. If they were to know that a claim that "he is repugnant to me" sufficed to ensure an immediate divorce from their husband, they would make use of it. Whatever the real reason for their wish to divorce, the woman could easily force her husband to give her a *get*. Evidently, Maimonides thought that, if one was in fact dealing with a physical revulsion of the woman toward her husband, any attempt to restore domestic harmony was doomed to failure, particularly in light of the fact that in this case the woman forfeits her *ketubah* money. However, the strong economic position of women in most of the European communities reduced the validity of this line of reasoning.

3. The Proliferation of Divorce in Ashkenaz in the Thirteenth Century and Thereafter

During the thirteenth century, there was a marked increase in the number of "rebellious" women in Germany who wished to divorce their husbands. This is a fascinating chapter in the social history of the period, which has not yet been properly studied. Due to the scattered nature of the relevant sources, the pattern indicative of this phenomenon has heretofore not been recognized. During the mid-thirteenth century, one of the sages of Regensburg appealed to R. Meir of Rothenburg, asking him to take action to reduce the large number of women who had "rebelled against their husbands" and sought divorce at their own initiative. The interlocutor referred to these women as "becoming arrogant to their husbands." He suggested to Maharam that in cases such as these, in which the "rebellious" woman refused to have sexual relations with her husband and wished to divorce him without any real justification, the ban of Rabbenu Gershom Meor Hagolah be waived and the husband be allowed to marry a second wife. This sanction would, in his opinion, stem the increase in "rebellious wives."[16] R. Meir agreed that a change for the ill had taken place in the character of women in his day: "In these generations, when the daughters of Israel are not modest as they were in earlier generations . . ." Some of Maharam's disciples quoted these words in an even harsher manner with regard to the women: "But in these generations when the women are loose, it is not fitting to believe them."

The second source pertaining to this subject appears in certain remarks of the leading disciple of R. Meir of Rothenburg, R. Asher ben Yehiel. He explained why, in his opinion, it is impossible to continue to maintain the above-mentioned edict of the Babylonian Geonim. This *taqqanah* was made, as he puts it, at a time when the women were "modest," whereas in his own day (end of the thirteenth and beginning of the fourteenth century) they are "brazen," so that were they to be allowed to divorce at their own initiative, not a single Jewish woman would remain with her husband; all of them would rebel and get divorced.[17] This is a rare and very harsh generalization. It is difficult to imagine that he would have used terminology of this type, had he not been aware of the large number of divorces in Jewish society and the danger they presented for the familial framework.

In all of the sources that we have seen, all of which stem from the same period, the women are depicted as "arrogant toward their husbands," "brazen," "immodest," and "loose"—all of these, terms used by men. Were we to have been privy to even something of the voices of the women, the picture received would certainly be very different.

The third source is found in the words of another disciple of R. Meir, R. Hayyim ben Yitzhak Or Zaru'a, which describes the strong action taken by R. Meir of Rothenburg against the women. *Or Zaru'a* relates that R. Meir, in contrast to the *taqqanah* of the Geonim, ruled that a "rebellious" woman who wishes to be divorced does not receive any of her *ketubah* money. But according to this author, that *taqqanah* did not help, and R. Meir was then forced to take a more drastic measure. In concert with other sages, he introduced a far-reaching ordinance—one that in fact contravened fundamental halakhic conceptions—to deprive the woman even of whatever private wealth she had brought with her from her parent's home as a dowry or as a gift.[18] According to the halakhah, not only is the husband required to return these monies to his wife in the event of divorce (or his heirs return them if he dies and she is widowed), but if they were lost he is required to pay their value to his wife from his own pocket. The fact that leading figures proposed such a far-reaching edict, opposed not only to Talmudic halakhah but to what had long been accepted both in the Ashkenazic communities and outside of them, clearly indicates the great social crisis underway and the panic felt by the leadership.

The fourth source describes an additional step, more severe than the two that preceded it: At the end of his life, R. Meir issued an edict that would remove from the woman's possession those properties that she had brought from her father's home, even if they were no longer in her husband's possession but in her own keeping—and this too against an explicit rule in the Talmud. The fifth source is preserved in the halakhic compendium of R. Mordekhai ben Hillel, likewise one of Maharam's disciples. This refers to another edict introduced at that time (mid-thirteenth century): Namely, that every couple who wished to become divorced cannot do so, even if the local rabbinic authority agreed to approve the *get*, but need to attain the consent of rabbis from other communities as well.[19] This practice remained in effect into the fifteenth century.

The edict also stipulated that the couple must pay a substantial sum of money to the sages in the various communities in exchange for their agreement. This edict also has no likes in the Jewish diaspora, and is likewise indicative of the depth of the crisis and the large number of divorces in German Jewish society at the end of the thirteenth century and thereafter.

Assembling all these diverse sources, we receive a double picture: (a) There was a large number of divorces in Ashkenazic Jewish society during the period in question, often at the initiative of the women. While we do not have exact numerical data, it is clear that one is speaking of a high percentage. S. D. Goitein found a divorce rate of about 20 percent in the Cairo Genizah records, which we shall discuss below. In my opinion, in thirteenth century Germany, the rate was even higher. (b) The sages undertook unsuccessful attempts to circumvent the divorce boom. The number of divorces in Germany in later generations, especially during the fifteenth century, was evidently even greater than that at the end of the thirteenth century. The situation in the fifteenth century goes beyond the framework of our present discussion, and we shall suffice with a brief presentation of the main features, which also shed light on the events of the thirteenth century. R. Seligman of Bingen strongly attacked the large number of divorces in his day, the early fifteenth century. His edicts and letters, not only demonstrate that the phenomenon of divorce was very common at the time, but there are clear hints therein of erotic infidelity on the part of the husbands and romantic adventures of the wives. He even accused the couples of arranging new marriages while still within the framework of their old marriage and before writing the *get*.[20] It is not clear whether such phenomena were in fact common in the fifteenth century, or whether R. Seligman was engaging in hyperbole. The latter view seems more likely, but it is clear that he would not have voiced accusations of this type without some factual basis.

R. Seligman also protested against other phenomena, such as that the making of a new match for the woman or her "*qiddushin*" took place immediately after the divorce, whereas according to halakhah she is required to wait at least three months. He and his colleagues issued an edict prohibiting engagements for second marriages until three months had passed since the divorce. The fact that divorce was already quite common among German Jewry during the twelfth and thirteenth centuries also serves to explain the admonitions found in *Sefer Ḥasidim* against men divorcing their wives, except in cases of infidelity.

What was the background for the high rate of divorce and the initiative of many women to break up their family unit and "rebel" against their husbands? As is the case with many other historical phenomena, it is difficult to isolate one single factor. In my opinion, five principal factors joined together here:

I. The first factor affecting the divorce rate was the improvement in the economic status of Jewish women in Germany and France beginning with the eleventh century. The woman played an important role in supporting the family, particularly during the thirteenth and fourteenth centuries, when many women were engaged in money-lending to non-Jews. The women also received substantial dowries and inheritances from their parents, which were in effect the woman's private property. As she was not economically dependent upon her husband, divorce did not affect her economic situation. Maharam and his colleagues had good reason to use economic sanctions against women in an attempt to limit their initiation of divorce.

II and III. Early marriage and the great mobility of Jews related to their means of earning a living, as mentioned above in chapter 2, contributed to divorce. The usual marriage age for girls was between twelve and sixteen, and some married even younger. On the other hand, many husbands and families were forced to uproot themselves for economic and other reasons. This phenomenon increased in the fourteenth and fifteenth centuries, when many Jews migrated to northern Italy and Poland. We have already noted the dilemma this presented to the young couple, and especially to the wife: to join her parents who were departing for a new place, or to remain with her husband and never again see her parents. Under the conditions of communication that existed in that time, the significance of such a move was in practice, in most cases, to be cut off from them forever. The alternative was to divorce the young husband and to find a new spouse in the new locale of the parents. From this, it would seem likely that many of those getting divorced were still relatively young. The large number of divorces prevented the feeling of shame, on the one hand, and increased the number of available bridegrooms, on the other. As soon as the phenomenon of divorce became common, other couples were also prepared to take this step, even if they may have hesitated initially. In a society in which divorce was common, there was no real harm to the social status of a man or woman who had been divorced.

IV. A general improvement occurred in the status of the Jewish woman in Ashkenaz beginning from the eleventh century. This improvement found its expression in many and varied areas, including that of the role of women in performing the commandments and in religious life generally. Their wealth and the general improvement in their status raised their self image.

V. A parallel and very interesting phenomenon took place in the neighboring Christian society. Because of its importance, we shall discuss this point separately.

4. "Rebellion" of Women in Christian Society

Medieval European Christian society, particularly in the eleventh century and thereafter, was marked by an interesting phenomenon that indirectly relates to the rebellion of women in Jewish society. During that period, a religious revival swept over Europe, which did not pass over the women. There were Christian women who wished to refrain from sexual relations with their husbands and, for various, primarily spiritual reasons, to live in a state of celibacy. As is known, the attitude of the Christian church toward sexuality has a definite negative aspect. Marriage was perceived as a lower form of life than celibacy. Those men and women who chose to forego marriage and sexual life, particularly after they already had children, were seen as choosing a more Christian way of life, one that brings man closer to God. Complete abstinence within the family framework and by mutual agreement was seen as the ideal to be striven for, because sexual relations, even within the family, disturb the spiritual development of both man and woman.

In the extant documents are found accounts of Christian women who, after the birth of a number of children, "rebelled" against their husbands and sought to refrain from sexual relations, in the hopes of fulfilling their longings for a more spiritual life. Frequently this took place as part of a process of penitence. Generally speaking, they succeeded in convincing their husband to respond to their request, but at times this involved a harsh struggle, to the point of "rebellion" in the literal sense.

Certain thinkers feared that accepting the woman's demand to cease sexual relations would reduce the husband's authority over his wife, which would in turn upset the social order generally. There are only few cases in which the husband initiated the abstinence in family life. In most cases, the woman took this step, and it was she who in practice forced the husband to accept her view.[21]

Two conclusions that emerge from the phenomenon of "rebellious" women in European Christian society are significant for its relationship to the phenomenon in Jewish society: the willingness of the Christian women to rebel against their husbands and to refrain from sexual relations after they failed in convincing their husbands to accept their view; and the fact that abstinence improved the woman's position within the Christian family, including her freedom of movement, alongside an improvement in her overall self-image. Offhand, the phenomenon seems similar to the large number of "rebellious women" in Jewish society, but it is nevertheless doubtful whether a direct connection existed between the two types of "rebellions." In any event, the motivations were different. We do not find women refusing to have sexual relations with their husbands on religio-spiritual grounds in the Jewish sources. The Jewish sages were in any event strongly opposed to the phenomenon, whereas in Christian society many thinkers and spiritual guides encouraged it. Nevertheless, the two rebellions reflect a certain mood that was widespread in society in those days, and both of them drew upon a certain shared common cultural atmosphere, including the recognition that one needs to take account of the woman's wishes in family life, and both of them indicate an improvement in the woman's self-image.

The heavy concerns of the Ashkenazic sages regarding the large number of divorces needs to be seen in a broad historical perspective. This was a period of decline in the political and social standing of the Jews generally. In 1215, harsh ordinances were introduced against the Jews by the Fourth Lateran Council. During the second half of this century, a further precipitous decline began in the status of German Jews, which reached its nadir in the statement of the German Emperor Rudolph, that the Jews were subjugated to him in both their bodies and property (*cum personis et rebus suis*). It was only natural that the sages would make efforts to strengthen the community from within in light of the harsh external pressures.

5. Divorce in Spain

The extant sources do not indicate far-reaching changes regarding the subject of divorce in Spain similar to those that occurred in Ashkenaz. True, many sources from the halakhic literature and from the responsa of the Spanish sages deal with the subject of divorce, indicating clearly that there too one of the principal—and perhaps the most important—grounds for divorce was the large amount of travel for commercial reasons, which often led to extended absences on the part of the husbands. Married women waited a long time for their husband's return, but once the absence became excessively protracted, they took the initiative and sought a divorce. This was particularly true during the eleventh and twelfth centuries. Travels and migrations occurred due to the political and economic changes in Spain, and particularly the establishment of the Christian principalities in northern Spain. The fact that most of the questions addressed to R. Yitzhak Alfasi (Rif) concerning divorce refer to the journeys and absences of the husband, clearly indicates the connection between the two phenomena. It is no accident that some women asked their husbands to take an oath, even before the marriage, that he would not abandon them and go elsewhere without their agreement.

Questions relating to the appointment of emissaries to receive the divorce writ from the husband, who was staying in a distant place, are one of the main subjects that appeared in responsa literature of the eleventh and twelfth century, as we have already noted above. In Spain, these lengthy journeys and absences often involved another particularly difficult aspect: namely, that at times the husband married a second wife in his new place of residence, something allowed by the halakhah and accepted in Spain and in the Muslim countries. These marriages were often an important factor in the wives' suit for divorce. They were often prepared to tolerate the husband's extensive absence in the hope that he would return to them and the family would be reunited, but once they learned that he had taken another wife in his new locale, they were no longer willing to sit patiently and wait.

These absences had a deleterious effect on family life in general, even when they did not cause the break up of the family unit. While the husband could marry a second wife during his absence and thereby take care of his personal needs, many women were left abandoned. At times, they sought lovers outside of the framework of marriage—a fact to which there are a number of testimonies in the responsa literature.

In this discussion, one needs to remember that the dozens of questions concerning divorce addressed to the Spanish sages in the eleventh to thirteenth centuries deal with specific problems that arose from a dispute between the partners or due to halakhic questions connected with the writing of the *get*. Those divorces that were executed without raising any special problems were not addressed to those sages, and we have no means of knowing their numbers. The ethical literature written in Spain during this period does not contribute information on this subject similar to what we have found in the parallel Ashkenazic Musar literature. It follows that any attempt to estimate the dimensions of divorce in Spain, notwithstanding the great interest elicited by the subject, is purely conjecture.

It is true that the sources preserve hints indicating that during the fourteenth century there were those among the Jewish sages in Spain who saw the situation of women as good and fortunate, to the point of complaining about their exploiting their good situation for ill, while emphasizing their self-confidence. We have already mentioned the words of R. Asher (the Rosh), written in Spain, concerning the "arrogance" of Jewish women in his day. He writes elsewhere that, "Because of our sins the daughters of Israel in these days are loose and one must be concerned lest they put their eyes on another man."[22] Similar complaints were articulated by the son of the Rosh, R. Judah ben Asher, who served as rabbi of Toledo in the mid-fourteenth century. But one is speaking here of linguistic hyperbole and, with all their importance, one needs to exert great care in relying upon them. They provide a clear indication of the strong position and self-confidence displayed by women from prestigious families in relation to their husbands, but it is difficult to build anything substantial upon them. The women from prominent families exploited the high status of their families and their connections with Christian courtiers to impose divorce upon their husbands. Rosh criticized the behaviors of these families in a variety of areas, including the misuse of their high status vis-à-vis weaker classes in society.

The divorce rate among the Jewish communities in the Mediterranean basin was also quite high, as follows from the findings of Shlomo Dov Goitein. His card file, based upon the Cairo Genizah documents, contains 243 references to

the family status of women who were married.[23] The division was striking: 103
were married for the first time ("virgin bride") as against 140 who were married for the second time. Thus, more than 60 percent of the marriages in Jewish society, according to this file, were second marriages. True, this finding
cannot be taken as indicative in any exact way of the situation in general, as
one is not speaking here of a systematic scientific study but only of random
data, but it is nevertheless significant. Even more interesting is the breakdown
of the 140 women who married for the second time: widows—32; divorcées—
23; divorcées remarrying their first husband—22; second marriages for which
there is no notation as to whether they were widows or divorcées—63. Thus,
the number of divorced women of whom it is explicitly stated that they remarried was 45. That is, at least 20 percent of the women mentioned in the lists
were divorced from their husbands, although it is clear that the number is
greater, as the 63 women who married a second time without any notation of
their prior status also included divorcées among their number. The fact that
some of the divorcées remarried their first husbands does not reduce the value
of this finding and its implications for the place of divorce in Mediterranean
society at that time. These women evidently divorced their husbands when
they traveled to distant places in connection with their business and remarried them, upon their return.

   The conclusion that follows from this discussion is that the family unit in
most Jewish communities was not at all stable, and that the idyllic descriptions
found in a number of studies have no basis in fact.

6. The Attitude to the Divorcée

What was the attitude of Jewish society to the divorced woman? The issue of
the social standing of divorcées directly relates to the frequency of divorce. It is
a well-known sociological fact that the more widespread and accepted a given
phenomenon is in society, the less negative its image is likely to be. In fact,
this serves as a kind of vicious circle: The more widespread divorce became, the
less negative its image, and in turn it became even more common. Many men
and women arrived at the conclusion that the suffering that fell to their lot in
their shared life did not justify the effort and self-restraint involved in maintaining their family unit. It was preferable to separate, as other acquaintances
of theirs had done, even if there was no weighty justification for divorce.

   The willingness of the medieval woman to be divorced was related to three
main factors: society's attitude to the divorcée, her opportunities for remarriage, and her economic status. In a conservative society, in which the attitude
toward the divorcée was negative, many women preferred continuing to bear
their suffering in silence, particularly when this was accompanied by serious

fears of harming their own family's prestige and weighing down their children's marriage prospects.

As mentioned, the frequency of the phenomenon in itself greatly blunted its sting. Many other respectable people were in the same status of divorce, as a result of which there was nothing about which to be ashamed. Support for this assumption is to be found as well in the fact that we do not find any reservations about marriage with a divorcée in the writings of the sages of Ashkenaz and Spain, of the same type as found in the Babylonian Talmud. The fact that there is no real opposition to such marriages in *Sefer Ḥasidim* as well is of particular importance. This book contains a great deal of advice to the pietists about the choice of the desired wife, such that the fact that it does not list divorcées among those with whom marriage is undesirable calls for explanation. Similarly, in R. Nissim ben Jacob of Kairouan's work *Hibbur Yafeh meha-yeshu'ah* there is no denigration of the divorced woman, even though it speaks at length of "bad women."

The economic status of the divorcée was a function of the money she brought with her from her parents' home and of the reason for the divorce. The divorcée had three main sources of income: the money and property she had brought with her from her parents' home at the time of her marriage; those that she had inherited; and payments she received from her husband at the time of the divorce. In many cases, the divorcée enjoyed a favorable economic situation, because the woman was generally speaking entitled to receive back the money she had brought with her from her parents' home. The extent to which this was a dominant factor in the economic situation of the divorcée may be seen from the fact that, when R. Meir of Rothenburg and his colleagues wished to combat the phenomenon of excessive divorce, they did so by attempting to hurt the woman's right to take this money with her, as mentioned above. This attempt was unsuccessful in reducing the number of divorces—yet another sign of the economic independence of the divorcée. One may assume, with a high degree of probability, that the high divorce rate specifically led parents to seek means of assuring that the monies they gave their daughters at the time of marriage would in all events remain in her hands and not pass over into "alien" hands. The edict accepted in Ashkenaz communities in the eleventh century, evidently under the initiative of R. Gershom Meor ha-Golah, not to divorce a woman against her will, made it even easier for her to get money from her husband. In the negotiation that accompanied the divorce process, she enjoyed a position of greater equality than in the past. The strong economic basis enjoyed by many divorced women strengthened their social position and, as mentioned, also contributed to the relative increase in divorces found in Jewish society.

CHAPTER TWELVE

The Widow and the "Murderous Wife"

1. The Large Number of Widows

The number of widows in medieval Jewish society was considerable, and many of them were still quite young. This was the result of four main factors. First, the death rate in those days was relatively high, particularly as a result of plagues and natural disasters. During the course of the antisemitic violence in Ashkenaz and Spain, particularly during the fourteenth and fifteenth centuries, many thousands of Jews, both men and women, were killed, leading to the ubiquity of widowhood. Also, many Jews engaged in trade during this period. Some of those who travelled afar never returned to their homes, particularly during the ninth to eleventh centuries: some died in natural disasters, while others were murdered by highway robbers. Finally, the life expectancy of women in Europe, beginning from the thirteenth century, was longer than that of men, as shall be discussed below. It is therefore hardly surprising that the lot of widows and "chained women" and their legal and social status was widely discussed in the responsa literature, far more so than that of men who had been widowed. The difference stems from difficulties relating to the legal status of women, which raised weighty halakhic problems, particularly concerning the verification of her husband's death and the collection of her *ketubah*.[1] Such questions did not arise in relation to men.

A fifth factor, of lesser weight, was that of the marriage of young girls to men who were decades older than them, particularly in Muslim countries, a phenomenon that we have already noted in our discussion of marriage age. Due to the relatively short life expectancy in those days, some women were already widowed at an early age. In general, the phenomenon of marriage at an early age, common in Jewish society in both Muslim and Christian countries, contributed its part to this problem. The extant sources do not enable us to definitively establish the number of widows in Jewish society in the Middle Ages, nor how many of them chose to remain widows and how many waited for the proper time to remarry. Nevertheless, the picture that emerges from the Cairo Genizah and from other sources supports the assumption that the number fluctuated around 20 percent of the Jewish women, similar to that of widows in the general population of Christian Europe. The relative frequency of divorce, noted in the previous chapter, and the large number of widows and widowers, explain the large number of second marriages in Jewish society, as follows from the Cairo Genizah sources, from folk literature, and from the various branches of halakhic literature.

In this chapter, we shall focus upon three central subjects in the life of the widow: her place in society and in the family; her economic status; and the lot of the "murderous," twice-widowed wife (*qatlanit*).

2. The Biblical and Talmudic Heritage

The Bible places no restriction upon the remarriage of a widow (with the exception of barring her marriage to the high priest). Moreover, there is a specific injunction in the Bible not to oppress the widow and not to harm her dignity or her rights; however, these rights are not spelled out. She and the orphan are listed among the weakest sectors of the society; there was hence an ethical obligation to care for her. A similar concern is expressed in the Code of Hammurabi and in other laws of the ancient Near East. The repeated injunctions in the Torah and the adjurations of the prophets against harming the widow and orphan indicate the difficulties to which the widow was subjected, her weakness, and her lowly standing in society. It is clear that these things did not apply to women from wealthy and well-established families.

The Talmud contains a detailed discussion of the economic rights of the widow. We cannot undertake a detailed discussion of this subject here, and will suffice by alluding to a few facts with implications for the status of the widow in the Middle Ages. According to Talmudic halakhah, the property of the dead husband was not inherited by the widow, but rather by his sons and other relatives. So long as the woman did not remarry and did not sue for her *ketubah* money in court, the husband's heirs were required to provide her with food, clothing, and medical care, in accordance with the standard to which she was accustomed in her husband's home. She was likewise allowed to continue living in the home where she had lived with her husband, and to use the utensils and servants she had in the past. The *ketubah* of a widow who remarried was half that of a virgin, and her wedding day was also different: a virgin was married on a Wednesday, and a widow on a Thursday. This practice, which originated in the Mishnah, was preserved in a number of places until the Middle Ages, resulting in a feeling of insult on the part of some widows.

The fundamental Talmudic understanding regarding the widow's psychological world and her place in society was that the widow would very much want to remarry. She found her status difficult, and therefore would be willing to settle for a husband who was far from being a model of perfection, so long as she did not remain a widow. In general, the Talmudic sages thought that "more than the man wants to marry, the woman wants to be married." This was particularly true regarding a widow. This fundamental view, entailing a stereotypic and uncomplimentary perception of the widow and her mental world, also affected Jewish scholars in the Middle Ages.

The intense desire of the widow to remarry is also emphasized in Rabbinic homilies, which saw it in a positive light, and even praised those who assist her to do so. The sages emphasized that the obligation to be sensitive to the widow's dignity because of her suffering applies even to a wealthy woman, indeed, even to the widow of a king. One must be careful to speak to a widow in gentle tones, and to be lenient with her even in the economic realm, enabling her to receive from the heirs the food and drink that she was used to receiving in the past when her husband was alive, even if these are expensive—and thus did the sages behave in the Middle Ages.

Nevertheless, the sages were concerned about the possibly permissive way of life of widows. Their attitude toward the "murderous" woman (*qatlanit*), that is, one who had already buried two or three husbands, was particularly harsh, as we shall discuss below. Another reservation concerning the remarriage of a widow or divorcée appears in the words of R. Akiva, based upon the fear that a woman might make comparisons between the pleasure derived from intimate relations with her first husband and those with her second husband. While this was only a piece of practical advice and not a halakhic ruling, it is nevertheless difficult to imagine that advice given by one of the greatest tannaim did not leave some impression in the hearts of people even in the Middle Ages. This motif is repeated in the *fabliaux* literature of the high bourgeois widespread in France and Germany during the thirteenth century.

In the stories of Ben Sira (late ninth or tenth century) we find opposition to marriage with a widow, based on the suspicion that she had been sexually loose. This weighty consideration against marrying a widow was raised in *Sefer ha-Zohar*, but does not appear in Talmudic literature. It alludes to harm committed against the spirit of the first husband, who is attached to his wife even after death, a point to which we shall return below.

3. The Situation in Non-Jewish Society

The early Christian Church did not have a positive view of the remarriage of widows and widowers, whom Paul advised not to remarry, but in the Middle

Ages remarriage of a widow was perceived within Christian society as a natural thing.[2] Many women from all levels of society married for a second and third time—in the city, in the villages, and among the ranks of the high nobility. There were, however, those who counseled them not to marry a second time until a full year had passed since the death of the first husband. However, in various regions, particularly in the villages, young people and especially bachelors expressed their displeasure with the marriage of widows and widowers in the framework of an accepted and well-known ceremony, the *charivary*. In this ceremony, musical instruments and warblings were used to gave vent to their complaints that they had been rejected while prospective marriage partners were snatched up by others, who already had offspring yet nevertheless remarried.[3]

Officially, the widow was entitled to the protection of the Church because she was considered to be among the "unfortunate." In practice, many women preferred the status of being a widow to that of a married woman, so long as they had some means of subsistence. Unmarried women and widows enjoyed greater freedom than married women. The widow enjoyed great personal freedom and was also legally independent. On the one hand, she had left the control of her husband, but was no longer subject in practice to the authority of her father, whose control she had left years earlier. There were even women who were willing to pay their feudal lord for the privilege of not marrying a second time.

The widow's financial rights were, generally speaking, guaranteed by the *dos*. This stated that she would take possession of a considerable portion of her husband's property—between one-third and one-half—so long as she was alive. To this was to be added the property she had received from her parents as inheritance. The widow was allowed to manage her property as she wished, to serve as guardian of her small children, and to conduct their economic affairs as well. It is not surprising, therefore, that some women would prefer to remain widows rather than to remarry. All these phenomena had many interesting parallels in Jewish society in Germany and France. However, already at the end of the twelfth century, and in particular during the thirteenth century, the widow's rights in Christian society were gradually restricted, first in the Italian cities and later in other parts of Europe. While the dowry that she brought with her from her parents' home actually increased, her rights to her husband's estate were severely limited.[4]

In Muslim society as well, care was taken that the widow not be deprived of her rights to inherit, and it was even forbidden for a husband to impair her economic rights by divorcing her in the event of illness.

4. Life Expectancy in Europe

The status of widows was greatly affected by the life expectancy of men and of women. During the fifth to seventh centuries, women's death rate was extremely high due to the difficult conditions of life in the villages, the primitive state of medicine, inadequate nutrition, and complications arising from pregnancy and childbirth. The number of women was smaller than that of men, whose ability to survive was greater. It should not be surprising, therefore, that in German tribes during that period it was common for the parents of brides to receive high dowries for them.[5] There was a slight improvement between the eighth and tenth centuries, and life expectancy increased somewhat, but the number of men was still greater than that of the women. The conditions of life for women in the villages were quite difficult, particularly regarding childbirth and the rais-ing of children. It may also be that parents invested greater efforts in caring for the welfare of their sons, who were considered more productive labor power.

During the tenth century, a certain improvement took place in the technique of agricultural labor (e.g., greater use of horses and of water mills). These new inventions greatly increased the agricultural harvest and the quantity of food consumed by all members of the typical family, as well as improving its quality. In particular, the quantity of protein and iron increased, as did that of protein from legumes. The family diet became more nutritious and the life expectancy of all its members increased, particularly that of the women. The death rate in childbirth also declined significantly. As a result, during the eleventh to thirteenth centuries the proportional number of men decreased. Statistical data from this period indicate, for the first time, a more or less equal number of women and men in European society. One of the explicit indicators of this was the decline in the sum of the bride-price paid by bridegrooms and the increase in the size of the dowry provided by the bride's parents. But the high death rate in the mid-fourteenth century due to the Black Plague decimated all strata of European population. In any event, statistical data from the fourteenth and fifteenth centuries indicate an increase in the number of women relative to that of men. Thus, for example, in Bologna (Italy) in 1395 there were 96 men for every 100 women, while in Nuremburg (Germany) there were only 84 men per 100 women. According to some sociologists, the increase in the number of women—that is, the increase in the "supply"—somewhat weakened their social and familial status. These data, which refer to the cities, are relevant to Jewish society, which was predominantly urban. From *Sefer Ḥasidim,* which depicts Jewish society in Germany of primarily the thirteenth century, as well as from other sources, it clearly follows that the dowry paid by the bride's parents at the time of her marriage became more important.

5. The Situation in Jewish Society: The Attitude to the Widow's Remarriage

The widow was harshly affected by the disaster that befell her upon her hus-band's death, which brought in its wake pain and loneliness. This subject is mentioned often in the Genizah sources, but is discussed but little in the responsa, whether those of the Babylonian Geonim or of the European sages. This should not be surprising, as by its very nature responsa literature deals with halakhic questions and disputes between people, rubrics that do not include the emotional and mental world of the widow.

But even in those places where the sages were able to display empathy to the feelings of the widow and to her inner world, they did not always do so. Such is the case in the discussion of her lot in *Sefer ha-Zohar,* which evinces explicitly "male discourse" in which the woman occupied a strictly secondary place. First and foremost, one must remember the reservations against marriage with a widow expressed in the *Zohar,* on the grounds that the spirit of her dead first husband was still attached to her, as we shall discuss below.

Another objection, that to marriage with a widow whose husband died a martyr's death, was raised by certain circles in Ashkenaz in the eleventh century:

He who was killed for the sanctification and unification of the Name, may He be blessed, whether at a time of persecution or not at a time of persecution . . . and gave himself over to death, and was killed or crucified or burned for the Sanctification of the Name: once he has sanctified the Name with his body and soul, all Israel are obligated to rent their garments for him, and to mourn for him and to eulogize him in the synagogues and the study houses. And his wife shall never marry again, for the honor of Heaven and for his honor.[6]

This surprising halakhah, which sees the martyr as a king whose wife is forbidden to remarry, is cited by the Ashkenazic sages in the name of *Sefer ha-Mikzo'ot,* evidently a compendium of halakhot that originated in Ashkenaz. In any event, this rule has no basis in ancient sources, and does not seem to have left a concrete impression upon Jewish society in Ashkenaz, in which there were many martyrs in the Middle Ages.

Another indirect objection—drawing upon an approach similar to that proposed by the *Zohar*—was raised by R. Yom Tov Lipmann Mülhausen of Prague, ca. 1400. He discusses the question, with which husband a widow who has remarried will find herself at the time of the resurrection of the dead. He ruled that the latter husband was the one who would remain with her, basing his ruling upon the biblical prohibition against a divorced woman who had remarried returning to her first husband "after she had been defiled" (Deut. 24:4).[7] It follows from this that a widow's sexual relations with her new husband entailed an element of defilement, nullifying the right of the first husband to return to her. Therefore she may no longer live with him, not even in the messianic age. It may well be that people whose first marriages were happy, were influenced by these things not to remarry following their spouse's death. But there is no evidence in the sources to indicate that this subject exercised a significant influence upon the mental world of the Jews during the late Middle Ages.

6. The Commonness of Widowhood and its Social Significance

As we stated, the number of widows in Christian and Jewish society fluctuated around 20 percent of the total female population, many of whom were still relatively young. Moreover, the high divorce rate in Jewish society created a further pool of available women who had been previously married. On the one hand, the social pressure on the widow to remarry was reduced, as the unmarried state became a widespread social phenomenon; on the other hand, the large number of unmarried women increased the competition to find suitable mates. An interesting indication of the number of widows who remarried is preserved in the Genizah sources. In Goitein's card file—which is admittedly random and unrepresentative from the statistical viewpoint—32 women are listed as widows who remarried, plus an unknown number of the 63 women who remarried without notation of whether they were widows or divorcées, out of a total of 243 marriages recorded in the card file. If we assume that about half of the 63 were widows—an assumption for which there is no real proof—then the number of widows who remarried was 60: that is, about a quarter of all women who married.[8] It should not be surprising that there was such a large number for, as mentioned, many women were widowed when they were still young and the death of husbands was common, not only due to the relatively low life expectancy in the Middle Ages, but also because of natural disasters that befell the husbands when they travelled for business purposes. This phenomenon was of considerable social significance, since as a result a relatively large number of women became heads of families and ran them.

7. The Widow's Economic Rights

The main problem that the widow needed to confront—in addition to feelings of loss, isolation, and concerns for her children—was the protection of her economic rights: maintaining a suitable standard of living and her rights of inheritance, receiving her *ketubah* money, holding her own against other creditors who sued for a portion of the husband's estate, and running the family business. This subject is far-reaching and comprehensive. Due to limitations of space, we shall address here only a few main points. In our discussion of women's economic status (above, chapter 6), we noted the firm economic basis of many Jewish women in medieval Europe, due both to the significant sums promised in her *ketubah* and to the inheritances they received from their parents later on. In all of the European communities, we find Jewish women who participated in the support of their families, continuing to work even after their husbands' death. Some of them continued in the business in which they had been, in effect, full partners even before they were widowed. We find that husbands often undertook commitments to give all or most of their property to their wives after their own deaths. However, collecting this money often involved extensive litigation with sons, daughters, sons-in-law, and other family members.

The economic situation of widows from poor families was particularly difficult. Various testimonies to that effect are preserved in the sources, particularly those from the Cairo Genizah.[9] On the other hand, in prosperous families or in those that belonged to the middle class, which constituted the majority of medieval Jewish families, their economic position remained quite strong.

Many couples lived with their parents, particularly during the period immediately following their marriage, as we noted in our discussion of age at marriage. There was a certain advantage to this: In the Middle Ages, the grandmother played an important role in the education and care of her grandchildren. If they lived with the parents of the wife who was then widowed, this made things much easier for her both in terms of child care and in terms of the emotional support received from her family. Feelings of loneliness and isolation were also reduced somewhat. If, however, she lived with the parents of her deceased husband—which was true in the majority of cases—the picture was more complex. The extant sources preserve dozens of testimonies about family disputes, originating in the mother-in-law's interference in the life of the young couple. The sages even recognized disputes between mother-in-law and daughter-in-law as a factor that justified uprooting the residence of the young couple. The continued residence of the widow with her in-laws was not always fortuitous; moreover, Talmudic literature raises the possibility that under certain circumstances the woman may have been responsible for her husband's death because of her own bad luck, as we shall discuss below.

Some husbands, in anticipating their deaths, saw in their mind's eye their children—at times from previous marriages—to whom they wished to pass on all of their property, thereby depriving the wife of her share. Several Ashkenazic sages dealt with this question in the eleventh century, strongly criticizing such acts and the claims of the husbands. Many disputes that arose between widows and children were rooted in the Talmudic distinction between *ketubah* money and money for her support, and the issue of the woman's right to monies she had brought into the marriage as dowry, and inheritance she received later.

The woman's active role in supporting the family was also a source of friction. A widow often continued to engage in money-lending and commerce even after her husband's death, but before the division of the estate between herself and the other heirs had been clarified. As mentioned, this was often the result of her extensive involvement in the business even during her husband's lifetime. Some sons claimed that the mother was not conducting the business properly, thereby causing losses involving property that also belonged to them. Another claim was that the mother's profits derived from the estate, which belonged to the entire family. Postponement of the division of the estate only increased these ambiguities. One of the main causes of disputes between the widow and her children was the fear that the mother would remarry and the family property thereby pass over into the hands of strangers. Sometimes the sons and daughters arrived at a compromise with her whereby she continued to hold the property alone, on condition that she not remarry.

Another common subject of conflict even among wealthy families concerned the "widow's oath." According to Talmudic law, the heirs could require the widow to take an oath that she had not received any of the *ketubah* money, either in whole or in part, during her husband's lifetime or after his death. Some women were afraid of this oath and preferred to refrain from it as much as possible. Sources from the Cairo Genizah even mention women who made an explicit condition at the time of their marriage that they be exempt from it. Moreover, it was often difficult for the woman to distinguish clearly between money she used that originated in the family as a whole, and that which she had received as an inheritance or a gift from her parents. The heirs' suspicions were particularly great when the woman had children from previous marriages, a phenomenon that was quite common in those days.

The woman usually wished to preserve the high standard of living to which she had become accustomed during her husband's lifetime. Indeed, her right to this was already acknowledged in principle in the Talmud, although its application sometimes caused disputes. R. Solomon Ibn Adret (Rashba) was asked whether a widow who was supported by her husband's assets was allowed to have "two or three maidservants and their expenses, as she did during her husband's lifetime, or whether she is given only one servant to serve her." According to his ruling, it all depends upon the standard accepted in the family as a whole. "If the women of the family are accustomed to having two or three servants, the widow is given a similar number." If not, she must make do with one servant.

The wish to maintain several maidservants did not derive from economic need alone. From the Genizah sources, it follows that at times women had close connections of friendship with their household servants and it was difficult for the members of the household to fire them even when their economic situation took a turn for the worse. Thus, for example, a dying woman asked her sister to assure than her daughter would in any event not need to dismiss her maidservant. In our case, too, the widow may have enjoyed a close friendship with her servants and found separation from them difficult.

Others who challenged the widow's rights were her late husband's creditors. Talmudic law gave them precedence in collecting their debts from the husband's estate, so that people would loan money, knowing that their money was assured. In a bourgeois or petit-bourgeois society such as those of medieval European Jewry, this was a major subject of concern. Many loans and partnerships are mentioned in the sources, primarily in the responsa literature. It follows that the problem of debt collection was a real one and that creditors needed to worry about the fate of their money. The custom of husbands to give a large part of their property to their wife prior to their death did not help her in this case to bypass the creditors. Rashba, who was rabbi in Barcelona, was asked about a woman whose husband gave her "houses as a complete gift, to do with them as she wished, even during his lifetime."[10] The woman's attempt to rely upon this "complete" gift was rejected by Rashba, who ruled that in this case as well the creditors have first claim.

In certain cases, the widow confronted another kind of dilemma: the need for *yibbum* (levirate marriage) when the couple did not have any children. There were great controversies among sages from the various Jewish diasporas concerning the issue of *yibbum* and *halizah* (release from *yibbum*), and there was no uniform practice regarding this matter. However, in most places in the eleventh to thirteenth centuries, it was customary to have levirate marriage, as discussed above at length (see chapter 4). Particularly grievous was the situation of those widows in Spain who were subjected to *yibbum* with a married man, unwillingly and not to their benefit. Due to pressures of family and society, it was difficult for the woman to refuse *yibbum,* which was thought of as an act of concern for the soul of the childless deceased husband.

Another oppressive factor related to society's attitude towards widows from among the weaker sectors of society. There were those who did not treat the marriage ceremony with such women with the proper respect. A responsum of Rashba tells of a woman who refused to agree to the norm that was accepted in her place regarding some widows: "and she did not agree to marry him in the disrespectful way, like other women . . . so that she not be humiliated before her neighbors, and they not behave with her according to the custom of widows."[11]

8. The "Murderous Wife"

A woman, two of whose husbands had died, was classified as a *qatlanit* ("murderous wife") and, according to Talmudic law, was not allowed to marry for a third time. The validity of this prohibition was the subject of polemics among the Sages, particularly during the twelfth to fourteenth centuries. The issue has important implications for the status and image of the woman in Jewish society, the tension between halakhah and reality, the relationship between spiritual ideas and halakhic rulings, and the relationship among various Jewish diasporas in medieval Europe. The fears entailed in marriage with a wife or husband who had been widowed are not restricted to the Jewish people alone, but are part of the folklore of human culture generally, and appear among other peoples as well.[12]

The Talmudic Heritage

The Bible does not make reference to the "murderous" woman. True, in the Middle Ages some sages thought that Judah's refusal to marry his son Shelah to Tamar was due to the fear that she was a "murderous" woman (see Gen. 38:11), and that this served as the basis for the prohibition against marrying a two-time widow. However, the relevant verses in the Book of Genesis indicate that Er and Onan, and not Tamar, were guilty in their own deaths—and this is one of the important morals that follows from the incident.

The Babylonian amoraim (in *b. Yevamot* 64b) deliberated the question of the motivation for the prohibition against marrying a *qatlanit*, offering two explanations. The view of Rav Ashi was that it was the bad luck of the woman that caused the death of her husbands, and this bad luck would endanger anyone who might marry her in the future. Rav Huna believed that her husbands' deaths were caused by sexual relations with her.

Anyone studying this Talmudic passage may well arrive at the conclusion, based upon the rulings of such great sages and on the basis of the story of the death of the amora Abbaye, who married a woman whose first two husbands had died, that it is indeed dangerous to marry such a woman.

The Talmudic discussion concerning the destiny of the *qatlanit* harmed the image of the woman. She was perceived as one who is capable, through magical powers, of harming her husband. Moreover, no corresponding concept of a "murderous" husband exists in the Talmud or the halakhic literature. A man may marry as many times as he likes, even if he has buried several wives. It follows that many of the women who were widowed—even if only once—began to fear that they carried bad luck or that there was danger in sexual relations with them. It was sufficient for the second husband to fall ill for these fears to become stronger. One may assume that these fears were also felt by the husband who married a widow, and among his relatives and friends. It is no coincidence that in both the medieval period and in modern times some sages advised against marrying a widow altogether. The death rate during the Middle Ages was quite high, even among young people. Plagues frequently broke out and, in the absence of solid medical knowledge and with an increasing store of folk beliefs, a fertile ground was created for the emergence of fears of this type.

One may conjecture that the psychological state of a twice-widowed woman was very hard. In addition to serious objective difficulties—loneliness, care of children, the yoke of supporting the family, and pain and mourning for her dead husbands—she needed to deal with the painful feeling that she might have been guilty in their deaths. One may assume that some of the parents of husbands who died and their families did in fact see the woman as playing a role in the death of their loved one, and that their attitude towards her was colored by this.

The *Qatlanit* in the Middle Ages

Beginning in the twelfth century, medieval Jewish sages discussed the question of the *qatlanit* extensively. This was a real, actual question, not only because of the great death rate but also due to two factors that were peculiar to the Jewish society: the extensive travel for commercial purposes, particularly during the fourteenth and fifteenth centuries, and the murder of Jews in various outbreaks of violence. Surprisingly, there is no discussion of the *qatlanit* in the thousands of extant responsa of the Babylonian Geonim. However, it would appear that the Geonim were strict with her and did not allow her to remarry a third time. The sages in Egypt are even mentioned in Maimonides' responsum on the subject as those to whom it was clear that a "murderous woman" is forbidden to remarry, and who ruled so in practice.

The Situation in Spain During the Eleventh and Twelfth Centuries

During the twelfth century, a significant change occurred in Spain in relation to the "murderous" woman, which had a decisive impact upon future generations, testimony to which is found in one of Maimonides' responsa. In his view, the fear of marrying the *qatlanit* was based "upon divination and magic alone," and he ruled that there is no prohibition to marry a woman who is a *qatlanit,* and only people who are unhealthy in body and soul and plagued with fear think it forbidden to marry such a one. According to Maimonides, it was only to such cases that the Talmudic sages were referring when they opposed the marriage of a *qatlanit.* He pointed out that, in the lands of Spain, they found a way to allow a *qatlanit* to marry, out of the fear that she would seek satisfaction outside of marriage. There is no objective basis to the fear of marriage with a *qatlanit.*

Maimonides emphasized, not only that the court must advise the woman how to bypass the halakhah in a roundabout way, but that the judges ought to take an active part in the act of marriage. He advised that the *qiddushin* of the couple be solemnized outside of the court, and that thereafter the judges write her *ketubah* and recite the seven blessings. Why did he insist that this be done by a Rabbinic court, notwithstanding the difficulty involved in judges assisting in an act that is opposed to the halakhic ruling? Evidently, his purpose was to improve the image of the *qatlanit* and her status in society. He did not consider it sufficient to resolve the legal-judicial halakhic problem, but wanted to ensure that the woman's relatives would not perceive her as a "murderous" woman who should be feared. Maimonides' words imply that he wished to uproot totally the fear of the *qatlanit,* which, due to his principled position regarding superstition, he completely rejected and to which he did not attribute any importance. He similarly feared that women who were widowed a second time when they were still young would find themselves lovers outside of marriage. This follows explicitly from his words "and how can we agree that the daughters of Israel go to evil ways"?[13]

In his responsum, Maimonides mentioned that R. Yitzhak Alfasi (Rif) and R. Joseph Ibn Migash had already advocated the same approach. This testimony is problematic, as his position is rather different from their extant responsa on the subject. Both of them attributed more weight to the prohibition against marriage with a *qatlanit* than did Maimonides. They explicitly spoke against such marriages and did not allow one who wished to marry a *qatlanit* to do so. The only leniency in their position was that post factum the husband is not forced to divorce her.

Two factors evidently combined here leading to the change in Spain, and to the willingness—at least retroactively—to allow a husband not to divorce a *qatlanit:* the proliferation of early marriage in Jewish society, and the rise of rationalism. To these must be added the dangers that confronted husbands who travelled long distances on business, who were subject to death by natural disasters or at the hands of brigands, thereby increasing the number of such women in both Spain and in Ashkenaz.

Philosophical study and interest in sciences had been widespread in Spanish Jewish society beginning in the tenth century, primarily within the circles of courtiers and in the cultural elite, due to their cultural and social proximity to Muslim culture. People raised on rationalism could not accept the notion that the bad luck of the "murderous" woman had caused the death of her husbands, and that she was therefore forbidden to marry again. Moreover, the multiple widower was allowed to marry as many times as he liked. Jews' extensive involvement in medicine also made it more difficult for them to see the *qatlanit* as responsible for her husbands' deaths and to insist upon the taboo on marrying her.

Maimonides' responsum and his testimony on the attempts made in Spain to find a way to allow the *qatlanit* to remarry had great impact upon the sages who acted after him in Spain and in the Oriental lands, as well as in the Ashkenazic periphery, even though they were aware of the fact that they thereby were violating the words of the Talmud. Their refraining from unequivocal opposition to such marriages stemmed, from the fear that they would not be listened to, as well as from the feeling that the prohibition against the marriage of the *qatlanit* was excessively stringent for both them and for society in general: The women would remain alone till the end of their lives, and this at a time when many of them were still young.

The Situation in Spain in the Thirteenth and Fourteenth Centuries

Many Spanish sages referred to the subject of the *qatlanit,* particularly during the thirteenth to fifteenth centuries, as did their descendants who were exiled

from Spain to the Oriental countries following the Expulsion. This is indicative of the concrete nature of the issue, on the one hand, and the misgivings
relating to it, on the other. The high mortality rate during the Black Death
(1348–49) and the violence of 1391 greatly increased the number of widows in
Jewish society, raising the question whether the husband's death in the plague
or as a martyr led to his widow being classified as a *qatlanit*. In these numerous discussions, one can see the powerful impression left by the above-mentioned words of Maimonides in the responsum. Several sages explicitly expressed
their astonishment at Maimonides' ruling, even though they accepted his decision with reservations. Only a minority totally opposed his permission. On the
practical level, the opposing position did not carry much weight, and those who
wished to marry a *qatlanit* were able to find sages who followed Maimonides'
approach and were willing to marry them.

The *Qatlanit* After the Persecutions of 1391

An extensive polemic over the subject of the *qatlanit* was conducted in Spain
and outside of it after the harsh persecutions of 1391, in which numerous Jews
were killed and the communities were harshly affected. In wake of these difficult events, the number of women widowed for a second time and considered
qatlanit grew significantly. While the number of widowers also increased,
they were not defined as "murderous" and there was no hesitation about marrying them. Many of the Spanish sages of the period debated this question. The
main issue that troubled them was whether the men who had died as martyrs, such as those killed in the various persecutions, were to be treated like any
other person who died, so that their wives, if previously widowed, would be
considered *qatlaniot,* or whether Kiddush Hashem is different, and is not to be
included under the category of the *qatlanit,* if the husband died as a martyr
or in the plague.

The sources clearly indicate the great contemporary interest in this question
under the prevailing circumstances and the deliberations and differences of
opinion among the Spanish and North African sages regarding this issue. Several responsa of the Spanish and North African sages dealing with this matter
are gathered together in Bodleian-Oxford MS 820. According to R. Hasdai
Crescas, the spiritual and political leader of Spain at that period, a person
who dies as a martyr does not make his wife a *qatlanit.* Moreover, the same
holds true for any man who caused his own death, including one who committed suicide. R. Joseph Albo, R. Hasdai's disciple, also held the same view. To these
one should add the view of Ribash (R. Yitzkak ben Sheshet) who ruled that
death for Kiddush Hashem is not a sign of bad luck but, on the contrary, a very
meritorious deed, so that in that case one cannot argue that the woman's luck
caused her husband to die.

The Widow and the *Qatlanit* in the Teaching of the *Zohar*

Sefer ha-Zohar expresses a negative attitude toward the remarriage of a widow generally, even if only one husband had died. The perspective is that the dead husband had not "given up" on his wife. His spirit is found within her, and continues to conduct a powerful and ongoing struggle with the new husband; if the former is victorious, the second husband will die, and if the second is victorious, the former will abandon his wife and his soul wander about in the world. Therefore, "One who marries a widow is like one who sets to sea in a ship while there is a strong wind without ropes, and he does not know if he will pass over in peace or sink down to the depths."[14]

One may reasonably assume that this line of argument created fears of marriage with a widow. Not only would the new husband have reason to fear a magical force that might harm him, but these arguments introduced a new dimension into the discussion, casting heavy doubts into the heart of one who married such a woman, lest by his acts he might push aside the spirit of the first husband who longs for his wife and is still connected to her with strong bonds.

Moreover, in that same context in the *Zohar* one finds an idealized picture of the husband who had died waiting for his wife. After her death, he will go out to meet her from Paradise and bring her in with him to his place. This also hints at the idea that it is proper that the widow await the spirit of her first husband so as to unite with it after death, when they shall again shine together. For all these reasons it is preferable not to marry a widow, and all the more not to marry one who is so twice-over.

We thus find intense and explicit opposition in *Sefer ha-Zohar* to the marriage of a *qatlanit*, related to the belief in metempsychosis. Here, one is no longer speaking of insubstantial fears. If the reasons offered in the Talmud for not marrying a *qatlanit* were somewhat vague, that offered here was stronger in that it involves not causing harm to another person. The death of the second husband indicates that the spirit of the first husband still resides in the woman and refuses to abandon her. His victory over the second husband is testimony to his powerful hold over the woman and his ability to defeat and kill any man who attempts to marry her.

Toward the end of the Middle Ages, the Kabbalah spread and enjoyed great influence both in Spain and beyond it, particularly among those who had been exiled from Spain. We may conclude from this that there were those, particularly among the Kabbalists and those close to them, who viewed with suspicion the remarriage of a widow in general and of a *qatlanit* in particular. In any event, many sages during the late Middle Ages and at the beginning of the modern period strongly opposed marriage with a widow in general, and with a *qatlanit* in particular, the majority of whom were influenced by the words of the *Zohar*. Others were influenced by the position of R. Asher ben Yehiel (the Rosh), who also strongly opposed the marriage of a *qatlanit,* as we shall see below. It is difficult to assume that things of the sort written by the Rosh, who described marriage with a *qatlanit* as a grave "danger," did not leave echoes and suspicions in the hearts of people, particularly in light of his great influence in Castille.

The conclusion that follows from all this is that there was a certain withdrawal from Maimonides' ruling in Spain during the late Middle Ages, and in practice from the end of the thirteenth century. True, those women who were considered *qatlaniot* could still find themselves various solutions and turn to courts that were more lenient and followed the approach of Maimonides. After the Black Death, the situation in Spain became particularly difficult. There were many double widows, thought of as *qatlaniot,* whom we may assume that men were reluctant to marry due to the opposition of the Kabbalists, the Rosh, the Ritba, and other sages. It was for good reason that many sages came and argued that one who dies in a plague or as a martyr, does not cause his wife to become a *qatlanit.*

The Situation in Ashkenaz in the Eleventh and Twelfth Centuries

No reference to the issue of the *qatlanit* appears in the responsa of the early sages of Ashkenaz and France from the eleventh and twelfth centuries. This is surprising, in light of the fact that in both Germany and France the practice of marriage at a very early age was quite common, on the one hand, and that a large number of men who made lengthy commercial journeys did not return home, on the other. From these facts, we may assume that the issue of the *qatlanit* was a real one in these two centers as well. It is difficult to give a simple, unequivocal explanation for this surprising silence, especially in light of the fact that responsa literature generally reflects the life milieu and reality. This is even more surprising in light of the extensive discussion of this issue in Spain. True, the argument from silence (*argumentum ex silento*) is problematic: responsa concerning this subject may have been lost. Nevertheless, the question remains in principle. How is it possible to explain the total ignoring, over a period of some two hundred years, of such a central question in the life of society and the family? Moreover, the violent acts directed against the Jews of Germany and France during the Crusades certainly created a problem similar to those that appeared in Spain in the persecutions of 1391, which, as mentioned, are expressed in the responsa literature of Spain and North Africa.

The silence of the early sages in Germany and France would seem to derive from the fact that they were not accustomed to allowing the "murderous wife" to remarry, continuing the ancient tradition that was evidently observed in Babylonia during the Geonic age. Unlike their brethren in Spain, they were not raised in a rationalistic spirit and on philosophical inquiry, and did not think that, notwithstanding the harm this caused to the woman, there was any way of getting around the explicit Talmudic prohibition against remarriage of a *qatlanit*. It is quite likely that in Ashkenaz too there were those who found a way to bypass this prohibition, but the silence of the responsa literature seems to reflect the prevalent situation in the eleventh and twelfth centuries: the unwillingness of the sages to participate in the marriages of "murderous" women and their opposition to this act. But it may also be that the rather close connections with Spain during the twelfth century led in practice to their adopting the same means of bypassing the prohibition, although we have no concrete proof of this.

Opposition in Ashkenaz to the Marriage of the *Qatlanit*: Hasidei Ashkenaz and the Rosh

During the thirteenth century, the Ashkenazic sages were divided in their opinion on this issue. Hasidei Ashkenaz strongly opposed the marriage of the twice-widowed woman. *Sefer Ḥasidim* refers to the subject a number of times, from which it follows that, like the Kabbalists in Spain, they saw marriage with the *qatlanit* as fraught with real danger. One of their strongest expressions depicts one who marries such a woman as guilty of bloodshed, for which he will have to render account.[15] On the other hand, *Sefer Ḥasidim* also contains some lenient positions and innovations that were intended to limit and reduce the force of the prohibition. If the woman had children from one of the deceased husbands, she is not considered a *qatlanit* and it is permitted to marry her. Another lenient ruling that astonished later rabbis was that the prohibition against marrying a woman who is a *qatlanit* only applies to the third or fourth husband, but not to a fifth husband.[16]

R. Asher ben Yehiel (the Rosh), one of the greatest Ashkenazic sages of the end of the thirteenth century and beginning of the fourteenth century, who immigrated to Spain, expressed stringent opposition to the marriage of a *qatlanit*. He stated that, not only is one not to permit the marriage of a *qatlanit* in any manner whatsoever, but that a man who married her must be forced to divorce her, because she brings danger upon himself.[17] This indicates how strongly he was convinced that there was a danger in marrying a *qatlanit*, a conclusion clearly based upon the Talmudic discussion in general, as described above. He may have expressed here an Ashkenazic tradition, as he did in many of his rulings in Spain. As mentioned, *Sefer Ḥasidim* contains an opinion similar to that of the Rosh, not only in its general contents but also in its detailed reasons, but one cannot make any definitive statements on this matter. The Rosh was in the habit of turning to the Talmud itself and inferring the halakhah from it directly, more so than others in his day, who relied extensively on the precedents of earlier sages.

The Rosh's staunch position toward the *qatlanit* strengthens the assumption that in Ashkenaz, as in Spain, there were various opinions in the thirteenth century regarding the twice-widowed woman. Had the Rosh known that all of his teachers in Ashkenaz allowed the "murderous" woman to remain with her husband post factum once she had been married, it is doubtful whether he would have opposed Maimonides' ruling so vociferously, to the extent of saying that even after the fact the husband is required to divorce her. We know that R. Asher held an extremely negative attitude toward philosophy, which he rejected wholeheartedly, so that his strict approach on this issue also may have stemmed from his opposition to rationalism. He knew well that the lenient approach, which began in Spain in the eleventh century and reached its peak in the ruling of Maimonides, drew largely upon a rationalistic world view. In any event, his position on the issue of the *qatlanit* is to be seen as representing that of an Ashkenazic sage even after he migrated to Spain, just as we have seen in many places in his responsa and halakhic rulings.

During the first half of the fifteenth century two of the greatest medieval Ashkenazic sages debated the issue of *qatlanit:* R. Israel Isserlein and R. Jacob Weil. Their views were similar and both of them tended to be lenient, being evidently influenced both by Maimonides' approach to this issue and the situation in their own locale. From the words of both, one many infer that in their day it was customary in Ashkenaz to be lenient and to find a way to marry off the *qatlanit,* and that in practice the sages accepted this situation, even if they did not have a coherent teaching and clear justification for the lenient view. R. Isserlein's interlocutor explicitly stated: "We have seen several great Talmudic scholars and decent men who were not strict about this and married a woman, two of whose husbands had died, and no one protests or criticizes them."[18] In his responsum, R. Israel Isserlein takes exception to this practice and states that one ought to refrain from marriage with a *qatlanit.* In his words, "our rabbis" stated that one should be careful, and that they were astonished at "those few scholars" who were not insistent on this. However, he too sought ways to be lenient.

He invokes three reasons for leniency regarding the law of the *qatlanit.* First, he points to the small number of Jews and the need to encourage the creation of new families, the bearing of children, and to care for the cohesion of the community. Second, he quotes the verse, "the Lord protects fools" (Ps. 116:6); Finally, he mentions the importance of preventing young women who were twice-widowed from being "anchored"—that is, unable to marry—and thereby falling into bad ways. In the end, he specifically rejects the ruling in *Sefer Ḥasidim* that a fifth husband is allowed to marry her, and testifies that in "some countries" suggestions had been raised to be lenient if the husband "died due to change in climate in a pestilence, or if he was killed and burned for Kiddush Hashem," as in such cases the death may not be attributed to the woman's evil luck. We have already seen how similar ideas were raised in Spain one generation earlier, after the violence of 1391.

R. Jacob Weil, who was active at the same time in Germany, responded specifically to the opinion of Maimonides. He also did not know of any "clear reason" upon which those sages who were lenient relied to allow the marriage of the *qatlanit*, but it clearly follows from his remarks that in his day many Ashkenazic sages were not strict about this matter.[19] A similar picture is derived from the responsa of R. Moshe Mintz, who was active during the same period in Germany.

It would appear that the violence that became exacerbated in Ashkenaz during the fourteenth century and the plague in the middle of that century served as a stimulus for finding a way to ease the lot of the *qatlanit,* who was unable to marry. At the end of the thirteenth century, there took place the harsh persecutions of Rindfleisch, in which more than 140 communities were severely harmed. During the years 1336 to 1337, the persecutions of Armelder descended upon the Jews, in which more than one hundred communities were affected. In the mid-fourteenth century, the Black Death struck all the inhabitants of Europe, including the Jewish communities. The Jews were also blamed at that period for poisoning the wells, and in the violence that followed more than three hundred communities suffered badly. The fourteenth century generally was a very difficult time for the Jewish communities of Ashkenaz from both the political and security viewpoint. As marriage at an early age was common in this period as well, the problem of the *qatlanit*—a relatively young twice-widowed woman— became a concrete problem that confronted the rabbinic leadership of Israel in a dramatic way. Ashkenazic Jews were now ready, more so than in the eleventh and twelfth centuries, to accept the solution that had been propounded by their brethren in Spain. But while many women also died in the violence and the plague, whereas the man who became a widower was able to remarry a second or third time as he wished without any external obstacles, women faced difficulties in remarrying because of their perception as being *qutlaniot.*

The willingness to allow a "murderous" woman to remarry is deserving of special notice. People in the Middle Ages believed in supernatural powers that acted in and influenced all areas of life. A world view not based upon supernatural factors was alien to the zeitgeist. Their understanding of science was also very limited. They were unable to offer an explanation for wars, catastrophes, disease, or death. All these are influenced by hidden powers that are the true causes. Reality is no more than a smoke cloud through which different images are reflected, but the actual forces pulling the strings and activating events in reality are concealed from human eyes.

During the thirteenth century, a certain retrenchment from rational thinking took place in Christian Europe. During this period, people were greatly influenced by the crusader ideal and a popular religious revival took place that was affected in part by the activities of the mendicant friars, the Dominicans and the Franciscans. During the thirteenth to fifteenth centuries, the power of popular superstitions gradually increased in European Christian and Jewish society. The women suffered greatly from this development. The fear of demonic powers, which were allegedly present within women, was greater in the fourteenth and fifteenth centuries than in the earlier period, and many accusations were lodged against women due to their alleged involvement in magic and their use of magical means (*Maleficium*) to cause harm to man, to animals, and to harvests. There was also a turn for the worse in the position of the Church regarding this matter in the fourteenth century. It acknowledged magic as a covenant with the Devil; the Devil was seen as the one who gave the witch her power to perform evil.

These folk beliefs in women's connection to demonic powers left their clear mark on the works of Hasidei Ashkenazic. Yet notwithstanding this cultural development in Europe, we do not find any greater strictness with regard to the *qatlanit* in Ashkenazic Jewish society of the fourteenth and fifteenth century.

CHAPTER THIRTEEN

Summary: Woman's Status in Historical Perspective

I n this concluding chapter, we shall examine the status of the medieval Jewish woman in a general historical perspective: In what areas was there an improvement in their situation in comparison to that found in rabbinic literature and the teachings of the Babylonian Geonim, and in what areas was there a retrenchment or "treading water." We shall suffice with a brief overall view, as the subjects have been discussed in detail in the earlier chapters of this book.

During the course of this book, I discussed ten main areas of positive change, in which the status of women improved in an appreciable manner, particularly compared with the picture reflected in the Babylonian Talmud. The advice and legal rulings of the Talmudic sages were seen as bearing an aura of sanctity, so that deviation from them was no trivial matter. Thus, this indicates that there were weighty historical circumstances that led to the new reality. As opposed to that, there were three negative changes in the status of women.

1. The Positive Changes

1. The *"edict of the moredet,"* introduced in Babylonia in 651, acknowledged the woman's right to initiate divorce and even to force it upon her husband without losing her *ketubah* money. This *taqqanah* was in effect for more than five hundred years, and in certain locales even longer. The husband no longer had the exclusive right to undo the family unit, as he did in Mishnaic and Talmudic law, but the woman now enjoyed "equal rights" in this important area. In practice, the woman could initiate divorce and force it upon the husband as she wished. Even following a certain retrenchment from this edict in the twelfth century, the woman could still force divorce on the grounds that she found her

husband repugnant, although in this case she generally speaking forfeited her *ketubah*. Moreover, according to many sages, one is speaking of real coercion, with blows ("whips"), executed by hired Gentile thugs. Even if the woman did not actualize her right of coercion in the case of a violent and oppressive husband, her very ability to threaten to do so and collect her *ketubah* strengthened her position within the family.

II. *The herem* (ban) *of Rabbenu Gershom Meor Hagolah*, issued during the eleventh century, prohibited divorcing a woman against her will. Together with the retention of the *taqqanah* of the *moredet*, this created a far-reaching transformation as against the situation in the Mishnah, Talmud, and Geonic period. For the first time in the history of the Jewish people, the woman had the upper hand in this important area. In practice, the woman could divorce her husband against his will without losing her economic rights, while he could not take similar measures against her, but had to convince her to agree to divorce. Thus, the sages of Ashkenaz and France in the twelfth century had good reason for wishing to nullify *taqqanat moredet*. The combination of the woman's right to force divorce, her economic independence, and her ability to remarry easily in an open society were a proven recipe for increased divorce, as follows clearly from the sources.

III. *Rabbenu Gershom's* herem *against polygamy.* While Ashkenazic Jews in any event did not marry two wives, the *herem* prevented traders who came from other places where this was the custom to take a second wife from among the local women, and prohibited the Jews of Germany, France, and England from doing so or using it as a threat against their wives. The prohibition was imposed with the force of a ban and thereby prevented exceptions. As we have already seen in Egypt, where there was no such *herem,* but community regulations (*taqqanot*) against taking a second wife, some people found various ways of getting around the prohibition and marrying another wife. In our above discussion (chapter 4), we saw a number of examples of the power of the *herem* and its importance as barrier against inventive arguments by husbands who wished to marry another woman.

IV. *The important role played by Jewish women in economic activity* and in supporting their families, and the freedom of movement that was given them in Christian Europe. The way of life of a bourgeois or petit-bourgeois society generally speaking exerted a positive influence on the status of women. The involvement of many Jews in Babylonia in the areas of trade and finance greatly improved the status of women. However, the change in Christian Europe was incomparably greater, among Spanish and Provençal Jewry, and more so in Germany, France, and England. In chapter 5, we cited dozens of testimonies to this situation and the influence it exerted in strengthening the status of the woman both at home and in society. Of all the factors leading to the improvement of the status of Jewish women in Christian Europe during the Middle Ages, this is in my opinion the most significant one, whose importance it is difficult to exaggerate. The woman's right to leave her home as she wished and to meet with traders and leaders of state was of great significance.

Did women also exert influence upon community leadership? It is told of certain women, mentioned by name in the sources, that they had great influence in the royal courts, and according to the description that follows from the sources exerted even greater influence than did the men. Thus, for example, a chronicle concerning the violent acts of 1096 describes a woman who enjoyed very senior stature among the circles of Gentile rule: "and there was an important woman there whose name was Madame Mina . . . whose name was well-known, for all the great ones of her city and the princes of the land had dealings with her."[1] At the time of the imprisonment of the Jews in Blois in 1171, a certain Jewish woman assured the others that no harm would come to them, as she had strong connections with the rulers "who liked her very much."[2] Even making allowances for the tendentious nature of this writing, the very willingness to portray women in these terms indicates their place in society. In the source from Blois, R. Ephraim of Bonn depicted what he saw and heard in his day, and it seems likely that there is at least a core of historical truth in his words. It is difficult to imagine that women enjoying economic and political standing of this sort would not exploit their power to influence communal life, since everyone needed them and their connections with the Gentile rulers. Medieval sources from both Europe and the Muslim countries indicate the extent to which the community made use of those Jews who were close to the monarch. It is thus very likely that those Jewish women who were close to the king were also marshalled to this task.

v. *The relaxation of the prohibition against teaching Torah to women* and the seeking of various ways to teach them Torah, if only somewhat. The connection drawn by the Talmud between teaching Torah to women and the fear that this would lead them from promiscuity also prompted the quest for ways to permit it. The Jews in most European communities knew their wives as people whose prime concern was the support of their family and education of their children, who guarded their modesty even when in a Gentile environment, and even in captivity. This point has been discussed extensively in the discussion of the role played by women in martyrdom (chapter 9). Study of Torah did not "ruin" them. Thus, they thought that in their time the above-mentioned suspicion was no longer valid.

vi. *Women's increased share in performing the mitzvot,* particularly their right to recite blessings over time-linked positive commandments. We noted above (chapter 8) that Jewish women in Germany, and thereafter in France and other places, struggled for the right to say such blessings, even though they were exempt from doing so according to the halakhah. Various outstanding sages, including Rashi's own teachers, already recognized this right in the second half of the eleventh century. This was not a purely religious matter, as it also entailed a clear recognition of woman's central place in society. Even if one cannot speak of actual equality in these areas, the very struggle and recognition of women served to improve their image in their own eyes and those of the environment.

vii. *Imposition of the* herem *and corporal punishment upon physically abusive husbands.* In France, during the twelfth century and thereafter, a rule was established that constituted a definite improvement in women's status: A man who beat his wife was considered like one who struck his neighbor. At the same time, it was determined in Ashkenaz that one must be even stricter with him than with one who struck a stranger, and in certain cases to impose upon him corporal punishment, to cut off his hand, and to place him in *herem.* The woman thereby changed from a person subject to the authority and control of a master, to an independent person, harming whom was considered a serious sin— also toward Heaven—even if in practice they were not always insistent upon suitable punishment to husbands who beat their wives.

viii. *Effective abolition of the prohibition against marrying a "murderous" wife* (i.e., one who had buried two husbands). The ignoring of the explicit Talmudic halakhah that one is not to marry a *qatlanit,* beginning in Spain in the eleventh century and greatly strengthened by Maimonides' position, gradually came to influence other Jewish diasporas. True, the Spanish Kabbalists, Hasidei Ashkenaz, and others refused to abolish this prohibition, but they were in the minority: Most of the sages followed Maimonides' approach. The improvement in the status of the woman regarding this subject involves two aspects: first, her right to marry a third time; second, that she was no longer perceived as responsible for the death of her husbands, with all that implies. The phenomenon of the *qatlanit* was more widespread in the Middle Ages than in modern times. It exerted a harsh influence upon the image of women, and the de facto ignoring of the prohibition against marrying her improved her status.

ix. *The large number of* mordot *(rebellious women) in Ashkenaz during the thirteenth century,* and the struggle against this phenomenon. Women's ability to initiate divorce and their resistance to the *taqqanot* of R. Meir of Rothenburg indicate their great self-confidence and economic independence. Moreover, this fact indicates that society generally saw divorce as a "natural and accepted" phenomenon, which does not harm the image of the woman involved.

x. *The important place of women in the teaching of the Kabbalists,* both in family life and in the picture of the Afterlife, within which marital relations were also understood as an important religious value. The woman facilitates the relationship of "mating" between her husband and the Shekhinah. As Moshe Idel put it: "From this point of view, one is to assume that the woman is considered not only as an addition to the man, who requires her for his own perfection, but also a comprehensive and necessary element for the existence of reality, whose activity has a decisive influence upon the situation of the universe as a whole."[3]

It is hard to imagine that such outlooks did not influence the attitude toward women on the part of those close to Kabbalistic doctrine. Some of these changes, particularly those relating to the place of women in religious life, fit in well within the general atmosphere of Christian Europe during the twelfth century, in which women played a more respectable role in religious life than they had in the past, and the individual played a greater role in society.

2. Negative Changes

We have enumerated ten positive changes in the status of women, but in several areas discrimination and inequality remained, and in three areas the situation even worsened:

I. *Greater insistence on exaggerated customs of modesty* in the Muslim countries. These were noted above (chapter 5) in our the discussion of the restrictions on movement imposed upon women. Limitations on freedom of movement and against appearing in public places had a clearly negative impact upon the status of woman. The ability to come into contact with strangers and to participate in social activity is a basic element of an open society, in which women are also allowed to be involved. These limitations did not affect the Jewish woman in Christian Europe in a negative way, and even in the Muslim countries there was not total insistence upon their observance.

II. *Greater strictures in relation to menstrual laws.* During the Middle Ages, there was an exacerbation in the laws of menstrual separation, particularly in Ashkenaz. This was not only a matter of physical distancing. The attitude toward the menstrual blood and its association with "dangers" inherent therein indicate the increase in the power of magic in Jewish society. It is no coincidence that Hasidei Ashkenaz were more concerned than were their predecessors with the association of woman with acts of magic. In the late Middle Ages, the belief in magic and enchantment reflected a high point in terms of its influence within European Christian society, and it is not surprising that this influenced Jewish society.

III. *The negative attitude toward women* of several medieval Jewish thinkers who were trained in philosophy. Philosophy flourished mostly in Spain and in Provence, and one might have expected these thinkers to see the place of the woman in society and in the family with greater openness and equality than did those sages who relied upon the words of the Midrash and the Talmud in a more literal way; dozens of harsh expressions speaking ill of women appear in these literatures, while there are relatively few positive expressions. But it was specifically the Kabbalists in Spain and the pietists in Germany who did not make extensive use of these negative expressions and generally ignored them. They showed greater admiration and respect for the woman than did several of the Jewish philosophers in Europe and the Muslim world during the Middle Ages.

Moreover, in the opinion of a thinker such as R. Yitzhak Abravanel, the nature of the woman is opposed to that of the man and harms him, and it is only through means of heavenly merit that a man finds a wife who is suitable to and helpful to him.[4]

From an overall historic perspective, greater weight must be given to the opposite camp. The views of Rashi, R. Simhah of Speyer, R. Meir of Rothenburg, Hasidei Ashkenaz, and the Spanish Kabbalists, who saw marriage as a holy covenant between two partners, in which God is not merely a witness but also an active partner, made a great impression. Harming the woman—who in the words of Rashi is "the seed of God"—is like harming the honor of heaven. The words of the prophet Malachi (2:14) that the woman is "your companion and your wife by covenant," served as the foundation for this viewpoint. It also suited that which was accepted in the Christian world from its beginnings, namely, that betrothal and marriage are a holy covenant. This viewpoint became increasingly strong in Europe during the tenth to twelfth centuries.

3. The Silencing of Creativity

In one area, that of the spiritual life, women had a decidedly inferior position. Throughout the Middle Ages, which continued for about a thousand years, we do not find so much as a single Jewish woman of importance among the sages of Israel. The Bible mentions women who influenced the course of history and were numbered among the important figures in the history of the Jewish people. The Talmud also mentions some isolated women, who became a symbol for future generations of women's ability to reach a position of prominence in the area of spiritual life. The best known among these was Beruriah, wife of the tanna R. Meir. But one seeks in vain for an analogous figure in medieval Jewish history. The names of hundreds of learned Jewish men and sages from this period have been eternalized, because of their outstanding life work in the areas of spiritual and social life, but not a single woman is to be found among them. While we did mention above (chapter 7) a number of Jewish women from the Middle Ages, none of them enjoyed real renown. Moreover, over a period of a thousand years, not a single Jewish woman wrote a halakhic, literary, theoretical, mystical, ethical, or poetic work, with the exception of a handful of poems written by Jewish women in Spain.

This fact is even more surprising if we compare the absolute silence of Jewish women with the significant creativity of women in Christian society, particularly in the area of mysticism. This difference does not seem restricted to the realm of creativity alone. One is speaking here of a profound and important indicator of their place in society. About 14 percent of the saints of the Catholic Church are women.[5] Moreover, as we have seen above in chapter 7, in Muslim culture too mention is made of women who transmitted religious traditions. The silence of Jewish women thus speaks volumes.

This is particularly true of Jewish mysticism, in which it was impossible to engage without profound knowledge of Talmud and halakhah. We have not found any record of women who engaged in mysticism or were creative within this field, as compared to Christian society, in which women were involved and creative within this field and occupied an important and respected place therein. Among the hundreds of Jewish Kabbalists, no mention is found of the name of even a single woman.

Offhand, this situation might be explained on the basis of the argument that in any event Jewish women did not create any literary works in the Middle Ages. But this does not help to resolve the mystery, as Jewish women were excluded from involvement in mysticism in all periods.[6] Not only do we have no works of women in the field of mysticism, but there are not even any testimonies to indicate that they engaged therein. By contrast, in other areas of Jewish religious life at least a few isolated women did take part, as we indicated above. Gershom Scholem observed, not only the absolute distance of women from involvement in Kabbalah, but also the damage caused to Jewish mysticism as a result. He suggested that this was caused by the ancient connection drawn by the sages between women and demonic forces.[7]

More recently, Moshe Idel has turned to this subject from a different perspective. In his opinion, the discussion of the absence of women from involvement in mysticism should not be separated from their complete silence in all areas of cultural creativity. In his opinion, this silence derives from two main causes.

The first reason is technical: In European Christian society, monastic houses were set up for women, which served as hothouses for the cultivation of mysticism: Most of the female mystics were nuns, and they had the free time to immerse themselves in sacred studies, to engage in meditation like the monks who became mystics, and to create a literature that expressed their thoughts and experiences. By contrast, it is impossible to find a parallel framework allowing for the cultivation of a life of solitude and study for Jewish women.

The second factor relates to the scale of values that Jewish society presented to women. With the women's full agreement, the society set the highest value upon giving birth to children, educating them for Torah and good deeds, and the strengthening of the Jewish family, under conditions of life which were at times quite difficult. Their happiness and satisfaction in the fulfillment of these tasks was equivalent in the eyes of the women to any other benefit and blessing that would ensue from involvement in any other cultural creativity.

"In a religious culture whose central values are raising families and the study of Torah on the part of men, one may assume that even Jewish women saw a merit to themselves in attaining these goals. They certainly saw themselves as enjoying a life of self-fulfillment and an experience of fullness, no less so than the Christian female mystics, who sought a life of a different type."[8]

There is no doubt that the two factors mentioned by Idel exerted great influence. However, it seems to me that these are insufficient in themselves to explain the compete absence of women from spiritual activity in general, and from mysticism in particular. There were widows who had already fulfilled their reproductive function and that of assisting their husbands in studying Torah, and others, the conditions of whose life allowed them to engage in mystical activity, without affecting their obligations toward their family. Moreover, there were learned Jewish women who devoted much of their strength and energy to the study of Torah. Why did none of these see fit to create works of their own?

It seems to me that to the reasons listed by Idel and other scholars one must add the heavy fears of women studying mystical works, which were considered particular sacrosanct, during the time of their menstruation. In the Hebrew version of this book, I cited a number of examples indicating the grave fear that a woman would unintentionally touch a book containing mystical secrets, all the more so that she would deal with this literature in depth. *Megillat Ahima'az* tells of a disaster that befell an entire family because a menstruant woman touched *Sefer ha-Merkavah*. This and similar stories indicate the depth of the fear of involvement of women in works characterized by holiness and mysticism.[9]

4. Between "Pious" and "Rebellious" Women

The concepts of "pious" and "rebellious" women cover a multi-faceted range. The Jewish female martyrs, who occupied an important place in the violent events of 1096, enjoyed the rare titles of "saintly women," "distinguished," "righteous," "holy," "pure," and "daughters of kings."

Under the rubric of "rebellious" women one may include quite a distinguished group of women. First and foremost one must mention those who demanded divorce of their husbands; these were the classical *moredot*. They were given this title on the basis of the Talmudic terminology, because they refused to have marital relations with their husbands or to perform their household duties as required by halakhah. Due to their large number and their strong position, they were referred to in the thirteenth century by such noted scholars as R. Meir of Rothenburg and R. Asher as "arrogant" and "loose," as we saw above in chapter 11.

However, there were also rebels of an entirely different type, who were unwilling to obey the rulings of the sages. For example, the Jewish women in Egypt and in Byzantine who refused to immerse themselves in the *mikveh,* according to the instructions of the sages; or the Jewish women in Ashkenaz, who continued to serve as *sandeqaiot* for their grandsons or sons, despite the explicit command of R. Meir of Rothenburg, the leading sage of thirteenth century Ashkenaz, to refrain from doing so (see above, chapter 8).

In a certain sense, "Rabbanit" Bruna may also be seen as a "rebel." She wore *zizit* (a fringed garment) in opposition to the express opinion of the Maharil, the leading Ashkenazic sage in the fifteenth century, as did other women at the same time (see above, chapter 8). The power of their "rebellion" may be indicated by the fact that Maharil refused to chastise her personally, because of the fear that she might refuse to listen to him.

A completely different kind of "rebellion" involved the refusal of young girls to marry, against their will, bridegrooms their parents had picked out for them. There were those who persisted in their refusal, even though the father had made an oath to give her to the bridegroom that he had chosen. Records of this are found from Spain and Germany. In several passages, *Sefer Ḥasidim* warns parents not to force marriage upon their daughters and sons, which may indicate that this was not a rare phenomenon.

These "pious" and "rebellious" women had many shades, and their definition is not simple. Is the refusal of Rabbanit Bruna to obey the ruling of the Maharil and refrain from wearing *zizit* to be seen as an act of rebellion? Or was it perhaps actually an act of piety, indicating her deep attachment to *mitzvot* that she was not obligated to perform by law? This doubt emerges with greater force regarding girls whose parents tried to force upon them marriage with a partner that they did not wish. The definition of "rebellion" is thus largely subjective. In any event, both the "pious women" and the "rebels" are indicative of women's self-awareness and their great confidence in their own power.

During the fifteenth century, Victor von Karben, a Jewish convert to Christianity, claimed that the intense devotion of Jewish women to their religion, and the decisive role they played in martyrdom, originated specifically in their feeling of deprivation. In his opinion, as they were not commanded regarding circumcision they did not merit eternal life. Their great zeal came to appease God and to atone for their inferiority.[10] Due to the tendentious nature of Von Karben's writing, it is difficult to know how much truth there is in his words. A comprehensive examination of the behavior and way of life of Jewish women is liable to cast much doubt upon his explanations. Nevertheless, his testimony that the women influenced the Jewish men to persist in their faith and to refuse to convert to Christianity, is of importance. Further testimony of this has been preserved in various and varied Jewish and Christian sources that are to be seen as reliable, as stated above in chapter 9. Hence, the paths of the pious women and the rebellious ones did not always diverge from one another, and at times they even took part together in the sacred task, which seemed to them to serve as surety for the continued existence of the Jewish people.

Notes

Introduction (pages 1–7)

1. *Sefer Ḥasidim,* ed. Wistinetzki, §1301 (321).
2. *Teshuvot ha-Geonim,* ed. Assaf (Jerusalem, 1927), §2.
3. "We find no real barriers to the capacity of women to exercise power; they appear as military leaders, judges, castellans, controllers of property." McNamara and Wemple, "The Power of Women," 94.
4. "In the aristocratic household based on the conjugal unity, women engaged in a variety of activities: supervising the rearing and marriage of children, dispensing patronage and gifts, receiving visiting dignitaries... performing lordly functions in their husbands' absence... As feudal lords, women settled disputes involving vassals, garrisoned and fortified castles, raised and commanded troops, and sometimes even rode into battle at the head of the host." Evergates, *Aristocratic Women in Medieval France,* 4–5, and ibid., 180, n. 2, for a survey of the polemic concerning this issue.
5. See what has been written on this recently by Rosen, "Circumcised Cinderella," and further bibliography there in the notes. See also the discussion of the image of woman, below, Chapter 1.
6. *Teshuvot ha-Ritba,* §61 (69).
7. Goitein, *A Mediterranean Society,* esp. vol. 3. For Friedman's studies, see the bibliography at the end of this book, and cf. Kraemer, "Women's Letters from the Cairo Genizah."

Chapter One. The Image of the Woman (pages 8–32)

1. *b. Shabbat* 62a. In the source, the sense is that women have forms of ornamentation unique to themselves.
2. *Gen. Rab.* 17.2 (ed. Theodor and Albeck, 151–52).
3. *b. Qiddushin* 29b.
4. *b. Pesahim* 113b.
5. "The characteristic medieval attitude could only have arisen in an age in which clerical and aristocratic groups were able to impose their point of view on society. If public opinion had been formed from the bottom upward, rather than from the top downward, the prevalent dogma might have been different." Power, *Medieval Women,* 10.
6. Rabad, *Ba'alei ha-Nefesh,* 14–15.
7. *Perush Ralbag al ha-Torah,* in *Miqraot Gedolot ha-Keter* (Jerusalem, 1997), 45. In his view, the woman is lacking in "perfection of the intellect," and therefore is on an intermediary level between animals and man, as shall be discussed below.
8. *Ba'alei ha-Tosafot al ha-Torah,* ed. Y. Gellis (Jerusalem, 1982), 1:111.

9. R. Bahye, *Perush ha-Torah* (Jerusalem, 1977), 73, 83. The perception of the woman as matter alone, because of her "passivity," also appears in the words of Maimonides and of the sages who belonged to the neo-Platonic circle that existed in Spain in the fourteenth century.

10. R. Yitzhak Aboab, *Menorat ha-Maor,* 368; cf. his words there, 371–73.

11. Abravanel, *Perush ha-Torah,* Gen. 1:27.

12. *Ralbag, Perush Ralbag* to Gen. 3:20, ed. Haketer, 55.

13. Ralbag's attitude to women has been examined by Menahem Kellner in "Philosophical Hatred of Women," 119–27, where he also compares the approach of Maimonides and others. He notes the tangible influence of Aristotle on Ralbag's attitude to women. On Aristotle's approach, see M. C. Horowitz, "Aristotle and Women," *Journal for the History of Biology* 9 (1976), 183–213; G. Freudenthal, *Aristotle's Theory of Material Substance: Heat and Pneuma, Form and Soul* (Oxford, 1995), 24, 37–39; and cf. P. Allen, "Plato, Aristotle and the Concept of Women in Early Jewish Philosophy," *Florilegium* 9 (1987):89–110.

14. See the Hebrew version of this book: Grossman, *Ḥasidot u-Mordot,* 30–31.

15. Schwartz, *Yashan be-Qanqan Ḥadash,* 239. See his discussion of the hatred of women and of sexual relations, ibid. 231–39. Apropos their rejection of intercourse, the sages used contemptuous expressions regarding women themselves.

16. *Perush Rabbenu Bahya le-Pirkei Avot,* in *Kitvei Rabbenu Bahya,* ed. H. D. Chavel (Jerusalem, 1970), 503.

17. b. Shabbat 146a: "When the snake copulated with Eve he cast into her contamination. When Israel stood on Mount Sinai their contamination ceased."

18. Maimonides, *Guide* 3.8.

19. *Miqraot Gedolot Haketer;* vol. I: *Bereshit* (Jerusalem, 1997), on Gen. 3:16, p. 53.

20. *Perush Ramban al ha-Torah,* in *Miqraot Gedolot ha-Keter,* ibid., 55.

21. R. Bahye, *Perush ha-Torah,* 81, and see the editor's notes there.

22. See the summary of Tishby, *Mishnat ha-Zohar, vol. 2,* 510.

23. *Aqedat Yizḥaq,* Pt. 9., 73b.

24. *Hadar Zeqenim* (Leghorn, 1840), 7.

25. On the position of women in Greek and Roman culture, see the bibliography in Horowitz, Freudenthal, Allen cited above, n. 13; Barkai, "Greek Medical Traditions," and the literature cited there, 139, nn. 38–39. On her position in midrashic and Talmudic literature, see e.g. D. Biale, *Eros and the Jews;* Boyarin, *Carnal Israel;* Ilan, *Ma'amad ha-Ishah ha-Yehudit be-Erez Yisrael;* Ahdut, *Ma'amad ha-Ishah ha-Yehudiyah be-Bavel,* esp. 23–99. Extensive further bibliography is cited in the notes there.

26. *Perush Rabbenu Sa'adya Gaon le-Qohelet,* ed. Kapaḥ (Jerusalem, 1962), 250.

27. Abravanel's *Commentary* to Jdg. 17:4 (Jerusalem, 1955).

28. Ahdut, *Ma'amad ha-Ishah,* 65.

29. See Schwartz, *Yashan be-Qanqan Ḥadash,* 232.

30. For examples, see the Hebrew edition of this book, 38–40.

31. For all these sources, see: *b. Yevamot* 63b; *Bava Batra* 145b; *Eruvin* 41b; *Eruvin,* ibid.

32. Aboab, *Menorat ha-Maor,* 357–364.

33. See Shirman and Fleischer, *Toldot ha-Shira ha-Ivrit bi-Sefarad ha-Nozrit,* 99ff., and n. 16 there with extensive bibliography on the *maqamah;* Rosen, "Minhat Yehudah."

34. On the image of the woman in medieval literature, see also Dishon, *Dimui ha-Nashim ba-Sifrut ha-Ivrit;* Baskin, *Images of Women in Sefer Hasidim.*

35. Borchers, *Jüdisches Frauenleben.*

36. See, e.g., *b. Sanhedrin* 66a; *b. Yevamot* 63b; *b. Berakhot* 57b; *b. Sotah* 47a. On the Iranian literature, see Ahdut, *Ma'amad ha-Ishah.* 56–60.

37. For all these, see *Masekhet Sofrim*, 15.7, ed. M. Higger (New York, 1937), 282; *m. Avot* 2.7; *b. Sanhedrin* 67a; *b. Pesahim* 111a; *b. Gittin* 45a.

38. R. Bahye, *Perush ha-Torah*, 1.765; cf. *Gen. Rab.* 17.21 (ed. Theodor and Albeck, 157).

39. See Tishby, *Mishnat ha-Zohar* vol. 2, 610.

40. *Sefer Ḥasidim*, ed. Wistinetzki, §§174, 380, 1456, 1465, 1466, 1468.

41. Dan, *Demonological Stories*, 278–86.

42. *Sefer Ḥasidim*, §§172, p. 70.

43. For a detailed discussion of this subject see Barkaï, "Greek Medical Traditions."

44. The attitude of Jewish tradition to the menstruant is discussed in various papers and articles. See especially Dinari, "The Impurity Customs of the Menstruate Women"; idem., "Profanation of the Holy."

45. Barkaï, "Greek Medical Traditions," 129; on the attitude toward menstruation in various cultures from the anthropological viewpoint, see Buckley and Gottlieb, *Blood Magic: The Anthropology of Menstruation.*

46. On Muslim law, see Quran 2.222; Farah, *Marriage and Sexuality in Islam*, 108–10; Roded, *Women in Islam*, 163. On the attitude of Christianity, see Brundage, *Law, Sex and Christian Society*, 283.

47. *Ketubot* 61a.

48. *Or Zaru'a*, 1.§460 (p. 96).

49. As found in the Cairo Genizah, Goitein, *Sidrei Ḥinukh*, 24–25.

50. See also Marcus, *Rituals of Childhood.*

51. See MS. NY-JTS, R. 356. The Talmudic source is *b. Berakhot* 17a.

52. *Siddur Rashi*, ed. Freiman (Berlin, 1912) §267, p. 127.

53. On the role of women in religious revival in Christian society, see Bynum, *Holy Feast and Holy Fast*, 13–72, and below, chapter 8.

54. See, e.g., Exod. 38:8; Num. 26:64.

55. ed. Müller, *Teshuvot Ḥakhmei Ẓarfat ve-Lutir*, §40, p. 24.

56. See *b. Qiddushin* 30b; *b. Niddah* 31a.

57. Tishby, *Mishnat ha-Zohar*, vol. 2, 607–12, which forms the basis for most of the statements brought here.

58. *Zohar* III.167a–b.

59. On the key position of marriage and of woman in Kabbalah and of erotic symbols connected with ecstatic and theosophic Kabbalah, see Idel, "Sexual Metaphors and Praxis"; Liebes, "Zohar and Eros"; Wolfson, "Woman—The Feminine as Other in Theosophic Kabbalah."

60. *Zohar* III.167a.

61. Meislish, *Shirat ha-Roqeaḥ*, 226–232. And cf. Kraemer, "Women's Letters from the Genizah"; and the discussion of woman as wife and mother, below, chapter 6.

62. On the sermons and their nature, see Horowitz, "Preachers, Sermons"; Saperstein, *Decoding the Rabbis.*

Chapter Two. Age at Marriage (pages 33–48)

1. The following several studies deal with marriage age in medieval Jewish society: Goitein, *A Mediterranean Society*, 76–79; Friedman, "The Ethics of Medieval Jewish Marriage," 83–102; Agus, *The Heroic Age*, 277–84; Grossman, "Child Marriage." According to Agus, there were many cases of betrothal and marriage at a young age, before the girl had reached the age of twelve and a half, so much so that it may be seen

as a general phenomenon in eleventh century Franco-Germany: "Girls were usually married before they reached the age of twelve and one half" (278). This statement, that the phenomenon characterized Jewish society in Germany generally, is somewhat exaggerated; in any event, there is no proof of this in the sources themselves. On marriage age in Jewish society of the Second Temple, Mishnaic and Talmudic periods, see Schremer, "Man's Age at Marriage"; Katzoff, "The Age of Marriage of Jewish Girls."

2. "It was an insignificant social phenomenon"—Goitein, *A Mediterranean Society*, 79. He is apologetic for the very fact that he devoted space to the discussion of such a rare and insignificant subject in Mediterranean society.

3. *Yevamot* 62b, and see below; and cf. Tosafot to *Yev.* 96b, s.v. *nasa ishah.* R. Yitzhak ben Shmuel—one of the leading Tosaphists of the twelfth century—interpreted this as implying that a person is obligated to find a wife even for "his minor son," that is, one who has not reached the age of thirteen.

4. *Qiddushin* 41a. I shall discuss below this ruling as it was issued by the amora Rav. This was done merely as a reminder of the saying, without giving preference of any kind to this tradition.

5. *Avot de-Rabbi Nathan*, Version II, ch. 48, p. 66. The concern is that the young girl may become pregnant and die as a result.

6. See the various opinions and the discussion thereof in Katzoff, "The Age of Marriage of Jewish Girls," 11–12, and Schremer, "Man's Age at Marriage" (above, n. 1).

7. The questions addressed to R. Moshe (the Gaon at Sura beginning in 825) and to R. Amram (the Gaon at Sura beginning in 858) refer to the phenomenon of betrothal and marriage of "minor" maidens. Even though we do not have sources from the early Geonic period (seventh century), one may assume that the phenomenon of child marriage existed at that time as well.

8. "Weddings were often arranged and sometimes solemnised when children were in their cradles . . . A father took the earliest opportunity of marrying his child in order that the right of marriage might not fall to the lord. Innumerable examples might be quoted." Power, *Medieval Women*, 39. See also Goody, *The Development of the Family*, 64, 185 ff. The practice of feudal rulers to involve themselves in the marriage of their subjects at times affected Jews as well. *Sefer Ḥasidim* tells of "a wealthy man who by means of his deputies forcibly took to wife a 'daughter of good family,' without the consent of either the woman or her parents" (§1879, 456).

9. Similar conclusions are reached by Shulamith Shahar in *The Fourth Estate*, 112, 121–123. For historical and sociological aspects connected with marriage age in Europe, see Hajnal, "European Marriage Patterns"; D. I. Kertser and D. P. Hogan, "Reflections on the European Marriage Patterns," *Journal of Family History* 16 (1991): 31–45. Hajnal's conclusion on the difference between the higher marriage age in Western European Jewish society during the late Middle Ages, as opposed to that in Eastern Europe, does not match the reality of Jewish society. It is difficult to find a distinction of this type, and it is clear that there were many marriages at a young age in Jewish communities in Europe, as will be discussed below.

10. Herlihy, *Medieval Households*, 103–11. Herlihy noted the changes that took place in the age of marriage in urban and rural society. (ibid., 74–78) In the early Middle Ages in Europe, the marriage age was very high. Many men even married in their thirties. This age decreased in the High Middle Ages. During the eleventh to thirteenth centuries far-reaching changes began to occur in Europe: The size of the population grew extensively and there were impressive developments in the spiritual and cultural life. These developments found their expression also in the structure of the family and its

arrangements. The need for agreement of both partners to marriage began to be recognized, a subject we shall elaborate in the next chapter. The age gap between the two marriage partners was likewise reduced. This is implied by the extant statistics of the number of men and women in the estates in Europe (see, for example, the summarizing table in Herlihy, ibid., 77). On marriage age in the late Middle Ages, see A. Borst, *Lebensformen im Mittelalter* (Frankfurt, 1982), 70–71.

11. Herlihy, *Medieval Households,* 101–103; "Medieval society in the central Middle Ages was acquiring a marked plurality of women over men . . . In the towns of Flanders and the Rhineland, from the late twelfth century, unattached, unmarriageable women reached extraordinary numbers, raising what historians traditionally call the Frauenfrage, the 'woman question'" (ibid., 102).

12. R. Hanokh served as the rabbi of Cordova between 965 and 1014, but in practice he served as the spiritual leader of all of Jewry in Muslim Spain.

13. *Teshuvot Geonei Mizraḥ u-Ma'arav,* §184, and its source in MS. Montefiore 98; ibid. §186.

14. Ibid., §187. While Miller, in his notes there, was uncertain as to the identity of the respondent and preferred the assumption that one was speaking of one of the Babylonian Geonim, it is impossible to agree with him. The use of the singular ("I read your letter and I understood . . . I was astonished"), the style of writing, and the location of the responsa in MS. Montefiore 98, indicate that one is dealing with an early Sephardic sage, who from the context must be R. Hanokh.

15. Research literature suggests a model of marriage in the Mediterranean countries characterized by a low marriage age for women, as opposed to a higher age for men. See P. Laslett, "Family and Household as Work Group and Kin Group," in *Family Forms in Historic Europe,* ed. R. Wall, J. Robin, and P. Laslett, 526–27 (Cambridge, 1983). I do not know whether this model is valid for the High Middle Ages. In any event, it fits the marriage age of Jewish maidens during this period, in both Muslim countries and European ones.

16. *Teshuvot ha-Rambam,* II, §427, p. 705.

17. In practice, the bridegroom and those supporting him rely upon the rule that custom overrules halakhah (*j. Yevamot* 12c), even though they do not mention this rule explicitly. There is no room for a claim of this sort if one is dealing with isolated and unusual individuals who did so.

18. *Tosafot* at *Qiddushin* 41a, s.v. *asur le'adam* (italics mine).

19. *Kol Bo,* §65.

20. Isserleim, *Sefer Terumat ha-Deshen,* §253.

21. Zeldes, "As One Who Flees from a Snake," 54.

22. Maimonides, *MT, Ishut* 3.19; and cf. ibid, §11–13.

23. *Sefer Ḥasidim,* ed. Wistinetzki, §1144, p. 290.

24. *Teshuvot ha-Rashba,* 4, §169, in the question. Cf. there, in *Teshuvot ha-Rashba:* "so small that she does not know . . ."

25. Maimonides, *MT, De'ot* 5.11.

26. See the comments on this source in Schremer, "Man's Age at Marriage," 53, and ibid., 48–49, for further sources in praise of marriage of boys at an early age.

27. *Sefer Ḥasidim,* ed. Wistinetzki, §1084, p. 275. Further on he again calls upon the father not to take to himself or to his sons really small girls, who are as yet unable to become pregnant—and we have already seen that "grown" girls refers to those aged thirteen and up, who are capable of giving birth. The repetition of this motif suggests that there were those within Jewish society who married "minor" girls, that is, below this age.

28. *Sefer Ḥasidim,* ibid., §1894, p. 458.

29. R. Yitzhak Aboab, *Menorat ha-Maor,* 353.

30. Regarding Spain, dozens of examples of marriage of girls at a young age, including marriage of minors, appear in Elon, *Ha-Mafteaḥ ha-Histori,* I:16, 28, 30, 68, 69, 71, 116, 187, 188, 189; idem., II: 130–132.

31. Characterizing these marriages at a young age, Agus writes: "Child marriages were not the result of a pessimistic and gloomy outlook on life. Quite the contrary. Such marriages were the concomitants of prosperity, well being, financial success, and supreme confidence in a bright future" (*The Heroic Age,* 281). In principle he is right, even though there is an element of exaggeration in this generalization.

32. *Teshuvot ha-Rambam,* §34. On the power of the family in medieval European society, see Heers, *Le clan familial;* Herlihy, "The Making of the Medieval Family." On its power in Jewish society, see Grossman, "From Father to Son."

33. Teshuvot ha-Ran, §15.

Chapter Three. Engagement, Betrothal, and the Choice of a Marriage Partner (pages 49–67)

1. The following is the major literature dealing with the subject of engagement: Freimann, *Seder Qiddushin ve-Nissuin,* 31–33; Katz, *Masoret u-Mashber,* 165; Falk, *Jewish Matrimonial Law,* 86–112; Goitein, *A Mediterranean Society,* III.65–71, 91–92; Friedman, "Match-making and Betrothal."

2. Engagement as a prior stage to marriage is depicted in the Talmud as obligatory. See, e.g.: *b. Qiddushin* 12b; cf. Freidman, "Match-making and Betrothal," 57.

3. "Since it is shameful for the bridegroom and his relatives if they do not make a large feast and celebrate the entire day, some people make the *erusin* and *qiddushin* together so as to discharge their duty for both of them in one feast on one day" *Ma'aseh ha-Geonim,* 52–53.

4. *Teshuvot ha-Rif,* §118 421. On the seriousness of this phenomenon in Genizah sources, see: Goitein, *A Mediterranean Society,* III. 336–41 (including travels of women).

5. *Teshuvot Ḥakhmei Ẓarfat ve-Lutir,* §27 (14a).

6. See Friedman, "Match-making and Betrothal," esp. 163.

7. *Sefer ha-Shtarot le-Rabbi Yehudah Barzeloni,* §72 (128); §49 (72).

8. Gulak, *Ozar ha-Shtarot,* 7.

9. See below near footnote 20.

10. Freimann, *Seder Qiddushin ve-Nissuin,* 32.

11. New York - JTS, MS. Rabb. 1077 (*Hilkhot R. Abraham b. R. Moshe*), §574. Prof. Haym Soloveitchik drew my attention to this source. Abalon evidently refers to Avallon, in Burgundy. On this community, see Gross, *Gallia Judaica,* 17.

12. See *b. Yevamot* 37b ("R. Eliezer b. Jacob said: A person should not marry a woman with the intention to divorce her"). However, at ibid., 52a, it states that such a marriage is valid.

13. This follows from a number of sources, some of which are cited in my book, *Hakhmei Ashkenaz ha-Rishonim,* chs. 2, 3, 5.

14. *Teshuvot Geonei Mizraḥ u-Ma'arav,* §195. Müller, in his notes there, was uncertain whether to attribute this responsum to R. Meshullam or to R. Gershom Meor Hagolah, and left the point undecided. But the style and subject matter of the responsum, as well as its location within the manuscript itself (MS. Montefiore 98), within a bloc of

responsa of early Spanish sages—prove that it is Spanish. The method of writing and style of things are very suitable to that of R. Joseph Ibn Avitur.

15. *Ha-Manhig: Hilkhot Erusin ve-Nissuin,* 537. Cf. *Ozar ha-Geonim* to *Ketubot, Heleq ha-Shut,* §§67–68 (22), and the notes there.

16. See G. H. Goyce, *Christian Marriage* (London, 1948), 85.

17. See *Ozar ha-Geonim* to *Qiddushin,* §§283–288 (124–126).

18. Oxford - Bodleian, MS. Heb C 23, fol. 27r.

19. *Teshuvot ha-Rashba,* I. §771; IV. 174. A similar situation is described in *Teshuvot ha-Ribash,* §198. No less serious, in terms of the ability of the girl to choose her husband freely, is an event repeated several times in the responsa literature in which family members and other relatives frightened young orphan girls and made them take an oath not to marry anyone except in accordance with their advice.

20. Gulak, *Ozar ha-Shetarot,* 6. The document was from England, 1249.

21. Hameiri, *Beit ha-Behirah, Qiddushin,* ed. A. Sofer (Jerusalem, 1963), 206.

22. *Sefer Hasidim,* ed. Wistinetzki, §1894 (458).

23. Ibid. §§1102, 1104, 1131. For the source of these things, see *b. Sanhedrin* 76a; *Yevamot* 4a.

24. *Sefer Hasidim,* §1104.

25. Ibid., §1897 (459).

26. Ibid., §1086 (276).

27. *b. Qiddushin* 41a. For a detailed discussion of the stance of R. Joseph Colon, see J. R. Woolf, "Towards as Appreciation of Elijah Capsali as a Halakhist" [Hebrew], *Tarbiz* 65 (1996), 174–87.

28. *Teshuvot Mahariq,* §166.

29. *Sefer ha-Yashar le-Rabbenu Tam,* §101 (209).

30. *Ibid.* 210

31. *Teshuvot ha-Rambam,* §364. The public nature of engagements ("before a large public") was intended to make its nullification more difficult, and also to combat secret marriages, which were usually love matches between the partners.

32. *Ozar ha-Geonim, Qiddushin,* 109. The question was sent from Kairouan. R. Estori ha-Parhi (first half of fourteenth century) also complained that "most of the people" ignore the Talmudic prohibition (*b. Qiddushin* 41a) against marrying a woman before one sees her. A different prohibition that it was customary to ignore, according to him, was that against betrothing a minor girl who had not yet reached maturity, without her father's knowledge (see Freimann, *Seder Qiddushin ve-Nissuin,* 51). It is not clear whether this testimony refers alone to the practice of the Land of Israel, or whether it was also the custom of the Diasporas that he visited, or of other Diasporas from which people immigrated to the Land of Israel.

33. *Hibbur Yafeh meha-Yeshu'ah,* §15 (49).

34. Bonfil, *Bemarah Kesufah,* 200. And see the discussion of marriage, ibid., 196–203.

35. A great deal has been written on this subject. See especially Brundage, *Law, Sex and Christian Society;* Herlihy, *Medieval Households,* 80–82; Sheehan, "Marriage Theory and Practice"; Murray, "Individualism and Consensual Marriage," and ibid., 124–25, for additional bibliography.

36. A fundamental critique of his position appears in Raymond Decker, "Institutional Authority versus Personal Responsibility in the Marriage Sections of Gratian's *A Concordance of Disconcordant Canons," The Jurist* 32 (1972), 51–65.

37. "While individualism posed a challenge to both the feudal hierarchy and the patriarchal family, it nevertheless became increasingly important and influential throughout

medieval society; consensual marriage was but one manifestation of this individualism"; Murray, "Individualism and Consensual Marriage," 127.

38. For another different opinion, which downplays the importance of these sermons, see P. P. A. Biller, "Marriage Patterns and Women's Lives: A Sketch of a Pastoral Geography," in *Woman is a Worthy Wight: Women in English Society, c. 1200–1500*, ed. P. J. P. Goldberg, 60–107 (Gloucester, 1992).

39. Murray, "Individualism," 145, and the bibliography cited there in the notes.

40. Ralbag's (R. Levi ben Gershon) Commentary to *Hayyei Sarah, To'elet* §11, ed. H. Brenner and A. Freimann (Ma'aleh Adomim, 1993), 327; Kellner, "Philosophical Hatred of Women," 118.

41. On the institution of matchmaking, see Shiloh, "The Matchmaker in Jewish Law," 361–73. He describes the development of this institution in a convincing way. I have added here a discussion of the historical factors that led to the growth and development that took place therein.

42. *Or Zaru'a, Pisqei Bava Qamma*, §457 (72), in the responsum.

43. *Sefer Ḥasidim*, ed. Wistinetzki §1131 (286).

44. *Teshuvot ha-Ribash*, §268.

45. Yuval, "An Appeal Against the Proliferation of Divorce," 190.

46. On the professional rabbinate, see Agus, *Teshuvot Ba'alei ha-Tosafot*, Introduction, 24–25; Yuval, *Ḥakhamim be-Doram*, 11–20, 398 ff. At ibid., 398 n. 201, further bibliography is cited.

47. *Teshuvot Maharil ha-Ḥadashot*, §189 (296).

Chapter Four. Monogamy and Polygamy (pages 68–101)

1. See Friedman, *Ribbui Nashim be-Yisrael*, 8–10. For selected bibliography dealing with the subject of monogamy and bigamy in medieval Jewish society, see the notes in the Hebrew edition of this book: Grossman, *Ḥasidot u-Mordot*, 119–88; and see M. S. Berger, "Two Models of Medieval Jewish Marriage; A Preliminary Study," *Journal of Jewish Studies* 52 (2001), 59–84.

2. *Avot de-Rabbi Nathan*, Version B, ch. 2, ed. S. Schechter (New York, 1967), 5a, and the notes there; Friedman, *Ribbui Nashim*, 8–9. This idea also appears in the words of some of the Jewish sages of the Middle Ages.

3. *b. Yevamot* 65a.

4. Friedman, *Ribbui Nashim*. His main discussion concerns the Genizah sources, including publication of new sources. Among other things, he discusses there the obligation of the husband not to marry a second wife; agreements with the first wife prior to marriage to the second; prenuptial agreements with the second wife; marriage to a second wife in a different country; supervision by the communities; maidservants.

5. Kupfer, *Teshuvot u-Pesaqim*, §147 (222–223), and parallels; and ibid., Kupfer's notes.

6. *Teshuvot Rashi*, §74.

7. Raban, *Sefer Even ha-Ezer*, 244d. Elsewhere in his book (*Ketubot*, 261c), Raban writes: "In our generations, when a married man doesn't take an additional wife," without mentioning Rabbenu Gershom as author of the edict. In my opinion, the use of the formulation "our generations," in the plural, strengthens the assumption that one is speaking of a known and long-accepted custom, and not of an innovation of his own time.

8. Finkelstein, *Jewish Self-Government*, 149: "We who live in Troyes and our surrounding communities issued an edict with an oath and a ban and severe sanctions . . . ," meaning, that the edict applied to Troyes and its environs, but not to the communities of northern France.

9. On Rashi's relation to Rabbenu Gershom, see Grossman, *Hakhmei Ashkenaz*, 107; idem., *Hakhmei Zarfat*, 252–53.

10. See Westreich, "Temurot," 145–50.

11. *Teshuvot ha-Rosh*, §43.8.

12. Raban, *Sefer Even ha-Ezer*, 261c; compare *Teshuvot Maharam*, §946.

13. *Siddur Rashi*, §222 (106), and parallels. On the collation of Rashi's teaching by his disciples, and especially by R. Shemaiah, see Grossman, *Hakhmei Zarfat*, 403–405.

14. For sources for these opinions and detailed citations, see Grossman, "The Historical Background to the Ordinances on Family Affairs."

15. On Rabbenu Gershom's responsa, see *Teshuvot Ragmah*, and Introduction, 46–52; Grossman, *Hakhmei Ashkenaz*, 151–58; On the responsa of R. Judah ha-Cohen, see ibid., 195–210. On the important role played by the Jews of Germany and France in international commerce during the tenth and eleventh centuries and their travels to distant places for extended periods, see Agus, *The Heroic Age*, 23–77. The sources themselves are analyzed by Agus in his book, *Urban Civilization in Pre-Crusade Europe* (New York, 1965), Vols. I–II.

16. I describe several examples of this in my book, *Hakhmei Ashkenaz*, 56.

17. Finkelstein, *Jewish Self Government*, 168.

18. *b. Yoma* 18b; *b. Yevamot* 37b. Admittedly, there were some medieval talmudic commentators who thought that these sages did not have sexual relations with the women they married for such a brief time, but that this was a kind of psychological trick so as not to involve themselves in sexual thoughts, but in terms of the subject itself this is certainly irrelevant; people understood these things in the literal sense.

19. *Teshuvot ha-Rambam*, II. § 347 (624).

20. S. D. Goitein, *Letters of Medieval Jewish Traders* (Princeton, 1973); idem., *Jews and Arabs* (New York, 1967), 89–124; Gil, *Be-Malkhut Yishma'el*, 611–35.

21. Finkelstein, *Jewish Self-Government*, 140–141.

22. Havlin, "The Taqqanot of Rabbenu Gershom," 231, from MS. Jerusalem. R. Joseph Colon (an Italian rabbi of French origin) mentions this tradition in his responsum, *Teshuvot Mahariq*, §101.

23. *Teshuvot ha-Rif*, §67.

24. Ibid., §120. For a discussion of additional sources related to the possible existence of monogamy in Muslim Spain, see the Hebrew edition of this book, Grossman, *Hasidot u-Mordot*, 138–40.

25. Alfasi was active in Spain at the end of the eleventh century, and it is inconceivable that at that time an edict would have been described as being from "the days of the early ones" if it had not been accepted at least two generations earlier.

26. On the desertion of wives in Egypt and in North Africa in Genizah sources, see Goiten, *A Mediterranean Society*, 195–97. He comments there that the phenomenon was common to all levels of society. On the desertion of wives in Spain in later generations as well, see Neuman, *The Jews in Spain*, 48–51.

27. *Teshuvot ha-Rif*, §118.

28. *Teshuvot ha-Ri mi-Gash*, §§58, 73, 122, 123, 135. Most of these were because of postponement of marriage.

29. Havlin, "The Taqqanot of Rabbenu Gershom"; Assis, "Double Marriages in Spain."

30. MS. Oxford-Bodleian 2550, fol. 194a. Havlin, "The Taqqanot of Rabbenu Gershom," 234–235.

31. Assis, "Double Marriages in Spain," 261.

32. Ibid., 272–74.

33. *Teshuvot Ḥakhmei Provinziah*, §63 (218); Havlin, "The Taqqanot of Rabbenu Gershom," 207. On R. Moshe Nasi, see Gross, *Gallia Judaica*, 407.

34. Havlin, ibid., §64.

35. Goitein, *A Mediterranean Society*, 3: 209–210; Friedman, *Ribbui Nashim*, 271–289. Another important source from the Cairo Genizah, published by Zvi Malachi, will be discussed below.

36. Malachi, "An Autobiographical Scroll, " 190–191.

37. *Teshuvot ha-Rosh*, 43.7.

38. *Teshuvot ha-Ribash*, §302; Assis, "Double Marriages," 266; Lamdan, *Am bifnei Azman*, 121.

39. *Teshuvot ha-Ran*, §48; *Teshuvot ha-Ralbah*, §27; Lamdan, op cit., 122.

40. Assis, "Double Marriages," 266.

41. *b. Yevamot* 101b.

42. *Teshuvot ha-Ri mi-Gash*, §139.

43. *Teshuvot ha-Rosh*, 52.6.

44. Katz, "Livirate Marriage *(Yibbum)* and *Ḥaliẓah*."

45. Kupfer, *Teshuvot u-Pesaqim*, §§141, 143. On R. Judah ha-Cohen and his senior status in Mainz, see: Grossman, *Ḥakhmei Ashkenaz*, 175–210.

46. Rashi, at *b. Yevamot* 39b.

47. Maimonides learned from this example that deformities alone are considered a legitimate reason for refusal to undergo *yibbum*. MT, *Yibbum ve-Ḥaliẓah*, 2.14.

48. *Teshuvot ha-Ralbah* (Venice, 1565), §36.

49. On the figure of Rashi, see Grossman, *Ḥakhmei Ẓarfat*, 136ff, and the bibliography cited in the note there.

50. Grossman, "'From the Genizah in Italy': Remnants of R. Joseph Kara's Torah Commentary" [Hebrew], *Peamim* 52 (1992), 16–36. The quotation is on page 28.

51. R. Yitzhak ben Yehudah Halevi, *Pane'aḥ Raza* (Warsaw, 1860); *Ki Tezei*, 62b.

52. *Teshuvot Maharam*, Prague ed., §866.

53. *Teshuvot Mahariq*, §91; *Teshuvot Ziqnei Yehudah*, ed. S. Simensohn (Jerusalem, 1956), §80 (116).

54. To clarify the position of Rabad and other Provençal sages, see: Katz, "Levirate Marriage *(Yibbum)*," 66–68.

55. *Teshuvot ha-Rambam*, 2. §373 (654).

56. *Teshuvot ha-Ribash*, §320.

57. *Teshuvot ha-Rashba*, 4.§36.

58. Ibid., 7. §421.

59. Ibid., 1. §802.

60. Goitein, *A Mediterranean Society*, 3: 210–211. On the Genizah sources, see Friedman, *Ribbui Nashim*, 129–52.

61. Katz, "Levirate Marriage *(Yibbum)* and *Ḥaliẓah*," 81. Katz wrote this before M. A. Friedman, in his book *Ribbui Nashim*, published some Genizah sources that contradict his opinion. One may assume that, had he known these additional sources, his conclusion would have been less definitive.

62. *Teshuvot ha-Rambam*, §373 (651). The hesitations and the varieties of opinions are found there, 650–655.

63. Friedman, *Ribbui Nashim*, 137.

64. Goitein, *Ha-Teimanim*, 307; Friedman, op cit., 150–151.

65. *Teshuvot ha-Rashba*, 4. §36.

66. For a detailed discussion of this issue, see: Tishby, *Mishnat ha-Zohar*, 2: 614–617. On the law of the "murderous" woman, see below, ch. 12. The quotation is from the Zohar II.106a.

67. Regev, "The Reasons for *Yibbum*."

Chapter Five. Feminine Modesty and Women's Role in Supporting the Family (pages 102–122)

1. *Midrash Leqah Tov* on Genesis, ed. S. Buber (Vilna, 1880), 174 (s.v. *vehalvai shelo noldah*). R. Toviah here took a personal stance on the controversy in *b. Bava Batra* 16b.

2. *m. Ketubot* 7.6.

3. *b. Gittin* 90a, s.v. *Papos b. Yehudah*. Rashi's comments there are not required for understanding the issue, nor do they even allude to it; rather, they are an exegetical addition, reflecting Rashi's personality. He also wrote to educate people to refrain from excessive strictness and suspicion, which would upset the harmony of their homes.

4. The sources for all these are found in S. D. Goitein, "Minority Self Rule and Government Control in Islam," *Studia Islamica* 31 (1970): 104.

5. Wilson, "Glimpses of Muslim Urban Women," 6–7.

6. In Wilson's words: "This official legally made everyone's business his business." On the nature of these sources, see especially his remarks there, ibid., 5–6, and the bibliography mentioned in his notes.

7. "The Hisba manuals . . . serve to challenge the traditional thesis of the secluded Muslim woman within classical Islamic society. Indeed, Muslim urban women, according to these accounts, defied the system's efforts to keep them silent and invisible" (Ibid., 11).

8. *MT, Ishut* 13.11. On the attitude toward female modesty in Jewish society in Muslim countries during this period, especially according to Genizah sources, see Friedman's detailed discussion in his paper, "The Ethics of Medieval Jewish Marriage."

9. R. Shlomo ben Abraham Ibn Parhon, *Mahberet ha-Arukh* (Jerusalem, 1970), 57b; Friedman, ibid., 93.

10. *Sivuv R. Petahya mi-Regensburg*, ed. E. Grinhout (Frankfort a/M, 1905), 8.

11. On the role of women in supporting the family and their appearance in court, see Goitein, *A Mediterranean Society*, III, 324–341; Friedman, "The Ethics of Medieval Jewish Marriage."

12. *Teshuvot ha-Rambam*, I. §34 (49–53). Compare: R. Levine Melammed, "He Said, She Said: A Woman Teacher in Twelfth-Century Cairo," *AJS Review* 22, 1997, 19–35.

13. Compare the discussion of the Jewish family in Kairouan, by Menahem Ben-Sasson "The Emergence of the Jewish Community in Muslim Countries," 122–38.

14. Important material concerning the inner world of the woman and her role in the family according to the Genizah sources appears in Goitein, *A Mediterranean Society*, III: 312 ff. But despite its great importance, this goes beyond the framework of our discussion here.

15. Meislish, *Shirat ha-Roqeah*, 226–232. The same elegy repeatedly emphasizes Dulca's social activity among the Jewish women in her community of Worms. From his remarks, it follows that she went out in public for purchases and ran the physical plant of her husband's yeshiva. Even though it was a small yeshiva, its administration

and supervision of the needs of the students demanded extensive activity both within and outside of the yeshiva.

16. Compare Goitein, *A Mediterranean Society,* III: 312–359.

17. *Teshuvot ha-Rambam,* II. §242 (434–444).

18. The subject is discussed below in Chapter 8. Cf. Cohen, "Purity, Piety and Polemic."

19. See at greater length in Grossman, *Ḥasidot u-Mordot,* 187.

20. Assis and Magdalena, *Yehudei Navarra,* 15–16, 72–75, 176–179.

21. For a discussion of women's involvement in trade in Santa Coloma, see Assis, The *Jews of Santa Coloma,* 29, 99; for a discussion of lending on interest on the part of women in this community, see ibid., 36–37, 48, 62.

22. *Teshuvot ha-Ritba,* §120.

23. Ibid., § 139.

24. Ibid., § 154.

25. Evergates, *Aristocratic Women in Medieval France.*

26. *Ma'aseh ha-Gezerot ha-Yeshanot,* in Habermann, *Gezerot Ashkenaz ve-Ẓarfat,* 97.

27. *Teshuvot ha-Maharam,* §880, concerning a question that was addressed to R. Judah Ha-cohen, R. Gershom Meor Hagolah's disciple.

28. *MT, Issurei Bi'ah* 22.4.

29. Tosafot to *b. Avodah Zarah* 23a, s.v. *vetu la middi.*

30. *Sefer Ravyah; Teshuvot,* ed. D. Dablitzky (B'nai Berak, 1989), §920.

31. See Shatzmiller, *Jews, Medicine and Medieval Society;* Barkaï, *Les infortunes de Dinah;* Baumgarten, "'Thus Say the Wise Midwives.'" On the involvement of Christian women in midwifery, see M. Green, "Women's Medical Practice and Health Care in Medieval Europe," *Signs,* 14 (1989), pp. 434–473.

32. See Yair Bachrach, *Teshuvot Havot Yair,* ed. S. B. Z. Kost (Ramat Gan, 1997), I. §73 (220), and cf. ibid., §66.

33. For a detailed discussion of the role of Jewish women in loaning on interest to Gentiles, see Jordan, "Jews on Top"; Marcus, "Mothers, Martyrs and Moneylenders."

34. "Loans by Jewish women—mostly widows—were not uncommon; such women were involved in a total of 61 loans recorded in the registers" Emery, *The Jews of Perpignan,* 26. On Jewish women in England, see M. Adler, *Jews in Medieval England* (London, 1939), 17–42. See especially his discussion of the activity of Licoricia of Oxford and other women who loaned money to the nobility and even to the king. They also took an active role in the public and economic life of England (ibid., 39–42). On Sicily, see Zeldes, "'As One Who Flees from a Snake,'" 51–53. Cf. Tallan, "Medieval Jewish Widows"; Yuval, "The Economic Arrangements of Marriage."

35. Rabban, *Sefer Even ha-Ezer,* §115; compare *Or Zaru'a,* Vol. III: *Pisqei Bava Kamma,* §§348–349, 353.

36. *m. Bava Kamma* 8.4.

37. Raban, *Sefer Even ha-Ezer,* §115.

Chapter Six. Woman as Wife and Mother and
Her Economic Status *(pages 123–153)*

1. The Genizah sources contain a relatively large number of sources relating to this subject. See Goitein, *A Mediterranean Society,* III, 312–359; Kraemer, "Women's Letters from the Cairo Genizah"; Friedman, *Ribbui Nashim be-Yisrael.*

2. Maimonides, *MT, Ishut* 15.20. In ibid., §19, he enumerates the husband's obligations to his wife. He must "honor her more than his body, love her like his own body,
and not impose upon her excessive fear, and he should speak with her gently and not
in an impatient or angry manner."

3. *Ozar ha-Geonim, Ketubot, Heleq ha-Teshuvot,* §428 (169–70).

4. On this mistaken attribution, see my book, *Ḥasidot u-Mordot,* ch. 10, n. 17.

5. Tishby, *Mishnat ha-Zohar,* II. 611.

6. Aboab, *Menorat ha-Maor,* 367.

7. *Teshuvot Rid,* (Jerusalem, 1967) §62 (320). "In all the communities of Romania"
refers to the communities of Byzantium, and perhaps to a certain part of Italy. A clear
identification is impossible. On the background of this severe polemic, see Cohen,
"Purity, Piety and Polemic."

8. *Megillat Aḥima'aẓ,* 16, 26. On the historical value of this scroll, see Bonfil, "Myth,
Rhetoric, History?"

9. Meislish, *Shirat ha-Roqeaḥ,* 227–229. Compare Marcus, "Mothers, Martyrs and
Moneylenders." Baskin, Dolce. Regarding the nature of the Ashkenazic yeshiva and its
relation to the home of the Rosh Yeshiva, see M. Breuer, "Toward the Investigation of
the Typology of the Western Yeshivot in the Middle Ages" [Hebrew], in *Peraqim be-
Toldot ha-Hevrah ha-Yehudit* (Jacob Katz FS; Jerusalem, 1988), 45–55.

10. See *b. Ketubot* 61b–62b; Maimonides, *MT, Ishut* 14.1–4. The Quran and Muslim
law similarly recognize the obligations of the husband towards his wives in the realm
of sexual life. This was especially elaborated by Al-Ghazali, one of the major Muslim
thinkers of the twelfth century. See Schacht, *An Introduction to Islamic Law,* 161–168;
Roded, *Women in Islam,* 161–67 and further bibliography there.

11. *b. Yevamot* 62b; Maimonides, *MT, Ishut* 15.19.

12. Rabad, *Ba'alei ha-Nefesh,* 120–122; compare *b. Nedarim* 20b. He elaborates
there at length on the husband's obligation to have relations with his wife. However,
in his discussion of means of intercourse, he objected to techniques that would not
bring the husband to full satisfaction "so that he will not think of another woman"
(p. 120), and he ignored the question of whether such techniques might not detract
from the woman's pleasure. Cf. Jeremy Cohen's discussion of the Rabad's approach
in comparison with those of medieval Christian thinkers: Cohen, "Rationales for
Conjugal Sex."

13. Tishby, *Mishnat ha-Zohar* II, 611–612.

14. Kupfer, *Teshuvot u-Pesaqim,* §156 (243).

15. Fleisher, "On Dunash ben Labrat"; Goitein, *A Mediterranean Society,* V, 468–470;
Taitz, The JPS Guide, 58–60.

16. *Ma'aseh ha-Geonim,* 50.

17. *Maharil,* Minhagin ed. Spitzer, 610.

18. *Teshuvot Maimoniot: Hilkhot Qedusha, Ma'akhalot Asurot* §5.

19. Maimonides, *MT, Ishut* 21.17. The source is in *b. Ketubot* 102b.

20. *Teshuvot Rashba ha-Meyuhasot la-Ramban,* §38.

21. *Teshuvot ha-Ri mi-Gash,* §71.

22. *Teshuvot ha-Geonim,* ed. A. Harkavi (Berlin, 1887), §553 (275).

23. *Zikhron Yehudah,* §78 (28a).

24. *Teshuvot ha-Rashba,* III, §312.

25. On prostitution, concubinage, adultery, and homosexual relationships in Christian and Muslim Europe, see Brundage, *Law, Sex and Christian Society;* Roded, *Women
in Islam,* 159–67; Wilson, "Glimpses of Muslim Urban Women."

26. Bullough, "The Prostitute in the Early Middle Ages"; the metaphor of the palace, ibid., 36. On the impact of Augustine's position upon thinkers and lawmakers in subsequent generations, see ibid., 36–37.

27. *Teshuvot Mahari Minz u-Maharam Padua* (Cracow, 1882), §5.

28. R. Yitzhak Aramah, *Aqedat Yizhaq: Bereshit* (Pressburg, 1849), 145.

29. Assis, "Sexual Behavior in Medieval Hispano-Jewish Society."

30. *Teshuvot ha-Geonim, Sha'arei Zedeq* (Jerusalem, 1966), Pt. 3, Sect. 6, §38.

31. *Teshuvot ha-Rambam*, II, §211 (374–375); see M.A. Friedman, "Halakha as Evidence of Sexual Life Among Jews in Muslim Countries in the Middle Ages," *Pe'amim* 45 (1990), 89–107.

32. Friedman, *Ribbui Nashim*, 28.

33. R. Moses of Coucy, *Sefer Mizvot Gadol: aseh* §3; *lo ta'aseh* §112.

34. R. Jonah Gerondi, *Sha'arei Teshuvah*, Sect. 3 (123–124). He wages war against those Jews who held Jewish concubines on the basis of the claim that the ancient kings of Israel and Judah did so. In his words, the courtiers are not kings, and anyone who gives his daughter to them as a concubine encourages licentiousness and is subject to a great punishment.

35. R. Judah ben Asher, *Teshuvot Zikhron Yehudah* (Berlin, 1846), §17 (3b).

36. See Brundage, *Law, Sex and Christian Society*; idem., "Prostitution in the Medieval Canon Law."

37. See Wilson, "Glimpses of Muslim Urban Women."

38. R. Judah ha-Cohen's responsum is found in *Teshuvot Maharam*, §912.

39. *Sefer Ḥasidim*, ed. Wistinetzki, §§1107, 1108; ed. Margaliot, §§ 561, 1117, 1118.

40. Ibid., ed Wistinetzki, §1187.

41. Ibid., §1896.

42. Ibid., §19, (25). He elaborated there at length about the gravity of sexual relations with Gentile maidservants, including the concern that they would become pregnant and bear him children. He likewise advised a penitent to refrain from "excursions" because such activities lead one "to sin with women" (ibid., 24).

43. *Sefer ha-Agudah*, 85c. The case brought before Maharam is also related to accusations against the husband of fornication with Gentile women.

44. On these three cases, see Yuval, *Ḥakhamim be-Doram*, 329–330. As he notes there, there is no full assurance that all these incidents occurred in reality. It is possible that at least some of them were based upon malicious slander.

45. Bregman, *Shevil ha-Zahav*, 65–66.

46. Bonfil, "Myth, Rhetoric, History?" 94–95; one must nevertheless remember that only a small minority of the cases involving sexual relations between Jews and Christians were discovered, and these alone were brought to the attention of the authorities. It follows that this discovery is of great importance.

47. It was usually possible to change a death sentence for a monetary fine. Bonfil, ibid., 94. Such was also the case in Christian Spain. See Assis, "Sexual Behavior."

48. Bonfil, "Jews of Venice," 71, quoting MS. Montefiore 94.

49. I. Yuval, "An Appeal Against the Proliferation of Divorce in Fifteenth Century Germany" [Hebrew], *Zion* 48 (1983), 177–216.

50. *Teshuvot Ḥakhmei Provinzia*, §27 (108).

51. R. Eleazar of Worms, *Sefer Roqeaḥ*, §100 (56–57).

52. Finkelstein, *Jewish Self-Government*, 251–256.

53. *Teshuvot Maharam,* §442. Cf. *Teshuvot Ba'alei ha-Tosafot,* §59 (137): "It was customary in our kingdom to write the same amount for all the virgins."

54. Finkelstein, *Jewish Self-Government,* 163–164; Y. Cohen, "Communal Edicts," 144 ff.

55. *Teshuvot Maharam Mintz,* (Jerusalem, 1991) §45.

56. Assaf, "The Husband's Inheritance," esp. pp. 84–91. The quotation is from there, 83.

57. For a detailed discussion of this development, see Herlihy, *Medieval Households,* 98–103, and the literature cited in his notes there. "From the middle twelfth century, the governments of the Italian urban communes moved to limit the claims of wives upon their husband's properties" (ibid., 98). Herlihy enumerates one after another the new legislation in the Italian cities that discriminated against women. A similar development occurred in Spain, if slightly more gradually (98–99).

Chapter Seven. Women's Culture and Education (pages 154–173)

1. The main literature dealing with this subject is Goitein, *A Mediterranean Society,* III, 344–58; V, 468–71; idem., *Sidrei Ḥinukh mi-Tqufat ha-Geonim,* 64–73; Morris, *Ha-Hinukh Shel Am Yisrael,* II, 168–183; Zolty, *"And All Your Children Shall be Learned;"* Baskin, "The Education of Jewish Women," and cf. the literature mentioned in the footnotes to this chapter in the Hebrew edition.

2. *b. Sotah* 21b.

3. See Power, *Medieval Women,* 80; Shahar, *The Fourth Estate,* 155.

4. *j. Sotah* 19a.

5. *b. Hagiggah* 3a. He nevertheless distinguished between men, who come "to learn," and women, who come "to hear."

6. *j. Sotah* 24c.

7. A discussion of Beruriah's actions and the attitude towards her in the Babylonian Talmud is beyond the scope of the present discussion, and has been widely discussed in recent years. See, e.g., T. Ilan , "The Quest for the Historical Beruriah, Rachel and Ima Shalom," *AJS Review* 22,/no. 1 (1997): 1–7; Boyarin, *Carnal Israel,* 183–194. It is surprising that several of the scholars mentioned interpreted the citation of these stories in the Babylonian Talmud as intended to convey an extremely negative message of the Talmudic sages against Torah study by women. It was as if the woman who studies Torah was destined to err and to distort its path. If this happened to the extraordinarily learned Beruriah, who was ultimately unfaithful to her husband and committed suicide, then there is an even graver fear regarding other women who study Torah. But this entire structure is very shaky. R. Nissim ben Jacob of Kairouan had a completely different tradition of the interpretation of "the incident of Beruriah" in *b. Avodah Zarah* 18b, according to which Beruriah was not unfaithful and did not take her life. R. Nissim received his exegetical tradition from the Babylonian Geonim, and preceded Rashi by two generations! See the detailed discussion in the Hebrew version of this book, pp. 269–271.

8. On the education of Muslim women, see: R. Roded, *Women in Islamic Biographical Collections: From Ibn Sa'd to Who's Who* (Boulder, 1994), 131–134; and further bibliography there; Ahmad, *Early Islam and Women.*

9. Roded, ibid. On education in Islam and the transmission of oral traditions, see also: J. Berkey, *The Transmission of Knowledge in Medieval Cairo* (Princeton, 1992).

10. On these conjectures, see Roded, ibid., 18–19.

11. See Bell, "Women Medieval Book Owners," esp. the summarizing table on p. 151. In this article, she repeatedly emphasizes the significant activity of women who owned books, not only for European culture but for other centers as well: "Women frequently bought and inherited religious as well as secular books, and spent considerable time reading them. In particular, as readers of vernacular literature, as mothers in charge of childhood education, as literary patrons who commissioned books and translations, and as wives who married across cultural and geographical boundaries, women had a specific and unique influence . . . There are numerous examples of women book owners who functioned as cultural ambassadors throughout medieval centuries." Ibid., 150, 175.

12. Maimonides, *MT, Talmud Torah* 1.13.

13. On Maimonides' ambivalent attitude toward women, see A. Melamed, "Maimonides on Women: Formless Matter or Potential Prophet?," in *Perspectives on Jewish Thought and Mysticism,* ed. A. Ivry et al., 99–134 (Amsterdam, 1998).

14. *Sefer Ḥasidim,* ed. Wistinetzki, §§796 (200).

15. R. Samuel Archivolti, *Sefer Ma'ayan Ganim* (Venice, 1553), §10.

16. *Sivuv R. Pethaya mi-Regensburg,* ed. A. Greenhout (Jerusalem, 1905), 9–10.

17. Her history and activity has recently been discussed in detail by Uri and Renée Levine Melammed, "Rabbi Asnat—A Female Yeshiva Director in Kurdistan" [Hebrew], *Pe'amim* 82 (2000), 163–178.

18. Three of her poems are extant. See Goitein, *A Mediterranean Society,* V. 468–470, and the discussion there of her conjectured identity as the daughter of R. Samuel Hanaggid; J. A. Bellamy, "Qasmuna the Poetess: Who was She?" *Journal of the American Oriental Society* 103 (1983), 423–424; Taitz, The JPS Guide, 57–58.

19. "Teshuvat Schondlein," in *Leqet Yosher* II, 19–20. Notwithstanding the great interest in the stance of R. Israel Isserlein, it is beyond the chronological framework of our work. His position is examined thoroughly by Yuval, *Ḥakhamim be-Doram,* 313–318, who concludes that: "It [Schondlein's teshuva] indicates the existence of a silent class of intelligentsia among the Jewish women in Germany, who managed to learn through their own efforts and without any organized study framework, the same material which the men learned from their rabbis and in their yeshivot" (ibid., 615). In *Teshuvot Maharil* (§§76, 118), there is mention of a woman who challenged Maharil's ruling and polemicized with him.

20. *Sivuv R. Petahya* (above, n. 16), 8.

21. Goitein, *Sidrei Ḥinukh,* 63, 66. On the place of women in the synagogue, and pious women and their contribution to charity, see ibid., 67–74; idem., *A Mediterranean Society,* III, 355–359; David Sperber, *Women Pray on Their Own* (Jerusalem, 2002), 5–11, and the bibliography there in the notes, 28–29.

22. S. D. Goitein has already commented on this in his book, *A Mediterranean Society,* II, 358: "The influential position of women of the higher class seems not to have been matched by spiritual attainments. Neither the literary nor the documentary Genizah seems to contain a single piece of writing, religious or otherwise, attributable with certainty to a woman. Tens of thousands of pieces of liturgical poetry have been preserved in the Genizah, but we never hear of a female poet."

23. *Sefer Ḥasidim,* ed. Margaliot, §588 (384). Cf. Tosafot at *b. Berakhot* 45b, s.v. *shanei hatam*; Meir of Rothenburg, *Teshuvot pesaqim,* §1 (181).

24. *Teshuvot Ḥakhamei Provinẓia,* §7 (41).

25. *Teshuvot Maharil ha-Ḥadashot,* §93 (92–93).

26. B. Smalley, *The Study of the Bible in the Middle Ages* (Oxford, 1952), 78.

27. *Sefer Ḥasidim*, ed. Wistinetzki, §835 (211), and cf. ibid., §1501 (362): "and he should not allow his grown daughters to study before unmarried youths, that they might not sin with them, but he should teach them." Study occurred within the family home.

28. MS. Bodelian 1566, fol. 178a.

29. Meislish, *Shirat ha-Roqeaḥ*, 292.

30. S. Salfeld, *Das Martyrologium des Nürnberger Memorbuches* (Berlin, 1898), 36.

31. L. Lewynsohn, Sechzig Epitaphien von Grabsteinen des israelitischen Friedhofes zu Worms, (Frankfurt, 1855) 85–86.

32. Abrahams, *Hebrew Ethical Wills,* 211. R. Eliezer died in 1357; Meislish, *Shirat ha-Rokeaḥ*, 230–231.

33. R. Jonah Gerondi, *Iggeret ha-Teshuvah*, III. §51 (261).

34. Ibid., §68 (268).

35. Ibid., §51 (261).

36. D. Bregman, *Shevil ha-Zahav*, 67–68.

37. The subject goes beyond the framework of our discussion here, and has been examined recently by H. E. Adelman, "Rabbis and Reality: Public Activities of Jewish Women in Italy during the Renaissance and Catholic Restoration," *Jewish History* 5 (1991): 27–40.

38. David and Hartum, *Iggerot R. Ovadiah,* 40.

39. Zeldes, "As One Who Flees from a Snake," 54.

*Chapter Eight. The Role of Women in Religious Life
and in Family Ceremonies (pages 174–197)*

1. 1 Corinth. 14:34–35.

2. "I permit no woman to teach or to have authority over men; she is to keep silent. For Adam was formed first, then Eve; and Adam was not deceived, but the woman was deceived and became a transgressor"1 Timothy 2:12–14.

3. On the implications of these changes upon the understanding of the institution of marriage, see Gold, "The Marriage of Mary and Joseph"; Duby, *Medieval Marriage.* Duby pointed out the tension between the understanding of marriage in aristocratic circles and its understanding in the Church. Only in the latter half of this century was there a convergence between these two models.

4. Bynum, *Holy Feast and Holy Fast.*

5. *Maḥzor Vitry,* ed. S. Hurwitz, (Berlin 1895), 413–414, and parallels.

6. For an explanation of the various halakhic approaches to this question, see Ta-Shma, *Halakhah, Minhag u-Meẓiut,* 262–279.

7. *Mordekhai, Shabbat* §286; cf. Tosafot at *b. Erubin* 96a, s.v. *dilma.*

8. *b. Haggigah* 16b; and cf. Tos. ad loc., s.v. *laʿasot nahat ruah.*

9. On the place of women in the synagogue, see Taitz, "Women's Voices, Women's Prayers"; D. Sperber, *Women Pray on Their Own: The Spiritual and Cultural World of Women in Light of Jewish Art* (Ramat Gan, 2002).

10. *Kol Bo, Hilkhot Tishʿah be-Av,* §62.

11. Hints of the existence of a separate women's synagogue adjacent to that of the men are preserved in the words of medieval Jewish synagogues. Remnants of the women's synagogue in a number of Provençal communities (including Carpentras) indicate that they were located beneath the men's synagogues and that the women viewed the Torah scrolls "through latticed grill windows." See Wischnitzer, *The Architecture of the European Synagogue,* 71–73.

12. *Sefer Ḥasidim*, ed. Wistinetzki, §468.

13. Maharil, *Minhagim*, 286.

14. Abrahams, *Hebrew Ethical Wills*, 208–209.

15. On the strictures regarding menstruants, whose source is in German Hasidism and in its ancient traditions, see Dinari, "Profanation of the Holy"; Ta-Shma, *Halakhah, Minhag u-Meẓiut*, 280–288. Ḥasidei Ashkenaz and the Jewish mystics who preceded them were very meticulous about [not] allowing women to have contact with holy books.

16. *Maharam me-Rotenberg: Teshuvot Pesaqim u-Minhagim*, ed. Y. Z. Kahana (Jerusalem, 1960), 149.

17. Ibid., 262. And see there in the notes.

18. This theory was suggested by Elisheva Baumgarten.

19. Maimonides, *MT, Berakhot* 5.7.

20. *Mordekhai, Berakhot*, §158. On the place of women in the teaching of R. Simhah, see A. Grossman, "Woman in the Teaching of R. Simhah of Speyer" [Hebrew], *Mayim mi-Dalyav* 13 (2002): 177–189.

21. *j. Pesahim* 10.1 [37b]; *b. Pesahim*, 108a

22. "All of our women are important women, and they need to recline" *Mordekhai, Pesahim* 237b, in the name of Tosafot.

23. *b. Pesahim* 4a–b. On the subject as a whole, see A. ha-Cohen, "'Women Are Lazy'? 'Women are Important'!" [Hebrew], *Alon Shevut Bogrim* 11 (1998): 63–82.

24. Maimonides, *MT, Ḥameẓ u-Maẓah* 2.17.

25. *j. Pesahim* 1.5 [27b].

26. Meiri, *Beit ha-Behirah, Pesahim*, at 4a (ed. J. Klein; Jerusalem, 1965), 14.

27. The dispute appears in *b. Avodah Zarah* 27a. For a detailed discussion of this issue, see Spiegel, "Woman as Ritual Circumciser;" and cf. Sperber, *Minhagei Yisrael*, 1.66; 4.8–9. In vol. 4, ibid., he brings a source from 1 Maccabees concerning Jewish women who were executed in punishment for circumcising their sons. In *Megillat Antiochus*, as well, it is told of a woman who circumcised her son.

28. Tosafot, at *b. Pesahim* 4b. s.v. *heimanuhu*. From the context of the things it follows, that one is speaking of actual *sheḥitah* and not merely of their giving testimony to the *sheḥitah* performed by others.

29. R. Bonfil, " Jews of Venice."

30. *Sefer ha-Agudah*, 171.

31. In his glosses to *Shulhan Arukh, Yoreh De'ah* (*Hilkhot Shehitah*), 1.1; and see Sperber's remarks, *Minhagei Yisrael*, 4.10, that the reason for the later Ashkenazic sages' objecting to women slaughtering, was the sensitivity of women and their fear lest the act of slaughtering and the seeing blood would affect them and the quality of their *shehitah*. This reason fits in with other testimonies about the decline in women's status at the end of the Middle Ages.

32. *Or Zaru'a*, 2. §33.

33. Bynum, *Holy Feast and Holy Fast*, 42–49.

34. *Sefer Ḥasidim*, ed. Wistinetzki, §670 (177).

35. *Sefer Ḥasidim*, ed. Margaliyot, §874 (490).

36. *Kol Bo, Hilkhot Tish'ah be-Av*, §62.

37. Maharil, *Minhagim*, 588; *Teshuvot Maharil ha-Ḥadashot*, 14.

38. Avigdor Zarfati, *Perushim u-Pesaqim al ha-Torah* (Jerusalem, 1996), 172.

39. Yuspa Shamash, *Minhagei Vormeiza*, 49.

40. R. Yuspa Shamash, ibid., 186.

41. *Ozar ha-Geonim, Gittin*, 8–9.

Chapter Nine. *Women's Role in Jewish Martyrdom* (pages 198–211)

1. There is a substantial literature about the persecutions of 1096. See, for example, Chazan, *European Jewry and the First Crusade;* and the collection of studies in the volume, *Yehudim mul ha-Zelav: Gezerot tatn"u be-Historia uve-Historiographiya,* ed. Y. T. Assis et al. (Jerusalem, 2000). On the role of women in these events, see especially Noble, "Women in Jewish Martyrology"; Breuer, "Women in Jewish Martyrology"; Einbinder, "Jewish Women Martyrs." They deal with some of the subjects discussed here.

2. Habermann, *Gezerot Ashkanaz ve-Zarfat,* 35 (italics mine); and parallels to this in the other chronicles concerning the persecutions of 1096.

3. Ibid., 34.

4. Ibid., 33.

5. On the repercussions of this literature in Christian society during the period parallel to the composition of the Jewish chronicles concerning the events of 1096, see B. Gazelles, *The Lady as Saint: A Collection of French Hagiographic Romances of the Twelfth Century* (Philadelphia, 1991).

6. Meislish, *Shirat ha-Roqeaḥ,* 226.

7. A detailed discussion of the attitude of Christian society in Germany to Jewish martyrdom appears in the paper by Mary Minty, "Kiddush ha-shem in German Christian Eyes." She examined three kinds of Christian sources in detail: chronicles, annales, and theological treatises.

8. Rudolf von Schlettstatt, *Historiae Memorabiles,* ed. E. Kleinschmidt (Köln, 1974), 58; Minty, op cit., 238. Rudolf relates there that she was given over to Rindfleisch and executed.

9. *Monumenta Germaniae Historica* (Scriptores, n.s. 12; Berlin, 1967), 370–71.

10. H. Frankel-Goldschmidt, "On the Margins of Jewish Society—Jewish Apostates in Germany During the Reformation" [Hebrew]. In *Sefer Zikaron le-Hayyim Hillel Ben-Sasson,* ed. R. Bonfil et al. (Jerusalem, 1989), 623–54., esp. at 644. Victor von Karben explains the Jewish women's zeal for their religion by the fact that because they were not commanded regarding circumcision they would not enjoy eternal life, and therefore are more zealous for their religion than men.

11. See, e.g., *b. Gittin* 58a; *Ketubot* 66b.

12. On the conversions of the sons of these two sages, see Grossman, *Hakhmei Ashkenaz ha-Rishonim,* 90, 111–12.

13. The primary plausible reason for the women's refusal to convert—in addition to the element of faith—was their connection to their families. This connection was a major factor in their lives, particularly in light of the early marriage that was common in those days, as we discussed above in chapter 2.

14. On these few sources and their historical significance, see M. Ben-Sasson, "On the Jewish Identity of Conversos—A Study of Apostasy in the Almohid Period" [Hebrew], *Pe'amim* 42 (1990), 16–37; Grossman, "Kiddush Hashem." In this latter paper, I survey the sparse literature relating to these persecutions, and discuss the central question that arises from comparison between Kiddush Hashem in Ashkenaz and its almost complete absence in the Muslim countries and in Spain from the eleventh century on. In the persecutions of 1391 in Spain, the important role of the women in refusing to convert, to the point of dying for Kiddush Hashem, is emphasized.

15. Levine-Melammed has published several studies of this subject. See, for example, her book *Heretics or Daughters of Israel?*

16. Zeldes, "'As One Who Flees from a Snake.'"

17. Blidstein, "The Personal Status of Apostate and Ransomed Women."

18. *Teshuvot R. Hayyim Or-Zaruʻa*, §221.
19. Hameiri, *Beit ha-Beḥirah Ketubot*, 126.
20. Einbinder, "Jewish Women Martyrs," 114.

Chapter Ten. Violence Toward Women (pages 212–230)

1. For the principal literature on this subject, see Grossman, "Medieval Rabbinic Views on Wife Beating"; Graetz, *Silence is Deadly*; Frishtik, "Violence Against Women."
2. *t. Bava Qamma* 9.14.
3. Maimonides, *MT, Hovel u-Maziq* 4.16.
4. See R. Yitzhak b. Moshe from Vienna, *Or Zaruʻa; Pisqei Bava Qamma* (Jerusalem, 1968), §161.
5. Prov. 13:24. While some Jewish sages in the Middle Ages interpreted "his staff" as referring to words of chastisement and admonition, many others interpreted it literally, as beating with a stick.
6. Shahar, *The Fourth Estate*, 89–90.
7. Quran 4.38.
8. See Goitein, *A Mediterranean Society* III, 185.
9. *Ozar ha-Geonim; Ketubot*, 169–170.
10. Maimonides, *MT, Ishut* 15.19.
11. See *Ozar ha-Geonim, Ketubot*, 191–192.
12. *Teshuvot Maharam*, ed. Cremona, 1557, §291.
13. *Sha'arei Ẓedeq*, Pt. 4, Sect. 1, §13.
14. Ibid., §4.
15. Ibid., Pt. 4, Sect 4, §42.
16. Maimonides, *MT, Ishut* 21.10.
17. *m. Ketubot* 5.5.
18. In his glosses to *MT, Ishut*, op cit.
19. *Ibid.*, 21.2–3. Cf. *m. Ketubot* 5.5: "Rabbi Eliezer said: Even if she brought in her dowry one hundred maid servants—she is forced to work with wool, for idleness leads to licentiousness."
20. *Teshuvot ha-Rambam*, II, §385 (664).
21. *Teshuvot ha-Rashba*, Pt. 4, §113.
22. Ibid., Pt. 7, §477.
23. In Goitein's words, "Clearly the complaint about beating was secondary to the woman's general unhappiness with a husband unwilling or unable to provide for her properly" (*A Mediterranean Society*, III 186).
24. See Goitein, ibid., 186–189. He cites there letters from husbands who promise to behave properly with their wives in the future or other agreements intended to appease the battered wife.
25. Hameiri's remarks are quoted in *Beit ha-Behirah; Niddah*, ed. A Sofer (New York, 1959), 279.
26. Finkelstein, *Jewish Self-Government*, 216.
27. *Sefer ha-Neyar*, ed. G. Apfel (Jerusalem, 1995), 166 in gloss.
28. R. Simhah's words are cited by R. Yitzhak ben Moshe, *Sefer Or Zaruʻa; Pisqei Bava Qamma*, §161.
29. *Teshuvot Maharam*, §81. Cf. his responsum in *Teshuvot Maharam*, ed. Cremona, §291, which is a later responsum.

30. *Sefer ha-Agudah,* end of *Ketubot* (fol. 121d in the 1571 Cracow ed.).

31. *Teshuvot ha-Radbaz,* §1228.

32. *Sefer Ḥasidim,* ed. Wistinetzki, §1086 (277).

33. Ibid., §140 (64).

34. *Sefer Ḥasidim,* ed. Margaliot, §49, and cf. in his notes.

35. *Sefer Ḥasidim,* ed. Wistinetzki, §1024 (257).

36. *Or Zaru'a,* Pt. 3, *Pisqei Bava Qamma,* Ch. 8, §346.

37. R. Eliezer of Metz, *Sefer Yereim ha-Shalem; Issurim she-Ra la-Shamayim vela-Beriot* (Jerusalem, 1973), §217.

38. Isserlein, *Terumat ha-Deshen,* §218.

Chapter Eleven. The Divorcée and the "Rebellious Wife" (pages 231–252)

1. For a detailed discussion of the different opinions, see the Hebrew edition of this book, *Ḥasidot u-Mordot,* 403–13.

2. *Sefer Ḥasidim,* ed. Wistinetzki, §1887 (457). Elsewhere (ibid., §1110), the author saw divorce as something fundamentally wrong. Marriage creates a firm connection between the couple, which may only be undone under extreme conditions of infidelity. This ruling is closer to the view of Beit Shammai than to that of Beit Hillel.

3. See Tishby, *Mishnat ha-Zohar,* II, 609–10; Idel, "Sexual Metaphors and Praxis"; Wolfson, "Woman—The Feminine as Other"; and in the next note.

4. *Sefer ha-Zohar* I:229a; *Sefer Ḥasidim,* ibid., §1128 (285–286).

5. Maimonides, *Guide* 3.49 (394).

6. Hameiri, *Beit ha-Beḥirah; Gittin,* (Jerusalem, 1972), 374.

7. On the words of R. Seligman, see Yuval, "An Appeal," 189.

8. For a detailed discussion of the issue of impotence as grounds for divorce, see Shiloh, "*Koaḥ Gavra.*" In medieval Christian society, there were various means of adjudicating the contradictory claims of the husband and wife regarding this question. One of the most popular was the testimony of experienced and wise women, who were present at the time of sexual relations between the couple, as to the degree of truth of the woman's claim that her husband was impotent. See Brundage. *Law, Sex and Christian Society,* 144–45; D. Jacquart and Cl. Thomasset, *Sexuality and Medicine in the Middle Ages* (Princeton, 1988), 169–173.

9. *Teshuvot Maimoniot* to *MT, Hilkhot Ishut,* §6; on its influence on later sages, see Shiloh, "*Koaḥ Gavra,*" 356–357, 364.

10. Maimonides, *MT, Ishut* 15.7.

11. On barrenness and impotence in medieval Jewish medicine, see Barkaï, *Les infortunes de Dinah,* 92–97; Baumgarten, "'Thus Say the Wise Midwives,'" 67–73.

12. *Sefer ha-Agudah,* §77 (85b).

13. *Teshuvot ha-Rosh, kelal* 43, §3.

14. Maimonides, *MT, Ishut* 14.8–9, 14 (emphasis added).

15. This was Maimonides' principled stance towards those who were required by law to divorce their wives and refused to do so: "Whomever the law states that he is to be compelled to divorce his wife and did not wish to divorce her, the Jewish Court *in every place and in every time beats him* until he says 'I wish to do so,' and he writes the divorce writ, and it is a kosher *get.*" (*MT, Gerushin* 2.2).

16. *Teshuvot Maharam,* §946 (135a).

17. *Teshuvot ha-Rosh, kelal* 43 , §8

18. *Teshuvot R. Ḥayyim Or Zaruʻa*, §126.

19. *Mordekhai, Gittin*, §421.

20. MS. Oxford-Bodelian 973, fol. 75; Yuval, "An Appeal," 209, 213–14.

21. "Very rarely do we hear of a transition to chastity that is allegedly mutual . . . More often, the move to a spiritual marriage was initiated by one party. . . With a female initiator, the movement to chastity was frequently painful . . . Every potentially rebellious impulse is aligned with diabolical force" (Elliot, *Spiritual Marriage*, 252, 259). On the background to the "rebellion" of the married women and their means of struggle, see ibid., esp. ch. 5 (195–265). And cf. J. Coakley, "Gender and the Authority of Friars: The Significance of Holy Women for Thirteenth-Century Franciscans and Dominicans," *Church History* 60 (1991): 445–60.

22. *Teshuvot ha-Rosh, kelal, 43*, §6.

23. For these data, see Goitein, *A Mediterranean Society*, III, 274.

Chapter Twelve. The Widow and the "Murderous Wife" (pages 253–272)

1. On the widow in medieval Jewish society, see Tallan, "The Position of the Medieval Jewish Widow"; idem., "Medieval Jewish Widows."

⟶ 2. 1 Corinthians 7: 8–9, 39–40.

3. See, e.g., Klapisch-Zuber, *Women, Family and Ritual in Renaissance Italy*, 261–82; C. Ginzburg, *Ecstasies: Deciphering the Witches' Sabbath* (London, 1991), 182–97. According to Esther Cohen and Elliot Horowitz, there were Jewish marriage customs particular to the widow that contained hints of criticism of the marriage per se, influenced by the above-mentioned custom in Christian society (*Charivary*). (See Cohen and Horowitz, "Marriage of Widows in the Middle Ages"). It is possible that influences of this type may be seen in Italian Jewish society at the end of the Middle Ages. However, in principle the different and special ceremony for the marriage of a widow in Judaism comes to show to all that the bride had been a widow, and therefore her *ketubah* is smaller, as stated already in the Talmud and in *m. Ketubot* 1.2. The fear was that the *ketubah* would be lost and that years later there would be no indication as to whether she had been a widow or a virgin.

4. On the harm to the inheritance rights of the widow, see Herlihy, *Medieval Households*, 98–103. Thus, for example, Herlihy summarized the development in England (100): "In the thirteenth century the English woman lost all capacity to own chattels or movables, which at her marriage passed completely under the ownership of her husband."

5. Herlihy, "Life Expectancies for Women," 5. Our discussion here relies primarily upon Herlihy's study. See also Goody, *The Development of the Family*, 64–65.

6. *Sefer ha-Mikẓoʼot*, ed. S. Assaf (Jerusalem, 1947), p. 10, §16.

7. *Sefer ha-Nizaḥon* of R. Yom Tov Lipmann Mülhausen (Jerusalem, 1983), 32. According to what is related in Matthew 22:22–30, the Sadducees addressed a similar question to Jesus, who answered that in the Resurrection there will not be marriage at all.

8. Goitein, *A Mediterranean Society*, III, 274. The divorced women were also counted separately, and there were 23 of them, plus another 25 who returned to their husbands after these had returned to their place. See the discussion of divorce, above, chapter 11. It follows from this that there is great likelihood in support of the assumption that a considerable number of the women who were married a second time without it being explicitly noted were widows.

9. See Goitein, *A Mediterranean Society*, III, 250 ff.

10. *Teshuvot ha-Rashba,* II, §210 (fol. 47d).

11. Ibid. III., §210.

12. On these fears in the folklore of various peoples, see H. Schwarzbaum, "The Hero Predestined to Die on his Wedding Day," *Studies in Marriage Customs* (Folklore Research Center Studies, IV; Jerusalem, 1974), 232–52, and further bibliography in the notes there. The folk literature that developed in Christian Europe contains various sayings expressing serious reservations about such marriages of widows and widowers. See Cohen and Horowitz, op. cit., n. 3.

13. *Teshuvot ha-Rambam,* II, §218 (386–87).

14. *Zohar* II, 202–203.

15. *Sefer Ḥasidim,* ed. Wistinetzki, §§1870–71 (452).

16. *Sefer Ḥasidim,* ed. Margaliot, §461 (316). And see the notes of the redactor, ibid.

17. *Pisqei ha-Rosh, Ketubot,* ch. 4, §gimel.

18. Isserlein, *Sefer Terumat ha-Deshen,* §211.

19. *Teshuvot R. Yaakov Weil* (Jerusalem, 1988), §183 (135).

Chapter Thirteen. Summary *(pages 273–281)*

1. *Ma'aseh ha-Gezerot ha-Yeshanot,* in Habermann, *Gezerot Ashkenaz ve-Ẓarfat,* 97.

2. R. Ephraim of Bonn, *Sefer Zekhirah,* in Habermann, ibid., 124. The ruler's wife was jealous of Pulcilina due to her connections with her husband.

3. Idel, "The Wife and the Concubine," 148–49.

4. Abravanel, commentary to Gen. 2:18.

5. See Schulenburg, "Sexism and the Celestial Gynaecum."

6. "Despite occasional references to women's spiritual visions, the circles of Jewish mystics through the ages (including the Hasidic groups in Eastern Europe of the eighteenth and nineteenth centuries) were exclusively male fraternities."Wolfson, "Woman—The Feminine as Other," 169. And see his discussion of this issue, ibid., 194–195 n. 115. Chavah Weissler has demonstrated that, in the eighteenth century, one can find allusions to the participation of Jewish women in Eastern Europe in streams of mystical thought, and there were apparently those who even acquired knowledge of Kabbalistic concepts. See Weissler, "Woman as High Priest."

7. "This exclusive masculinity for which Kabbalism has paid a high price, appears rather to be connected with an inherent tendency to lay stress on the demonic nature of woman and the feminine element of the cosmos." Scholem, *Major Trends,* 37. Cf.: Dan, "Samael, Lilith and the Concept of Evil," 503.

8. Idel, "The Wife and the Concubine," 142–43.

9. See *Megillat Aḥima'aẓ,* 30. But the main reason for this according to David Berger is that the Kabbalah could not be studied without extensive Talmudic background. See D. Berger, "Nahmanides' Attitude towards Secular Leaning and Its Bearing upon His Stance in the Maimonidean Controversy," M. A. Thesis (New York: Columbia University, New York, 1965), 113–14.

10. See Hava Frankel-Goldschmidt, "On the Periphery of Jewish Society: Jewish Converts to Christianity in Germany During the Reformation" [Hebrew], In *Sefer Hayyim Hillel Ben-Sasson,* ed. M. Ben-Sasson et al. (Jerusalem, 1989), 623–54, esp. at 644.

Glossary

Amoraim sages of the Talmudic period.

Bogeret a maiden who has passed the age of puberty, usually over the age of 12.

Dayyan judge in a religious court.

Erusin betrothal or engagement.

Genizah generically, a term used for a place where worn Torah scrolls and other holy objects and Hebrew manuscripts are stored. Specifically, it refers to the Genizah in the main synagogue in Cairo, where numerous Hebrew documents were discovered in the late nineteenth century. This collection, which is an invaluable source of information about Jewish life in the medieval period, is now located in various libraries throughout the world, particularly in Cambridge, England.

Get divorce writ, written by hand and serving as the instrument for Jewish divorce.

Halakhah Jewish law.

Halizah alternative to the ritual of *yibbum* (levirate marriage), in which the woman removes her brother-in-law's shoe and spits on the ground in front of him (based on Deut. 25:5–10).

Hamez leavened food stuff, forbidden to eat on Passover.

Herem ban, in which a person who has violated a major halakhic or communal norm is ostracized and excluded from various aspects of religious, social, and public interaction.

Huppah lit., wedding canopy. Refers to the wedding ceremony.

Ketubah wedding document, in which the bridegroom formally undertakes various obligations to his wife. The document also functions as a promissory note to the wife, giving her a certain sum of money upon the termination of the marriage, whether by divorce or the husband's death.

Miqveh Ritual bath, traditionally run as a communal institution, in which married Jewish women immerse themselves monthly after menstruation, as a prerequisite for resuming marital relations with their husbands.

Mishnah Codex of Jewish law, summarizing legal traditions of late tannaitic tradition. Edited by R. Judah the ha-Nasi ca. 215 CE, it serves as the starting point for the Talmud.

Miun Annulment: a special procedure allowed in the case where an underage orphan girl had been married off by her mother or brothers, in which she may annul the marriage prior to her majority without requiring a *get*.

Mitzvah commandment.

Mohel ritual circumcisor.

Moredet Rebellious wife, who refuses either to have sexual relations with her husband and/or to perform her household tasks.

Na'arah maiden, in most cases defined by the halakhah as one between the ages of 12 and 12.5.

Piyyut liturgical poem or poetry.

Poseq / posqim   Rabbinic decisor(s).

Public domain (*reshut harabbim*)   unenclosed public space within which, according to Jewish law, it is forbidden to carry objects on the Sabbath.

Qatlanit   "murderous wife." Category applied to a woman, two of whose husbands died while married to her.

Qetanah   minor girl who has not yet reached the age of twelve.

Qiddushin   Betrothal. The ceremony by which a woman becomes formally betrothed to a man; following it, the connection between them may only be undone by means of a formal divorce writ (*get*). Today, this ceremony is performed in conjunction with the wedding ceremony itself.

Responsum / Responsa (Heb., *Teshuvah / Teshuvot*)   Rabbinic reply to a question in Jewish law, or the literary genre consisting the record of such responses. These usually include the reasoning used in arriving at the decision.

Sandaq   godfather; i.e., the person who holds the baby infant on his lap during the circumcision ceremony. Considered the highest honor at that ceremony.

Shiddukh, Shiddukhin   Match; the act of engagement to be married.

Shohet   ritual slaughterer.

Taqqanah   edict or ordinance issued by the community or rabbinic leadership of a given town, district, or country.

Talmud   the central work of classic rabbinic Judaism, containing discussions of and elaboration of the Mishnah, new discussions that take off from there, and miscellaneous ethical maxims, stories about the sages, folklore, etc. (*aggadah*). Exists in two distinct compendia: the Jerusalem (or Palestinean) Talmud, and the Babylonian Talmud.

Tannaim   sages of the Mishnaic period.

Yibbum   Levirate marriage, in which the brother-in-law marries his brother's childless widow so as to perpetuate his brother's memory (see above, *halizah*).

Bibliography

This list includes those primary and secondary sources that appear in the book numerous times or that are of particular importance for the study of the subject. Those sources that are mentioned only once or twice in the book are cited in the footnotes with full details.

Aboab, Yitshak. *Menorat ha-Maor*. Jerusalem, 1961.

Abrahams, Israel. *Hebrew Ethical Wills*. Philadelphia, 1954.

Abravanel, Isaac. *Perush ha-Torah*. Jerusalem, 1964.

Agus, Irving A. *Teshuvot Ba'alei ha-Tosafot*. New York, 1954.

_____. *The Heroic Age of Franco-German Jewry*. New York, 1969.

Ahdut, Eli. *Ma'amad ha-Ishah ha-Yehudiyah be-Bavel bi-Tequfat ha-Talmud*. Jerusalem, 1999.

Ahmad, Laila. "Early Islam and the Position of Women: The Problem of Interpretation." In *Women in Middle Eastern History*, ed. N. Keddie and B. Baron, New Haven, 1991. 58–73.

_____. *Women and Gender in Islam*. New Haven, 1992.

Al-Syyid-Marsot, Afaf L., ed. *Society and the Sexes in Medieval Islam*. Malibu, Calif. 1979.

Arama, R. Yizhaq. *Aqedat Yizhaq*. Pressburg, 1849.

Assaf, Simha. "The Husband's Inheritance, Different Ordinances and Customs in the Husband's Inheritance of His Wife" [Hebrew]. *Mad'ei ha-Yahadut* 1, no.3 (1936): 79–94.

Assis, Yom Tov. "Double Marriages in Spain: The Ordinace of Rabbenu Gershom and polygamous Marriages in Spain" [Hebrew]. *Zion* 46 (1981): 251–77.

_____. *The Jews of Santa Coloma de Queralt*. Jerusalem, 1988.

_____. "Sexual Behavior in Medieval Hispano-Jewish Society." In *Jewish History: Essays in Honor of Ch. Abramsky*, ed. A. Rapaport-Albert and S.J. Zipperstein, London, 1998, 25–59.

Assis, Yom Tov, and Magdalena Ramon. *Yehudei Navarra be-Shilhei Yemei ha-Beinayim*. Jerusalem, 1990.

Avot de-Rabbi Nathan, ed. S. Schechter. New York, 1967.

Bahye ben Asher. *Perush ha-Torah*. Jerusalem, 1977.

Barkaï, Ron. *Les infortunes de Dinah, ou la gynécologie juive au Moyed-Age*. Paris, 1991.

_____. "Greek Medical Traditions and their Impact on Conceptions of Women in the Gynecological Writing in the Middle Ages" [Hebrew]. In *Eshnav le-Hayihen shel Nashim be-Hevrot Yehudiot*, ed. Y. Azmon, 115–142. Jerusalem, 1995.

Baskin, Judith R., "Images of Women in Sefer Hasidim." In *Mysticism, Magic and Kabbalah in Ashkenazi Judaism*, ed. J. Dan and K. E. Grözinger, 93–105. Berlin and New York, 1995.

_____. "Jewish Women in the Middle Ages." In *Jewish Women in Historical Perspective*, ed. J. R. Baskin, 101–127. Detroit, 1998.

_____. "The Education of Jewish Women in the Lands of Medieval Islam and Christendom" [Hebrew]. *Pe'amim* 82 (2000): 31–49.

_____. "Dolce of Worms: Women Saints in Judaism," in *Women Saints in World Religions*, ed. Arvind Sharma, Albany N.Y. 2000, 39–69.

Baumgarten, Elisheva. "'Thus Sayeth the Wise Midwives': Midwives and midwifery in Thirteenth-Century Ashkenaz" [Hebrew], *Zion* 65 (2000): 45–74.

Bell, Susan G. "Women Medieval Book Owners: Arbiters of Lay Piety and Ambassadors of Culture. "In *Women and Power in the Middle Ages*, ed. M. Erler, 149–61, Athens and London, 1988.

Bellamy, James A. "Sex and Society in Islamic Popular Literature." In *Society and the Sexes in Medieval Islam*, ed. A. L. Al-Syyid-Marsot, 23–41, Malibu, Calif. 1979.

Ben-Sasson, Menahem. *The Emergence of the Local Jewish Community in the Muslim World, Qayrawan, 800–1057*. Jerusalem, 1996.

Berger, David. *The Jewish Christian Debate in the High Middle Ages*. Philadelphia, 1969.

Biale, David. *Eros and the Jews, from Biblical Israel to Contemporary America*. New York, 1992.

Biale, Rachel. *Women and Jewish Law: An Exploration of Women's Issues in Halakhic Sources*. New York, 1984.

Blidstein, Yaakov. "The Personal Status of Apostate and Ransomed Women in Medieval Jewish Law" [Hebrew]. *Shenaton ha-Mishpat ha-Ivri* 3–4 (Jerusalem, 1976–1977): 37–116.

Bonfil, Reuven, "Jews of Venice: Aspects of the Social and Spiritual Life of the Jews in the Venetian Territories at the Beginning of the 16th Century" [Hebrew], *Zion* 41 (1976): 68–96.

_____. "Myth, Rhetoric, History? A Study of *Megillat Aḥima'aẓ*" [Hebrew] In *Tarbut ve-Ḥevrah be-Toldot Yisrael be-Yemei ha-Beinayim*, ed. R. Bonfil, M. Ben-Sasson, and J. Hacker, 99–135 H. H. Ben-Sasson FS.; Jerusalem, 1989.

_____. *Bemarah Kesufah; Ḥayyei ha-Yehudim be-Italyah be-yemei ha-Renasans*, Jerusalem, 1994.

Borchers, Susanne. *Jüdisches Frauenleben im Mittelalter: Die Texte des Sefer Chasidim*. Frankfurtam Main, 1998.

Boyarin, Daniel. *Carnal Israel: Reading Sex in Talmudic Culture*. Berkeley, 1993.

Bregman, Dvora. *Shevil ha-Zahav*. Jerusalem, 1995.

Breuer, Mordechai. "Women in Jewish Martyrology" [Hebrew]. In *Yehudim mul ha-ẓelav*, ed. Y.T. Assis et al., 141–149 Jerusalem, 2000.

Brundage, James A. "Prostitution in the Medieval Canon Law." In *Sisters and Workers in the Middle Ages*, ed. J. M. Bennett et al, 79–99, Chicago and London, 1976.

_____. *Law, Sex and Christian Society in Medieval Europe*. Chicago, 1987.

Buckley, Thomas, and Alma Gottlieb, ed. *Blood Magic: The Anthropology of Menstruation*. Berkely and Los Angeles, 1988.

Bullough, Vern L. "The Prostitute in the Early Middle Ages," *Sexual Practices and the Medieval Church*, ed. V. L. Bullough and J. Brundage, 234–42. New York, 1982.

Bynum, Caroline W. *Holy Feast and Holy Fast*. Berkeley, 1987.

Chazan, Robert. *European Jewry and the First Crusade*. Berkeley, Los Angeles and London, 1987.

Cohen, Esther, and Elliot Horowitz. "Marriage of Widows in the Middle Ages: In Search of the Sacred: Jews, Christians and Rituals of Marriage in the Later Middle Ages." *The Journal of Medieval and Renaissance Studies* 20 (1990): 249–55.

Cohen, Jeremy. *"Be Fertile and Increase, Fill the Earth and Master It": The Ancient and Medieval Career of a Biblical Text.* Ithaca and London, 1989.

———. "Rationales for Conjugal Sex in RaABaD's *Ba'alei ha-Nefesh.*" Jewish History 6 (1992): 65–78.

Cohen, Shaye J. D. "Purity, Piety, and Polemic: Medieval Rabbinic Denunciations of 'Incorrect' Purification Pracitce." In *Women and Water: Menstruation in Jewish Life and Law,* ed. R. R. Wasserfall, 82–100. Hanover and London, 1999.

Cohen, Yedidyah. "Communal Edicts: The Inheritance of a Wife of Her Husband in the Communal Enactments" [Hebrew]. *Shenaton ha-Mishpat ha-Ivri* 6–7 (Jerusalem, 1979–1980): 133–75.

Dan, Joseph. "Demonological Stories in the Writings of R. Judah he-Ḥasid" [Hebrew]. *Tarbiẓ* 30 (1961): 273–89.

———. "Samael, Lilith and the Concept of Evil in Early Kabbalah." *AJS Review* 5 (1980): 17–40.

David, Abraham, and Menahem Hartum. *Me-Italyah le-Yerushalayim; Iggerotav shel R. Ovadyah mi-Bartenora me-Erez Yisrael.* Ramat Gan, 1997.

Dinari, Yedidya. "The Impurity Customs of the Menstruate Women—Sources and Development" [Hebrew]. *Tarbiẓ* 49 (1980): 302–24.

———. "Profanation of the Holy by the Menstruant, and Ezra's Edict" [Hebrew]. *Te'udah* 3 (1983) 17–35.

Dishon, Judith. "Images of Women in Medieval Hebrew Literature." In *Women of the World, Jewish Women and Jewish Writing,* ed. J. R. Baskin, 35–49. Detroit, 1994.

Duby, George. *Medieval Marriage: Two Models from Twelfth-Century France.* Baltimore and London, 1978.

———. *The Knight, the Lady, and the Priest: The Making of Marriage in Medieval France.* New York, 1983.

Eidelberg, Shlomo. *R. Yuspa Shammash de-qehilat Wormaisa.* Jerusalem, 1991.

Einbinder, Suzan L. "Jewish Women Martyrs: Changing Models of Representation." *Exemplaria* 12 (2000): 105–127.

Eleazar of Worms. *Sefer ha-Roqeaḥ.* Jerusalem, 1967.

Elliot, Dyan. *Spiritual Marriage: Sexual Abstinence in Medieval Wedlock.* Princeton, 1993.

Elon, Menahem, *Mafteaḥ ha-Sheelot veha-Teshuvot shel Ḥakhmei Sefarad u-Ẓefon Afriqa; Ha-Mafteaḥ ha-Histori.* 2 vols. Jerusalem, 1981–87.

Emery, Richard W. *The Jews of Perpignan in the Thirteenth Century.* New York, 1959.

Evergates, Theodore, ed. *Aristocratic Women in Medieval France.* Philadelphia, 1999.

Falk, Ze'ev W. *Jewish Matrimonial Law in the Middle Ages.* Oxford, 1966.

Farah, Madelain. *Marriage and Sexuality in Islam: A Translation of al-Ghazali's Book on the Etiquette of Marriage from the Ihya.* Salt Lake City, 1984.

Finkelstein, Louis. *Jewish Self-Government in the Middle Ages.* New York, 1964.

Fishman, Talia. "A Kabbalistic Perspective on Gender-Specific Commandments." *AJS Review* 17 (1992): 199–245.

Fleisher, Ezra. "On Dunash ben Labrat, his Wife and his Son: New Light on the Beginnings of the Hebrew-Spanish School" [Hebrew]. *Meḥuerei Yerushalayim be-Sifrut Ivrit* 5 (1984): 189–202.

Friedman, Mordechai A. "The Ethics of Medieval Jewish Marriage." In *Religion in a Religious Age,* ed. S. D. Goiten, 83–101. Cambridge, Mass., 1974.

———. "Match-making and Betrothal According to the Cairo Genizah Documents" [Hebrew]. *Divrei Ha-Qongress ha-Olami ha-shevii le-Mad'ei ha-Yahadut; Meḥqarim be-Talmud Halakhah u-Midrash,* 157–73. Jerusalem, 1981.

———. *Ribbui Nashim be-Yisrael.* Jerusalem, 1986.

Freimann, Aharon H. *Seder Quiddushin ve-Nissuin*. Jerusalem, 1965.

Frishtik, Mordechai. "Violence Against Women in Judaism." *Journal of Psychology and Judaism* 14 (1990): 131–53.

Gen. Rab. = *Midrash Bereshit Rabbah*, ed. J. Theodor and Ch. Albeck. Jerusalem, 1996.

Gerondi, R. Jonah. *Iggeret ha-Teshuvah*. Jerusalem, 1991.

_____. *Sha'arei Teshuvah*. Jerusalem, 1991.

Gil, Moshe. *Be-Malkhut Yishma'el bi-Tequfat ha-Geonim*. 4 vols. Jerusalem, 1997.

Goitein, Shlomo D. *Sidrei Ḥinuch mi-Tequfat ha-Geonim ad Beit ha-Rambam*. Jerusalem, 1962.

_____. *A Mediterranean Society*. Vol. 3: *The Family*. Berkeley and Los Angeles and London, 1978.

_____. *Ha-Teimanim*. Jerusalem, 1983.

Gold, Penny S. "The Marriage of Mary and Joseph in the Twelfth-Century Ideology of Marriage." In *Sexual Practices and the Medieval Church*, ed. V. L. Bullough and J. Brundage, 102–17. New York, 1982.

Goody, Jack. *The Development of the Family and Marriage in Europe*. Cambridge, 1983.

Graetz, Naomi. *Silence is Deadly: Judaism Confronts Wifebeating*. Northvale, N.J. 1998.

Gross, Henri. *Gallia Judaica*. Amsterdam, 1969.

Grossman, Avraham. *Ḥakhmei Ashkenaz ha-Rishonim*. Jerusalem, 1981.

_____. "From Father to Son: The Inheritance of the Spiritual Leadership of the Jewish Communities in the Early Middle Ages" [Hebrew]. *Zion* 50 (1985): 189–220.

_____. "The Historical Background to the Ordinances on Family Affairs Attributed to Rabbenu Gershom Meor Hagolah (The Light of the Exile)." In *Jewish History: Essays in Honor of C. Abramsky*, ed. A. Rapoport-Albert and S. Zipperstein, 3–23. London, 1988.

_____. "Child Marriage in Jewish Society in the Middle Ages until the Thirteenth Century" [Hebrew]. *Pe'amim* 45 (1990): 108–125.

_____. "Medieval Rabbinic Views on Wife-Beating, 800–1300." *Jewish History* 5 (1991): 53–62.

Ḥakhmei Zarfat ha-Rishonim. Jerusalem, 1995,

_____. "Kiddush Hashem" = "Martyrdom in the Eleventh and Twelfth Centuries: Between Ashkenaz and the Muslim World" [Hebrew]. *Pe'amim* 75 (1998): 27–46.

_____. *Ḥasidot u-Mordot; Nashim Yehudyot be-Eropah be-Yemei ha-Beinayim*. Jerusalem, 2001.

Gulak, Asher. *Oẓar ha-Shtarot*. Jerusalem, 1926.

Habermann, Abraham M., ed. *Gezerot Ashkenaz ve-Zarfat*. Jerusalem, 1971.

Halivni Weiss, David. "Torah Study for Women" [Hebrew]. In *Mayim medalyav*, ed. Y. Ben-Sasson, 15–26. Jerusalem, 1997.

Ha-Manhig (R. Abraham ben Nathan ha-Yarḥi), ed. Y. Raphael. Jerusalem, 1978.

Hameiri, R. Menahem. *Beit ha-Beḥirah: Ketubot*. Jerusalem, 1947; *Quissushin*, Jerusalem, 1963.

Harris, Monford. "The Concept of Love in Sepher Hassidim." *JQR* 50 (1959–1960): 13–43.

Havlin, Shlomo Z. "The Takkanot of Rabbenu Gershom Meor Hagolah in Family law in Spain and Provence (in the Light of Manuscripts of Responsa of Rashba and R. Isaac de-Molina)" [Hebrew]. *Shenaton ha-Mishpat ha-Ivri* 2 (1975): 200–57.

Heers, Jack. *Le clan familial au Moyen Age*. Paris, 1974.

Herlihy, David. "Life Expectancies for Women in Medieval Society." In *The Role of Women in the Middle Ages*, ed. R. Morewedge, 1–22. Albany, 1975.

_____. "The Making of the Medieval Family: Symmetry, Structure and Sentiment." *Journal of Family History* 8 (1983): 112–30.

_____. *Medieval Households.* Cambridge, Mass., 1985.

Ḥibbur Yafeh meha-Yeshu'ah le-Rabbi Nissim ben Ya'akov. Jerusalem, 1970.

Horowitz, Carmi. "Preachers, Sermons and Homiletic Literature in Spain" [Hebrew]. In *Moreshet Sefarad*, ed. H. Beinart, 309–20. Jerusalem, 1992.

Hyman, Paula. "Gender and Jewish History." *Tikkun* 3, no. 1 (January-February 1988).

Idel, Moshe. "Sexual Metaphors and Praxis in the Kabbalah." In *The Jewish Family*, ed. D. Kraemer, 197–224. Oxford, 1989.

_____. "The Wife and the Concubine: The Woman in Jewish Mysticism" [Hebrew]. In *Barukh she-Asani Ishah?*, ed. D. Y. Ariel et al, 141–57. Tel Aviv, 1999.

Ilan, Tal. *Ma'amad ha-Ishah ha-Yehudit be-Eretz Yisrael bi-Tequfah ha-Hellenistit Romit.* Jerusalem, 1991

Isserlein, Israel. *Sefer Terumat ha-Deshen.* Jerusalem, 1991.

Jordan, William C. "Jews on Top: Women and the Availability of Consumption Loans in Northern France in the Mid-Thirteenth Century." *Journal of Jewish Studies* 29 (1978): 39–56.

Kanarfogel, Ephraim. *Jewish Education and Society in the High Middle Ages.* Detroit, 1992.

Katz, Jacob. *Masoret u-Mashber; ha-Ḥevrah ha-Yehudit be-Moẓa'ei Yemei ha-Beinayim.* Jerusalem, 1958.

_____. "Levirate Marriage (*Yibbum*) and *Ḥaliẓah* in Post-Talmudic Times" [Hebrew]. *Tarbiẓ* 51 (1982): 59–106; reprinted in his *Halakhah ve-Qabbalah*, 127–74. Jerusalem, 1984.

Katzoff, Ranon. "The Age of Marriage of Jewish Girls During the Talmudic Period" [Hebrew]. *Te'udah* 13 (1997): 9–18.

Kellner, Menahem. "Philosophical Hatred of Women in the Middle Ages: R. Levi b. Gershon vs. Maimonides" [Hebrew]. *Meḥqerei Yerushalayim be-Maḥshevet Yisrael* 14 (1998): 113–28.

Klapisch-Zuber, C. *Women, Family and Ritual in Renaissance Italy.* Chicago and London, 1985.

Kol Bo. Naples, 1490.

Kraemer, Joel L. "Spanish Ladies from the Cairo Geniza." In *Jews, Christians and Muslims in the Mediterranean after 1492*, ed. A. Meyuhas Ginio, 237–67. London, 1992.

_____. "Women's Letters from the Cairo Genizah: A preliminary Study." In *Eshnav le-Ḥayeihen shel Nashim be-Ḥevrot Yehudiot*, ed. Y. Aẓmon, 161–81. Jerusalem, 1995.

Kupfer, Efraim, ed. *Teshuvot u-Pesaqim me-et Hakhmei Ashkenaz ve-Ẓarfat.* Jerusalem, 1973.

Lamdan, Ruth. *Am bifnei Aẓman.* Tel Aviv, 1996.

Leqet Yosher le-R. Yosef b. R. Moshe, ed. Y. Freimann. *Ḥeleq Oraḥ Ḥayyim*, Berlin, 1903; *Ḥeleq Yoreh De'ah*, Berlin, 1904.

Levin-Melammed, Renée. *Heretics or Daughters of Israel?* Oxford, 1999.

Libson, Gideon. "Legal Status of the Jewish Woman in the Geonic Period: Muslim Influence—Overt and Covert." In *Developments in Austrian and Israeli Private Law*, ed. H. Hausmaninger et al., 213–43. Wien, 1999.

Liebes, Judah. "Zohar and Eros" [Hebrew]. *Alpayim* 9 (1994): 56–119.

Ma'aseh ha-Geonim, ed. A. Epstein. Berlin, 1910.

Maharil, *Minhagim* = Moellin, Jacob, *Sefer Maharil, Minhagim*, ed. S. J. Spitzer. Jerusalem, 1989.

Maimonides, Moses. *Moreh ha-Nevukhim* [Guide for the Perplexed] ed. and trans. J. Kapah. Jerusalem, 1977.

Maimonides, Moses. *MT = Mishneh Torah la-Rambam: Sefer Nashim*, ed. N. L. Rabinovitch. Jerusalem, 1997.

Malachi, Zvi. "An Autobiographical Scroll by a Youth Found in the Cairo Genizah" [Hebrew]. *Mikhael* 5 (1978): 190–91.

Marcus, Ivan G. "Mothers, Martyrs and Moneylenders: Some Jewish Women in Medieval Europe." *Conservative Judaism* 38 (1986): 34–45.

_____. *Rituals of Childhood: Jewish Acculturation in Medieval Europe*. New Haven, 1996.

McNamara, Jo Ann and Suzanne Wemple. "The Power of Women through the Family in Medieval Europe, 500–1100." *Power in the Middle Ages* (Athens, 1988): 83–101.

Megillat Aḥima'aẓ, ed. B. Klar. Jerusalem, 1974.

Meir of Rothenburg. *Teshuvot Pesaqim u-Minhagim*. Jerusalem, 1957,

Meislish, J. *Shirat ha-Roqeaḥ; Piyyutei R. Eleazar mi-Vormaiza*. Jerusalem, 1993.

Metzger, Theresa, and Mendel Metzger. *Jewish Life in the Middle Ages, Illuminated Hebrew Manuscripts of the Thirteenth to the Sixteenth Centuries*. New York, 1982.

Minty, Mary. "Kiddush ha-Shem in German Christian Eyes in the Middle Ages" [Hebrew]. *Ẓion* 59 (1994): 209–66.

Mordekhai = Sefer ha-Mordekhai to tractate Kiddushin, ed. J. Roth, Jerusalem, 1990; To tractate Gittin, ed. M.E. Rabinowitz, Jerusalem, 1990.

Morris, Nathan, *Ha-Ḥinukh shel Am Yisrael*, 3 vols. Jerusalem, 1997.

Moses of Coucy. *Sefer Miẓvot Gadol*. Venice, 1547.

Müller, Yoel, ed. *Teshuvot Ḥakhmei Ẓarfat ve-Lutir*. Wien, 1981.

Murray, Jacqueline. "Individualism and Consensual Marriage: Some Evidence from Medieval England." In *Women, Marriage and Family in Medieval Christendom*, eds. C. M. Rousseau and J. T. Rosenthal, 121–51. Kalamazoo, Mich., 1998.

Neuman, Abraham A. *The Jews in Spain*. 2 vols. Philadelphia, 1944.

Noble, S. "The Jewish Woman in Medieval Martyrology." In *Studies in Jewish Bibliography, History and Literature in Honor of I. E. Kiev*, ed. C. Berlin, 347–55. New York, 1971.

Or Zaru'a; Pisqei Bava Qamma le R. Yiẓḥaq b. Moshe me-Wien. Jerusalem, 1998.

Ozar ha-Geonim, ed. B. M. Lewin. *Gittin*, Jerusalem, 1941; *Ketubot*, Jerusalem, 1938; *Qiddushin*, Jerusalem, 1939.

Power, Eileen. *Medieval Women*. London, 1975.

Rabad (R. Abraham ben David of Posquières). *Ba'alei ha-Nefesh*, ed. J. Kapah. Jerusalem, 1968.

Raban (R. Eliezer ben Nathan), *Sefer Even ha-Ezer*, ed. S. Albeck. Warsaw, 1905; ed. S. Z. Ehrnreich. Samloi, 1927.

Ralbag (R. Levi ben Gershon). *Perush al ha-Torah*. Jerusalem, 1992–2000.

Rapoport-Albert, Ada. "On Women in Hasidism: S. A. Horodecky and the Maid of Ludmir Tradition." In *Jewish History: Essays in Honour of Chimen Abramsky*, ed. A. Rapoport-Albert and S. Zipperstein, 495–525. London, 1988.

Regev, Shaul. "The Reasons for *Yibum*—Philosophy and Kabbalah" [Hebrew]. *Da'at* 28 (1992): 65–86.

Roded, Ruth. *Women in Islam and the Middle East*. London and New York, 1999.

Rosen, Tova. "Circumsized Cinderella: The Fantasies of a Fourteenth-Century Jewish Author." *Prooftexts* 20 (2000): 87–110.

_____. "Minhat Yehudah." = "Sexual Politics in a Medieval Hebrew Marriage Debate." *Exemplaria* 22 (2000): 157–84.

Saperstein, Marc. *Decoding the Rabbis*. Cambridge, Mass., 1980.

Schacht, Joseph. *An Introduction to Islamic Law*. Oxford, 1964.

Scheindlin, Reuven. *Wine, Women and Death*. Philadelphia, 1986.

Scholem, Gershom G., *Major Trends in Jewish Mysticism*. New York, 1967.

Schremer, Adiel. "Man's Age at Marriage in Jewish Palestine of the Hellenistic and Roman Period" [Hebrew]. *Zion* 61 (1996): 45–66.

Schulenburg, J. T. "Sexism and the Celestial Gynaecum from 500 to 1200." *Journal of Medieval History* 4 (1978): 117–133.

Schwartz, Dov. *Yashan be-Qanqan Hadash*. Jerusalem, 1997.

Sefer ha-Agudah le-R. Alexander Zuslin ha-Kohen. Cracow, 1571.

Sefer ha-Shtarot le-Rabbi Yehudah Barzeloni, ed. S. J. H. Halberstam. Berlin, 1898; photo ed.: Jerusalem, 1967.

Sefer Hasidim, ed. J. Wistinetzki. Frankfurt a. M., 1924.

Sefer Hasidim she-Hibber Rabbenu Yehudah he-Hasid, ed. R. Margaliot. Jerusalem, 1964.

Sefer ha-Yashar le-Rabbenu Tam; Heleq ha-Teshuvot, ed S. P. Rosenthal. Berlin, 1898.

Sefer ha-Zohar, ed. R. Margaliot. 3 vols. Jerusalem, 1984.

Sha'arei Zedeq = Teshuvot Geonim Sha'arei Zedeq. Jerusalem, 1966.

Shahar, Shulamith. *The Fourth Estate: A History of Women in the Middle Ages*. London and New York, 1983.

Shatzmiller, Joseph. *Jews, Medicine and Medieval Society*. Berkeley, Los Angeles ad London, 1994.

Sheehan, Michael M. "Marriage Theory and Practice in the Conciliar Legislation and Diocesan Statutes of Medieval England." *Mediaeval Studies* 40 (1978): 408–60.

Shiloh, Shmuel. *"Koah Gavra*; Impotence as Grounds for Divorce" [Hebrew]. *Divrei ha-Qongress ha-Olami ha-Hamishi le-Mad'ei ha-Yahadut* 3 (Jerusalem, 1972): 353–67.

———. "The Matchmaker in Jewish Law" [Hebrew]. *Mishpatim* 4 (1972): 361–73.

Shirman, Hayyim, and Ezra Fleischer. *Toldot ha-Shirah ha-Ivrit bi-Sefarad ha-Nozrit uve-Darom Zarfat*. Jerusalem, 1997.

Siddur Rashi, ed. S. Buber and J. Freimann. Berlin, 1911.

Soloveitchik, Haym. "Three Themes in the Sefer Hasidim." *AJS Review* 1 (1976): 311–57.

Soloveitchik, Haym. *Shu't ke-Maqor Histori*. Jerusalem, 1990.

Sperber, Daniel. *Minhagei Yisrael*. 6 vols. Jerusalem, 1989–1998.

Spiegel, Jacob S. "Women as Ritual Circumciser: The Halakhah and its Development" [Hebrew]. *Sidra* 5 (1989): 149–57.

Stow, Kenneth R. *Alienated Minority: The Jews of Medieval Latin Europe*. Cambridge, Mass., 1992.

Taitz, Emily. "Kol Ishah—The Voice of Woman: Where Was It Heard in Medieval Europe?" *Conservative Judaism* 38 (1986): 46–61.

———. "Women's Voices, Women's Prayers: Women in the European Synagogue of the Middle Ages." In *Daughters of the King*, ed. S. Grossman and R. Haut, 59–71. Philadelphia, 1992.

Taitz, Emily, Sandra Henry, and Cheryl Tallan. *The JPS Guide to Jewish Women*. Philadelphia, 2003.

Tallan, Cheryl. "The Position of the Medieval Jewish Widow as a Function of Family Structure." *Proceedings of the Tenth World Congress of Jewish Studies*, Division B, II, 91–98. Jerusalem, 1990.

———. "Medieval Jewish Widows: Their Control of Resources." *Jewish History* 5 (1991): 63–74.

Ta-Shma, Israel M. *Halakhah Minhag u-Meziut be-Ashkenaz*, 1000–1350. Jerusalem, 1996.

Teshuvot Ba'alei ha-Tosafot, ed. I. A. Agus. New York, 1954.

Teshuvot Geonei Mizrah u-Ma'arav, ed. J. Müller. Berlin, 1888.

Teshuvot Hakhmei Provinzia, ed. A. Sofer. Jerusalem, 1967.

Teshuvot Ḥakhmei Ẓarfat ve-Lutir, ed. J. Müller. Wien, 1881.

Teshuvot ha-Rambam [Responsa of Moses Maimonides], ed. J. Blau. 4 vols. Jerusalem, 1958–1989.

Teshuvot ha-Ran [Responsa of R. Nissim of Gerona], ed. A. L. Feldman. Jerusalem, 1984.

Teshuvot ha-Rashba [Responsa of R. Solomon Ibn Adret]. Vol. 1: Wien, 1812; Vol. 2: Livorno, 1657; Vol. 3: Livorno, 1778; Vol. 4: Salonica, 1803; Vol. 5: Vilna, 1884; Vols 6–7: Warsaw, 1868: hamyuhasot la-Ramban, Jerusalem, 1976.

Teshuvot ha-Ribash [Responsa of R. Isaac ben Sheshat]. Jerusalem, 1975.

Teshuvot ha-Rif [Responsa of R. Yitzhak Alfasi], ed. W. Leitter. Pittsburgh, 1954.

Teshuvot ha-Ri Mi-Gash = Teshuvot Rabbenu Yosef ha-Levi Ibn Mi-Gash, ed. S. Hasida. Jerusalem, 1991.

Teshuvot ha-Ritba [Responsa of R. Yom Tov al-Ishbili], ed. J. Kapah. Jerusalem, 1959.

Teshuvot ha-Rosh [Responsa of R. Asher ben Yehiel. Venezia, 1553.

Teshuvot Maharam [Responsa of R. Meir ben Barukh of Rothenburg], ed. M. A. Bloch. Prague, 1885.

Teshuvot Maharil [Responsa of R. Jacob Moellin], ed. J. Setz. Jerusalem, 1980.

Teshuvot Maharil ha-Ḥadashot, ed. J. Setz. Jerusalem, 1977.

Teshuvot Mahariq [Responsa of R. Joseph Colon]. Jerusalem, 1973.

Teshuvot Ragmah [Responsa of R. Gershom Meor Hagolah], ed. S. Eidelberg. New York, 1956.

Teshuvot Rashi, ed. I. Elfenbein. New York, 1943.

Teshuvot R. Ḥayyim Or Zaru'a. Jerusalem, 1960.

Tishby, Isaiah. Mishnat ha-Zohar, 2 vols. Jerusalem 1971–75.

Toch, Michael, "Die jüdische Frau im Erwerbsleben des Spätmittelalters." In *Zur Geschichte der jüdischen Frau in Deutschland*, ed. J. Carlebach, 37–48. Berlin, 1993.

Weissler, Chava. "Woman as High Priest: A Kabbalistic Prayer in Yiddish for Lighting the Sabbath Candles." *Jewish History* 5 (1991): 9–26.

Westreich, Elimelech. *Ribbui Nashim = Temurot be-Ma'amad ha-Isha ba-Mishpat ha-Ivri*. Jerusalem, 2002.

Wilson, Boydena R. "Glimpses of Muslim Urban Women in Classical Islam." In *Woman and the Structure of Society*, ed. B. J. Harris and J. K. McNamara, 5–11. Durham, 1984.

Wischnitzer, Rachel. *The Architecture of the European Synagogue*. Philadephia, 1964.

Wolfson, Eliot R. "Woman—The Feminine as Other in Theosophic Kabbalah: Some Philosophical Observations on the Divine Androgyne." In *The Other in Jewish Thought and History*, ed. L. J. Silberstein and R. L. Cohen, 166–204. New York and London, 1994.

Yassif, Eli. *Sippur ha-Am ha-Ivri*. Tel Aviv, 1995.

Yuval, Israel Y. "An Appeal against the Proliferation of Divorce in Fifteenth-Century Germany" [Hebrew]. *Ẓion* 48 (1983): 177–215.

_____. *Ḥakhamim be-Doram*. Jerusalem, 1989.

_____. "The Economic Arrangements of Marriage in Ashkenaz in the Middle Ages" [Hebrew]. In *Dat ve-Kalkalah: Yaḥasei Gomlin*, ed. M. Ben-Sasson, 191–207. Jerusalem, 1995.

Zeldes, Nadia. "As One Who Flees from a Snake: Jewish Women in Sicily in the Generation of the Expulsion Confront their Husbands' Conversions" [Hebrew]. *Pe'amim* 82 (2000): 50–63.

Zikhron Yehudah. Berlin, 1846.

Zolty, Shoshana P. *"And All Your Children Shall Be Learned": Women and the Study of Torah in Jewish Law and History*. Northvale, N.J. 1993.

Index